SEEING THE LORD

Resurrection and Early Christian Practices

Marianne Sawicki

FORTRESS PRESS   *Minneapolis*

SEEING THE LORD
Resurrection and Early Christian Practices

Biblical quotations, unless otherwise noted, are from the Scholars Version taken from *The Complete Gospels*, copyright © by Polebridge Press and used with permission.

Portions of this book are based on the author's previous research: "How to Teach Christ's Disciples: John 1:19-37 and Matthew 11:12-15," *Lexington Theological Quarterly* 21 (1986) 14–26; "Recognizing the Risen Lord," *Theology Today* 44 (1988) 99–118; and "Educational Policy and Christian Origins," *Religious Education* 85 (1990) 455–77. Used by permission of the publishers.

Cover design: Cindy Cobb-Olson
Cover art: *Pietà*, a color linoleum block print by Sybil Andrews, 1932. Printed by permission of the Mary Ryan Gallery, New York.

Library of Congress Cataloging-in-Publication Data
Sawicki, Marianne.
    Seeing the Lord : Resurrection and early Christian practices / by
Marianne Sawicki.
      p.   cm.
    Includes bibliographical references and index.
    ISBN 0-8006-2709-1 (alk. paper)
    1. Jesus Christ—Resurrection. 2. Christianity—Origin. 3. Bible. N.T.
Gospels—Criticism, interpretation, etc. 4. Body, Human—Religious
aspects—Christianity. 5. Women in Christianity—Palestine. 6. Women in
Christianity—History—Early church, ca. 30-600. 7. Sex role—Religious
aspects—Christianity. 8. Lord's Supper. 9. Palestine—Church history. I. Title.
BT481.S28   1994
232'.5—dc20   93-40947
                                                        CIP

Manufactured in the U.S.A.   AF 1-2709

98   97   96   95   94   1   2   3   4   5   6   7   8   9   10

For Sam
and for his generation

Contents

Preface

1. Introduction   1

Part One   Reconstruction:
Practices of Recognizing Jesus

2. Like Nursing Babies   27
3. For Teachers a Teacher   51
4. Empty Text as Empty Tomb   77
5. Son of God's Slavewoman   95
6. Hearing in Israel   119
7. Grooming Messiah for Death   149

Part Two   Interpretation:
Theories of Corporality, Textuality, and Humanity

8. Bodies Born and Grown   185
9. Scripts Written and Read   215
10. A Frontier Anthropology   243

Part Three   Application:
Christology, Liturgical Theology, and Catechetics

11. A Resurrection Theology   279
12. Copy Who Copies   301

Bibliography   337
Index of Ancient Texts   357
Index of Subjects and Names   363

Preface

THIS INQUIRY into Christian origins is my attempt to determine whether to continue to teach that Jesus of Nazareth is risen bodily from the dead.

Bodies and teachings are fragile. Our century has not been gentle to either. Textual criticism of various kinds has jeopardized our capacity to say anything meaningful about our past. Texts have been unmasked as implements of power, and canons of every sort have been discredited. Even the friendly critique of multiculturalism has evoked a paralyzing pessimism among the church's teachers, or at least among those who are brave, aware, and conscientious enough not to have barricaded themselves behind dogmatic denial. On the other hand, theologians who dare attend to the fate of textuality—few though they be—have retreated from the tradition and now merely mine it for nostalgic motifs and literary allusions. I think that that is a tragic mistake in light of what is happening to human bodies.

The onslaught against the human body in our century has been massive and sustained. Racism, genocide, and ethnic cleansing; famine, joblessness, and substance abuse; rape, heterosexism, and sexual exploitation: these are not individual aberrations but policies systemically engineered and implemented in the pursuit of political advantage. Bodies are radically at risk. Their defense requires more than words. The Christian tradition of bodily resurrection offers more than words, more than literary motifs. It is a way of life that cherishes the human body and resists whatever threatens the bodies of children, women, and men on this planet.

Yet much that has called itself Christian in our history has declined to affirm life and has defected from the defense of the body. Christians too often have pursued murderous pogroms, crusades, and purges. Some observers would assert that there is no criterion to distinguish between these and a "true" Christian stance. What is "Christian," they would say, is whatever Christians happen to have done.

On the contrary, I argue that we can discover a criterion to discipline and certify the Christian way of life. This norm is not simply the Scripture but something that is more subtle than text, something to which the scriptural text itself nevertheless points. Nor is it simply the defense of the body, but something more basic that volunteers itself in defense of the body. It is a competence that we first practice and only secondarily describe, a competence that has been shared across space and time since the death of Jesus. It is the competence for recognizing what God has done with Jesus—if you will, the competence for allowing God to have done it and to persist in doing it. The Gospels are not *this;* they are merely descriptions or *specifications of* this. The resurrection of Jesus is a bodily competence that is still happening to us and still making us make it happen.

This competence is the norm governing its own propagation. As such, it does not need historical recovery and reconstruction, for it is quite available in the present in the ongoing activities of ecclesial life. The church does not go a-questing for the historical Jesus. Yet historical questions confront those of us who, on behalf of the church, work to provide professional training for its ministers.

Thus the present inquiry into Christian origins also was motivated by my growing dissatisfaction with the academic field in which I taught at the postgraduate level during the decade of the 1980s: the field of Christian religious education. To be sure, the job of teaching the churches' teachers is a superbly challenging one, no less today than when I began. Teachers need competence in theological and pastoral disciplines as well as in secular studies such as history and communications. What imparts unity to their multidisciplinary preparation must be profound love for the church, based on thorough understanding of what ecclesial existence entails for those who commit their lives to following the way of Jesus of Nazareth.

Yet, I found, fear was eroding that love. Fear is institutionalized within structures and practices of Christian education at all levels across a wide spectrum of the Protestant and Catholic churches with whom I have worked. For example, pastors who received excellent training in exegesis themselves nevertheless continue to preach distorted information to avoid disturbing their people. Congregations commission teachers to ensure that the youth will adopt their parents' lifestyles, not reevaluate them. Theologians ignore the findings of anthropology and history. Church historians cling to androcentric, ethnocentric, and bourgeois presuppositions. All seem to collude in denying what any catechist knows: that the resurrection isn't over yet, and the Risen Lord still walks through locked doors. It takes tremendous energy to sustain the fable that "Christian origins" occurred just once, long ago in the first century, through processes nevermore to be repeated. Fear of the resurrection is what supplies that enormous energy, and at its core is despairing disbelief.

If you once let go of that prejudice, however, then you can see that the Gospels are describing catechetical processes of Christian initiation essentially similar to those in practice today. Faith arose for the churches of the New Testament in ways that are rather like the ways in which it still arises. That means that questions about the intergenerational transmission of faith constitute something more than mere contemporary pastoral concerns; they offer an avenue of approach into the phenomenon of the origination of Easter faith at the birth of the church. Ideally, this points toward the possibility of professional collaboration between Scripture scholars, historians, and theologians, on the one hand, and theorists and practitioners of Christian education, on the other. In fact, such collaboration is impeded by the disciplinary boundaries observed within seminary faculties and university departments.

The work that I have undertaken in this book, then, stems from my acute dissatisfaction with those disciplinary taboos. But I must admit that I am deeply dissatisfied as well with my own research as it is reported in the present book. In so many instances, my own skills were not equal to the challenges that I saw in the texts. I was too alone to write this book well—despite the help I received from many friends and colleagues. My sincere hope is that readers also will be dissatisfied with this book and will find ways of working collaboratively on issues of gender, race, and class that I have perhaps succeeded only in disclosing by stumbling over them here.

Thanks are due to several institutions and individuals who have helped me with aspects of my research. In expressing my gratitutde, however, I must acknowledge that none of those whom I have the privilege of naming here would endorse all that I say within these pages. In fact, some have warned me earnestly against aspects of the methodology that I employ or the conclusions that I espouse.

The studies that made this book possible were supported by a sabbatical leave from Lexington Theological Seminary 1988–89; by the kind hospitality of Princeton Theological Seminary while I served as Guest Professor of Christian Education 1989–90; and by a presidential fellowship in the department of philosophy at the University of Kentucky 1990–92. At Kentucky, I benefited from participation in Monica L. Udvardy's seminar in Anthropology of Gender, and in other activities within the interdisciplinary program in Social Theory coordinated by Theodore R. Schatzki, who was friend and mentor to this work in its final stages of composition. Thanks also are due to Peggy M. Akridge of the University of Kentucky's Computer Center, Academic User Services, for assistance with electronic analysis of ancient texts.

Portions of the research reported in this book were first presented and discussed at meetings of the Society of Biblical Literature, the North American Academy of Liturgy, the Catholic Theological Society of America, the American Academy of Religion, and the Association of Professors and Researchers in Religious Education. Comments and suggestions received on those occasions were very helpful, and in particular I must acknowledge the criticisms of Clarisse Croteau-Chonka, Francis Schüssler Fiorenza, Gordon Lathrop, Bernard Brandon Scott, and Robert Sokolowski. Earlier versions of three of the exegetical studies appeared in *Lexington Theological Quarterly* (1986), *Theology Today* (1988), and *Religious Education* (1990), respectively. My questions about ecclesial access to Jesus were first formulated in my 1984 doctoral dissertation at the Catholic University of America, which was directed with preternatural fortitude by Mary Collins, Kevin Seasoltz, and William Cenkner. I remain in their debt.

It was Mary Gerhart, however, who helped me to see that this scattershot work was converging upon an aesthetic approach to Christian origins. She is the godmother of this book, for without her friendship and encouragement it could not have come together. My acquaintance with Mary was occasioned by the kind invitation of Peter C. Hodgson, Robert H. King, and Edward Farley to collaborate with them and their colleagues in the Workgroup on Constructive Theology. The original membership of the Workgroup, now senior scholars, decided in 1986 to admit several junior colleagues and, moreover, generously to sponsor our participation through the royalties from their prior publications. Since then, conversations with the Workgroup at its periodic meetings have been a continuing source of stimulation, for which I am deeply grateful.

I also had the privilege and pleasure of working with James F. Strange and his associates on the University of South Florida Excavations at Sepphoris in Israel for the 1989 season. They opened my eyes to the significance of material reconstruction for the interpretation of the past and gave me a practical foundation for further research in anthropology and social theory. My gratitude goes especially to Joan Keller, my supervisor and teacher on the dig, and to Marilyn Power, my confidante and roommate in Nazareth during that summer of grace.

A year after I returned from Israel, my father died suddenly. Grief, together with gratitude for his life and for the one he had given me, imparted new urgency to the questions about death and resurrection that I was pursuing in my research. I had also the joy of many afternoon discussions with my nephew Sam, who recalled his grandfather with a child's clear-sighted perspective on death, life, love, and time. The liturgical community at Holy Spirit Parish, the Newman Center at the University of Kentucky, has profoundly imprinted my ecclesiology and has leavened my academic preoccupations. In its Catechumenate I worked for several years with people who were learning to see the Lord. Much of what I know about the volatility of the resurrection has come from observance of Easter Vigil with them, both in years of sorrow and in years of promise.

The manuscript has benefited hugely from the suggestions of Bruce Chilton and Robert J. Miller, each of whom gave portions of it a very rigorous reading. Robert Funk generously permitted the use of the Scholars Version, Polebridge Press's translation of ancient Christian texts. David Seeley argued through several of the scriptural interpretations with me but so far has failed to convince me to try writing novels instead of history.

Marianne Sawicki
Lexington, Kentucky
Feast Day of Mother Seton

1

Introduction

A BOOK'S introduction, like a travel brochure, should entice readers to come along on a journey by describing the challenges ahead. Welcome to an adventurous but difficult book. Ours will be a journey back into the origins of Easter faith. Some portions of the trip will traverse space and time, taking us into consideration of historical events that occurred long ago in Greco-Roman Palestine. But the resurrection is not to be discovered there in the past. The distinctive reality of the resurrection requires something more than a historical approach. What happened to Jesus is not the sort of thing that can be over, done, completed, and closed like a historical event. Therefore other portions of this book's journey will survey contemporary practices that, quite like those uncovered in Gospel texts, embody strategies for recognizing the Risen Lord.

The church knows these strategies. In fact, a short definition of what is meant by "church" might be this: the community of competence to recognize Jesus as Risen Lord. Church is know-how. If this book is a journey, it is a journey that we mean to make *as* and *in* this church. While the scholarly investigative strategies through which we shall attempt to grasp the church's competence are not identical with that competence itself, they must closely accommodate it.

The information encoded in the Gospel texts and in liturgical and cate-chetical practices is of two kinds: theoretical content and practical strategy. In order to grasp what the church means by the doctrine of the resurrection, we must correlate the verbal contents of this notion, "resurrection," against the strategies that position people so that any such contents become intelligible, meaningful, and effective for them. The verbal information and the practical information have been co-defining and interdependent throughout the Christian tradition. The church *is* the accessibility of the ancient wisdom required for seeing Jesus as Lord. What wisdom is that? Ecclesial wisdom embraces dimensions of memory, desire, and practice. The church retains the ancient memory of Jesus of Nazareth: what he said, how he lived, how he died. The church knows the loss of Jesus: it mourns him, and out of that mourning it yearns to see him again. The church maintains the competence to reach Jesus: it knows how to propagate the ability to see the Lord.

This ecclesial wisdom is such that it cannot be expressed adequately in words alone. Much of it is practical competence. The wisdom of resurrection is not the possession of a privileged clerical hierarchy, nor does it provide a shortcut to avoid the hard work of critical investigation. In the Christian tradition, genuine seeking always is prerequisite to finding. In this book, the intent is to seek an understanding of Christian origins in an intellectually rigorous and academically credible way. On the one hand, this investigation should be in harmony with the church and should take account of the interests and the methods that have been traditional for the church. On the other hand, this investigation is also an investigation of the church's own quest for Jesus. We must employ scholarly methods that would be neither necessary nor appropriate for someone simply seeking Jesus—for example, a child or a catechumen approaching Easter baptism. The catechumen enters a church that, even as it seeks the Risen Lord, already knows how he is found. In contrast, we as scholarly investigators can examine the seeking and the finding separately, abstracted from each other, for the sake of critical understanding.

Hardheaded historical investigation is no enemy to faith. On the contrary, since it develops out of the church's own constitutive yearning to know the Lord, a historical quest for Jesus of Nazareth can be an act of faith. In this book, however, our quest is *not* for historical knowledge of Jesus of Nazareth as he might have been known before Calvary. Rather, we are targeting for investigation those ecclesial practices or disciplines that developed during the first few decades after Calvary. On a time line, the emergence of those practices would fall after the crucifixion (about 30 C.E.) but before the final edition of the earliest canonical Gospel, the Gospel of Mark (about 70 C.E.).[1] Those practices, which include ways of teaching and imagining, are canonized "between the lines" of the canonical Gospels, as it were. They also have been transmitted both ritually and catechetically, as

---

1. The designation C.E. (common era) replaces the ethnocentric A.D. (*anno Domini*). The centuries B.C. (before Christ) are designated B.C.E.

well as textually, down to the ecclesial communities of our own day; yet they cannot adequately be translated into words.

While the descriptive verbal accounts and the effective practical strategies are distinguishable, they are also correlated and should be understood as such. The necessity of critically relating our own and our predecessors' descriptions to their practices is an interpretive challenge to scholars across the human sciences.[2] For example, anthropologists recognize that their ethnographic verbal descriptions of a people's experiences, and even the explanatory stories that the people themselves may tell, always fall short of capturing the full meaning carried in the efficacy of the strategies by which the people conduct their common life. Much of what people "know" is known with their hands and feet, blood and bones. What enters consciousness as a strategy is the mere tip of an iceberg of unreflected know-how. The seasonal cycle of agricultural tasks is more than the calendar that can be charted on paper; the plotting of betrothal, kinship, and economic reciprocity defies codification in any book of laws or customs. Life is waged, not recited. Essential meaning is embodied nonverbally in the competences that are brought into engagement as social moves are schemed up, gamed out, and enacted. In fact, the purely verbal formulations inevitably spun off in this process are dangerously misleading if the practical competences are left out of account.

Anthropologists and other social scientists—sociologists, economists, psychologists, historians—continually refine their methods of investigation in an effort to achieve more and more adequate understandings of the human phenomena that they study. Biblical studies, as an academic discipline, is not a purely social science, although for a generation now it has increasingly borrowed both the findings and the methods of the social sciences. Thus, refinements in contemporary social theory continue to spur the development of what is known as historical-critical method for the scholarly study of Scripture.

Besides social theory, the other principal contributions to recent refinements in historical-critical method have come from textual studies, including advances in literary theory and criticism, as well as philological study of the ancient languages and their secular and sacred literatures. It is clear, then, that the New Testament when read in the academy requires interdisciplinary, sometimes bewilderingly eclectic, methods of study. No

---

2. The anthropologist Pierre Bourdieu has insisted on this distinction. See Pierre Bourdieu, *Outline of a Theory of Practice,* trans. Richard Nice (Cambridge: Cambridge University Press, 1977). This landmark in recent social theory is based on and illustrated by Bourdieu's fieldwork with the Kabyle, a Semitic village-dwelling people in North Africa.

single scholar today can pretend to master all the disciplines needed for an adequate treatment of the subject matter.[3] Increasingly, therefore, a collaborative way of working and a conversational style are emerging in biblical studies.

The book that is introduced here, then, is more a pilot study than a methodological manifesto or a definitive commentary. We will examine only six cases drawn from Gospel materials. Those cases do not even constitute a representative sample of the relevant material, yet we shall see that they are singularly significant. Moreover, the investigation will show that certain lines of questioning promoted by contemporary social theory are indispensable for understanding the New Testament texts and the practices out of which they come. These social-theoretical considerations will further demonstrate their significance as we move from the text studies into a theological appropriation. Theology too has become more methodologically interdisciplinary in recent decades. Our investigation means to arrive at a theology of resurrection coherent with contemporary social theory and also faithful to the historical witness of Gospel materials.

Terminology

This book is inductively oriented, which means that the gist of the argument will flow from the data of concrete cases, into a synthetic theoretical statement, and then into applications for systematic and pastoral theology. Wherever possible, then, terms should be allowed to define themselves as we go along. Nevertheless, for a good start it is helpful to un-define a few important terms, that is, to dislodge them from their customary meaning, to wipe them clean so they are ready to receive the meanings that emerge from the investigation.

The first problematic cluster of terms is "resurrection," "Risen Lord," and "rising from the dead." To make a fresh start here, we should suspend the imagination of resurrection as an event with a before-and-after structure, something that occurred at a definable point in the historical calendar, something that is narrated adequately in the Gospel tales about appearances and the finding of an empty tomb, something that

---

3. This principle is honored in the breach by John Meier, who states the intent of his recent Anchor Bible volume as expressing the consensus of a hypothetical conclave of scholars—for whom he presumes to speak alone and under an imprimatur. See John P. Meier, *A Marginal Jew: Rethinking the Historical Jesus*, vol. 1: *The Roots of the Problem and the Person* (New York: Doubleday & Co., 1991), 1–2.

could have been recorded on videotape (had videotape been invented), something that happened once and now is over.[4] In this investigation we shall discover that resurrection has to do with the identity and status of Jesus and especially with his continuing availability to the church despite his death. There were indeed "events" connected with the resurrection, and they manifested the astonishing salvific intervention of God, but they were events of poiesis or imaginative construction, events of the transformation of human social practices. The resurrection has a history, and the early decades of its ecclesial unfolding are the target of investigation here.

"Church," then, is a term always to be used correlatively with "resurrection." The church is all those who know how to recognize the Risen Lord as Jesus of Nazareth, and how to acknowledge the Spirit of that Jesus as the tangible agency working in their midst. To belong to church is to have a competence for a knowledge as well as a competence to propagate such competence. It is the church that initiates people into the availability of Jesus as Risen Lord. Mother church reproduces herself as she reproduces the practices collectively called "seeing the Lord."

In targeting for investigation the historical era between Jesus' execution at Calvary and the final editions of the Gospels, we shall be focusing on social and poietic innovations that made possible both the Gospel texts in the forms in which they have come down to us and the ecclesial institution that finally congealed around them. But these decades in the latter half of the first century C.E. are not the only period of Christian origins. The beginnings of the Jesus movements in human history exhibit certain characteristic patterns that also imprint both the origin of Easter faith within any individual believer and the founding of any new Christian community.

Thus as we un-define terms, we note that the origin of resurrection competence requires engendering certain capabilities, whether the case under consideration is that of the earliest churches, that of mission churches planted in ninth-century Europe or nineteenth-century Africa, that of an adult catechumen in an American urban parish, or that of a child in a Christian home. Theology of Christian origins must cover all such cases and illuminate the structures they have in common. Therefore in un-defining the term "Christian origins," which ordinarily denotes the

---

4. The reimagination of the resurrection has been under way for quite some time by theologians and biblical scholars. Two works that provide both surveys and constructive proposals are Pheme Perkins, *Resurrection: New Testament Witness and Contemporary Reflection* (Garden City, N.Y.: Doubleday & Co., 1984); and Francis Schüssler Fiorenza, *Foundational Theology: Jesus and the Church* (New York: Crossroad, 1984).

scholarly field of study focused on the emergence of Jesus movements in first-century Judaism, we affirm the necessary complementarity between exegesis of the New Testament, on the one hand, and catechetics and liturgical studies, on the other. A two-way street runs between them. Not only are the latter fields informed by historical data but catechetical and liturgical considerations for their part often provide the exegetical clues to decode practices that underlie scriptural texts.

In what, then, does the competence to see Jesus as Lord consist? We shall discover, through investigation of the Gospels' Easter narratives, that seeing the Lord is an event of recognition that has two fundamental preconditions: proximately, a run-in with an indeterminate locus of empowering intimacy within the community; and remotely, information about the details of Jesus' person and message. Then there follows an act of recognition to forge a connection between the two: *that* and *this* are the same. In other words, *this* matches up with *that* remembered profile of a particular man from Nazareth who met a particular fate.

It is clear, then, what must be provided if the possibility of such a recognition is to be prolonged, expanded, and shared. There must be ways to reproduce real time engagement with some intense and intimate experience of empowerment in the midst of the community, and there must also be ways of preserving information about who Jesus was. The term "access" will serve in this book as the shorthand way of indicating the production of present pneumatic and even bodily encounter; the term "identity" will indicate the specification of who Jesus was.

Although distinguishable in analysis, the two provisions were in practice accommodated to each other. Jesus' identity was recalled in an increasingly creative project of portraiture that was geared to facilitate the occurrence of precisely that flash of recognition, that "seeing" of Jesus as Risen Lord, comprising the Easter experience—or conversely, as some Gospel texts indicate, to dampen it or rein it in or discipline it. At the same time, dramatic healings, impressive feedings, and transgressive social conduct set up an ominously escalating resonance in the brittle networks of custom and coercion that were barely restraining the multicultural volatility of mid-first-century Palestine. Such practices could connect explosively with a dangerous memory at the invocation of the name of Jesus.

In reading Gospel portrayals of Jesus, and especially Gospel claims about the conditions of risen presence, we must keep in mind that these texts were never written to stand alone in the twentieth century but rather to precipitate recognition of something outside themselves occurring in the first century. As texts, they simply do not contain all that is needed for "seeing the Lord" in the way their writers intended.

As texts, moreover, these Gospels were sophisticated enough to carry indications of the extratextual, body-accessible components that together with the texts would make up the complete ecclesial strategy of propagating the possibility of Easter faith. Gospel portraits of Jesus, in fixing the contours of his identity, operate not out of some detached objective historical interest but rather as part of the ecclesial strategy of opening access to Jesus as Risen Lord. They carry information about how that strategy worked.[5] They intend and project the very context they need in order to make sense.

The final term that requires some comment here is "Gospel." The four Gospels in the canon of the New Testament all are life and death stories of Jesus that identify his significance for the reader. That which those narratives are "about" includes Jesus, the reader's response to Jesus, and the constitution of the church. Besides the texts of Matthew, Mark, Luke, and John that are most familiar, we know at least a dozen other Gospels. Some are older, or contain familiar material in versions that seem to have undergone less editing before they were written up in final form. Some Gospels are biographical narratives, while others are simply lists of sayings attributed to Jesus.

All of those ancient texts are valuable for historical reconstruction of what was going on in the Jesus movements during the decades under investigation here. Moreover, these Gospels themselves are actually our predecessors' reconstructions of Jesus and the details of his life and teachings. Virtually all of the information about Jesus that is textually available to us comes by way of the editorial work of historians who were vitally interested in propagating the conditions for the possibility of recognizing Jesus as risen, that is, as still speaking and still opening up the way to reconciliation with God despite the scandalous death on the cross. That interest was complex and sometimes compromised by rivalry and repression.

It is notoriously difficult for historians today to untangle the strategically motivated modifications of those early storytellers from the bare facts of Jesus' career, teachings, and death. Luckily, recovery of the historical Jesus is not our task in the present investigation. Not Jesus, but the anonymous first and second generations of Jesus' disciples are the focus of our interest. The premise here is that those people knew how to see

---

5. As we shall see, there were competing portraitures of Jesus and competing strategies of establishing access to him—some of which involved suppression of others. It is futile to ask whether the portraits and the strategies that survived were in any wise the best or most genuine. That is an impossible question, because one would have to climb out of the stream of history to achieve the perspective for answering it.

Jesus as Risen Lord (whatever that formula may have meant to them) and that competence of theirs was transmitted and can be described thanks to the very modifications they made in the information about Jesus that they themselves had received. Our investigation does not try to penetrate behind Calvary to the historical Jesus. Instead, it examines the progressive remaking of the Jesus traditions and lets their textual variations disclose the strategies for propagating Easter faith that were pursued in some of the early Jesus movements.

Ecclesia Pietà

What is intended here is a reconstruction of the early reconstructing of Jesus. Exactly how and why were the various Gospel portraits designed? The Jesus traditions lent themselves to continuous revision during the decades after Calvary as they were performed orally in a variety of social settings. After versions of the Jesus materials began to be committed to writing (by a few atypical intellectuals, it now seems), there emerged strands of textual dependence that still are detectable. What could be made of Jesus was determined partly by what he had in fact said and by what in fact happened to him. But to an increasing degree, the makeover of Jesus also was determined by the possibilities of imagination, expression, and practice inhering in the different cultural layers of Palestinian society and the wider world of Hellenistic civilization. Therefore it is of crucial importance to pay attention to the character of those layers and of their interfaces.

These two kinds of factors—the events of Jesus' life leading to Calvary and the cultural embroidery of Hellenism—when taken together still do not add up to an explanation of how Jesus could be "seen" as risen Lord. Seeing the Lord was rendered possible through *making* the Lord, in all the senses that "making" carries in colloquial American English usage: to construct, to recognize, to confect, to coerce, and even to sexually abuse.

The Gospels *constructed* Jesus. These verbal portraits are artifacts made up according to the writers' designs and interests. The very madeness of these texts, their character as written works, is their most salient feature for the critical historian. Second, the intent of the evangelists who did the textual makeovers of Jesus was precisely to enable Jesus to be made—that is, to be *discovered, recognized, identified, apprehended* in circumstances subsequent to Calvary where otherwise his involvement would go unnoticed. Third, ancient liturgical tradition linked the recognition of Jesus' risen body with the provision of the elements of the eucharistic celebration, shared bread and wine. When eucharist was *confected,* Jesus was made out of these things, so to speak. The sacrificial sacramental elements were made out to be him so that the worshiping assembly could be made into one body. The eucharist made the church, made it the body of the Lord. Fourth, the Christian tradition *manipulated* Jesus. In its burgeoning memories, the figure of Jesus was conscripted to say and do things that likely would have astounded the Jew from Nazareth. This Jesus had given himself over into the hands of others. Submissively, or so we are told, he accepted the manner of this death. Submissively he now remained available after death for what others had the power to do with him. The body, blood, soul, and divinity became narratively malleable.

Fifth, Jesus was sexually *abused.* As a political prisoner who was "disappeared" by a death squad, he was utterly vulnerable to the torture with which the imperial mercenaries amused themselves after his clandestine arrest and midnight trial. In daylight Jesus died naked and cold and bloodied and torn, under the contemptuous gaze of the men who had overpowered him. Their gaze upon the crucified has persisted aesthetically in western traditions of religious image-making. The writhing corpus on the gilded cross and the squirming baby on madonna's knee are familiar to us as stereotypical artistic representations of the human sexuality of Jesus, through which he was as vulnerable as any of us. His fragile humanity was the screen upon which the passions of others were projected and played out. The objectifying gaze of the abuser was not yet a seeing of the Risen Lord, but it was a precondition for such seeing. The abusive gaze made Jesus mere meat fit for slaughter; that is precisely the view that the vision of resurrection disrupted and canceled out. Made into a victim, Jesus was identified with other victims, who made use of him to contest and subvert the hurtful practices that constituted relations of gender, race, and class throughout first-century Greco-Roman society.

The reality of the bodily resurrection necessarily embraces all these dimensions of the making of Jesus. Greek-speaking Jews of Jesus' day called God *patēr kai poiētēs,* "father and maker"; in neither capacity had God finished with Jesus at Calvary.

Resurrection is at once a textual and a bodily event. The body of Jesus is heavily inscribed. In its fragility, it continues to offer itself for reinterpretation. After Calvary, the church has Jesus on her hands. The body of Jesus that came down from the cross fell into the lap of the teaching church. Michelangelo's carving of the Pietà represents mother church as well as mother Mary. The church receives the totality of Jesus' life in his death. After Calvary, the church has responsibility for what will textually and bodily happen to the crucified.

This responsibility generates the ecclesial interest that goes to work in the crafting of the Jesus tales. At Calvary, it is still hundreds of years too early to call this interest "authority," or to attach it to discrete individual leaders, or even to think of "the church" in the singular. Multiple constituencies take hold of the dead body of the Lord, and he is carried along in many diversifying traditions. That peaceful moment captured in the Pietà, if it ever occurred, cannot have lasted very long. The evidence shows a vigorous textual tug-of-war over the body of Jesus, his words and his customs. The one thing that the church could not do after Calvary was to sit serenely with dead Jesus in her lap. The body needed burial, and the words needed remembering. Yet the dislocation of both began almost immediately. As the first resurrection witness tearfully complains in John 20:13, "They've taken my Master away, and I don't know where they've put him."

But was the body stolen, or is he moving under his own power? Does the corpus of Jesus sayings grow and diversify through counterfeiting, or is the Lord indeed still speaking after death? The disciples claim the latter: the body is alive again and the mouth is speaking new words. Among our sources, only Luke thinks of placing a spatiotemporal limit on where the risen body can go and what it can say. Luke reports a departure of the body, either on Easter evening (Luke 24:51) or forty days later (Acts 1:9), after which time Jesus can be seen and heard no more—although still there are exceptions (Acts 7:56 and 9:3-6).

Luke's hypothesis of an ascension is part of a strategy of certifying Jesus, that is, of distinguishing the authentic Jesus from impostors. Thus in the Lukan reconstruction the departure of Jesus is localized in time, and access to him is restricted thereafter. He no longer is literally visible or audible but must be sought in another fashion. Other communities devise other strategies, as we shall see. For now, the point is made that the ecclesial interest in the Jesus tales extends beyond mere "information" about the historical Jesus. In addition, modalities of access to the Risen Lord are devised, debated, challenged, and revised within the communities that transmit Jesus traditions. They contest not only who he was, but *how one can know* who he was or is. They have divergent practical knowledge of certain protocols of approach to the Risen Lord. This too is information carried in the New Testament canon itself.

The Gospel texts, then, carry both "who" information and "how" information. Much of the latter concerns the proper way to lead people into position to "see" Jesus as Lord. It is technical information, although it is not always technically presented or clearly labeled for what it is. Indeed, much of the "how" information has been carried bodily, within the practices of

Christian communities, because it is not the kind of thing that can be satis-factorily reduced to written text at all. Examples must be sought in the lives of those who serve the poor.

Written texts are best adapted for transmitting theory. We as inheri-tors of Western culture share in the bias of the ancient Greeks toward *theōria*. Theory is a kind of knowledge in which the knower is detached and separated from the known. The root meaning of the word is to gaze, like spectators watching a baseball game from the bleachers. The theorist watches the big picture, with all the parts composing an intelligible whole. We tend to prize this sort of knowledge as the most reliable and objective. But its very objectivity can be its most disabling feature. Be-cause theoreticians actively interrogate reality according to their own agenda, they risk forgetting that any agenda, while imparting structure to the data, may at the same time cloak important features. At its extreme, theory denies the limitation of perspective and the necessary involvement of the knower in the construction of anything known.

History is a task of *theōria*. That is, the historian tries to simulate the viewpoint of a detached observer floating over a field of "events" that are plainly available for one's viewing and describing. While, at best, objectiv-ity can be only approximated, nevertheless the reporting of events is vitally important to a tradition. Even reports with an acknowledged unobjective point of view, like the four canonical Gospels, can convey valuable informa-tion. In fact, it is precisely because we understand the viewpoints and inter-ests of the Gospel writers that we can reconstruct some extremely interesting "facts" that they do not directly tell.

Among those facts are the evidences for two other kinds of knowing in the early Jesus communities, which can be called by the Greek names *poiēsis* and *praxis*. *Praxis* means a doing, a business affair, or a transaction. It comes from a root that means to achieve or to complete, which also gives us the English words "pragmatic," "practice," and "practical." *Praxis* entails the skill and competence to do something habitually. It is businesslike know-how. On the other hand, *poiēsis* means a making, a creation, a genera-tion, a fiction. It comes from a root that means to produce, to make, to bring to pass, or to compose. Our English word "poetry" significantly reduces this range of meaning. *Poiēsis* entails creative talent and imagination. It means literacy in the fuller sense, as when we speak of "computer literacy." Perhaps a good way to distinguish and relate *poiēsis* and *praxis* would be this: *praxis* lets you do the same thing effectively over and over again, while *poiēsis* lets you do new things with established themes and genres. *Praxis* looks toward maintenance, while *poiēsis* looks toward re-creation. Clearly, both involve competence, and both also rely on the "factual" knowledge of

theōria. The canonical Gospels indicate that all three epistemic modes are
involved in seeing Jesus as Risen Lord.

Race and Class

All three of these epistemic modalities were engaged by the early Jesus
movements to carry their Gospels or "good news." The wake of the resurrection across first-century Palestine shows up as progressive disruptions
in the interwoven systems of gender, race, and class in that society, in a
pattern that propagates around the continual remaking of Jesus. While
the complexity of these systems will emerge from the case studies in the
chapters that follow, it will be helpful here to give an overview of what we
have to deal with.

Class distinctions have to do with whether and how people control
their own time, their labor, and the goods they produce. In the United
States we have a relatively simple and stable economic class structure. Class
is commonly equated with income level. Traditional differences between
white-collar and blue-collar occupations are fading from common awareness, as is the conscious distinction between agricultural and industrial
work. Yet there is also a growing concern about a permanent urban underclass that has no hope of employment, while a few people are extremely
wealthy and do not work at all.

American society, which, despite its diversity, is still comparatively
undifferentiated by class, gives us only a rather inadequate model for
imagining the economic class structure of even a simple agrarian society
in which wealth for the most part comes directly from the land.[6] And
Palestine of the first century was not purely agrarian in its economic
structure. It was instead in a transitional state of imperial colonization,
with an agrarian base overlaid by a system of world trade, Roman taxation, and planned urbanization. The closest analogues we know today

6. John Dominic Crossan, in his superb work on Jesus in the context of the ancient
world, uses Gerhard Lenski's generalized model of agrarian society, with its nine distinct
classes, to analyze the economic realities of first-century Palestine. See John Dominic Crossan,
The Historical Jesus: The Life of a Mediterranean Jewish Peasant (San Francisco: HarperSanFran-
cisco, 1991); and Gerhard E. Lenski, *Power and Privilege: A Theory of Social Stratification* (New
York: McGraw Hill Book Co., 1966). But one can adjust Lenski's model to give a better fit for
Greco-Roman Palestine by taking appropriate comparative studies into account. Data on soci-
eties in economic transition can be found in Jane L. Parpart and Kathleen A. Staudt, eds.,
Women and the State in Africa (Stanford, Calif.: Stanford University Press, 1989); and Haleh
Afshar, ed., *Women, State, and Ideology: Studies from Africa and Asia* (New York: Macmillan Co.,
1987). These studies show the co-variance of economic, racial, and gender practices.

come from the recent economic histories of the nations of Africa, many of which made rapid and difficult transitions from decentralized kin-controlled agriculture, to king-client states, and/or to colonization linking them into the pressures of world trade. Colonial and state policy favored the greater efficiency of capitalized industrial ownership, the migration of labor to cities or to the large plantations of absentee landlords, and the consequent erosion of kinship as an economic system.

In the African experience, traditional practices such as family subsistence farming and women's management of regional markets persisted alongside the urbanizing, imperialist, and capitalized economic structures forcibly imposed from abroad. International trade networks, penetrating African societies even before European maritime contact, could siphon off the labor of a region, but they had to distort and exploit the hereditary life-support systems in order to do so. Traditional kinship-based spheres and capitalized urban spheres therefore coexisted, and still coexist, in an uneasy parasitical relation that drains the life out of the home and the village but does not kill them outright. People can move between the two spheres, with a certain amount of hardship, at different points in the year or in their life cycles.

First-century Palestine was something like that. The pressure of world markets and imperial taxation was felt everywhere. Under Roman policy, urban administrative centers took control of most civil, economic, and cultural functions. Cities were either built from scratch or reorganized along the lines of the Greek polis, at Tiberias, Caesarea, Sepphoris, and even Jerusalem. Whatever worldly Hellenistic culture had to offer was available wherever the roads penetrated and the cities were organized. In Palestine, that was everywhere. Yet the persistence of traditional kinship-based social transactions in the villages made it possible to avoid the cities almost entirely, if one wanted to do so.

So we must understand Galilee in the first century as offering its people a range of economic options, any of which had important social and cultural implications. Movement from village to city and back again might occur daily, seasonally, once in a lifetime, or never. Villagers were generally poorer than city dwellers, having relatively limited access to consumables. Yet the village was a network of kinship, providing both emotional and economic security because cousins, unlike mere neighbors, cannot be permitted to starve.

Especially in the cities, the people living in Galilee and Judea were racially diverse. They included Jews, who differed greatly in their religious observances; Syrians and other Semitic peoples who settled there after army service or came on business; and citizens, freedmen, and slaves from all over the empire. Villages may have been predominantly Jewish; yet even at the village of Capharnaum there was a Roman garrison to collect taxes from merchants using the nearby road.

One cannot, then, make an airtight association of village, poor, and Jew. Some Jews were wealthy, traveled abroad in the empire, and enjoyed the cultural richness of the Hellenistic cities. Some villagers may have farmed their plots in season and then worked as journeymen on estates for cash. Perhaps small-scale cottage industry was the rule in the villages; yet we know that the pottery workshops at Kfar Ḥananya (near Sepphoris) supplied both Galilee and Judea, while salted fish from Magdala (Tarichaeae) was exported throughout the empire.[7]

Beyond Palestine, the racial realities of the first century were comparable in complexity to those of our own society. It is somewhat misleading to speak of a unified Mediterranean culture, for the peoples positioned around that very navigable body of water recognized very acute differences among themselves. Jewish racial identity was a matter of kinship, inherited through the mother, while Greek identity had become more of a cultural choice. The Romans, who were not Greek, wanted to be. Some Jews also aspired to Greek culture. The Greeks recognized the Jews as a Semitic people, like the Egyptians. Egyptians, for their part, resented the comparatively well-off and hellenized Jews who lived in expatriate settlements around Egypt. In Alexandria, the city that the Greeks built on the Egyptian coast, Jews developed a scholarly tradition of Greek learning; but those Alexandrian Jews were bitter economic and political rivals with the expatriate Greeks themselves at the expense of the indigenous Egyptians.[8] Egyptians for their part preserved economic and kinship practices that linked them into the rest of Africa. It was in everyone's interest to keep the lid on racial conflict, because rioting or civil unrest could bring down brutal punishment from Rome.

Palestine was thoroughly integrated with the Roman Empire both economically and culturally. Its racial makeup was as complex as its economics. Like class, race too exists more as a repertoire of possibilities for action than as a coherent pattern fully describable in words. If being a

---

7. On the economics of Galilee, see Sean Freyne, *Galilee, Jesus, and the Gospels: Literary Approaches and Historical Investigations* (Philadelphia: Fortress Press, 1988). The distribution of pottery has been studied by David Adan-Bayewitz of Bar-Ilan University. See his recent contributions to *Israel Exploration Journal* and his forthcoming monograph *Common Pottery in Roman Galilee.*

8. See E. Mary Smallwood, "The Jews in Egypt and Cyrenaica during the Ptolemaic and Roman Periods," in *Africa and Classical Antiquity,* ed. L. A. Thompson and J. Ferguson (Ibadan, Nigeria: Ibadan University Press, 1969), 110–31.

villager brought certain economic options but closed off others, so racial identity had its own possibilities and disabilities. Language differences give us today some indication of what those possibilities and disabilities might have been like. Three languages are important encoders of the racial and class configurations of first-century Palestine: Hebrew, used by upscale scholars and in the Temple liturgy; Greek, for business, international politics, and secular culture; and, for traditional village life, Aramaic, of which there were different dialects in Galilee and in Judea. As people moved among Mediterranean cities or between city and village, so some important texts moved by translation from one language to another. Our investigation must remain alert to the difference in social practices signaled by an urban or a rural provenance and by Hebrew, Greek, and Aramaic cultural possibilities.

Languages

These considerations, as we shall see, become enormously significant when we inquire into making Jesus. It matters tremendously whether his story is told in a village or in a city, in Aramaic or in Greek, by those who manage their own labor or those who do not. We can understand the portraits that actually do come down to us only by mapping them against the range of words and deeds that could have been claimed for Jesus, given options afforded by the economic and racial scripts that the Jesus makers were playing out.

The three language communities with which we have to deal for first-century Palestine—the Hebrew, the Aramaic, and the Greek—do not exactly coincide with economic classes or with races, yet there are important correlations. Moreover, individual members of each group could communicate with people in other groups with some degree of fluency, ranging from a few words of greeting like *šālôm* and *chairete* to advanced trilingual and tricultural competence.[9] There were Jews in all three groups, and they differed in their economic status, their educational practices, their uses of texts, and their ways of observing the traditions of ritual and custom. The first disciples of Jesus came from among those Jews, and their languages are an index to their poietic capacities.

9. My transliteration system for the Hebrew alphabet is adapted from C. L. Seow, *A Grammar for Biblical Hebrew* (Nashville: Abingdon Press, 1987). The transliteration system for Greek comes from Maurice Balme and Gilbert Lawall, *Athenaze: An Introduction to Ancient Greek* (New York and Oxford: Oxford University Press, 1990). *Šālôm* is pronounced "shalom."

Hebrew is the ancient ancestral language of the Jews. The Jewish Scriptures are written in it. It is one of the Semitic languages, and to the native speaker of English it can seem both fluidly poetic and earthily concrete. Its words are formed from relatively few basic roots, and many of those roots are shared with other Semitic languages as well. Roots usually consist of three consonants, written right to left. Two of the Hebrew consonants are guttural stops that have no equivalent in English but are transliterated with the signs ' (for the letter 'aleph) and ' (for the letter *'ayin*). In the first century, vowels were not yet part of written Hebrew. Verbs in Hebrew are wonderfully flexible. Where English has two voices, active and passive, Hebrew has seven main patterns, or *binyānîm*. Thus one root—for example, *nś'*—with slight variations can cover a range of meanings: to raise, to rise, to pardon, to show one's face, to be kindly, to lift one's hand against, to contain, to carry, to support.

When the Jewish population of Palestine was deported to Babylon in the sixth century B.C.E., they adopted the language of that land for their everyday speech. Although many of the exiles returned home within a generation or two, for most Jews the Hebrew language had become something that one learned in school and heard at public worship in the reading of the Torah. Outside Palestine, in the Diaspora, many Jews knew scarcely a word of Hebrew.

At the same time, Hebrew continued as a language of theology and religious law. Although it had ceased to be a mother tongue used in everyday family communication, Hebrew was a living scholarly language that grew and adapted to changing times—but conservatively, since scholarship always focused on the classical language of the Torah. Both in Palestine and abroad, there is an unbroken line of literary production in Hebrew from the Babylonian exile down to the present day, some two and one-half millennia. Jews never went through the kind of loss of literacy and learning that Christian Europe experienced as the "dark ages."

In the first century C.E., great teachers were active at several centers in Palestine. After the destruction of Jerusalem's Temple in the year 70 C.E., those scholars regrouped and established academies in several cities, and to them we owe the organization of rabbinic Judaism. The Hebrew scholars interpreted the history, law, and traditions of the people by means of learned discussion in academic circles. This was a living discussion (and still is); our critical access to it, however, is chiefly by means of a textual record beginning with the Mishnah and continuing in the Talmuds.

The Hebrew scholars, or *Tannaim*, were rabbis in the generic sense of the word: a great one, a sage, a teacher. In the first century they were not officially ordained, but their authority was popularly recognized

nevertheless. Gradually they would assume responsibility for oversee-
ing and certifying the teaching activities of another language group, the
Aramaic speakers, and eventually their texts as well.

Aramaic is a Semitic language, like Hebrew. It seems to have been the
everyday language of the streets and the homes in first-century Palestine,
at least in villages that had not been politically targeted for hellenization.
Because of the shared word roots and other similarities, Aramaic is much
closer in spirit and imagination to Hebrew than Greek is. Nevertheless,
without school training an Aramaic-speaking Jew could not understand
the Scripture passages that were read in the local synagogue. That difficulty gave rise to a distinctive practice at public worship. After a Hebrew
text was read, an interpreter would tell the people what it meant in Aramaic. The interpreter was called a *meturgeman,* and his version of the reading was called a *targum,* or translation.

To make plain the distinction between Scripture and interpretation,
the Hebrew reader was required to keep his eyes on the scroll, while the
meturgeman had to look up and recite the targum from memory. The targums were interpretive, catechetical, even homiletic. They updated the sacred text by supplying details, such as mentioning some recent historical
event that plausibly was the referent intended by an ancient prophecy. As
oral performances, the targums could vary considerably from the written
text of the Bible, and also from one rendition to another; yet standard versions seem to have been congealing by the middle of the first century. In
later centuries, under the direction of the rabbis, traditional targums were
collected and written down, often in several stages.[10]

By turning these oral pastoral performances into text, the rabbis were
able to regulate the practice of the *meturgemanin* and to guarantee some
standard of fidelity to acceptable interpretive procedures. Given that fact, it
is enlightening to see that the rabbis did not insist on a strict translation of
the Hebrew, which would have been technically rather easy for them to do.
But the rabbis were not pedants and did not violate the people's sense of
ownership of these cherished recitals with too much scholarly tinkering.

Today we can compare the Hebrew and the Aramaic versions of the
Bible and thus glean a great deal of information. We can discover what
trends of interpretation were considered acceptable. We can see what concepts or antique customs were still intelligible to the people and which ones
needed to be explained or even revised. The targums are a window into the

---

10. A new series of English translations of the targums is being published by Michael
Glazier Books, of the Liturgical Press. The availability of these sources portends a revolution in the study of Christian origins by English-speaking theologians and historians.

religious sensibilities, imaginations, and liturgical experience of the ordinary people—including many of those who affiliated with Jesus movements in one way or another. Often an Aramaic targum sheds light on some point in the New Testament that seems dissonant with the "official," Hebrew Scripture.[11] Many of the early Christians did not read a Hebrew Bible; they recited and heard an Aramaic one. It has been argued that Jesus of Nazareth developed his own distinctive style of popular preaching using the meturgemanic tradition.[12]

Greek is an Indo-European language, which means that it is quite different from the Semitic languages in vocabulary and in the ways that it provides for the making of meanings. Unlike Hebrew, Greek is part of the linguistic family line from which modern English has developed. Classical Greek has continued to influence our own language into the present century, because the majority of men whose writings make up the canon of English literature were taught to read and write Greek as schoolboys. Western civilization's literary legacy from the ancient world includes many works of history, drama, mathematics, science, poetry, and philosophy written in the several dialects of ancient Greek.

After Alexander's military conquest of the Mediterranean basin and Asia Minor during the fourth century B.C.E., Greek became a common language for business and administration throughout the conquered territory. This was a simplified form of the language, called the *koinē*—or common Greek. The Christian Scriptures were written in this language, and other surviving examples of it include correspondence and records of business transactions. The *koinē* can be thought of as part of a "middlebrow" or popular literary communications technology; the elite educated class disdained it and tried instead to write like Plato, while the uneducated laboring classes did not write at all.[13]

---

11. In some instances a targum may preserve an older version of the Hebrew text than the one incorporated by the Masoretic Text, the standard version of the Jewish Scripture. See, e.g., John Gray, "The Masoretic Text of the Book of Job, the Targum and the Septuagint Version in Light of the Qumran Targum (IIQtargJob)," *Zeitschrift für die alttestamentliche Wissenschaft* 86 (1974): 331–50. Gray estimates that the Qumran targum was composed in the latter half of the second century B.C.E. That dating would make it nearly as old as the Septuagint. Gray suggests that the Septuagint may sometimes reflect an older Hebrew manuscript than the ones used in compiling the Masoretic text.

12. This was suggested in Bruce Chilton's introductory work *A Galilean Rabbi and His Bible: Jesus' Use of the Interpreted Scripture of His Time* (Wilmington, Del.: Michael Glazier, 1984). It seems clear that targums have influenced certain sayings attributed to Jesus.

13. For a discussion of the language and genre of the Gospels in the context of Hellenistic literary productions, see David E. Aune, *The New Testament in Its Literary Environment* (Philadelphia: Westminster Press, 1987).

Like Hebrew, Greek supported both classic texts and a rich scholarly tradition in which those classics were studied and interpreted. The city of Alexandria in Egypt, on the Mediterranean coast, has been called a "university town" because of its great library and its superb academic culture. People of many nations, including Jews, worked there and participated in the research and the literary production of the city.

The synagogue of Alexandria (which was of course an association of people, not merely one or several buildings) was particularly significant for the development of Jewish and Christian religious thought. The Jews of Alexandria had the same pastoral problem at worship as the Aramaic-speaking Jews in Palestine: most of them could not understand the Hebrew Bible. Therefore they undertook to translate the Bible into Greek. This translation project, however, followed a very different process from the one that produced the targums. The Alexandrian community wanted more than something to support popular piety at Sabbath services. They wanted a text that could stand up to critical study by Platonists, yet could also display its orthodoxy before the skeptical Hebrew scholars in Palestine.

For people were reading Greek in Jerusalem, too. Alexandrian Jewish scholars were in dialogue with their confreres in Eretz Israel. Travel between Alexandria and, for example, the Galilean city of Sepphoris was not difficult at all, and exchanging texts was rather easy. Scholarly circles of Greco-Jews based in a multicultural trading city like Sepphoris were the natural transmission points between Hebrew scholarship and Greco-Jewish scholarship.

The texts that have come down to us preserve only a small portion of that lively life of the mind and soul. The Septuagint is the third- and second-century (B.C.E.) compilation of the Greek versions of the Jewish scriptural books, plus some other texts. On the one hand, the Septuagint often attempts a more literal translation than the Aramaic targums.[14] On the other hand, it is more conceptually and imaginatively distant than the targums, partly because a Greek text could hardly be otherwise and partly because it programmatically overlays Moses with Plato. If some of the earliest Christians knew the Bible as an Aramaic recitation, others knew it as a set of Greek philosophical and historical treatises. The Septuagint was not the only or the last compilation of biblical books in Greek; moreover, we cannot always be certain that the text we receive is identical with the text available to first-century Jews. Nevertheless, comparing the Hebrew and the Greek

---

14. There are exceptions, however. As John Gray points out, the Qumran targum of Job is comparable to the Septuagint in its attempt at strict translation. See Gray, "Masoretic Text," 339.

texts of today may give us insight into the sensibilities of Diaspora Judaism and particularly into the conceptuality of the New Testament documents. The question of Aramaic textual influence thickens the plot.

Frontiers

Linguistically attested practices from first-century Palestine yield information for us about the society's class and racial diversity. The languages clue us in to the options that were available for negotiating economic survival and cultural identity. Moreover, the interface of the languages discloses for us certain important facets of the relationships among classes and races. Languages translate, but only imperfectly, and only by warping the viable social strategies of one society to allow for their representation to another. Luckily for our project of historical reconstruction, comparing the "before" and "after" versions of a textual translation permits us to understand something of the contours of the social frontier between two groups of people—or, in this case, among three.[15]

Perhaps the single most critical issue in understanding the ancient Mediterranean world, and Palestine as an integrated part of it, is finding an adequate working model to conceptualize the character of the social frontiers of class, race, language, and, as we shall presently see, gender. Those frontiers were like membranes that, as in the example of linguistic translation, subtly altered whatever was able to pass across them. At the same time, those interfaces themselves were mutating even as they brought people into contact, for Hellenistic civilization was a dynamic melting pot heated by the frictions of historical change.

Among contemporary scholars there are several current options for conceptualizing the structure of such social, cultural, and economic interrelationships. Most simple—and least adequate—is the commonplace assumption that although Greco-Roman society was pluralistic, the boundaries separating racial and economic groups were completely transparent and permeable. On this assumption, it would make no difference

---

15. The three Jewish groups are (1) a scholarly and religious elite who could read, write, and debate in Hebrew, although they likely spoke Aramaic at home and conducted business and political affairs in Aramaic and in Greek; (2) a large peasant population who spoke either of the two Palestinian dialects of Aramaic but knew enough Greek to get along at market and enough Hebrew to say their prayers; and (3) business people, pilgrims, bureaucrats, visiting scholars, and others from the Mediterranean Diaspora, who spoke and read Greek but perhaps picked up a little Aramaic.

whether someone read the Hebrew text of Isaiah, heard an Aramaic rendition of Isaiah, or debated in Greek with aphorisms lifted out of Isaiah. It would make no difference whether Mary was betrothed in the polis of Sepphoris, in the village of Nazareth, or out of Sepphoris into Nazareth.

A somewhat more complex modeling lays out the different racial and economic groups as strata or levels, with a narrow top and a broad bottom recognized by everyone in the pyramid. Peasant agricultural workers and artisans are supposed to be on the lowest rung. Petty officials and retainers are placed above them. Next come knightly or equestrian classes, and families with senatorial rank. Royalty sits on the top. Analogously for languages, Aramaic is placed at the bottom, Hebrew in the middle, and Greek on top. This stratification model surely reflects the upper-class perception, then as now; but it is nevertheless inadequate to the complexity of the situation that obtained in first-century Palestine. The directions of "up" and "down" were not uniformly perceived at each rung of the alleged ladder. For example, Aramaic, although spoken by villagers, was also a privileged language of scholarship and trade in the East, just as Greek was in the West. There is no reason to suppose that a village elder saw himself as the social inferior of an imperial centurion, notwithstanding the centurion's opinion. Moreover, the stratification model is inherently a static one. It does not help us to understand how the interaction of people across group boundaries could precipitate historical changes.

A third proposal would conceive of disadvantaged groups as pockets of muted knowledge and practice that were engulfed but not submerged by the dominant group.[16] From the perspective of the latter—for example, Greek literati—the muted groups appear to be poor, disparaged, and devalued. Muting is a strategy of the dominant group to discredit the alternative knowledges propagated by the subjected group. Yet, from their own perspective, members of the muted group operate by an entirely different calculus of valuing. Muted groups are like bubbles within the dominant society. Because they are all around in the midst of the dominant group, and because they make available an alternative construal of the "up and down" of social relations, these groups are dangerous to the dominant group. The written records that come down to us give information about both dominant and muted groups. Recognizing the textual

---

16. This model was proposed by the anthropologists Edwin Ardener and Shirley Ardener in *Perceiving Women,* ed. Shirley Ardener (New York: John Wiley & Sons, 1975). Although it was designed to conceptualize the interface of genders in contemporary societies, it is readily adaptable to describe class and racial relations in the ancient world.

disparagement of muted groups for what it is, we are led to pursue the disadvantaged group's view of itself and to watch for its creative uses of the distinctive semantic strategies open to it.

A muted group typically conserves its own meanings and practices but does not actively set out to challenge and change those of the dominant group. Therefore this model needs some modification if it is to fit the situation in first-century Palestine, where the bubbles, so to speak, of a certain muted group turned into storm fronts and moved out like wedges of turbulent weather across the horizons of the society.

The muted group that precipitated this social displacement was women, according to the evidence in the Gospels. The roots of resurrection lie on the far side of the gender front from the place where our texts now stand when they tell the story. To investigate resurrection, we have to recover the muted knowledge of women disciples. We need to understand what practices were available to them for making Jesus. Like class and race, gender too is a social construction and a repertoire of strategies for negotiating interpersonal transactions. Moreover, as a set of options, gender differs according to race and class. We must investigate the sorts of life strategies available to village women in comparison with the options of urban aristocratic Greek women. Could they read? Did they cook? Would they nurse? How did they manage their homes? To whom would they speak? What latitudes did custom allow, and how could these be manipulated to accomplish the women's purposes? Most important, how did women relate to one another, and what did their friendships mean to them?

Such information was deemed insignificant by the dominant, literate gender and is largely unavailable in the Gospels. Fortunately, the canonical Gospel materials do permit inferences that can be corroborated by information preserved in other Gospels, in non-Christian literature, and in the archaeological record. It will be possible for us to reconstruct a great deal of significant information about the strategies practiced by women in the first century. Without those strategies, without taking account of friendship among women as a crucial factor in the earliest propagation of Easter faith, it is impossible historically to explain Christian origin, that is, the beginnings of belief in resurrection and the first instances of recognizing Jesus as Lord.

Investigation of resurrection, then, entails a crossing of the gender frontier that extends through racial and class distinctions. We must trace backward along the pathway that the good news of Jesus followed. Quite simply, we must investigate what women can have made of Jesus.

A Look Ahead

This book is organized in three stages: (1) an inductive recovery of early practices of recognizing Jesus; (2) a synthetic discussion placing those practices in the context of a formal theorization of text and body and a cultural anthropology of gender, race, and class in Hellenism; and (3) a theological application embracing Christology, liturgy, and catechetics.

The investigation begins with six case studies of stories selected from the canonical Gospels. The first three studies establish that practices of access to Jesus were an important consideration in the production of those Gospel texts. Chapter 2 traces the career of a saying about nursing that traveled through variant Jesus traditions. Chapter 3 examines early theorizations of teaching as a strategy for putting people in touch with Jesus. Chapter 4 reads the appearance and empty tomb stories as critical reflections on catechetical practice. The second set of case studies explores early strategies used for identifying Jesus. Chapter 5 reconstructs litigation concerning the kinship of Jesus. Chapter 6 recovers the rhetorical contest over Jesus between constituencies from different economic classes. Chapter 7 watches a woman make something out of Jesus.

These six studies provide the embarkation point for the next major section of the book. There it becomes possible to summarize what has been learned about the early interdependent practices of identifying Jesus and providing the means of access to him. Contemporary scholarly approaches to text and body will be surveyed as helps for organizing this information and grasping its significance. The textual and bodily aspects of the distinctive gender, race, and class systems in Hellenistic society will then be reviewed. This middle part of the book is designed to set up the conceptual materials needed for the theological work of the third part.

The third and final section of the book formally presents the theology that the inductive and synthetic parts have prepared for. This theology transgresses the gentlemen's agreement that would distinguish so-called systematics from pastoral theology, with the former controlling the latter. We will instead treat Christology as the outcome of liturgical and catechetical practice, today as it was in the earliest Christian communities whose strategies define the rule of faith for us. Christological identity depends on liturgical and catechetical access.

Part One
Reconstruction

Practices of Recognizing Jesus

2

Like Nursing Babies

THE CHALLENGE of understanding divine availability and divine activity in this world has piqued religious imaginations in the West for several millennia. In relation to this issue, the postulate of bodily resurrection from death historically has been a theme of theological speculation shared by Judaism, Christianity, and Islam. But in Christianity, the stark assertion that Jesus rose from his tomb itself emerged as the culmination of a process that had its beginnings in a different thematization of divine availability and activity: the concept of the kingdom of God. The contemporary scholarly consensus about the Jesus sayings indicates that Jesus' own teaching before Calvary used this metaphor, divine monarchy, as the centerpiece of a message about the kind of God it was who was ruling the world, the kind of rule being divinely practiced, and the kind of world in which divine agency was at large.[1]

On Jesus' lips before Calvary were the words of blessing taught to him by his Jewish family. These same words are still recited several times daily by all who cherish the Mosaic covenant: "Blessed are you,

---

1. There is an extensive literature on the concept of God's kingdom in the Jesus traditions. The masculine term "kingdom" and the metaphor of monarchy both are troublesome. See the careful discussion of this metaphor as "founding axiom" of Christian theology in Edward Farley, *Ecclesial Reflection: An Anatomy of Theological Method* (Philadelphia: Fortress Press, 1982). The Scholars Version translation of the New Testament, which I have generally followed in this book, uses the terms "imperial rule" and "domain" instead of "kingdom" in order to capture the connotations of irresistible power and active governance. I have chosen to retain the archaic term "kingdom" because in the 1990s it is still the term most commonly and unselfconsciously used by scholars and students of Scripture, even those who criticize it. In these pages, the Scholars Version translation has been adjusted accordingly.

Lord our God, King of the Universe . . . ." *"Bārûk ʾatāh ʾadōnāy ĕlōhênû, melek hā-ʿôlām . . . ."* Like many of his contemporaries, Jesus speculated about the kingdom of this *melek hā-ʿôlām:* what it was, where it was, and how to get into it.

In the Aramaic idiom of villages like Nazareth where Jesus grew up, it was improper to refer directly to the deity. The targums typically render Hebrew terms meaning "God" as "glory of God," "name of God," or simply "the glory" or "the name." Readers of Matthew's Gospel are familiar with a similar practice, the substitution of "heaven" for "God" in the Matthean phrase "kingdom of heaven."

Thus on the one hand, to say "kingdom of God" in Jesus' neighborhood was a pious periphrastic for avoiding too direct a mention of the deity. To say "The kingdom of God is within you" was to say "God is within you."[2] On the other hand, the phrase "kingdom of God" also tends to throw the emphasis onto a divine activity of governance while deflecting attention from the theoretical question of the static substantial attributes of the deity. God is known through practices both divine and human rather than through appearance and contemplative gaze. Jesus' parables offer illustrations of how God works and of human ways of operating that bring people into the sphere of divine influence. Access to God is imagined—by Jesus' disciples, if not by himself—as an entering of God's kingdom.

Therefore in the Jesus traditions the collected sayings about entering the kingdom and its whereabouts merit particular attention. Kingdom is a metaphor of divine activity and human access to it. Jesus' own extraordinarily creative human imagination must have delighted in playing with this metaphor before Calvary. Yet the productive output of Jesus' imagination itself is not what concerns us here, although it lies in the background of our investigation. We are interested in how Jesus' poetic constructions stayed alive after Calvary, branched out, grew, and spread. The imagination of an accessible kingdom for God continued to propagate in the various constituencies of the Jesus movements.

The passage of that kingdom access metaphor through the semantic frontiers of economic class, gender, and race has left an interesting trail, which this chapter means to investigate.[3] But there are several

---

2. Johannes Weiss argued in *Die Predigt Jesu vom Reiche Gottes* (1892; Göttingen, 1964) that the concept of a kingdom of God was a means of avoiding anthropomorphic claims about the deity. Bruce Chilton also makes a case for this interpretation in his 1976 Cambridge doctoral dissertation, *God in Strength: Jesus' Announcement of the Kingdom* (Sheffield: JSOT Press, 1987), 272, 277–85. Chilton concludes that the phrase "kingdom of God" "refers in the first place to God's self-revelation and derivatively to the joy of men in His presence."

3. An earlier version of this study appeared in *Religious Education* 85 (1990): 455–77.

methodological stipulations that, although discussed at more length else-where in this book, ought to be stated here. First, the sayings of Jesus made their transit through Palestine and across what I have called social frontiers for the most part as oral recitations, not as written texts. Today our recovery strategies must work backward from texts, to be sure; yet these texts should be read as traces of oral practices occurring before the writing, continuing alongside the writing, and often persisting indepen-dently after the writing. Each saying had plenty of variants, and they could bundle with other sayings or stand alone, depending on the needs of the occasion. A Gospel writer had quite a selection to choose from; or, to put it another way, the writer had ample precedent to mix and match and improvise in accordance with traditional oral practices.

Second, there was a time when a textual, written Gospel was an odd-ity, a curious innovation amid the Jesus movements. Sayings of and about Jesus ordinarily were recited to the accompaniment of certain distinctive practices, which could not be replicated in texts. The textual practice of writing itself does not come from Jesus; writing Gospels was an innova-tion introduced in several early churches. This "new" way of remember-ing Jesus severed the traditional interaction among spoken words and their context. The "old" way, the way that arguably came from Jesus, was to vary the sayings about God's kingdom and to improvise. The texts that we have today still preserve variations in the stories, although of course they permit no further variation now.

The third methodological reminder is that the metaphor of God's kingdom is a semantic work of imagination. Different groups had differ-ent poietic resources available for doing that work, and so they left dis-tinctive fingerprints on what they touched. These fingerprints tell us about the kind of people who were building the Jesus traditions; knowl-edge of the social circumstances of those men and women in turn helps us to bring their traditions into sharper focus. Fourth, where we go to look for these fingerprints is to the stories about Jesus' career, which we re-ceive in versions that were captured on vellum or papyrus at least forty years after his death. What people were making of Jesus during those four decades is narratively projected back before Calvary, and to recover it we work constantly against the grain of the historical fiction of the Gospels. The stories purport to convey information about Jesus before Calvary, but from them we infer information about subsequent generations.

The fifth, and most theologically compelling, premise is that two generations of Jesus makers felt perfectly justified in attributing things first said after Calvary to the one who had died there. This practice attests to the character of their resurrection faith: that Jesus who died *is identical with* this one who is speaking and acting now in our midst. This premise of identity and access is the generative principle of the literary form that we call a Gospel.

In the first decades after Calvary, it was feasible to propagate historically accurate information about what Jesus had said and done. Yet as far as we can tell, the proclamation of the Gospel *never* meant propagating historically accurate information about what Jesus had said and done. His availability to the churches was never that of someone whose life had closed. He never was remembered as someone out of the past. He was not gone, and to know him as gone would be not to know him at all. From the beginning, then, the church had to mount a distinctive poiesis and praxis in order to introduce people to who the Jesus who had been now was. The beginning of the church is the inception of that poiesis and praxis, providing access to Jesus. However, those procedural competences developed quite gradually and not without conflict.

Paideia, Law, and Nature

The Gospels, like all texts, are essentially rewrites of earlier texts. They are patchworks in which one can still discern the textures of earlier weavings, stitchings, and wearings. By the time the canonical Gospels reached the final forms in which we receive them, many rewrites of Jesus already had been done.[4] Early versions of Jesus' message were progressively overlaid with messages about Jesus himself. The earlier theme of God's kingdom as the focus of the Jesus constituencies gradually gives way to the figure of Jesus himself in later layers of the Gospels. Or, if you will, the figure of Jesus is patched over the text of the reign of God. In the overlay, two message systems that had been conceptually separable were superimposed and ultimately fused.

This displacement seems to be a function of practices connected with the transmission of the Gospel. It appears as a textual shadow or trace of the development of distinctive teaching practices within the early Jesus movements. The emergence of those practices can be uncovered through an "archaeological" reading of the texts. The point of such a reading is not to

---

4. These revisions were more than mere rewrites, and at first they were accomplished without the technology of ink and vellum. Bruce Chilton persuasively describes the recitation or performance of Jesus materials (which he identifies generically as haggadah and halakhah) within homiletic or catechetical traditions that were both conservative and inherently varying. See Bruce D. Chilton, *Profiles of a Rabbi: Synoptic Opportunities in Reading about Jesus*, Brown Judaic Studies, no. 117 (Atlanta: Scholars Press, 1989).

uncover "the historical Jesus" as founder and foundation of the church. Rather, we turn 180 degrees away from the historical Jesus and look instead for the teachers in whose faces, activities, and words Jesus and his practices are reflected. This quest is for the earliest teachers, which is to say, the historical pedagogies of the earliest churches.

The context in which the Jesus movement erupted was Jewish Palestine, and specifically lower Galilee. This was a society experiencing political tensions but nevertheless enjoying prosperity and the influx of a remarkably rich mixture of cultural commodities. The language of the indigenous population was Aramaic, which facilitated contact between Palestinian Jews and Diaspora Jews living to the east in Babylon. Hebrew had become a language for prayers and learned exchanges. The Syriac dialect also was heard among veterans of the Roman army who lived in the gentile settlements ringing lower Galilee.

Greek, however, was the language that tied the society into the economic, cultural, and political network of the Mediterranean world. Diaspora Jews in great cities like Alexandria, Antioch, Ephesus, and Rome long had been enthusiastic participants in the Hellenistic way of life. For their part, upper-class Greek Gentiles included many who understood and respected Judaism as a philosophy with a strong ethical focus. Greek-thinking Diaspora Jews exerted upon the Jewish aristocracy of Jerusalem a pressure toward hellenization that probably was at least as influential as that of the Roman administration, which gathered its political strength from a long-standing policy of the urbanization of Palestine.

The Greek city, or polis, in Eretz Israel as elsewhere, was an ideal and a way of life as much as a place. Villages like Nazareth might retain their traditional council of elders and overseers, might support an elementary school, might provide for widows and the poor through complex kinship and charitable structures, and might even arbitrate property or labor disputes by the old traditional customs. Nevertheless Nazarenes had to walk three miles to the great polis of Sepphoris for market, for banking, for the writing of deeds, to file civil complaints, to consult the genealogical archives or a renowned rabbi, and often even to find work. It is likely that a family of builders, such as Jesus' family, would hire on for the massive construction projects undertaken by Herod Antipas in Sepphoris and Tiberias. In Mark 6:3, the word *tektōn*, often translated "carpenter," means a skilled craftsman and refers as well to a builder or a stonemason. Trees were scarce in lower Galilee, so limestone and basalt blocks were common materials used for houses and other structures. Once the stonemasons completed Sepphoris's five-thousand-seat theater, the people could go there to see the popular mime shows and hear entertaining orators.[5] There were both economic and cultural incentives for the people of the land to learn Greek.

The Greek city held further attractions for aristocratic families. The idea of the polis was linked to the ideal of public life. And in order to foster public life in the Hellenistic sense, one had to set up the Greek system of education, particularly the *gymnasion*. In the second century B.C.E., Jerusalem's upper class had established the ephebate: the order of young men in their late teens undergoing athletic and military training through the *gymnasion* system. It was this, together with the hellenization of the cult of Israel's God in the Temple, that had led to the Maccabean revolt.

Outside Judea, however, and especially outside Palestine, Jews of the great cities continued to take part in at least some of the stages of Greco-Roman education. At the elementary level, childen were instructed in basic Greek literacy at the city's expense. Parents who could afford it then sent their boys, in the company of the slave called the *paidagōgos,* to the grammarian to read the classical poets. Privileged young men finished off their education with a year or two in the *gymnasion.* Thus they came into possession of paideia, the cultured Greek way of life. The process of instruction, or "cultivation," by which they achieved this culture also was called paideia.[6] For those few headed into a career in politics, law, or civic administration, further training in public speaking and composition was obtained, at considerable cost, through private study with a rhetor. Alternatively, one might become the student of a philosopher.

Jews who attained a certain economic class, both among the Mediterranean Diaspora and within Eretz Israel itself, took part in this system at every level, including the theoretical debates about the very nature of paideia that went on interminably at the top of the pyramid. Here learned

---

5. The theater at Sepphoris is dated to the early first century by the archaeologist James F. Strange. For the opinion that Herod Antipas built this theater, see Richard A. Batey, *Jesus and the Forgotten City* (Grand Rapids, Mich.: Baker Book House, 1991), 94–100. But this opinion is disputed by another archaeologist working at the site, Eric Meyers, who believes that "the theater and other so-called pagan or Roman aspects of Sepphoris cannot be positively dated to the first century." See Eric M. Meyers, "The Challenge of Hellenism for Early Judaism and Christianity," *Biblical Archaeologist* 55 (1992): 88.

6. The classic treatment of the concept is Werner Jaeger's 1933 *Paideia: The Ideals of Greek Culture,* trans. Gilbert Highet, 3 vols. (New York: Oxford University Press, 1943–45). Jaeger opened the door for explorations of the ways in which the Jesus movements adapted Hellenistic educational practices and theories in his 1960 Carl Newell Jackson Lectures at Harvard University, published as *Early Christianity and Greek Paideia* (Cambridge: Harvard University Press, Belknap Press, 1961). But for a generation afterward, Christian paideia was treated as strictly a post-New Testament phenomenon. See, e.g., the article by T. P. Halton in the *New Catholic Encyclopedia.*

Jews felt that they had a special wisdom to offer to the other Greek philosophers. During the third century B.C.E., the Greco-Jews of Alexandria produced the Septuagint, a translation of the Hebrew Scriptures. This was a creative philosophical endeavor, a reinterpretation of both the Hebrew and the Greek concepts.[7] In the Greek rendering, *tôrāh* ("instruction") became *nomos* ("law"). *Lēb* ("heart," the organ of thought) became *dianoia* ("mind"). *Nepeš* (literally, "throat"; figuratively, the fragile and vulnerable totality of the breathing human person) became *psychē* ("soul"). And so the Pentateuch became a respectable philosophical treatise.

The upper-class Alexandrian translators came to regard Judaism itself as a paideia, or cultured way of life, and God as the teacher of Israel. But besides teaching, paideia can mean punishing. In that vein, the Deuteronomic history of God's "chastisements" of Israel was interpreted as one great program of paideia. Historical revelation, then, became a paideia for the upwardly mobile Greek Jews.

In the third century B.C.E. in elite academic circles within the Greek cities, the interpretation of *tôrāh* as *nomos* made very good sense and was a distinct theological advance. Three centuries later, however, the situation had changed. The classical philosophy of Plato had competition. Most significantly, the Cynic movement was criticizing the artificiality of law, social convention, and the vaunted Greek paideia itself, urging instead a return to nature, *physis*. Cynics favored simplicity in food, clothing, and lifestyle. Centers for the advancement of Cynic thought emerged in several Palestinian cities. And in the first century C.E., popularized versions of Cynic wisdom were in circulation through the efforts of unwashed, ragged, wandering philosophers who moved along the trade routes and found audiences in the market cities as well as in the villages and towns. They were popular speakers, they disparaged *nomos,* and they despised paideia.

Along the colonnaded avenues of Sepphoris one can imagine a lively argument between, say, a Cynic opponent of all law as unnatural and a scribe of the Pharisees bent on instructing Galilean villagers in how to apply Torah by tithing herbs. One can imagine a young stonemason, on his lunch break from theater construction, relishing such a debate enormously. Even more plausibly, the Cynics soon would hear much that they

---

7. The degree of hellenization varies in the different books of the Septuagint. (The Septuagint fell into disfavor among Jews by the end of the first century C.E., and other Greek translations were adopted.) Extremely helpful is Georg Bertram's article on the word group *paideuō/paideia* in Gerhard Kittel, *Theological Dictionary of the New Testament,* ed. Gerhard Friedrich, trans. and ed. Geoffrey W. Bromiley (Grand Rapids: Wm. B. Eerdmans Publishing Co., 1967).

liked from the young worker himself, once he laid down his hammer and took to preaching. Sayings of Jesus would find their way into Christian Greek literature in the form of *chreia,* or pointed anecdotes that were the stock-in-trade of Cynic rhetorical practice.

Thus when the term "paideia" is found in Greek Christian literature, it says something about economic privilege. An approving use of the term signals upper-class, perhaps Alexandrian, sympathies (or aspirations), while disparagement of the term or its avoidance might constitute the fingerprint of Greek Jews of a somewhat lower class, Cynic sympathizers. Behind either of these handlings, of course, may lie an even earlier Aramaic provenance.

What was said about (and maybe by) Jesus in Greek eventually took literary form in the Gospels. Alongside that transmission, and probably even before it, what was said by and about Jesus in Aramaic first took the form of haggadoth and halakhoth. Halakhah is instruction about living life before God, while haggadah is narrative illustration of a virtue or a teaching.[8] Of the two traditionings, Aramaic and Greek, the Greek one is more accessible to us because of our familiarity with its literary precipitate, the Gospels. The Aramaic traditioning of haggadoth and halakhoth, which differed from the Greek *chreia* not only in language but in its poietic strategies as well, will be discussed in a later chapter. But first we will attempt a reading of the praxis and poiesis that wrote Jesus up in Greek.

We begin with a first-century saying attributed to Jesus, one that can be interpreted against the popular Cynic background: "The Sabbath is made for people (*anthrōpos*), not people for the Sabbath." This saying is reported in Mark 2:27 (although not in the parallel passages, Matt. 12:5-8 and Luke 6:5). If read in its Greek literary context, it yields meanings different from those possible in spoken Aramaic. Philo of Alexandria, an older contemporary of Jesus who reflects the influential Greek exegetical traditions of the Alexandrian synagogue, pursues a similar line of thought when he explains how the Sabbath serves human well-being.[9] Although Philo (that is, his community) is generally credited with the first literary interpretation of the Greek concept of nature through the Jewish concept of divine creation, Mark 2:27 indicates the currency of that very interpretation at the popular, grassroots level. Within rabbinic literature, this view of the Sabbath would persist, perhaps not independently of the influence of popular

---

8. These are of course Hebrew technical names for modalities of oral teaching that were familiar to Aramaic-speaking villagers.

9. Philo, *De specialis legibus* 2. 60–70; cf. 71–115.

Hellenism. Rabbi Simeon b. Menasiah, who lived in Galilee in the second century C.E., is credited in the *Mekilta* with interpreting Exod. 31:14 to mean that the Sabbath is given to you, you are not given to the Sabbath.

What is the significance of finding this saying within a relatively early stratum of the Jesus traditions? The term *physis,* or "nature," is not found in the Gospels, and the absence has been attributed to "a deliberate theological decision that rests on the fact that there is no place for 'natural theology' in the thinking of the New Testament."[10] But this motive seems obvious only if one is theologically predisposed to deny any Greek influence in the Gospels. A more plausible explanation may be found in the fact that, unlike contemporary literary works produced by and for the upper classes—in which the term *physis* is quite common—the Gospels have no vested interest in reinforcing the fiction of the "naturalness" of various social constructions that disadvantage the working people. Thus the absence of the term *physis* supports the view that the Gospels originate outside the most privileged of the Greek intellectual classes.

By contrast, the Gospels are very interested in the naturalness that does not have to be constructed, that is, in the nonfictional human body itself. The texts need not assert that the body is natural; that fact is obvious. What must be asserted and defended are the claims of the body against the claims of social fictions. Within the slogan in question, Mark 2:27, the term "people" (*anthrōpos*) stands for the body and all its claims prior to the inscription of social texts, in this case the text "Sabbath."

The body's resistance to social inscription was a major preoccupation of Cynic thought. Thus the slogan "The Sabbath is made for people" makes sense as a point of contact between peasant Palestinian Judaism and popular Cynicism, that is, in the topography of the cultural frontier between them. The saying can be taken as a very clever strategy for resolving in one stroke both the opposition between *nomos* and *physis* on the Greek side and the semi-cognate opposition between halakhoth and the exigencies of village life on the Aramaic side. In Greek, it scores a point in favor of the nature-loving Cynic lifestyle; in Aramaic, it puts legalists in their place. The key to the resolution is found in one of the creation stories in Genesis, where God is the maker of both human nature, on day six, and the Sabbath law, on day seven. Thus the law is no less "natural" than men and women themselves, even though it comes into being after they do.

In the Jesus traditions, this saying has an affinity for situations where legal requirements conflict with human needs. "Nature" would cover all

10. See Helmut Koester, *"physis," Theological Dictionary of the New Testament.*

that goes with the divinely created human condition: hunger and the need for food, illness and the need for healing, childhood and the need for nurture, even menstruation and the need for respite.[11] These needs have a prior claim to that of the law. This solution makes sense on all sides of the social frontier. A Cynic could accept it because it privileges nature, in keeping with the Cynic program. A Sadducee could accept it because it is based in the Pentateuch and because it thwarts the Pharisees' modernizing project. And a Pharisee could not reject it without seeming to reject the divine wisdom and will at work in the design of human nature.[12]

Entering the Kingdom of God

The Sabbath saying played differently on different sides of important social frontiers in the first century C.E. The conflicting claims of law, nature, and culture were a common concern, although juxtaposed variously by various groups. The Jesus tradition tapped into a lively multicultural contestation in the first century C.E., one that reached throughout the Mediterranean Diaspora, into hellenized Palestine, and down to Lower Galilee itself. The exchange shaped up differently among urban and rural populations and among the peasant farmers, the artisans, and the ruling classes; but none was left out of it. As Jesus movements expanded through these economic classes and ethnic constituencies, the emerging Christian educational practices were profoundly affected by the ongoing renegotiation of these culturally contested realities.

The Gospel texts freeze this dynamic development at several points and give us cross-sectional glimpses of what in actuality was a vigorously flowing stream. The texts preserve indications of the material *content* of the Jesus traditions at selected points in time. But they also show something of

11. From an anthropological perspective, Sabbath itself is a stylized, textualized version of menstruation: a periodically recurring time of rest and renewal during which certain activities are proscribed. There are four or five Sabbaths a month, just as there are four or five days of menstrual flow, although Sabbaths are distributed throughout the month. Thanks to the text of Sabbath, everyone can enjoy a periodic respite such as that which the body requires for women.

12. Pharisees sought to expand the authority of the law to cover more recent interpretations and applications, while Sadducees resisted this expansion. The Sabbath slogan resembles Jesus' answer to the Sadducees about resurrection in Mark 12:26–27—a retort based on "the book of Moses," which Sadducees accept, rather than on more convenient references to resurrection in the Prophets and the Writings, which would not have been authoritative for Sadducees.

how the stream flowed, providing information about the evolving *process* of traditioning itself. Significant strands emerged in the development of Christian initiatory practices. They show up in successive modifications that a second dominical saying underwent while carried in oral traditions before achieving the several different textual forms that come down to us in the canonical Gospels. The career of this particular saying reflects the evolution of initiatory policy in the communities that were carrying the saying. Its mutation can be explained by reconstructing the teaching practices that it must have served in its various forms.[13]

The saying in question has to do with children and entering God's kingdom. It comes down to us in a number of different versions, and it is unique in several respects.[14] For example, this is the only one of the extant dominical sayings in which "entering the kingdom" is easy. Second, a version of the saying provides the only Johannine mention of God's kingdom. Third, it is one of very few dominical sayings to appear, in some form, in the Synoptics, in the *Gospel of Thomas*, and also in John.

Let us start with a form of the saying that likely is unfamiliar to many modern readers and that also may be the earliest of the extant versions: the one found in the *Gos. of Thom.* 22:1-2, which we have in Coptic translation from a lost Greek source.[15]

> Jesus saw some babies nursing. He said to his disciples,
> "These nursing babies are like those who enter the kingdom."

These terse lines provide only a minimal narrative setting for the saying. Yet they give us sufficient information to infer the ethnicity, the economic class, and some of the significant gender practices of the people who kept the saying current in this form. These inferences will help us to bring the nuances of the metaphor into sharper focus.

---

13. This approach presumes the evolution of something like the Sayings Source, Q, first as a repertoire of Aramaic halakhoth and haggadoth and then as a collection of Greek *chreiai*.

14. John Dominic Crossan has brought to light the affinities between the different versions of this saying by placing them together in numbers 158 and 446 of his *Sayings Parallels: A Workbook for the Jesus Tradition* (Philadelphia: Fortress Press, 1986). See also Crossan, "Kingdom and Children: A Study in the Aphoristic Tradition," in *Kingdom and Children, Semeia* 29, ed. Daniel Patte (Chico, Calif.: Scholars Press, 1983), 75–95; and the unique weighting he gives to the saying in his *The Historical Jesus*, 436.

15. To reconstruct the precanonical career of a saying, it often is necessary to take account of extracanonical versions. For this saying in the *Gospel of Thomas*, the Scholars Version has: "enter the < Father's > domain."

The first significant detail of the saying is that "babies" is plural. There are several babies. There is a group of nursing women. It is interesting that the women are not actually mentioned; they are invisible in the text although indispensable to the activity of nursing. The setting provided for the saying, then, is a group of women gathered for companionship as they suckle infants. By custom, those "babies" could be as old as three years. The scene that we are given to imagine is not a silent one. The women are conversing among themselves and speaking to the babies; some of the little ones may also be talking back, or playing, or napping.

Given this tableau, the reader wonders: Who are these women to one another, that they are found together nursing? Are they friends? Neighbors on a courtyard? Sisters-in-law or other kin? Slave wet nurses in a wealthy household? Who are they *to Jesus,* that he happens upon them at this domestic work? Are they his wife and sisters? Neighbors on his courtyard? Slaves of a wealthy host who is entertaining him?

To sort out these questions, we first must consider the varieties of nursing arrangements known in the ancient world. A nursing pair need not be a mother with her own offspring. Women able to nurse had a commodity to sell. Court records survive from hellenized Egypt of free women's contracts to provide nursing and other child-care services to clients.[16] Women were more likely to seek this kind of work in times of economic hardship than in times of plenty. We can only guess at the fate of the natural child when the mother was forced by hunger—her own and that of her older children—to take a job feeding someone else's baby.

In Hellenistic civilization, there were four situations in which a wet nurse was needed. First, a wealthy woman might want to transfer to a servant some or all of the work of nursing her highborn child. Second, illness or death might remove the natural mother of a highborn child. Third, a slave with specialized skills might be required by her master to return to work soon after childbirth and leave the nursing of her slave child to another. Fourth, a slave trader who took in an abandoned foundling would need a wet nurse to ensure that the child survived to be put to work.

---

16. For wet-nursing contracts, see Deborah Hobson, "The Role of Women in the Economic Life of Roman Egypt: A Case Study from First-Century Tebtunis," *Classical Views* 28 (1984): 373–90. Hobson found that more women hired out as wet nurses in years when the harvest was poor. For information on the duties of the wet nurse and on general child-care practices in Hellenistic civilization, see Aline Rouselle, *Porneia: On Desire and the Body in Antiquity,* trans. Felicia Pheasant (Oxford and New York: Basil Blackwell Publishers, 1988); Robert Garland, *The Greek Way of Life: From Conception to Old Age* (Ithaca, N.Y.: Cornell University Press, 1990); and Sandra Joshel, "Nurturing the Master's Child: Slavery and the Roman Child Nurse," *Signs* 12 (1986): 3–22.

While these four situations could in principle be served by either a free wet nurse or a slave, wealthy families preferred slaves. The slave nurse could become the object of affection particularly for highborn girls, who often took their old nurses with them when they married. Among Jews in Palestine we have no records of wet nursing contracts by free women. The Mishnah, however, knows of household slaves who are wet nurses.[17] But if there were a slave wet nurse in a Jewish home, she would have to be a Gentile, assuming halakhah were followed, because an Israelite slave girl must be set free at puberty and a mature Jewish woman could not be bought as a slave.

It is clear, then, that nursing need not imply kinship; it could also be an economic relationship or a condition of servitude. One cannot tell just by seeing some babies nursing. Moreover, the babies themselves do not really care about the status of the nurses beyond their availability as sources of food and comfort. If we want to know more about the women in the Jesus saying, we have to inquire further.

Exactly where was this group of nursing women when Jesus supposedly spied them? We know where they were not. They were not in the women's quarters or *gynaikōn* of a well-to-do hellenized home. Between puberty and menopause, Greek women of the better classes were supposed to keep to their own apartments.[18] Even in a household that had not the means to observe strict enclosure, a nursing group—whether slave, free, or mixed—would not gather where a male guest might see them. If a family, whether Jewish or gentile, was wealthy enough to afford a slave wet nurse, then it could afford a large enough domestic space to seclude her in her work.

The Land and the Body

Chances are, then, that the suckling envisioned in the Jesus saying is being done either by freelance wet nurses or by the babies' own relatives, or

---

17. The sages teach that a wife has the duty to nurse her own child unless she has brought two slaves with her to the marriage and one is a wet nurse (*M. Ketubot* 5:5). See Judith Romney Wegner, *Chattel or Person? The Status of Women in the Mishnah* (New York and Oxford: Oxford University Press, 1988), 76.

18. For details, see Susan Walker, "Women and Housing in Classical Greece: The Archaeological Evidence," in *Images of Women in Antiquity,* ed. Averil Cameron and Amélie Kuhrt (Detroit: Wayne State University Press, 1983), 81–91. Walker compares floor plans of two houses in Attica and one modern Islamic dwelling in Nigeria. See also Garland, *The Greek Way of Life.*

by both. The most likely setting seems to be a courtyard. In the villages of Galilee, a common architectural design was the *insula,* which today we would call an apartment house or tenement. Families occupied one or several rooms opening onto a common courtyard. The rooms were small and their stone walls were proportionately very thick, so as to regulate temperature both in summer and in winter. The courtyard was open to the sky and was the most pleasant place to work, eat, and visit.[19] Families sharing a courtyard might be kin to one another; but then, most of the village would be at least distant kin by one scheme or another.

"Jesus saw some babies nursing and said . . . ." The offhand tone of this scene-setting frame for the saying implies that (for whoever is repeating the saying in this form) there is nothing out of the ordinary in the premise that Jesus might be talking with his companions in a spot where they could see a nursing group. Who, then, are the tradents or tellers of this bit of Jesus lore? If we want to know what they understood to be Jesus' teaching on kingdom entry, then we have to understand what nursing babies meant to them.

Wet-nursing could mean slavery or economic exploitation in the ancient world, but we have already ruled that out as unlikely in this instance. Here, nursing may imply kinship, but it need not. Although one must be a mother in order to nurse, she need not be the mother of the baby whom she is nursing. One baby can displace another at the breast. Nursing is transgressive allocation of food, without regard to kinship or to the halakhah that governs all other nutritional transactions in Eretz Israel.

The productivity of the maternal body should be understood in the context of the cultural system of Palestinian village Judaism in the first century, of which the social construction of distinct gender definitions was part. No ethnographic reports about that culture survive, of course, but information in the Mishnah can provide a general sketch.[20] The land of

---

19. For illustrations of the ruins of such dwellings in Upper Galilee, see Eric M. Meyers, James F. Strange, and Carol L. Meyers, *Excavations at Ancient Meiron, Upper Galilee, Israel 1971–72, 1974–75, 1977* (Cambridge, Mass.: American Schools of Oriental Research, 1981), chap. 3. For Capharnaum, see Stanislao Loffreda, *Recovering Capharnaum* (Jerusalem: Edizioni Custodia Terra Sancta, 1985). The Mishnah's case law preserves fascinating glimpses of the life of village courtyards and the mishaps that could occur there.

20. The Mishnah was edited about 200 C.E. in Sepphoris, in Lower Galilee—more than a century after the Jesus traditions took shape. Thus the specific legal formulations of the tractates cannot be projected back to Jesus' time with absolute confidence. However, the cultural symbols reflected in them are much more enduring and can be used for an anthropological reconstruction of the society—especially when the underlying law was codified many centuries earlier. The following comments are based on Jacob Neusner, *The Economics of the Mishnah* (Chicago: University of Chicago Press, 1990).

Israel was the key cultural symbol to the sages whose traditions comprise the Mishnah. God was the principal owner of the land, but human landowners were treated like God's business partners. The land was regarded as having been allotted equitably in ancient times, and, at least in theory, it could never be permanently sold. In the seventh, or sabbatical, year debts were canceled and slaves went free, and at the fiftieth, or jubilee, year land returned to the family of the original owners.

Productive management of the land was more important than legal documentation in establishing ownership. In case of disputed title, if the owner of record was absent for three years while another farmed his plot, the squatter's claim was upheld. The technical term for this method of securing ownership is usucaption. Ownership, then, consisted in caring for the land and controlling its fruits. The system of tithing was critically important in supporting this conception. Tithes were owed to God as to the senior partner in a business deal, although they were in fact consumed by special castes in Israel: priests, Levites, and the poor. Tithes fell due at the time when the produce became available for consumption. It was the right and privilege of the landowner to present the tithe and to pronounce the ritual formula declaring his membership in Israel and his personal participation in covenant with God. Because women were excluded from performing that ritual, they did not have the cultural status of landowners in Israel. (But women were responsible for separating a tithe of dough from each loaf before they baked it.) Untithed food must not be eaten; to do so would be like cheating God. On the other hand, eating food that had been tithed was a celebration of the covenant fulfilled.

In the legal logic of the Mishnah, women are treated in some respects like the land.[21] Just as the firstfruits of the crops are sacred, so the firstborn of women and of the flocks have special cultic status. Land, a portion of the heritage of Israel, is handed down through the patriline, from father to male heirs, while membership in the people of Israel itself is handed down through the matriline, from mother to child. Neither the land nor the Jewish woman can be permanently sold. If a Gentile takes a woman captive or buys away some land, every possible effort must be undertaken to ransom her or it. The householder in Israel is responsible for keeping both the land and the women within the family. Moreover, just as one can acquire land from an absentee owner by usucaption (that is, by taking it over and making it produce), so one can acquire a wife by rape.[22]

21. Some of the details in what follows are taken from Wegner, *Chattel or Person?* although Wegner does not draw the parallel between women and the land.
22. For rape as usucaption, see Wegner, *Chattel or Person?* 42, on M. *Qiddušin* 1:1.

The cultural system represented by the Mishnah projected a more or less stable symbolic coherence for a privileged minority: male landowning villagers. For that constituency, God's dominion was Eretz Israel, the land farmed and harvested in accordance with rituals of tithing that confirmed the divine ownership and governance. But what about the majority? Their symbolizations are muted almost beyond recovery, for we have little textual evidence to go on if we inquire whether women or landless artisans might have construed some of these realities differently.

But we *do* have those nursing babies. What is being asserted in this claim that nursing babies are like those who enter the kingdom of God? Against the background of the cultural system reflected in the Mishnah, our Jesus saying acquires a new edge. For one thing, the babies are eating untithed food. That food is being produced independently of the covenant between God and landowning males. Moreover, kinship is irrelevant here. Any mama will do. Milk "belonging" to one baby can be had by another, in a primal usucaption. With this feeding, there can be no Sabbath preparation, no storing up in barns for the sabbatical year. Here is productivity that women control. It falls outside law and ritual. In effect, the nursing analogy implies that the way into God's dominion lies in the opposite direction from that defined in a dominant cultural system: tithing the fruits of the holy land. Moreover, the nursing analogy places kingdom entry prior to Torah. The age of weaning, when nursing ceased, was significant for the rabbis of the late first century C.E., because at this age a child began to be instructed in Torah and took on a new legal status.[23] Nursing babies are ignorant of divine law because they are too young to read.

It is plausible to suppose that nursing was a common enough activity for men to see and even discuss in a village like Capharnaum, yet something that would not have been invented by a scribal circle and might have been downright embarrassing to elite city dwellers trained in the technical niceties of rhetorical composition. The latter fact perhaps explains its absence from the canonical Gospels, which allow someone to *mention* nursing to Jesus but not to *show* it to him.[24]

---

23. The Mishnah records a disagreement between R. Eliezer and R. Joshua about the proper age for weaning (see *Ketubot* 60a; cf. 2 Macc. 7:27). Eliezer Ebner points out: "The names for the little boy and girl were appropriately *Tinok* and *Tinoket,* meaning 'suckling.' This name became a term of endearment, as it was applied to boys and girls who were beyond the nursing stage for a number of years." See Eliezer Ebner, *Elementary Education in Ancient Israel during the Tannaitic Period (10–220 C.E.)* (New York: Bloch Publishing Co., 5716/1956).

24. Even in the canon, however, a mention of nursing is linked to conditions for receiving the word of God (see Luke 11:27).

Whether or not Jesus historically uttered this saying before Calvary is beside the point. The saying permits us to infer that certain people were able to grasp the analogy between nursing and God's kingdom and were able to associate that analogy with the memory of Jesus. I have made a case that those people were landless villagers, including, especially, women. But this saying was destined to cross cultural frontiers because it also could resonate with somewhat differently defined issues current among upscale hellenized Jews.

The version of the saying in the *Gospel of Thomas* 22, which comes to us in Coptic through Greek, employs a strategy similar to that of the saying about the Sabbath discussed above. An Israelite idea, God's kingdom, is reconciled with a Cynic theme, naturalness. Therefore the saying about babies and God's kingdom is another frontier saying. Like "Sabbath for people," this saying plays into the nature versus law discussion, and it engages cultural values on both sides of the front between the Greek urban milieu and the Jewish village. While it seems likely that the saying originated in an Aramaic-speaking village, it definitely would appeal to Greeks with Cynic leanings because of the earthiness of infants suckling with a group of women in a place accessible enough for a teacher to be talking to his disciples there. The participle "nursing" itself reprises the tension between text and the bodily practices that text encodes. As a text, the verb "to nurse" demands a subject and a direct object: "*M* nurses *B*; *B* is nursed by *M*." Yet the bodily reality of nursing resists the grammatical separation of subject from object. Is it the mothers or the babies who are "nursing"? The reciprocality of the action itself confounds the attempt to textualize it. Are the babies nursing or being nursed? Are the mothers suckling or being sucked? The body presents instead a nutritional reality with two nonsymmetrical sides but without differentiation into an active role and a passive role. One uses the same word to encode what the babies do and what the mothers do simultaneously. Just so with God's kingdom: you enter it, it enters you. It is easier done than explained.

Tightening Up the Criteria

In the unchristological early form of the saying that we have been considering, the saying images God's kingdom as present to hand (or rather mouth), and not far off in time or space. The metaphor of nursing represents entrance into the kingdom as something that is easy and natural, something toward which the body actually inclines us. To enter is to have the kingdom enter you. You receive it as a baby receives milk: just do what comes natural, and down it goes. The metaphor suggests that God is like the nursing mothers, as eager to give the kingdom as the babies are to receive it—although the business angle cannot be ruled out, either. These aspects of the metaphor also attest to its age. Easy entry, natural affinity, and a mother-God all are more likely to have been written out of the Jesus traditions than to have been written into them. Most notably, in this sound bite Jesus is the observer of the kingdom *but not its bringer*. The saying in this form has yet to undergo what Bruce Chilton calls the Synoptic transformation, according to which Jesus becomes herald, advocate, and definer of the kingdom.[25]

That transformation was quite complex among the Greek-speaking Jesus movements. It happened in stages and differently for different communities. In this little saying, one can identify four distinct strands of development subsequent to the version at *Gos. Thom.* 22:2, which I take to be the earliest extant form and quite close to the predecessor of all members of the set. Three of the strands lead into the Synoptic tradition, where they are tied together again in Mark's text. The fourth leads into the expansion appended in the *Gospel of Thomas* and into John. (Figure 1 illustrates these four strands.)

Three of the trails that this saying has left through the thickets of the Jesus traditions all start off in the same direction: an evolution toward formulations that can justify the disciplinary practices of paideia. Paideia in the Hellenistic sense represented one distinctive option open to early churches as they developed their initiatory practices. This option was attractive, and the power of that attraction has significantly shaped the canonical texts. Competing options were present as well, however, and their proponents bequeathed to us the terminology that the New Testament commonly uses in association with teaching—for example, *akouō*, "hear, listen to, learn," and *manthanō*, which appears most commonly in a participial form, "one who is learning, disciple." This was not the vocabulary of paideia. The praxis of transmitting Jesus information must have been contested vigorously within the early communities, for the presence of these terms in the canonical versions signals that the developmental trajectory toward paideia was diverted and ultimately derailed.[26]

Why did the nursing version of the saying pass out of currency? Did it lose its ability to "be about" the propagation of the gospel in the generations

---

25. See Chilton, *Profiles of a Rabbi*, 152–54.

26. Yet the pattern of paideia exerted a significant influence in the composition of Mark's Gospel, as we shall see in the next chapter.

Figure 1.   Entering the Kingdom

These nursing babies are like those who enter the kingdom. (*Gos. Thom.* 22:2)
Entering is easy and natural.
To enter is to be entered: to receive and welcome.
The kingdom is present, tangible, there for the taking.
Kingdom entry occurs independently of Torah.
Jesus is an observer.

COMMON DEVELOPMENTS:

    Feeding metaphor is suppressed.
    Mothering metaphor is suppressed.
    Babies become children.
    Human initiative introduced.
    Kingdom becomes something objective.

"belongs"	**"like a child"**	**"hinder not"**

DEVELOPMENTS:
  Describes make-up of an entity, not an activity. Static, analytic.
 	
Of ones like these is the kingdom of God. (Mark 10:14b; Luke 18:16b; Matt. 19:14b)
	DEVELOPMENTS:
	  Generalization of status: all who enter kingdom have to be like children. Requirements introduced: become childlike.
	
	Then shall we enter the kingdom as babies? (*Gos. Thom.* 22:3)
	
	I swear to you, whoever doesn't receive God's kingdom like a child certainly won't ever set foot in it. (Mark 10:15; Luke 18:17)
	
	I swear to you, if you don't do an about-face and become like children, you will never enter the kingdom of heaven. (Matt. 18:3)
		DEVELOPMENTS:
		  Entry-as-taking becomes entry-as-approaching. The kingdom lies at a distance. Someone or something can get between you and the kingdom.
		
		Let the children come up to me, don't try to stop them. (Mark 10:14a; Luke 18:16a)
		
		Let the children alone. Don't try to stop them from coming up to me. (Matt. 19:14a)

"reprogramming"

DEVELOPMENTS:
  Kingdom becomes less accessible. Requirements are introduced. Nursing becomes pregnancy. Jesus becomes a teacher and dialogue partner.

When you make the two into one . . . then will you enter the kingdom. (*Gos. Thom.* 22:4)

DEVELOPMENTS:
  Possibility of hindrance. Nature becomes a problem.

How can an adult be reborn? Can you re-enter your mother's womb and be born a second time? (John 3:4)

DEVELOPMENTS:
  Entry-as-receiving becomes entry-as-seeing. Womb becomes water and spirit.

As God is my witness, no one can see God's kingdom without being mentored anew . . . no one can enter God's kingdom without being re-educated in water and spirit. (John 3:3,5)

Scholars Version translations have been adjusted to produce more literal correspondence with the Greek text.

after Jesus? May we infer that teachers within the post-Calvary Jesus movements discovered that entering the kingdom was in fact not as easy as nursing? Perhaps they offered the nipple of their gospel but found few hungry babies ready to suckle. Perhaps even their most willing disciples experienced difficulty in swallowing the kingdom. Perhaps in the evangelical wet nurse market there were more sellers than buyers. Moreover, Christian teachers had a vested interest in heightening the difficulty of entering the kingdom by concentrating the kingdom in Jesus, who was scarce after Calvary. For whatever reasons, the nursing metaphor ceased to lend intelligibility to the practices of kingdom entry that it had been designed to illuminate.

In the wake of disconcerting realizations such as those, several modifications were made in the statement: suppression of the food metaphor and the mothering metaphor; a weaning of "babies" (Coptic *kouei* in the *Gospel of Thomas*) so that they age into "children" (Greek *paidia* in the Synoptics) who are old enough to learn new Torah; and consequently a change from natural receptivity to a somewhat more deliberate effort. The kingdom itself becomes the object of speculative knowledge, a destination for human attainment. These developments may be read as evidence that teachers have been thinking with this saying. They have been using the saying, and therefore modifying it, in their attempt to interpret their experiences (including their failures as well as their successes) and to articulate principles to guide their practices. The statement mutates as the practices diversify.

After these early developments, there is a branching of the saying into two trajectories, with one of them undergoing a further three-way split. Thus we have four general forms of the saying in the texts that come down to us. In the first, a strategic practical concern with "entering" the kingdom is displaced by a judgment of constitutive affinity, almost a legal relationship between the kingdom and the children. We get: "Of ones like these is the kingdom of God" (Mark 10:14 and par).[27] No activity is envisioned; this is a matter of merely being: being a constituent of the kingdom. I call this the "belongs" form of the saying.

A second trail retains the activity of entering, in all its paradoxical reciprocity. You enter the kingdom by receiving or welcoming it as it enters you. Yet there are interesting modifications here, too. A generalization is made in regard to the status of those who enter the kingdom: they must be like children. This brings the concept of "kingdom" closer to the concept of paideia, for one characteristic of children (*paidia*) is that they

---

27. Here and in what follows, the Scholars Version translation is adjusted to retain the archaic but familiar term "kingdom" and to approximate the Greek text more literally.

are susceptible to instruction and vulnerable to punishment. Yet the requirement of becoming like a child remains implicit in the first two examples of
this trend. The *Gospel of Thomas* 22:3 offers a positive interrogative form:
"Then shall we enter the kingdom as babies?" Mark and Luke offer a negative declarative form: "I swear to you, whoever doesn't receive God's kingdom like a child certainly won't ever set foot in it" (Mark 10:15; Luke 18:17).
It is Matthew whose formulation makes the implicit requirement of suscep-
tibility to paideia explicit: "I swear to you, if you don't do an about-face and
become like children, you will never enter the kingdom of heaven" (Matt.
18:3). The desirability of a structured program of learning now emerges, as
the means of entering the kingdom. Entering is not natural; it requires discipline. A teacher becomes the indispensable guide. This allows Matthew to
lay down specific behavioral requirements elsewhere, as we shall see. I call
these three versions the "like a child" forms of the saying.

A third trajectory develops the saying in yet another direction. The
figure of Jesus himself now is set up as one pole of an attractive force exerted by the kingdom. Children occupy the other pole. Access or entry,
previously imaged as swallowing and then later as receiving, now is imaged in terms of approach across space. There is still a natural attraction
toward the goal, yet there is now also the sinister possibility of hindrance
by something or someone (disciples!) who stands between Jesus and the
ones being drawn to him. The Synoptics give us their version of the saying: "Let the children come up to me; don't try to stop them." I call this
the "hinder not" form of the saying.

It is worth noting here the startling implication of the bundling together of the "belongs" and the "hinder not" formulations as it occurs in
all three Synoptics. If the kingdom consists "of children," then we have
Jesus welcoming the kingdom when he welcomes children. *They* bring it to
him; and whoever stops the approach of the children is keeping the kingdom away from Jesus. On this reading, Jesus is still someone seeking
God's kingdom as well as someone who can recognize it when he spies it
nearby. The children here are still little opportunists, nonchalantly taking
possession by usucaption like the courtyard babies. The bundling of the
two sayings retains the same ambiguous bidirectionality as the nursing
metaphor: do you enter the kingdom or does it enter you? do you go up to
the kingdom or does it come up to you?

In our usual reading of this passage, one side of the paradox is suppressed by the Markan frame: "And they would bring children to him so
that he could lay hands on them . . . and he would put his arms around
them and bless them and lay his hands on them" (Mark 10:13, 16 and
par.). It is this frame which positions Jesus as the magnet and tends to

align *him*—rather than the children—with the kingdom as source of blessings and caresses. With this spin, the saying is handy for teachers because it gives them a way to conceptualize the failures that they occasionally experience in their practice. That is, Jesus stands for the kingdom and its attraction, so that a failure to contact means that someone has gotten in the way of the little ones who naturally are drawn to him. Despite its drastic modifications, the Markan frame retains something of the intimate physical contact that characterized the nursing tableau.

The fourth trajectory of the saying is rather different. Here the motherhood metaphor is not suppressed. Neither have those babies from *Gos. Thom.* 22:1-2 been weaned; on the contrary, the imagery here regresses them in time and places them inside wombs again. In this strand of development, Jesus acquires a higher profile as teacher or dialogue partner, but without displacing the kingdom itself. As in the other strands, the kingdom becomes less accessible and requirements for entry are introduced. Here these are of a markedly different kind, however. The nursing imagery of the early saying is transposed into what may have been a metaphor of pregnancy and gestation in *Gos. Thom.* 22:4.

> When you make the two into one, and when you make the inner like the outer and the outer like the inner, and the upper like the lower, and when you make male and female into a single one, so that the male will not be male nor the female be female, when you make eyes in place of an eye, a hand in place of a hand, a foot in place of a foot, an image in place of an image, then you will enter.

The imagery of pregnancy is more explicit in John 3, where it structures Jesus' exchange with Nicodemus. In this discourse, however, the pregnancy metaphor itself is the source of the hindrance to entering the kingdom—both in its literal sense and in the fact that its literal sense blocks Nicodemus from grasping its figurative sense. Nicodemus asks Jesus, "How can an adult be reborn? Can you reenter your mother's womb and be born a second time?" (John 3:4). The key to removing the hindrance is the fact that the verb *gennaō* has both a literal and a figurative, pedagogical sense. Literally it means either "to give birth to" or "to beget" (depending on the sex of the agent), but figuratively "to influence" as a teacher does.[28] This pedagogical sense of mentoring fits well here in the context of

---

28. This figurative sense is well attested in Greek literature, e.g., in Philo. See Walter Bauer, *A Greek-English Lexicon of the New Testament and Other Early Christian Literature,* trans. and adapt. by William F. Arndt and F. Wilbur Gingrich, 2d ed. (Chicago: University of

a dialogue between two teachers. Thus one could translate the Johannine form of our saying: "As God is my witness, no one can see God's kingdom without being re-educated. . . . No one can enter God's kingdom without being mentored by water and the Spirit."[29] Two final developments may be noted. Entry as receiving is displaced by entry as seeing, and the maternal womb becomes water and the Spirit. This fourth trajectory of development, unlike the others, does not move toward the establishment of a Christian paideia at all. The mentor/influence works independently of human effort, guidance, coaching, or correction—an interesting conclusion indeed, if it comes out of the experiences of Christian teachers. I call these versions the "reprogramming" form of the saying.

Kingdom as Monopoly

The four poietic trajectories outlined above were completed before Mark composed his Gospel, about 70 C.E. The first three forms of the saying are stitched together in Mark 10:14-15, indicating that they may already have fused in the Greek and possibly the underlying haggadic performance traditions.[30] The fourth form, "reprogramming," either was unknown to Mark or was rejected by him in favor of the paideia metaphor of sowing seed, which will be discussed in the next chapter.

Chicago Press, 1979), s.v. *"gennaō."* One might colloquially translate the *gennēthē anōthen* of John 3:3 as "be reprogrammed from above," or have new programming downloaded. In Plato's *Theaetetus*, Socrates uses the metaphor of the midwife to describe the art of the teacher, in the context of a summons to a potential disciple. See Vernon K. Robbins, *Jesus the Teacher: A Socio-Rhetorical Interpretation of Mark* (Philadelphia: Fortress Press, 1984), 89. Moreover, the Mishnah tractate *Sanhedrin* 19b says, "When a man teaches the son of another the Torah, the Scriptures treat him as if he had begotten him."

29. Paul will exploit the figurative, pedagogical sense of *gennaō* in Galatians 4. This sense is overlooked by J. Louis Martyn in his otherwise quite enlightening study, "The Covenants of Sarah and Hagar," in *Faith and History: Essays in Honor of Paul W. Meyer*, ed. John T. Carroll et al. (Atlanta: Scholars Press, 1990), 160–92. It may be that Paul is merely adapting a tradition that associated teaching and entering God's kingdom with birthing and nursing—a tradition, moreover, that would not tolerate severing the notion of divine rule from the motherhood metaphor that originally delivered it. Martyn points out that Paul shifts the verbs in his presumed source, the Septuagint, in order to position himself as the subject of the verb *gennaō*. Paul's usage also destabilizes traditional kinship and caste assignments.

30. These are originally three different strands (rather than one complex saying), because they configure Jesus/children/kingdom in distinct and mutually incoherent ways. The "hinder not" form is about the gravitational attraction between Jesus and children. The "belongs" form has children as constituents of the kingdom. The "like a child" form has children as exemplars: criteria invoked to limit access to the kingdom.

This chapter has proposed a model of the evolution of a Jesus saying through several stages and along four branches of development. This reconstruction has used materials that come down to us in texts. What has been reconstructed, however, is the *pre*-textual history of the saying as it circulated through communities that did not yet have any Gospel texts. Clearly, there was evolution in the content of the oral recitation, and that evolution was driven to a significant extent by strategies and interests and practices that never were codified into text as such. What "God's kingdom" meant had to change in tandem with changes in what "entering" the kingdom could mean and require.

More significant than any alteration we have observed so far was Mark's decision to curtail the process of alteration itself, by stabilizing and standardizing kingdom access into text. Mark wants Jesus to be the point of reference for God's kingdom: its definitive arbiter and interpreter. This is apparent in the Markan frame for the children sayings, where Jesus is the one to whom children are brought for blessing and loving contact. Therefore Mark needs a Jesus who will sit still, so to speak, a Jesus whose words do not change (as words inevitably do in oral storytelling). Mark does not want Jesus to be on the lookout for God's kingdom. He wants Jesus to have found it and to introduce it to others.

Mark's Jesus has to have a monopoly on the kingdom. Thus Mark has to deflect attention away from the implication that children bring the kingdom "of children" to Jesus. Mark makes Jesus the only child (Mark 15:39 and possibly 1:1). This move imports into the notion of God's kingdom those very factors which the nursing metaphor had made its antithesis: legitimate inheritance, kinship, caste, privilege. With the Markan concentration of God's kingdom into one child, Jesus, we get a drastic narrowing of access to it. Demand now will exceed supply, and Mark's text can corner the market. Instead of a ubiquitous kingdom confounding ownership, we get a king of the Jews (Mark 15:26). One enters the kingdom by approaching the king. With Mark, this approach is a way to be followed, and the map is narratively drawn in the Gospel text.

Mark's text, then, consolidates the translation of a metaphor from its origins in villagers' imaginations to its mobilization in support of the teaching practices of literate Greeks. The problem of access now centers on the figure of Jesus himself. And the utter scarcity of Jesus after Calvary is the crux of the problem.

3

For Teachers a Teacher

BETWEEN CALVARY and Mark's literary achievement, the kingdom of God was progressively reimagined, and the quest for it was redirected toward the figure of Jesus of Nazareth, of blessed memory. The continued bodily availability of Jesus after his death became a premise for the possibility of access to God's kingdom. For forty years the churches experimented and learned what it took to bring people into the possibility of recognizing Jesus in realtime. The necessity of the resurrection was apprehended strategically, in the midst of devising practices for propagating the Jesus movements. Teachers learned it not by thinking about the past but by doing in the present and building for the future.

It does not deny or diminish the traditional Christian announcement that Jesus is risen bodily from the dead if one can show how that claim resonated through the three epistemic modes of theory, poiesis, and praxis. My assumption is that precanonical communities had a certain know-how that we mistakenly assume is no longer extant in the churches: the ability to "see the Lord." This know-how has been encoded in the Gospel texts, right alongside the familiar historical information—although the latter is what we habitually take from them simply because that kind of information is all that we expect to read. My intention is to recover this know-how by illuminating traces of early Christian praxis and poiesis within the ancient documents.

It is often taken for granted that the definitive precanonical genre of Christian communication was kerygma. (The Greek word *kerygma* means a proclamation or public announcement formally delivered by a messenger or herald.[1]) This view seems plausible if one considers only the Pauline letters. Occasionally Paul does seem to be citing a kerygma, or short formulaic summary of information about Jesus, although he does not claim that that formula comes from Jesus himself. The epistles are notoriously lacking in detailed information about Jesus, when compared to the Gospels.[2]

But if one examines the Gospels instead of the epistles, "kerygma" seems quite an inadequate term to describe the many varieties of communication that are at work. The difference in textual genre reflects a difference of bodily practice. In contrast to the apparent Pauline method of moving on from a community after a brief visit, the Gospels presuppose more long-term, dynamic interpersonal relationships of nurture and cultivation. They reflect the experiences of communities discovering that it takes time and patience to learn to "see the Lord."

Rather than "kerygma," then, it seems plausible that "catechesis" might more adequately describe the principal genre in which information about Jesus was transmitted during the first decades after Calvary.[3] Catechesis is a distinctively Christian kind of teaching that both imparts information and transmits lifestyle. An interest in catechesis is discernible throughout the canonical Gospels. Their authors and their first readers were concerned with the question of how a teacher functions in the relationship between Jesus and Jesus' disciples after Calvary. The culturally available model of Hellenistic paideia served as a blueprint for catechesis in some sectors of the Jesus movements. In others, it was contested and rejected. No consensus emerged among the churches known to us through their literary productions. This alerts us to the possibility that teaching practices were a contested terrain on the frontier where economic or ethnic or even gender systems came into contact.

Jesus Keeps Talking

Controversy over the proper way to teach is what motivated the first evangelist to write, some forty years along in Christian history. Werner Kelber

---

1. For example, Rudolf Bultmann's program of demythologizing, or separating the kerygma from its cultural packaging, is summarized in his essay "New Testament and Mythology," in *Kerygma and Myth: A Theological Debate,* by Rudolf Bultmann and others, ed. Hans Werner Bartsch (New York: Harper & Row, 1961), 1–44.

2. For a thorough discussion of the different literary forms in which the New Testament texts express the fact of the resurrection of Jesus, see Perkins, *Resurrection.*

3. Bruce Chilton affirms this at the opening and the close (pp. ix and 178) of a work that supports this view; see Chilton, *Profiles of a Rabbi.*

has convincingly argued that Mark's intention in writing was to discredit the practices of the Christian prophets, along with the whole prophetic oral style of communicating the Gospel message. The prophets' way of working can be reconstructed roughly as follows. Christian prophets continued Jesus' Galilean practice of traveling among the villages, casting out demons, working cures, maintaining an open table fellowship in thanksgiving, and speaking "in Jesus' name."[4] Scholars today identify these prophets as the tradents of the Q sayings. They were active for a considerable portion of the time between Calvary and the end of the century, perhaps longer. One evidence of their persistence is the fact that their sayings collection, Q, was composed in at least two stages: an earlier layer representing sapiential utterance and a later layer that is apocalyptic in tone.[5]

The prophets did not preach the resurrection as a miraculous event that had happened to Jesus. Instead, they spoke on behalf of a living Jesus whose death was not preventing him from healing, exorcising, and uttering new words to fit the occasion and the needs of their constituencies. Never designed as a ministry of community building, the prophetic way must have been perceived, in certain circles at least, to be growing even more volatile and destabilizing when the prophets' message took its turn toward apocalyptic extremism as the political situation in Palestine deteriorated after the middle of the first century.

Those whom the New Testament calls "prophets" seem to have operated like itinerant Cynic philosopher-charlatans in some respects but in others like village *meturgemanin*. Perhaps what the Scripture remembers is a composite portrait of several styles and cultural bases. The *meturgeman* was a resident authoritative interpreter of the Hebrew Scripture into the vernacular Aramaic. His liturgical role was to deliver a targum, or homiletically enhanced translation, after the reading of the Hebrew Scripture in the synagogue. The targum was unlike the written Torah or Prophets in two respects: it was not supposed to be read off of a text and (in this era) it was not regarded as inspired by God's Spirit. One thing that distinguished the Christian prophets from other

4. This is the gist of Werner Kelber's proposal in *The Oral and the Written Gospel: The Hermeneutics of Speaking and Writing in the Synoptic Tradition, Mark, Paul, and Q* (Philadelphia: Fortress Press, 1983). For cultural comparisons, see also David E. Aune, *Prophecy in Early Christianity and the Ancient Mediterranean World* (Grand Rapids: Wm. B. Eerdmans Publishing Co., 1983).
5. See John S. Kloppenborg, *The Formation of Q: Trajectories in Ancient Wisdom Collections* (Philadelphia: Fortress Press, 1987).

traditional reciters of haggadah and halakhah was their claim that God's Spirit inhabited their speech.[6]

Either as haggadah or as prophecy, the oral performance of Christian prophets was a way of communicating adapted to the village ecology of Galilee and to ordinary folks. But the author of Mark was no ordinary villager. He belonged to the hellenized cultural elite and had had the advantage of advanced training in rhetorical composition.[7] From Mark's vantage point—within the polis, astride the divergence of several contrasting Jesus movements, amid violent insurrection and the brutal reaction of the Roman administration, and in the aftermath of significant failures to get Jews and Greeks to swallow Gospel teaching—it was clear that there had to be a better way. Mark chose the way of text.

Mark's text is one continuous, creative makeover of Jesus into a disciple-gathering teacher.[8] With their relatively privileged cultural background, Mark and his circle had the poietic competence to create this new portrait using both scriptural and nonscriptural literary sources, both Hellenistic and Israelite. The question is, Why did they paint Jesus *as a teacher?* Why did they do to Jesus what the Alexandrian synagogue scholars had done to Moses and to God? A plausible explanation is that Mark himself stood within (or stands for) the line of teachers who gave us the "hinder not" form of the kingdom entry saying. That is, Mark represents

6. The phrase "spirit of prophecy" often is used in the targum of Ezekiel in place of the Hebrew for "hand of God" in order to avoid the anthropomorphism. This indicates that prophecy connoted powerful agency, not merely verbal information. See the introduction to *The Targum of Ezekiel,* trans. Samson H. Levey, Aramaic Bible, vol. 13 (Wilmington, Del.: Michael Glazier, 1987), 14. David Aune says that some first- and second-century rabbis held that the spirit of prophecy had been withdrawn in their time, while others claimed to have the gift of prophecy or possess the Spirit of God. See Aune, *Prophecy in Early Christianity,* 104.

7. As Burton Mack and Vernon Robbins have shown. For a comprehensive treatment of recent research in Markan studies and a daring reconstruction of the inquiry, see Burton L. Mack, *A Myth of Innocence: Mark and Christian Origins* (Philadelphia: Fortress Press, 1988). See also Vernon K. Robbins, *Jesus the Teacher: A Socio-Rhetorical Interpretation of Mark* (Philadelphia: Fortress Press, 1984; with new Introduction, Minneapolis, 1992); Burton L. Mack and Vernon K. Robbins, *Patterns of Persuasion in the Gospels* (Sonoma, Calif.: Polebridge Press, 1989). Mack postulates the existence of six distinct early communities stemming from Jesus: Galilean itinerants, the twelve "Pillars" in Jerusalem, the family of Jesus, the Congregation of Israel, the synagogue reform movement, and a Christ cult. See Mack, *Myth of Innocence,* 84–102. I would identify the first and the last of these as primarily Greek, and the others as Aramaic or, in the case of scribes, Aramaic and Hebrew.

8. As Robbins demonstrates in *Jesus the Teacher.* But Bruce Chilton cautions against investing all this poiesis in one individual author, hypostatized as "Mark." Chilton holds that a relatively stable traditional performance of the halakhah and haggadah of Jesus already had congealed before it was captured in the text we know as Mark's Gospel.

those for whom *the person of Jesus could displace the notion of the kingdom of God*, a notion that was becoming both too theoretical and too imprecise.[9] As we have seen, in Mark 10:14-16 the "belongs" and the "like a child" forms of our saying are amalgamated to the "hinder not" form, within bracketing statements about affectionate touches by Jesus.

This choice to model Jesus as a Hellenistic teacher was at the same time a definitive rejection of two other Greek options: Jesus as personification of paideia and Jesus as recipient of paideia. As for the first option, the Markan frame-up of the "like a child" and the "hinder not" sayings actually did take a step toward making Jesus into paideia personified. The "like a child" saying merges the kingdom with paideia while the frame tilts the "hinder not" saying to superimpose the figure of Jesus upon the kingdom. It would have been an easy move to make; indeed, Philo does choose the option of making paideia the hypostasis or personification that will be "agent and mediator of the Old Testament revelation in the Greek world."[10] Yet Mark ultimately rejected the option of personifying paideia into Jesus—in favor of resurrection, as we shall see.

As for the second option, the canonical Gospels reject it as well: Jesus is not to be designated the target of divine paideia either. On the one hand, the infancy narratives of Matthew and Luke opened the conceptual possibility of Jesus' undergoing paideia, and in Luke's passion narrative Jesus receives a punishment from Pilate (*paideusas auton*, "teaching him a lesson," Luke 23:16, 22). Yet on the other hand, the gospel tradition ultimately refuses the option of explaining Jesus' passion and death as punitive instruction from God.[11] Instead, early Christologies cast around for other conceptual resources to interpret Jesus' execution. From the Septuagint they adopt the notion that prophets were rejected because they delivered the paideia (that is, instructive punishment) of God. It was this Deuteronomic theory of the rejected and persecuted prophet that supplied the christological option ultimately taken.

The prophet who brings divine paideia is, to the Greco-Jewish mind, a teacher. There are textual indications that portions, at least, of Mark's Gospel have an author who studied at length with a teacher—*not* Jesus but a rhetor of considerable skill. This background evidences itself in Mark's command of Greek literary compositional techniques (although not in his grammar). A man acquired rhetorical skill by lengthy and

9. Compare this poietic move with that of Paul, who in Galatians 4 promotes himself into the position of the mother who gives birth to churches.

10. According to Bertram, "*paideuō*," *Theological Dictionary of the New Testament*.

11. In contrast with other New Testament genres. See Heb. 12:5-11.

costly post-*gymnasion* training with a rhetor, one on one. The close personal relation with the teacher was the learner's vehicle for acquiring skills needed for a successful public career. Mark the author sets great store by the teaching strategy of facilitating access to the person of Jesus, although this intention already was shaping up as a stable feature of the oral traditioning stream that Mark taps. Because he prizes the teacher/learner relationship so highly, Mark wants a Jesus with sharp and clear outlines. He counts as hindrances the intrinsic variance of oral performance and particularly the growing number of dominical sayings that are being produced by the Christian prophets "in Jesus' name." Mark needs to shut the mouth of the Risen Lord and bury him in text, paradoxically so that "the real Jesus," textually certified, can be preserved for encounter. This is what the genre of the narrative Gospel, as Mark creates it, is designed to do.

The Trouble with Paideia

This Markan agenda arises from the conflicting implications of the mutating metaphor for divine accessibility, as "God's kingdom" turns into a paideia. On the one hand, if the kingdom is paideia and Jesus is not a student, then Jesus must be the rhetor imparting its competence: kingdom literacy. (Such an implication is operative, for example, in Matt. 13:52, which mentions a scholar "schooled in God's kingdom.") On the other hand, several facts about Jesus refuse to fit the model. For example, after the crucifixion he is absent from his disciples. Moreover, he left no successors, as a proper teacher would do. While Mark knows of people teaching the halakhah of Jesus, complete success is eluding their efforts—which should not happen if the paideia they were propagating were truly coextensive with the kingdom of God as taught by Jesus.

Mark did not invent the notion that the kingdom is paideia, but he undertook to cut through the conceptual knots it had presented. The experienced dissonance between a theory (kingdom as paideia) and a practice (teaching gone awry) motivates Mark's pedagogical concerns. His text imparts information, but it also prescribes *how* such information *is to be properly grasped and communicated*. The pedagogical instructions themselves become constitutive of the Gospel message.

Evidence internal to Mark's text, analyzed in the light of what is known of first-century Hellenistic teaching practices, points to a community that needed to come to grips with its failure to implement its own program of synagogue reform and redirection. What drives Mark's reworking of traditional materials is the need to refight and win, if only in hindsight, an argument that already had been lost in realtime—an argument about the social boundaries of God's people—while at the same time showing why that loss had to happen. Mark needs to rationalize the failure of Christian teaching.[12] Mark makes it clear through his parable of the Sower (Mark 4:2b-9) that the issues he wants to address are pedagogical. This parable is the key to everything else that Mark's Jesus has to say: "You don't get this parable, so how are you going to understand other parables?" (Mark 4:13). Plowing, and especially sowing seed, was a standard analogy employed in discussions of paideia in late antiquity. Everyone in the first century knew what Mark has Jesus explain in 4:14: "The 'sower' is 'sowing' the message." Mark is working in a tradition in which God's kingdom is something teachable. That teachability is "the secret of the kingdom of God" (Mark 4:11).

The parable as we have it cannot have been circulating during the first Christian generation, before the synagogue reform movement collapsed. It is a parable about the failure of a great deal of teaching, a parable that nevertheless holds out hope of eventual success in some form.[13] Once God's kingdom was construed as paideia, one could imagine that and how the kingdom still might eventually displace the two competing paideiai currently in force: Judaism in its several varieties and the Greco-Roman paideia. Over against its cultural competitors, God's kingdom becomes a kind of counter-paideia.

Mark's parable of the Sower goes to work on the issue of failed teaching in order to exonerate teachers from malpractice. Burton Mack observes that Mark has erased one traditional element from his depiction of Christian paideia in the parable of the Sower: the motif of labor. In Mark 4:26-29, the sower does not know how the seed grows; "the earth produces fruit on its own." Mack says: "Now the seed growing secretly fits with the apocalyptic theme, for the kingdom of God comes to harvest automatically, in contrast, that is, to a paideia characterized by work and visible accomplishment. . . . The Greeks would certainly have noticed that the essential point was missing: the imagery of cultivation, so important for the analogy to work." The parable of the Sower takes the teachers off the hook, for it asserts that the success of the teaching depends, not

---

12. This is the view of Mack, *Myth of Innocence*, 153–69. My argument here follows that of Mack and is supported by evidence he presents.

13. See Mack, *Myth of Innocence*, 166. As Mack says, "Social history is under review," and the parable betrays "deeply embedded concerns about the destiny of some Jesus movement that thought of itself as the bearer of the kingdom Jesus had announced" (p. 156).

upon the sower or the seed, but upon the character of the soil, that is, upon the learners.[14]

In distinguishing good from bad soils, Mark's parable explains a social division already in place in this community: that between a group of Jesus people and their former synagogue. By putting the parable into the mouth of Jesus, Mark is claiming that this division was foreseen by Jesus and was really there from the beginning, although time had to pass before it would be manifest.[15]

Not only in content, but in structure as well, does the parable of the Sower attest to the formative effect of pedagogical practices upon the Markan text. The chapter in which this parable appears, Mark 4, was carefully composed according to the pattern of a standard speech form that teachers of rhetoric called an "elaboration."[16] The components are these:

1. An introduction to the speech situation (Mark 4:1-2a)
2. A statement of the thesis (vv. 2b-9, the parable itself)
3. A rationale for the thesis
   —request for rationale (v. 10)
   —rationale given as direct statement (vv. 11-12)
   —rationale given as paraphrase of the parable (vv. 13-20, explanation of the terms of the parable)

---

14. See Burton L. Mack, "The Kingdom Sayings in Mark," *Foundations and Facets Forum* 3 (1987): 3–47, p. 25. Matthew and Luke, however, edit out Mark's comment that the sower "is unaware . . . the earth produces fruit on its own" because their communities have had more success in their pedagogical practices. (Unlike Mark, Matthew and Luke are writing in order to pass on wisdom about teaching praxis that is effective, as we shall see.) Mark C. Taylor is among those who have noted that the sower disappears from the parable as soon as the seed is sown; see Mark C. Taylor, *Erring: A Postmodern A/theology* (Chicago: University of Chicago Press, 1984), 119. Mark's Gospel thus becomes the first work of deconstructive criticism.

15. It is perhaps ironic that the third Christian generation finds that it must define social boundaries and devise criteria for discerning who is inside or outside the Jesus movement. Arguably, what had constituted the Jesus movement in the first place was a violation of such boundaries. See Robert J. Miller, "The Inside Is (Not) the Outside," *Foundations and Facets Forum* 4 (1988). According to Mack, the "social coding" of the grandparents and parents of Mark's circle had deviated from that of more conventional Jews principally in their reluctance to assign people a place predetermined by community boundaries. See Mack, *Myth of Innocence*, 222–24, 91–96. It is interesting that Edward Farley, working independently of recent historical-Jesus research, used phenomenological method to reach the conclusion that the essence of ecclesia, the church, is to be without boundaries. See Farley, *Ecclesial Reflection*.

16. This has been brought to light by Burton Mack in *Myth of Innocence*, 161–63, from which the outline that follows is condensed.

4. A testing of the rationale by setting up a contrast or showing that the converse is also true (vv. 21-23, the saying about the lamp and the bushel)
5. Providing an analogy or *parabolē* (vv. 30-32, God's reign is like a mustard seed)
6. Giving an example or *paradeigma* (vv. 26-29, God's reign grows like crops grow)
7. Offering a pronouncement, maxim, or precedent judgment from some authority (vv. 24-25, to one who has, more will be given . . .)
8. Summing up in a conclusion (vv. 33-34)

The experiences of teaching, then, have shaped the message about Jesus in several ways. A well-known format propounded by secular teachers of rhetoric has been used for the very structure of the chapter. Members of the ecclesial community image themselves as the receptive learners, the "good soil," in distinction from the untaught outside the community. God's kingdom is construed as growing seeds, that is, as paideia, which means both a way of life and a way of teaching. Finally, Jesus is modeled as a master rhetor, a teacher.

Making a Teacher Out of Jesus

If the fourth chapter of Mark's Gospel has the rhetorical structure of a Hellenistic "elaboration," that chapter is set within a work that, in its entirety, is designed to portray Jesus as a disciple-gathering teacher. This distinctive role, according to Vernon Robbins, was a recognized sociocultural pattern reflected in both Jewish and secular Greek literary sources. In Robbins's view, Mark's Gospel was preserved by the churches "because it perpetuated an image of Jesus, an understanding of discipleship and a teaching/learning cycle compatible with ideology in Mediterranean society."[17]

Such a portrayal customarily had three parts, which may be identified in Mark's Gospel. First was the introduction and initial phase of the teacher/disciple relationship, in which the disciples were called. This is illustrated in Mark 1:1—3:6.[18] Robbins shows parallels in Plato, Philo, Josephus, the Babylonian Talmud, and Philostratus but concludes that Mark's portrayal of Jesus combines Israelite and Greco-Roman characteristics into

17. See Robbins, *Jesus the Teacher*, 76, 209.
18. See Robbins, *Jesus the Teacher*, 75–123.

an original new profile. Summoning and luring young men into the role of disciple-companion is what *the Socratic teacher* does among the Greeks; in Israelite tradition, however, it is what *God* does. Robbins proposes that Hellenistic culture provides a conducive medium for the intermingling of Israelite traditions with teacher/disciple relational patterns. For example, Josephus portrays Moses and Elijah as teachers who select and train their successors. But they do so as prophets, that is, as men with specific and limited authorization from God. By contrast, Mark makes Jesus more autonomous, more like a Greco-Roman teacher than a Hebrew prophet. Robbins sees the Gospel of Mark as revolutionizing Jewish tradition by portraying a Jesus who takes over divine functions with divine sanction but without close divine supervision such as Israel's prophets bore. For Robbins, "a basic dimension of the 'messianic' nature of Jesus' activity in Mark arises from the adaptation of the autonomous stature of the teacher in Greco-Roman tradition and the subsequent importation of this emphasis on autonomy into Jewish tradition where God has been the dominant autonomous figure."[19] The opening chapters of Mark's Gospel establish for Jesus the profile of a teacher in whom both Greeks and Jews recognize something familiar and whom both would find unsettling.

The second or intermediate phase of the conventional teacher/disciple literary cycle was the portrayal of the actual process of teaching and learning. This is exemplified in Mark 3:7—12:44. Through direct conversation between Jesus and his disciples, Mark develops the profile of Jesus as distinctive teacher along Greco-Roman lines. As before, Robbins explores literary parallels in Xenophon, the Hebrew Bible, Plato, and Philostratus. He points out that the first Gospel "virtually eliminates interaction between God and Jesus and between God and the followers of Jesus in order to focus on the interaction between Jesus and his disciple-companions."[20] Mark's configuring of Jesus in the Greco-Roman mold has contributed to the eventual theological perception of Jesus as both divine and human.

The third and final phase of the conventional teacher/disciple literary cycle was the portrayal of the farewell and death of the teacher. This is exemplified in Mark 13:1—16:8. As before, Robbins finds both Israelite and Greco-Roman parallels against which one can observe how creatively Mark has reconstrued the meaning and significance of Jesus' death.[21]

Thanks to the work of Robbins and of Burton Mack we are in a position to appreciate how the generations between Jesus and Mark accomplished

19. See Robbins, *Jesus the Teacher*, 118–19.
20. See Robbins, *Jesus the Teacher*, 167. See also 162, 166.
21. See Robbins, *Jesus the Teacher*, 171–96.

the redesign of the Calvary incident and the Jesus who died there. The interpretations that come down to us in the canon do not exhaust the theological possibilities for what could be made of Jesus, nor do they represent all the viable readings of Jesus within different movements honoring his name. Mack points out that the very idea of a death with salvific significance is Hellenistic and would have seemed odd or obnoxious to many people in the Jesus movements. "The notion of a noble death is Greek. The notion of imitation is Greek. The logic of 'losing one's life in order to save it' is Greek."[22] Mack argues that the three passion predictions in Mark, which call on the disciple to follow and imitate, all are meant to construe Jesus' death as a martyrdom through persecution. He concludes that the notion that Jesus' death is vicarious, "a ransom for many" (Mark 10:45), is therefore a Markan fiction whose function is to provide common ground for alienated constituencies by joining the traditions of a Jesus movement with those of a Christ cult.

For his part, Robbins has done more than show that the organizing principle for Mark's composition derives from the fund of learning theory and praxis available in first-century Hellenistic society. Beyond that, Robbins's findings indicate that certain key christological and soteriological dimensions of Christian faith that we trace back to the first Gospel also derive from that same source: common teaching practices. Out of concerted reflection upon the nature of the peculiar kind of teaching that Christians do has come, not merely a secondary theological interpretation, but the very "fact" about Jesus itself.

The rhetorical analyses of Robbins and Mack, reviewed here, concern the profiling of Jesus in the *first* Gospel, that of Mark, where Jesus became exactly that teacher with distinctive authority whom the Jesus movements needed in order to validate their own teaching praxis. But what of the *second* Gospels, those of Matthew and Luke? They come from communities that already have had recourse to Mark's solutions for a generation, during which time new needs have arisen. One of the things that the fourth Christian generation needs is a way to permit Jesus to keep on teaching through the mouths of authorized Christian teachers. Matthew in particular worries deeply about this issue.

---

22. See the discussion in Mack, *Myth of Innocence*, 276–87, based on evidence presented in 1987 doctoral dissertations by David Seeley and Elizabeth Castelli. See also David Seeley, *The Noble Death: Graeco-Roman Martyrology and Paul's Concept of Salvation* (Sheffield: JSOT Press, 1990); and Elizabeth A. Castelli, *Imitating Paul: A Discourse of Power* (Louisville: John Knox Press, 1991). Before Paul and Mark, the death of Eleazar already had been portrayed in Jewish literature as a noble death in the Greek tradition: a death to benefit others.

The Kingdom as Not-Paideia

The failures of Christian teaching that prompt Mark to compose his text are not confined to the "hindrance" within the community comprised by freewheeling *meturgemanin* and prophets with loose lips. Mark's major reflection upon the failure of Christian teaching is presented when, in his fourth chapter, he has Jesus explain what happened when a sower went out to sow. By Mark's account, when Christian teaching fails to "yield a crop," it can be blamed on three likely causes: birds (Satan), poor soil (shallowness of character), or weeds (competing concerns). *How* the sower sows, that is, how the teacher teaches, is thus discounted as a factor in the success or failure of the teaching. The emphasis is drawn away from the "artificial" work of teaching and focused back upon the "natural" phenomena of seeds sprouting, birds gobbling, and sun shining.

In the sowing-teaching metaphor, this claim constitutes a curious denial of responsibility for pedagogical malpractice by Christian teachers (and neither Matthew nor Luke records it). Yet in adopting the metaphor of the sower to discuss Christian teaching, Mark has only followed the tradition established three centuries earlier by the Septuagint. For its Greco-Jewish translators, God was Israel's teacher, and salvation history was the paideia through which God both instructed and chastened the people. Mark retains the idea that God is the people's teacher; in fact, this very theme moves the Synoptic tradition toward asserting divinity for Jesus. At the same time, the idea of God as ultimate teacher tends to preclude any useful discourse about preferred methods for Christian teachers. Human malpractice wouldn't matter. We have, then, with Mark a reinterpretation of Christian teaching as a curious un-paideia, true to its Cynic pedigree in its reliance on the unfolding of natural processes.

Matthew, by contrast, is not so reticent. This Gospel takes another shot at discrediting the Christian prophets, but its overriding concern is to tell teachers how to teach. Matthew's tradition continues to use the cultivation metaphor to discuss Christian teaching but, unlike Mark, finds in it a way to evaluate the efficacy of various human means of communicating the Gospel. Quite simply, good communication is cultivation that produces good fruits (as in Matt. 7:15-20). Fruits are good deeds: that is, not sensational feats that the communicator might pull off to attract attention, but the common, ordinary, everyday good deeds that people do after they have received the communication. The trouble with the prophets, for Matthew, is that their deeds—flashy cures and exorcisms—do not teach the people to feed the hungry. Matthew cartoons the prophetic practices of claiming to speak "in the name of Jesus" and of evoking charismatic manifestations of the presence of the risen "Lord."

> Not everyone who says to me, *"Lord, Lord,"* will get into the kingdom of heaven—only those who carry out the will of my Father in heaven. On that day many will say to me, *"Lord, Lord,* didn't we prophesy *in your name?* Didn't we drive out demons *in your name?* Didn't we perform all those miracles *in your name?"* Then I will tell them honestly: "I never knew you; get away from me, you subverters of the Law!" (Matt. 7:21-23)[23]

Matthew's community accepts the Markan tilt to the "hinder not" form of the saying about the children; that is, Matthew agrees that access to the person of Jesus is the objective of Christian teaching.[24] Matthew 25 returns to the theme of judgment to reinforce this view. In the parable of the Last Judgment (25:31-46), those who shall have done the commonplace deeds of feeding the hungry and welcoming the stranger are the ones who shall receive the yearned-for summons from Jesus, "Come." Moreover, in Matthew's scheme of things, it turns out that Jesus has been available all along, although hidden, in the hungry and the stranger. While *prophets* might be able to evoke occasional intense experiences of the Risen Lord, *teachers* know the whereabouts of Jesus in the everyday. Thus, one needs a teacher to decode the presence of Jesus in the opportunities of ordinary life.

Matthew has perhaps taken the cue for his critique of prophecy from the Septuagint. But the critique had to be very carefully made, and with a certain ambivalence. Greek-speaking Jews regarded the Hebrew prophets as implements of the paideia of God, that is, interpreters of the punishments by which God corrected the people. To kill the prophets was to refuse to be educated. Matthew knows this tradition and has incorporated it (from Q) in Matt. 23:34-35 (although Matthew's addition of "scholars" to the list reflects his concern with his own kind of teacher).

> Look, that is why I send you prophets and sages *and scholars (grammateis).* Some you're going to kill and crucify, and some you're going to beat in your synagogues and hound from city to city. As a result there

---

23. The Scholars Version is adjusted to bring out the literal sense of the Greek that is important to the argument here.

24. "Matthew" is the designation of a text. An individual stands behind that text in a relationship to it that, while it resembles modern "authorship" in some respects, also is characterized by aspects of the traditional oral haggadah. Whether individual or corporate, however, the Matthean poiesis has strong elements of critical reevaluation of praxis.

will be on your heads all the innocent blood that has been shed on the earth, from the blood of innocent Abel to the blood of Zechariah, son of Baruch, whom you murdered between the temple and the altar.

Nevertheless Matthew may have found his authorization to reject the Christian prophets in the Septuagint version of Ezek. 13:9:

I will extend my hand against the prophets. . . . They will have no part in the education (*paideia*) of my people, nor will they be written in the writings of the house of Israel.

Yet it is also significant that Matthew knows and preserves the tradition that the prophetic way was used and authorized by Jesus. In Matt. 9:35, Jesus' mode of operating consists in traveling through villages (although Matthew adds cities, *poleis*), teaching, preaching, and working cures. In Matt. 10:1-15, the disciples are told to continue in that same mode: travel among Jews only, preach, work cures, and exorcise. Nevertheless Matthew has the Risen Lord revise these instructions specifically to exclude the characteristic prophetic wonderworks. In Matt. 28:18-20 the new policy is to go among Gentiles, to baptize, and to teach observant behavior.

Matthew's overall concern for teachers has long been recognized. The teacher is "the scholar who is schooled in the kingdom of heaven" (Matt. 13:52).[25] Teachers who both obey and teach the law will be called great in the kingdom of heaven (Matt. 5:19). Where Mark dismissed the problem of failed teaching as "bad soil," Matthew is obsessed with it. Significantly, to the parable of the Sower is added the parable of the Weeds (Matt. 13:24-30), in which malpractice is interpreted as bad seed sown by an enemy in secret.

Warnings to teachers are posted throughout the Matthean text. The Christian teacher's role is defined by comparison to two foils: the Christian prophet, as we have seen, and the Pharisee in Matt. 23:1-28. Without discounting the anti-Jewish tone of this passage or its tragic anti-Semitic career, we find that it is possible to read it as a list of "don'ts" for Christian teachers. Projected upon the Pharisees are the dangers of pedagogical malpractice to which any teacher in antiquity is tempted: to seek honors, to harp on trivia, to set impossible requirements, to lose substance amid

25. The word translated as "schooled" here derives from *manthanō* and *mathēteuō*, which connote being someone's pupil and therefore a scholar—*not* from *paideia* and *paideuō*, which carry the class-related connotations discussed above.

fancy words, to preach one thing while practicing another. If in Matthew's community a class or order of teachers is forming, Matthew is terrified of what this could portend.

The Gospels that made it into the canon of the New Testament come down to us because they formed, and are still carried by, churches whose political clout rides upon their viable teaching strategies. But besides transmitting approved teaching strategies, the Gospels also display traces of practices that were suppressed entirely. The Gospels' ambivalence about paideia may be just such a trace. Something almost forgotten is submerged beneath paideia and its metaphor of cultivation (sowing, weeding, reaping). The hidden bedrock underneath Christian un-paideia is the metaphor of nursing (and gestation) from that early saying about kingdom entry discussed in chapter 2.

These two metaphors, nursing and cultivation, do not ride comfortably together. Milk is "wild food" that needs no cultivation, and so nursing is easy and natural. But crops take work; unlike milk, the produce of the fields affords the opportunity to honor Torah and must be tithed. Now, teaching can be either like nursing or like sowing—not both. The canonical Gospels choose sowing, and they model no teaching practices based on the nursing metaphor. (As we shall see, this metaphor founds instead the liturgical practices of Eucharist and Baptism.) Nevertheless, when the Gospels tap into the cultivation metaphor to discuss teaching practices, incongruously something of the nursing metaphor is transferred to farming. Thus we get catechetical seed sown but not tended. In Christian teaching practices, the seed of the word is supposed to behave like wild food. Theorizing a curious un-paideia, the Gospels teach teachers how to teach but then undermine the significance of human effort for the quest to capture the kingdom. The inevitable cases of failure through malpractice bring this entire conceptual system crashing down.

Meanwhile, Jewish education was developing in response to the same cultural pressures that shaped early Christian education: Hellenistic paideia mediated through the Septuagint as well as the ubiquitous *gymnasion*, the hermeneutical principles of the Greek rhetors, the dialogue with Cynicism over law and nature, and the frictions between village and city ways of life. In the era of the sages, or Tannaim, knowledge propagated among Jews generally in ways not too dissimilar to the traditioning of Jesus material among early Galilean Christians. Interpretive traditions that we know from the targums evolved to make the Scripture accessible to ordinary lay people, whose language was Aramaic. The Mishnah, which was edited in Sepphoris, is a collection of sayings at first orally transmitted, some of which come from the first century C.E., attached to the names and authority of famous rabbis.

The notion of "God's kingdom" would have been unobjectionable to the Tannaim. Yet the step that differentiated Christian from Jewish teaching practice is the step that I have associated with the Markan tilt to the "hinder not" form of the kingdom entry saying: the superimposition of the figure of Jesus upon the kingdom. It is interesting that this displacement of the kingdom by Jesus was an artifact of the transmission process of the Jesus haggadah; it was not at first a thematic or material content proposed by it. Among the Tannaim, of course, no single sage takes on such significance. The living Torah abides instead in the circle of ongoing study within the circle of ongoing Jewish community life.

Sending Disciples to Jesus

For the Christian movements as they evolve, then, the express objective of teaching is to bring people into contact with Jesus. This contact is characteristically imaged as "seeing Jesus." The terms of the formula are mutually defining. To get at the real Jesus, you need to do the right kind of seeing. To train for the practice of proper seeing, you need the right kind of teaching. The Gospels employ a variety of devices in order to demonstrate how a Christian teacher operates. We have just examined one of them: Matthew's caricature of Jewish scholars as foil for the ideal Christian teacher that he wanted to produce.

Among the most ingenious Gospel devices for portraying Christian catechetical practice is the use of the figure of John the Baptist as a model of the kind of teaching practices that effectively send disciples to the Lord. The posthumous drafting of John into the Christian teacher corps serves two purposes. First, it redefines the earlier baptist movement by connecting it to the later Jesus movement. Second, it dramatizes the proper functioning of the teacher's intervention, if you will, in the formation of the disciple relationship between Jesus and his followers, between Christ and Christians.

The stories of the Baptist have been shaped by critical reflection upon the role of teachers within communities claiming competence for introducing people to the reality of resurrection. How does the Christian teacher avoid forming a circle of one's own disciples, as did other teachers in antiquity? How do teachers themselves remain disciples? How do they step aside to deflect attention toward the Lord? How does the teacher keep from becoming a kind of chaperone on the honeymoon, the third party who turns a couple into a crowd?[26]

The Gospel narratives make of John the Baptist a much more dynamic figure than a mere bystander to the event of discipling. In fact, there are two distinct (if not contradictory) portraits of John as teacher: that of the Fourth Gospel and that of the Q tradition as preserved in Luke's and Matthew's Gospels. A close look at those two Johns can reveal what they are meant to convey concerning the delicate task of teaching people so as to make them not one's own disciples but disciples of another.[27]

Against the background of first-century teaching practices, that was quite a remarkable ambition. In comparison, the schools or circles of noted rhetors, philosophers, and rabbis proudly cited the names of their teachers along with the lineage of teachers before them. Mishnah invokes the authority of the sages by name. From the Greeks we also have texts, anecdotes and *chreiai* as well as treatises, enshrining the names of famous teachers. Their schools might take pride, for example, in forming "Platonists." Yet it was hardly expected that a Platonist in training would have a relationship with Plato or that a Pharisee would "see" Moses.[28] The Greek world knew of visionary experiences, of course, such as the dream appearances of Asclēpios to heal pilgrims sleeping at Epidaurus, the Lourdes of antiquity. Yet other than general cultural conditioning, no special training was required to "see" Asclēpios.

This examination of the Gospel material concerning John is concerned less with what might be termed "the historical John the Baptist" than with how the Christian texts use him as a literary vehicle to demonstrate the way or ways in which a teacher can hand over disciples to the Lord. Specifically, the portraits of John make him the *teacher* amid a self-identified group of disciples—a role that contrasts with his status as a *prophet* broadcasting exhortations to whoever happens to pass by. Luke's Gospel asserts that John taught his disciples how to pray (Luke 11:1). People seeking baptism say to him, "Teacher, what should we do?" In response, John is able to translate his general prophetic exhortations into quite specific applications for the particular circumstances of property

26. In John's Gospel, the honeymoon metaphor is employed to liken the Baptist to the best man at a wedding who stands with the bridegroom "and is happy enough just to be close at hand" (John 3:29).

27. An earlier version of this study was published in *Lexington Theological Quarterly* 21 (1986): 14–26.

28. There is a report, however, that after the death of Apollonius of Tyana a young disciple had a dream in which the philosopher-mystic imparted a teaching. See Aune, *Prophecy in Early Christianity*, 236.

owners, tax collectors, and soldiers (Luke 3:10-14). John is said to have disciples who remain loyal to their teacher throughout his career, even during his final imprisonment, and who bury him after he is murdered (Matt. 14:12; Mark 6:29).

John the teaching baptizer is presented as a model for Christian teachers by both the Fourth Gospel and the Q tradition, through their distinctive dramatizations of the way in which he directs his own disciples to Jesus. It is interesting that the two traditions put forth contrasting accounts of the conditions under which a teacher sends disciples to the Lord. The texts are making use of the figure of John to convey something other than a historically factual account of his career. The contrasting portrayals of John suggest that the churches of the New Testament have devised at least two effective ways for teachers to send disciples to the Lord. Both accounts were received into the canon. The ancient churches intended to share with subsequent generations both practical information about how to send people to Jesus and the significant theoretical information that *the ways of doing so are multiple.*

An examination of the traditions about John the Baptist discloses that there are two textual versions of him. The Baptist of the Fourth Gospel (John 1:19-37) is a free man breathing the fresh outdoor air of Bethany beyond the Jordan. He is portrayed, at the height of his own career, as being absolutely certain about the identity and role of Jesus. When he catches sight of Jesus, he calls out, "Look, the Lamb of God, who does away with the sin of the world." Not once but twice does he point to Jesus as the Lamb of God. On the second utterance, two of John's disciples "heard him say this, and they followed Jesus." This John Baptist can identify Jesus with a certitude stemming from a personal revelation that he has received concerning Jesus, for he attests: "I have seen the Spirit coming down like a dove out of the sky, and it hovered over him."

The "other" John, however, does not know who Jesus is. The Baptist of the Q tradition is locked up in prison (Matt. 11:2-15). This John, although heralding the approach of *someone*, has had no access to the revelation of Jesus' identity, for in the Synoptic tradition (Mark 1:10-11 and parallels), Jesus' baptism involves no revelation for John.[29] The descent of the Spirit on Jesus is presented as a personal experience of Jesus alone (Matt. 3:16). This John too sends disciples to Jesus, but they go with a

---

29. This tradition rests more easily with some communities than with others. Matt. 3:14 has John balk at baptizing Jesus on grounds that "I'm the one who needs to be baptized by you." Even in this Gospel, however, it is Jesus, not John, who receives the revelation of sonship (Matt. 3:16-17).

question: "Are you the one who is to come, or are we to wait for another?" (Matt. 11:3).

Other contrasts in the content and structure of the two stories are readily apparent. In the Fourth Gospel, the Baptist denies that he is Elijah or the prophet (John 1:21), but in Matthew, Jesus emphatically insists that the Baptist is indeed Elijah and prophet (Matt. 11:9, 14). In the Fourth Gospel, the Baptist identifies Jesus with the words, "This is the one I was talking about" (John 1:15), but in Matthew it is Jesus who identifies John with "This is the one about whom it was written" (Matt. 11:10).

Amid these contrasts, one is most salient. With Q and the Synoptics, what sends the disciples to Jesus is the teacher's uncertainty, that is, the teacher's ability to ask a question. It is not the teacher but the disciples who "hear and see" the evidence of healings and preaching. These evidences, in turn, become the answer to the question of Jesus' identity. The Jesus of the Q tradition instructs the disciples to go back and share those evidences with their teacher in the prison. With the Fourth Gospel, on the other hand, it is the teacher's own experience of revelation that gives the teacher the certitude about the identity of Jesus out of which disciples are sent to the Lord. The teacher has seen the dove descending and has heard the voice. What the disciples hear is the teacher's witness to Jesus' identity, a witness based on the teacher's own inner revelation and certitude.[30]

The character of the heavenly "voice" as evidence is a question that takes us into the heart of the evolution of distinctively Christian teaching practice. In the first-century, some said that the spirit of prophecy had been withdrawn, so that no human being was then speaking authoritatively the word of God. Nevertheless divine communication might come occasionally through a disembodied echo of a heavenly voice. The *bat qôl,* literally "daughter of a voice," is explained by Bruce Chilton in this way:

> The *bath qol* . . . is viewed as an objective phenomenon in Rabbinica, where the echo was understood as a sound which proceeded from a heavenly voice, and so as the contemporary counterpart of God's address to his people through the prophets.[31]

The rabbis were not prophets but teachers, and numerous tales from the tannaitic period accord rabbis access to a *bat qôl.*

---

30. It is interesting that in the Q tradition the inquirers remain John's disciples after meeting Jesus, while in the Fourth Gospel allegiance is transferred from John to Jesus.

31. See Chilton, *A Galilean Rabbi and His Bible.* Chilton identifies the baptismal voice as an example of a *bat qôl;* see the discussion on pp. 125–31.

There is also a disembodied voice in Isaiah 40. It is, in Hebrew, "a voice of one calling, 'Prepare the way'" (Isa. 40:3). Again in Hebrew, "A voice says, 'Cry out'" (Isa. 40:6). All four canonical Gospels associate this voice with John. For Matthew and the Fourth Gospel, the Baptist not only hears the voice, he is the voice (Matt. 3:3; John 1:23). In Hebrew, the text was of course attributed *to* the eighth-century prophet Isaiah, but it was not *about* "prophecy" in the technical sense. Then why were the stakes so high when John—unlike a rabbi—was personally identified with the Isaian *bat qôl*? The Aramaic targum of the Isaian text holds the key. It indicates that popular homiletic interpretation likely was reading this text as an announcement of a reopening of prophecy in association with the revelation of the kingdom of God. This can be seen clearly in a comparison of a translation of the Hebrew text with a translation of its Aramaic reading:[32]

Figure 2.   Isaiah 40 in Bible and in Targum

From Hebrew	From Targum
v. 1	
Comfort, comfort my people, says your God.	Prophets, prophesy consolation to my people, says your God.
v. 2	
Speak to the heart of Jerusalem and proclaim to her . . . that her sin has been paid for.	Speak to the heart of Jerusalem and prophesy to her . . . that her sins have been forgiven her.
v. 6	
A voice says, "Cry out." And I said, "What shall I cry?"	A voice of one who says, "Prophesy!" And he answered and said, "What shall I prophesy?"
v. 9	
Get you up to a high mountain, you who herald good tidings to Zion . . . say to the towns of Judah, "Here is your God!"	Get you up to a high mountain, prophets who herald good tidings to Zion . . . say to the cities of the house of Judah, "The kingdom of God is revealed!"

If in the Gospels the disembodied Isaian *bat qôl* becomes incarnated in John, then according to the targumic reading such a claim would signal

---

32. The targum comes from *The Isaiah Targum*, trans. Bruce D. Chilton, Aramaic Bible, vol. 11 (Wilmington, Del.: Michael Glazier, 1987).

the appearance of the kingdom of God. Yet it does not close off the channel of the *bat qôl,* for the voice that identifies Jesus at his baptism is another instance of its operation.

There are, then, two witnesses to Jesus: the "prophet" John and the *bat qôl,* whether heard by the "prophet" or by Jesus himself. But John's witness, insofar as it consists in reciting the targum, is not what traditionally would have been recognized as Israelite prophecy; instead, it is teaching. John is interpreting the Isaian Scripture like a *meturgeman* in the synagogue, except that he does it out of doors. This popular homiletical teaching, which is to be distinguished not only from classical prophecy but also from the academic discourse of the Tannaim, is what occasions the disclosure of the identity of Jesus.

Nevertheless we get variant accounts of what John's teaching was like. John interests the Gospel traditions more as a demonstration of a praxis than as a source of content for Christian teaching. We have, then, from those adept Christian teachers who wrote down the Gospels, two distinct procedures for handing disciples over to the Lord. One model envisions a teacher who knows who Jesus is and whose infectious certitude leads others to experience the Lord. The other model works with teachers who have received no personal guarantee about who Jesus might be but nevertheless know how to give their disciples the questions, and point them in the right direction, to find out. Of the two Baptizers, Riverbank John teaches with answers, while Jailhouse John teaches with questions.

These contrasting methods are equally canonical. (That is, these are the procedures that survived the tug-of-war over Jesus during the first century and also the textual sorting process completed in the fourth.) The "two" John Baptists of the New Testament are modeling two different praxes, both of which are presented as appropriate for one whose job it is to turn over disciples to the Lord. But they have even more to demonstrate to the perceptive reader. They represent two different approaches to devising a program or curriculum, as it were, for Christian initiation. John-Baptist-by-the-River exemplifies liturgical catechesis, a form of Christian teaching that aims to facilitate the learner's encounter with the Lord in the midst of those who regularly gather for liturgical celebration. John-Baptist-in-Prison, on the other hand, exemplifies Christian initiation through experiences of liberating action on behalf of justice and human welfare. This distinction is of interest to contemporary theological discussions of Christian education, but it is quite startling to find it clearly laid out at such an early point in the tradition.

Teaching Worship and Care

In contemporary pastoral theology, consensus is forming that the criterion of effective teaching or preaching is its ability to coordinate, interpret, and sustain both the church's life of worship and its life of service to
the world. That is, the church's proclamation of God's kingdom is seen as
intrinsically linked to both its celebration and its actualization of God's
kingdom. The two teaching Johns of the New Testament can be cited in
support of that consensus, for they suggest that Christian teaching has
been characterized by this double linkage since quite early times.

Among the communities that wrote Gospels, it seems, the identity
of Jesus could be manifested in two kinds of experiences that they had
abundantly available to them. On the one hand, Christian beliefs about
Jesus were validated by intimate encounter with the personal presence of
the Risen Lord when the community gathered to read Scripture, hear
"prophetic" utterances—that is, haggadic performances—of the words of
Jesus, and celebrate his abiding presence in the rituals of Eucharist and
Baptism.[33] On the other hand, their beliefs about Jesus were validated by
their own empowerment to heal, exorcise, evangelize, and serve the material and spiritual needs of their sisters and brothers in Jesus' name.

As praxes, both of these evidences of the continuing availability of
God in Jesus—the intimacy of liturgical encounter and the caring service
to brothers and sisters in need—were sources of "content" for Christian
teaching within those early churches which gave us the New Testament.
Each of the two teaching John Baptists depicts the use of one of these
sources.

The Johannine story of the Baptist's witness by the river displays the
elements of what later would be called mystagogy or catechesis of the
mysteries. The little drama is staged with a downright liturgical structure. The setting where John speaks is the place where he baptizes (John
1:28).[34] The identifying formula, "Look, the Lamb of God," is ritually

33. This is not to beg the question. The structure of resurrection experience is such
that *whatever* it is that releases itself and goes at large in the midst of the Christian assembly,
that is what/who is identified as Jesus. The recognition that constitutes "seeing the Lord" is
the judgment or insight connecting the facts about Jesus, remembered from the past, with
whatever/whoever this is now.

34. The practice of offering mystagogical catechesis in the same location where the
community celebrates the liturgy is attested by archaeological evidence and in the textual
examples of patristic catecheses that have come down to us. The most vivid examples are
found in a fourth-century work, *The Catechetical Lectures of S. Cyril, Archbishop of Jerusalem*, A
Select Library of Nicene and Post-Nicene Fathers of the Christian Church, vol. 7 (Grand

repeated (John 1:29, 36). Lambs, of course, were liturgical animals par excellence within the ancient Jewish cult of sacrifice. The action unfolds in liturgical stages. On the first day, John gives his questioners a reading from the Hebrew Scripture (responding to their request in 1:22 that he identify himself). On the second day, John delivers a prophetic witness about a personal pneumatic experience of the Spirit that he has had, an experience that identified Jesus as "the one who baptizes with holy spirit" (John 1:33). Such charismatic testimony was a familiar feature of early Christian gatherings for worship. On the third day, John repeats the liturgical recognition formula, "Look, the Lamb of God," and his disciples go away with Jesus. Another familiar feature of early Christian worship was prayer inviting Jesus to return and take away those who were his own.

This is not to assert that the historical event of Jesus' baptism actually had this remarkably liturgical structure. Rather, a Christian community recalling that event has projected it onto the screen of its own liturgical practices. That church, whose memories the author of John's Gospel writes up, may have used its own emergent liturgy as a mnemonic outline through which to remember what was significant about the historical event of Jesus' baptism. Or more likely that church, while retaining no historical memory of the details of John's teaching practices, sketched them in according to the model of its own mystagogy. Its portrait of the Baptist is really a self-portrait of its own teaching practices.

What is perhaps most liturgical about the design of the riverbank scenario is the haunting phrase, "Right there with you is someone you don't yet recognize" (John 1:26). That statement focuses the strategy and the instructional objective of the Christian mystagogue. In liturgical catechesis, the teacher's task is to get the disciples to recognize the one who stands among them whenever they gather for worship as the Christian assembly.

It falls to the other teaching John Baptist, the one who is in jail, to dramatize pedagogical praxis that uses the other kind of evidence for the validity of Christian claims about Jesus: the church's activities of caring service to human need. We find this John teaching not in a liturgical place but in a place of injustice, repression, and misery. It is a place where Jesus himself cannot enter. The Synoptic story does *not* assert that Jesus is standing unrecognized among those who are there in the prison. In this

Rapids: Wm. B. Eerdmans Publishing Co., 1955). The liturgical space in which Cyril gave instructions actually had been built over the geographical sites of the passion and death of Jesus. While speaking, Cyril gave his catechumens a walking tour of Golgotha and the tomb of Jesus, which at that time were enclosed within the compound of a basilica.

place, John does not answer questions; he asks them. Nor does Jailhouse
John have access to any comforting private revelation about Jesus. The experience of captivity, frustration, puzzlement, and need is what generates
the teaching question.

In the riverbank story it was John who heard and saw and then told
his disciples. But here it is the disciples who hear and see and who are sent
back to tell their teacher what they have found out (Matt. 11:4). The evidence they witness is that "the blind see again and the lame walk; lepers
are cleansed and the deaf hear; the dead are raised up, and the poor have
the good news preached to them" (Matt. 11:5). Those are the evidences of
who Jesus is. In other words, the curriculum for Christian initiation reflected here consists in examination of the church's works of merciful care
for human beings in need. That is the kind of evidence that someone in
captivity can understand.

Moreover, the structure of the teaching event in the jailhouse version
is not a unidirectional transmission of revelation but a dialogical inquiry
into evidence. The disciples are empowered to see and hear for themselves, and moreover to return and share the fruits of their investigation
with their teacher. He has sent them to the Lord with a question, not with
certitude. But the question is the doorway through which they can reach a
certitude of their own.

If the portraiture of John the Baptist can be read as a deliberate profiling of models for catechesis, then the early churches must have initiated
Christians in a variety of ways. Two of those ways, at least, were demonstrated by John stories and became canonical through inclusion of those
demonstrations in Gospels that came to belong to the New Testament.
Therefore those methods are not simply described for the reader's information; they are prescribed as constitutive components of preparing people to recognize the Lord. The know-who depends upon this know-how,
as it were.

By excavating the John Baptist stories, we have disclosed two distinct
ways of making disciples for the Lord. Both of them involve a teacher
whose role it is to give the disciple over to Jesus. But the content, the
method, and the setting of the teaching differ. The way of teaching modeled by Riverbank John is mystagogical catechesis, an ancient term denoting instruction based on the church's experience of the presence of the
Lord when gathered for sacramental worship. The content of that teaching is the naming of "someone right there with you whom you don't yet
recognize." He is named Lamb of God and recognized as the son of God,
the only one, who does away with the sin of the world. The method of this
teaching is to witness to personal experience of the coming of the Spirit

and to personal encounter with Jesus particularly in the church's liturgical celebrations. The setting of this teaching is the assembly of disciples as they are gathered in the place of baptism. Mystagogy is a teaching of the mysteries, in the ancient sense of the mysteries of worship. This teaching focuses on the church when it is being most intensely itself: when it assembles to name the "someone" in its midst. This teaching is meant to foster intimate personal encounter with the Lord in worship and recognition of him as God's chosen one. Out of this encounter, discipleship develops.

But we have seen that the Gospels also model another way of teaching, with a different content, method, and setting. The way of teaching modeled by Jailhouse John might be termed an inductive action/reflection model. Its content is its method: a way of questioning. Rather than identifying one who is manifestly present in liturgical ritual, this way of teaching *wagers* the identity of Jesus upon the outcome of an investigation of the evidence. Whether Jesus is "the one who was to come" depends entirely on the presence or absence of the hallmarks of the kingdom of God: whether the disabled are accommodated, whether there is good news for the poor. The setting for this way of teaching is any situation where human freedom and well-being are hindered. The church can creditably offer a christological answer to the question of Jesus' identity only to the extent that it can show itself to be a place of healing and empowerment. Potential disciples will look and listen closely, and they will tell exactly what they do and do not see and hear.

The job of John the Baptist in the Gospels is to transmit, guide, and correct ecclesial initiatory practices. The two distinctive procedures that are dramatized by the stories of John are complementary. They also presuppose a third practice, the transmission of biographical information about Jesus through narratives. Stories about Jesus preserve some concrete facticity for the one who lived, taught, and then died at Calvary. Jesus was a real human being, and although the Gospel texts give us fictionalized versions of him no less than of the Baptist, still the textual Jesus is not a complete fabrication. There was someone there first to be fictionalized. The name connected to pneumatic liturgical experiences, the name in which afflictions continued to be healed, first was the name of a human body. The reality of that body, its actions and its fate, keep the text that is that name from floating off into fantasy.

If "entering God's kingdom" once was "like nursing," in this chapter we have traced the reinscription of the kingdom as a cultured way of life accessible only through a carefully defined program of cultivation. The teaching/learning transactions for inducting people into the kingdom now conform to the basic pattern of Hellenistic paideia, yet they incorporate certain elements of resistance to it. All the while God's kingdom was becoming this distinctive un-paideia, the figure of Jesus was also being reinscribed as a teacher—and being reinscribed directly upon the text of "God's kingdom." With Jesus made over into *the* teacher, Christian teachers found themselves in a ticklish situation. They needed a way to conceptualize their contradictory role: well-trained arbiters of the Jesus tradition, with its distinctive exegetical and initiatory practices, who nevertheless remained perpetual learners at the feet of another. They seized upon the figure of John the Baptist to illustrate how this contradiction could be worked out in practice. This fictionalization further contributed to defining procedures of access to Jesus and ultimately to designing also the "Jesus" who was being sought.

With the figure of the teaching Jesus superimposed upon the text of God's kingdom, to "enter" the kingdom must mean to "approach" Jesus. The ubiquity and accessibility claimed for God's kingdom in the Jesus movements now must entail ubiquity and accessibility for Jesus himself. Jesus requires *and acquires* a risen body. In other words, superlative accessibility is ascribed to Jesus' body after Calvary. But these developments emerge as practical initiatory strategies before they take shape as poietic textual artifacts. A later chapter will explore how such artifacts function to deflect creative energy back upon human bodies.

4

Empty Text as Empty Tomb

WHAT HAPPENED on Easter? The possibility of telling what happened on Easter arises out of the practices that effect Christian origin and specifically out of the canonized teaching practices that we have been reconstructing from Gospel materials. Easter means seeing Jesus alive despite crucifixion. But how? For the churches of the Johannine tradition, the teacher could see Jesus clearly by standing on the liturgical riverbank of baptism. For the Q tradition, Jesus showed his identity through actions relieving misery and thus matching the profile drawn by Christian teachers out of Hebrew Scripture. The presumption of the New Testament writers is that their texts will intervene in the pedagogical processes that equip people to recognize Jesus long after Calvary. These texts are reflexive, that is, self-conscious and deliberate in their intent to depict the teaching process itself as an essential component of the possibility of seeing the Risen Lord.

Nowhere is this intent plainer than in the Easter stories: the appearance narratives and the accounts of finding the empty tomb. If the Easter saga were a photograph, it would have the photographer's shadow crossing the foreground as a deliberate component of the composition. But these stories are words, so they break their frame in another way. They let a speaker address the reading audience while talking to other characters in the scene. This is done to lift *you and me* out of our seats and our time, to deposit us tombside with the witnesses. We arrive at the grave beside the Marys, but we are not they; yet our expectations, although different from theirs, are equally determinative of what we can find. If this is so for readers today, the same can be said equally well of the first generations

"Don't be afraid. For I know that you are seeking Jesus the crucified."

Who is speaking? These are the words with which *the Easter angel* startles the two Marys who, in Matthew's story, arrive at daybreak to sit shiva for their Galilean rabbi, on what is supposed to be their third and final day of mourning by his tomb. They already have seen terrible things on the first two days. These women watched the agonized death of Jesus at Passover, writes Matthew; and later that evening, it was they who observed the custom of watching over the sepulcher and the stiff, cold body within. The second day was the Sabbath, when the religious authorities went to work and sealed up the tomb, posting guards there.

Now on the third day the Marys are back again, as custom prescribes, to watch by the tomb once more. This time the disturbances are described in terms of earthquake, lightning, quite a drastic changing of the guard, and the approach of someone spectacular to take over the job of tomb sitting. But, says this angel, don't worry about all of that. I'm not here just to shake you up. This is happening because you're looking for somebody who most definitely is not resting in peace.

Who is speaking? These are the words of *the teaching church* to catechumens and to seekers of all kinds. It takes courage to look for Jesus—if what you want is not some comfortable counterfeit, but the real Jesus: that historic individual who expressed certain distinctive insights that irritated the religious establishment so much that they wanted him dead.

When people sincerely inquire about Jesus, the first words they need to hear are words of reassurance. To seek Jesus is indeed a hazardous project; no use denying it. Many are afraid to seek because they fear not finding him; or, worse, finding someone who is not really Jesus at all. For others, the implausibility of the project is overwhelming. How can we hope to find this man? We know hardly anything about him, he lived so long ago and far away. Still others are wary of facile and easy answers to their serious questions about the identity and whereabouts of Jesus.

The teaching church first affirms that these questions are serious indeed, and the route difficult. But *the church knows what the Easter angel knows*: seeking Jesus is the first step in finding him. One must expect to see him; one must go looking in the place of his last known address. But there will be earthquakes. And skittish guards, some of whom are us. Says the church: don't worry so much about all of that. The starting point is simply to come with some expectations.

Who is speaking? These are the words, finally, with which *the critical investigator* reassures theologian, bishop, and catechist. I know that there could be any number of reasons why you find yourself here in the midst of this paragraph, seventy-eight pages into a book that quakes the bedrock of Christian history. I know that you might not name "seeking Jesus" as your primary interest.

Perhaps you are looking for something that is not here. I don't have Jesus. I am writing this book because I am interested in "seeking Jesus." That is the religious story of my life. But more important for this work, on the level of critical scholarly inquiry I am interested in *what it means to seek* Jesus, and particularly in what the Gospels tell us about how one seeks Jesus after Calvary. Why are there earthquakes? Why are there guards? Why are women sitting by his tomb?

Why, indeed, are stones rolled in front of the places where we store Jesus? How does one get those stones to roll back so Jesus can once again go at large in the world?

who read the canonical Easter stories. And we must presume that the Gospel writers had them very much in mind.

As an experiment, then, let us allow the messenger from Matthew's Easter story to speak outside its frame, by listening to one line in three different ways.

There are three layers of epistemology to be read out of the *oida* ("I know") of Matt. 28:5. What the *angel* knows about seeking Jesus is simply the action or plotline of the narrative. What the *church* knows about seeking Jesus is more complex: the church knows both the desire of countless human beings who continue to seek and the ways of fulfilling that desire. What the *investigator* knows about seeking Jesus is that there is congruence between what the angel knows and what the church knows, that is, between the story of resurrection, on the one hand, and the church's initiatory and pedagogical praxis, on the other.

The thesis taking shape here is that the post-Calvary availability of Jesus is defined by certain protocols of approach. These are canonical, if you will. That is, Easter stories like the one that concludes Matthew's Gospel actually encode a pattern for seeking and seeing Jesus as the Risen Lord. This pattern of discovery and recognition, presented narratively as a plotline or action sequence within the text, will be picked up also in the structure of liturgical ritual and in the strategies of Christian pedagogy, as we shall see. It is this pattern or protocol which defines what "resurrection" itself means. In other words, risen life is that mode of availability of Jesus to the church that results from the enactment or realization of this pattern. The pattern is no human work but an instance of the incarnating mystery of Jesus Christ, God's true Son and our true brother, firstborn from the tomb. Resurrection doesn't happen *to* persons; it happens *between and among* them.

Ethnicity, Economics, and Easter

In this chapter we will be comparing Matthew's version and Luke's version of what happened on Easter, that is, their tomb stories and their accounts of appearances of a Risen Jesus to various people.[1] Before beginning that

---

1. The English word "Easter" comes from the name of a pre-Christian spring festival. It now names a liturgical feast day (or season) on which the resurrection annually is commemorated and on which new Christians are initiated into this mystery through baptism. Easter has a place on the liturgical calendar, but I do not mean to imply here that the resurrection of Jesus was an event that could just as neatly be located on the calendar of a year in

investigation, however, we do well to take note that these stories have crossed gender, ethnic, and class frontiers before settling into the Greek texts in which they have come down to us. A lot has happened to the stories of what happened "on Easter."

If we ask how transit across social frontiers may have altered the stories, one curious detail draws attention right away. Matthew's Marys are Galilean village women following traditional mourning customs; why, then, should they be having a Greek vision through their Jewish tears? Greeks get apparitions; Jewish villagers hear a *bat qôl*.[2] Greeks come to know things by seeing and reading; Semites, by hearing and tasting.

It is odd of Matthew to supply a visual description of the radiant messenger at the tomb, and there is much more at stake here than a quirk in the vocabulary of supernatural manifestation. The visual bias of Greek culture profoundly shapes all its expressions, from poetry to philosophy to science and history. In Greek grammar, the present tense of the verb "to know," *oida*, is the perfect-tense form of the verb "to see," *horaō*. Quite literally, to know means to have seen. The essential being of something is its *eidos*, the shape that it presents to the seeing eye. Our word "idea" comes from that term. Greek symbolism prizes whatever is bright, clear, light, open, dry, warm, or sunlit. Those qualities are associated with reality, rationality, truth, racial purity, and maleness. Anthropologists speculate that this semantic configuration is owing to the language's distant origins in northern latitudes with long dark winters. Since English belongs to the same language group, and inherits many words and concepts directly from Greek, it is difficult for us to grasp intuitively just how arbitrary and peculiar this symbolic bias is.

In contrast, Hebrew and Aramaic are Semitic languages encoding a symbolism that evolved beneath much more sunlight. Hebrew poetry associates shade, shadow, and shelter with the provident care of God. Moisture, dew, cool, and darkness are prized. The parched, the bleached, the bone-dry, the pale, and the sterile are considered repulsive. Divine communication would not accost one as dazzling brightness; rather, it would come like dew in the expectant darkness of early morning. The Hebrew

the first century. The "happening" of the resurrection cannot be apprehended apart from liturgical and initiatory practices.

2. Even Jewish women. An Aramaic story in which Mary hears a *bat qôl* is the likely antecedent of the annunciation stories in Luke and in the *Protevangelium of James,* as will be argued in chapter 5 below. Even when the classical literary Jewish prophets like Isaiah use the term *ḥazôn* (Isa. 1:1), sometimes translated "vision," they often intend an oracular perception, as the context indicates.

word translated "glory," *kabôd*, literally means heaviness—as in the heaviness of approaching rain clouds or the heaviness of pregnancy and lactation amid the flocks and the women.

Knowledge comes to Semitic peoples through hearing. The ear has a direct channel to the heart, which is for them what we and the Greeks would call the mind. Yet Greek and Jewish bodies are of course biologically identical in sensory function. For either, hearing is quite unlike seeing. To see, one steps back to achieve some objective distance. But to hear, one steps close and lets oneself be surrounded and saturated with the sound. In Hebrew, God often speaks but is never seen. In Greek, divine apparitions are a literary commonplace.

Greeks and Semites differ over the epistemological credibility of other senses as well. This makes for turbulence on the culture front between them. For example, in Genesis 3 when Eve tastes the fruit of the tree of knowledge, her motive is plainly the hunger for wisdom, and in fact the story indicates that she was satisfied. But a Platonist Greco-Jew like Philo, reading the Septuagint version and thoroughly immersed in the cultural system of a race not his own, cannot imagine how someone would gain knowledge by eating. Therefore he reads Eve as a mere glutton for sensual pleasure.[3] Philo's culturally bastardized invention of a "fall" through feminine sensuality determined how the West would read creation from that day to this.

The association between food and information may be a clue to differences of economic class as well as to racial differences. In observant Judaism, every meal was (and still is) a consummation of the covenant. Food encodes Torah through the system of tithing and *kashruth*. But as we surmise from the Mishnah, the poor widow and the single mother who got a tithed share ate themselves into a different social status than the landowner who donated it for them. Wild food, however, like fish or honey or mother's milk, was not part of that information system or the social stratification of Torah. It was free to carry other meanings. This cultural background enhances the plausibility of John Dominic Crossan's proposal that the canonical Christian eucharistic ritual of bread and wine submerges an earlier practice: informal outdoor meals on bread and fish.[4] This unwashed, unruly eating of unsown, unprocessed, untithable, unstorable fish would put across quite a different enactment of divine governance—God's kingdom—than did the orderly distribution of cultically apportioned grain.

3. See Philo, *On the Account of the World's Creation Given by Moses,* 46–59.
4. See Crossan, *The Historical Jesus,* 366–67.

Strategic Writing and Reading

The excavation of underlying social practices from beneath the smoothed-over surface of Gospel texts is enabling us to recover important information about the conceptual resources available to various constituencies in first-century Palestine. We need to know how those people could think and imagine, because upon their cognitive capacities depends everyone else's connection with the resurrection of Jesus. There is no other access to a living Jesus except through what they made of him. They knew it would be so. They knew, because it was *already* so within a short while after Calvary.

The teaching practices reconstructed in chapter 3 took shape in the urgency of the post-Calvary situation. Significantly, *reading a text* was not a component in any of the canonized procedures for educating Christians. One could learn to see the Lord without reading anything. Who, then, needed texts? Why did communities begin to produce written Gospels after several decades of effectively initiating people into the possibility of recognizing Jesus as Risen Lord? Perhaps communities discovered that they needed the texts for use in teaching the teachers.

The Gospels were drawn up less as primers than as professional training manuals. To be sure, they transmit some factual information about Jesus. But along with it they define just how that information is to be deployed, including the conditions under which it can come true for the learners or "disciples." Teaching doesn't work—doesn't deliver what it takes to recognize Jesus—unless certain material conditions are fulfilled. The Gospels specify the conditions for recognizing Jesus after Calvary. These specifications can be found throughout the narratives, but they are especially salient in the telling of the Easter stories. That is no accident. In large part, that is why they were written.

We proceed as before on the premise that early Christian communities knew how to see the Lord.[5] At least they knew how to do something that they called seeing the Lord. The phrase "Lordship of Jesus" expresses an insight into Jesus' significance for humankind. This insight arises as one identifies that man, in the very particularity of his earthly life and teachings, with the one whom God has raised to a new life compelling all lives and whose Spirit currently is at large in the community. But how is it that the community can connect these two: the one known to it from its historical traditions and the one known to it within its everyday practices?

---

5. An earlier version of this research was published in *Theology Today* 44 (1988): 441–49.

This is not a new problem; it was already at issue in the writing of the Gospels, where the normative or classic programs for recognizing Jesus are still to be discovered. These texts *about* the past are also texts *with* a past, and the past of the texts invites investigation. How and why did these particular words come to be written and revered? These texts specify the means of access to resurrection experience as the originating communities understood it: the possibility of identifying Jesus and Risen Lord in such a way that one's own destiny also becomes clear. The texts are, quite self-consciously, words. Yet curiously, the New Testament words assert that words are not sufficient for the possibility of resurrection. The insufficiency of text must be grasped in order to grasp the necessity of the other conditions.

What are those other conditions, besides words? *According to Luke-Acts,* what makes it possible to grasp resurrection is participation in a community whose members can be hungry, recognize hungry persons, and respond to their needs. *According to Matthew,* what is required is to put certain ethical teachings into practice. Both Gospels expressly link these conditions to recognition of the identity and significance of Jesus, while at the same time they discount the efficacy of merely verbal identifications—a highly ironic assertion to find in a literary text.

What is meant by the resurrection of Jesus in these Gospels? To inquire honestly, one should first attempt to bracket any present associations with the term "resurrection," particularly the notion that resurrection is an event calling for belief, and let the texts set up the referent or semantic range of this term. Does resurrection mean finding an empty tomb? seeing a dead man alive? being able to heal, exorcise, and teach "in Jesus' name" so as to evoke a realtime presence of the power of the living Lord? intuiting the significance of Jesus? suddenly recognizing a stranger? hearing a voice? meeting the Lord in the air? finding out after the fact that Jesus was really there in the little one whom you cared for? gathering and being sent out as church?

All of those options are supported by New Testament texts. Narratives present these experiences, which is to say that all are presented as having happened to someone else, not to oneself. Such narratives are needed to specify and define the experience; however, they are insufficient to open its possibility *for me.* The other conditions are also specified textually: not in narratives constructing historical events but in other textual features and details. One can grasp what resurrection is only after working through both the diverse narrative depictions of it and the non-narratively specified qualifications of those narratives.

How, according to the texts, does one recognize the Risen Lord? In the Gospel narratives, resurrection witnesses are asked to recognize *someone living, but unknown, as Jesus* who died. Retrojecting resurrection faith back before Calvary, the narratives also depict the disciples as being asked to recognize *Jesus as someone special*. But it was only after the narratives turned resurrection into a past event that subsequent generations were asked to recognize *someone dead—Jesus—as someone living*. The third recognition becomes possible only because of the prior two: identification of Risen Lord as Jesus, and of Jesus as Risen Lord. But how do these prior identifications become possible? Two kinds of assertions about this possibility are made in Luke-Acts and Matthew: (1) Words are not sufficient for it. (2) Sharing of the necessities of life is essential to it.

The Empty Text

Luke's story of the empty tomb (Luke 24:1-11) is a story about where Jesus is *not* to be found. Curiously, it is a story about how a story fails to bring people to the Risen Lord. Jesus obviously is not in the tomb, where the women expected him to be. But neither is the Lord in the text, the narrative. The question of Luke 24:5 applies equally well to those who seek Jesus in a tomb and those who seek him in the text: "Why are you looking for the living among the dead?" Tombs are for dead people; texts are for words already spoken in the past. In Luke 24:10-11 the women tell the apostles what happened at the tomb, "but their story seemed nonsense to them, so they refused to believe the women."[6] These first evangelists find that they cannot bring anyone to the possibility of resurrection through the mere telling of a story. The reprise of the empty tomb story in Luke 24:22-24 ends with the same outcome: "nobody saw him." This narrative about the futility of narrative gives us Luke's wisdom about the possibility of understanding what has happened to Jesus.

Matthew is more subtle, and he carefully preserves a modicum of efficacy for teachers' words. Teaching, for Matthew, entails the present application of reliable past words. Matthew's Gospel presents itself as an authoritative teaching text for the Christian community. Moreover, it presupposes that it, as a text, will be administered by a corps of Christian teachers—for whose governance it takes the trouble to encode some stern directives.

---

6. I am continuing to use the Scholars Version of the Gospel texts, with the same adjustments as before to make the translation more literal in places where a peculiarity of the Greek is important to my argument. The chief adjustments in this chapter are that *basileia* is "kingdom" and *dechomai* is "receive."

Matthew profiles the Christian teacher, or "scholar who is schooled in the kingdom of heaven" (Matt. 13:52), by contrasting him or her to the Pharisee, on the one hand, and to the Christian prophet, on the other. Both of these roles have been distorted for the sake of illustrating what the Christian teacher should avoid. The famous polemic in Matthew 23, pitched against Pharisees, is not meant for them alone. In effect, it warns the Christian teacher corps not to "invent heavy burdens and lay them on folks' shoulders," not to "pay tithes on mint and dill and cummin too, but ignore the really important matters of the law," and so forth. In Matt. 23:8, "you are not to be called Rabbi; after all, you only have one teacher."

More interesting is the corresponding polemic against Christian prophets, whom Matthew regards as a menace.[7] Prophecy in the early churches, as we have seen, was a ministry distinguishable from teaching. If Christian teaching was comparable to the Aramaic homiletic interpretive practice of the synagogue *meturgeman*, then early prophecy showed remarkable affinity with Greek Cynic rhetorical practice. By Matthew's time, which is relatively late in the day of Christian origins, these early heritages have been overlaid by decades of development. Yet certain traditions persist. Even in Matthew's time, Christian prophets are those who operate according to the instructions preserved in Matt. 10:1-14, and in imitation of Jesus' own way of working as represented in the verses immediately preceding, Matt. 9:35-38. That is, they travel, exorcise, heal, and preach, uttering new sayings of Jesus that are accorded authenticity equal to that of sayings remembered from before Calvary. Moreover, prophets do such things "in the name of Jesus." If the Aramaic imagination could incarnate in John the Baptist the *bat qôl* of the Isaian voice, then the Greek imagination could invest these prophets with the pneuma, or spirit, of Jesus.

Sociological reconstruction indicates that the prophets proclaimed resurrection as a realtime experience.[8] That is, they were able to evoke the presence, power, and life of the once-crucified Jesus, and to validate this experience, by wonderworks done through the mention of Jesus' name. In the heyday of the Christian prophets, there was as yet no story of resurrection as an event in someone else's past. Teachers later would narratize

7. The role and the practices of Christian prophets have been intensively investigated since M. Eugene Boring's landmark article "How May We Identify Oracles of Christian Prophets in the Synoptic Tradition? Mark 3:28-29 as a Test Case," *Journal of Biblical Literature* 91 (1972): 501–21. For cultural comparisons, see Aune, *Prophecy in Early Christianity.*

8. That is, the prophets did not replay or retell an event that had occurred previously. I have in mind particularly the work of Kelber, *The Oral and the Written Gospel;* and Gerd Theissen, *Sociology of Early Palestinian Christianity,* trans. John Bowden (Philadelphia: Fortress Press, 1978).

resurrection, but the prophetic way was simply to proclaim that one now lives and works among the people who is Jesus, who died.

The problem with Christian prophecy was that such a proclamation needed continuing dramatic exorcisms and healings to sustain it, or so historians surmise. The prophets were itinerant, but the resident leaders of the community faced a range of day-to-day difficulties ignored or even exacerbated by the prophets. Matthew's Gospel intends that resident teachers take over from prophets the proclamation of resurrection. (This project in fact succeeded, and today we have a Christianity based on the teachers' text, not charismatic wonder-working.) Matthew therefore defames the Christian prophets with the epithet *pseudoprophētēs*. Although some deference to prophets may be expressed in Matt. 10:40-42—"The one who receives a prophet as a prophet will be treated like a prophet"—this saying may be a vestige of older material (in any case, it is so ambiguous that it can be taken as a drollery). Matthew frets about damage sprouting from the words of the prophets. Alone among the Synoptics, he adds to the parable of the Seed (Matt. 13:18-23) the parable of the Secret Seed (Matt. 13:24-30, 36-43) in which an enemy sows weeds among good crops, the interpretation being that bad words are sown among good by the offspring of the evil one. In the eschatological scenario of Matt. 7:21-23, Jesus confronts the prophets on the day of judgment. They plead with him, "Lord, Lord, didn't we prophesy *in your name?* Didn't we cast out demons *in your name?* Didn't we perform all those miracles *in your name?*" The judge replies with a chilling "I never knew you." The prophets are called evildoers and told to get out. Although they recognize Jesus, he does not recognize them.

After having Jesus disclaim those who speak and work "in the name" as the prophets do, Matthew goes on to co-opt this magical phrase for his own purposes. In Matt. 18:5, "Whoever receives one such child *in my name* is receiving me." Given the Matthean spin, the kind of works to be done "in the name" are no longer wonderworks but deeds of justice and compassion.

Yet because he wants to establish Christian teaching authoritatively, Matthew cannot dismiss the efficacy of words entirely, as Luke seems ready to do. The words of Jesus must be authoritatively remembered along with the words of the Torah. In Matt. 5:17-19, Jesus says that every serif and iota of the law must be fulfilled; moreover, "Whoever then ignores one of the most trivial of these regulations *and teaches others to do so* will be called trivial in the kingdom of heaven; but whoever does them *and teaches them* shall be called great in the kingdom of heaven." Again, in Matt. 12:33-37, "On judgment day people will have to account for every thoughtless word they utter. Your own words will vindicate you, and your own words will condemn you." This contrasts curiously with Matthew's parable of the Last

Judgment, Matt. 25:31-46, where orthodox teaching does not appear among the criteria enumerated. The judge neglects to remark, "I was ignorant and you instructed me, lax and you admonished me," because by implication the judge is the teachers' teacher himself, Jesus.

The irony of Matthew is that teachers (unlike prophets) are supposed to have no authority or power in their own words; nevertheless their words ultimately come to outweigh all else. Theoretically Jesus retains authority; it is his words alone that have power. But *whose* Jesus is it who has authority? It is *Matthew's* Jesus, the one whose words are recorded for all time in Matthew's text. The written Gospel brings closure to what Jesus can say. Once the text is promulgated, prophets no longer can come up with new sayings of the Risen Lord. The text controls what teachers can teach. However, teachers control the text inasmuch as they wrote it by narratizing resurrection, and, in the days before widespread literacy and inexpensive printed Bibles, access to the text is through teachers alone. You need a teacher to reach and recognize the Risen Lord. But you need more than just a teacher's words.

The problem is, how can anyone have realtime contact with Jesus as Risen Lord, once he has been buried in the text? How can Jesus say anything new? Who gets to speak for Jesus? Matthew has established that speaking "in the name" is insufficient for recognition of Jesus as Risen Lord and the Risen Lord as Jesus. You need a narrative, and moreover that narrative needs to be taught in specific ways, in a specific context.

For Matthew, the way one gets to see the Lord is by following Jesus' instructions, that is, by obedience. In the scenario at the empty tomb, Matt. 28:1-10, those who wish to see Jesus must go to (a mountain in) Galilee, and Jesus comes to them there. The teacher's role is to lead people "to the mountain," that is, to the teachings of the Sermon on the Mount and to the authority of Jesus. Through the teacher, Christians can see what they literally cannot see: Jesus in the hungry, the thirsty, the strange, the naked, the sick, and the imprisoned.

Where does the text say that? The program that Matthew proposes for seeing the Risen Lord is found in the Easter narrative, Matt. 28:1-10, 16-20. The angel at the tomb tells the women, "I know you are looking for Jesus who was crucified." (This is precisely what the Christian seeks from the teacher.) "He is not here. You see, he was raised, just as he said. Come, look at the spot where he was lying." (The Christian first must accept the factuality of everything about the real Jesus, including his death.) "Run, tell his disciples that he has been raised from the dead. Don't forget, he is going ahead of you to Galilee. *There you will see him.*" Why Galilee? In v. 16, it is the location of the mountain "where Jesus had told them to go."

Throughout Matthew's narrative, mountains have been milestones on the way to establishing Jesus' divine authority as well as lodestones from which Jesus attracts the whole world. Two of these mountains are specifically located "in Galilee": the site of the teachings of Matt. 4:23— 6:29 and the site of the mass healing and feeding in Matt. 15:29-39.[9] In effect, the Christian who wants to see the Risen Lord is being directed away from the tombsite and toward what has transpired on those Galilean mountains. To see Jesus, one must observe the Beatitudes and the other teachings of the Sermon on the Mount. Moreover, seeing the Lord means witnessing the miraculous healings and mass feedings that manifest eschatological power.

The women who dash away from the tomb to fulfill the angel's instructions find their obedience confirmed and rewarded by a glimpse of Jesus in Matt. 28:8-10. The Risen Lord himself promises to be available on the mountain: "Go, tell my companions so they can leave for Galilee, where they will see me." In vv. 17-18, the Eleven do indeed see Jesus; the text says that he came to them on the mountain. Matthew 28 closes with the Great Commission of vv. 18-20, repeating themes that have been important to Matthew: "All authority has been given to me in heaven and on earth. . . . Teach them to observe everything I commanded. I'll be with you [you teachers, that is] day in and day out, as you'll see."

The terms of the mountaintop commissioning point the reader back toward the earlier mountain scenarios. "Authority" has been demonstrated by the healings of the sick and the feeding of the hungry. It has been certified by the voice endorsing Jesus as beloved son, in the presence of two witnesses, Moses and Elijah.[10] "Everything I commanded" has been acted out in the bodily care of Matt. 15:29-39 and laid out in the ethical teachings of Matthew 5–7:

> Congratulations to those who hunger and thirst for justice! . . .
> Congratulations to the merciful! . . .
> Congratulations to those who work for peace! . . .

---

9. Besides the three Galilean mountains, three other mountains are identified by Terence Donaldson: those of the temptation (Mark 4:8-10), the transfiguration (Matt. 17:1-9), and the discourse about end times (Matt. 24:3–25:46). Donaldson says that a Zion theology was the background for this theological motif in Matthew. See Terence L. Donaldson, *Jesus on the Mountain: A Study in Matthean Theology* (Sheffield: JSOT Press, 1985).

10. Bruce Chilton reads the mention of Moses and Elijah as the trace of a dominical saying that swore by deathless witnesses to the power of the kingdom. See Bruce D. Chilton, "The Transfiguration: Dominical Assurance and Apostolic Vision," *New Testament Studies* 27 (1980): 115–24.

> When someone slaps you on the right cheek, turn the other. . . .
> Give to the one who begs from you. . . .
> Notice how the wild lilies grow. . . .
> Don't pass judgment, so you won't be judged.

In this Matthean *epitomē*, or summary of the teacher's words, there is also mention of a variety of rewards for obedience: the merciful will receive mercy, those with undefiled hearts will see God, those who pray in secret will be heard, failures will be forgiven for those who forgive others. But it is not until the parable of the Last Judgment that we find out what really was at stake in obedience to these instructions: anyone who helps needy people has helped the Lord himself. The Lord is available in the needy, although, as the parable indicates, he is never literally "seen" in them.

In short, Matthew's advice to those who want to see the Risen Lord is to follow Jesus' teachings, trusting that the Lord is there in the person of the needy. To find out what Jesus' teachings are, one consults a teacher, who consults Matthew's text. And by the way, teachers themselves are supposed to follow these instructions as well as teach others to do so.

The Empty Stomach

Luke's prescription for recognizing the identity and significance of Jesus as Risen Lord resembles Matthew's in emphasizing ethical action, but the terms are rather different. As we saw above, Luke says that words do not lead anyone to recognize the Risen Lord. In fact, for Luke the ability to recognize a hungry person is the precondition for recognizing the Risen Lord.

Let us look at the texts. In Acts 10:40-41, Peter's catechesis to Cornelius specifies what it means to be a witness to resurrection: "God raised this man on the third day and openly displayed him, not to all the people but to God's pre-selected witnesses, to us who *ate and drank with him* after his resurrection from the dead." Checking back to Luke's Easter appearance narratives, one finds that eating was the key to recognition both in Emmaus and in Jerusalem.

With the Emmaus story, the eucharistic ritual overtones that are usually read into it should not be allowed to hide its other, more direct meaning. At Emmaus, "he took a loaf, and gave a blessing, broke it, and started passing it around to them. Then their eyes were opened and *they recognized him;* and he vanished from their sight" (Luke 24:30-31). Later on, back in Jerusalem, those who had the Emmaus experience report that Jesus was recognized "in the breaking of the bread" (24:35). Then, "while they were talking about this" (24:36), Jesus is there and sets about trying to convince his friends that it is really he. First he shows them his hands and feet; then he asks them to look at him and touch him, to see that he has flesh and bones. This doesn't work; "they still didn't know what to believe and were bewildered." Finally, Jesus hits upon something that is bound to convince them. "*'Do you have anything here to eat?'* They offered him a piece of grilled fish, and he took it and ate it in front of them" (24:41-43). "Then he prepared their minds to understand the scriptures" (24:45).

Why would hunger be a sure indication that this must be Jesus? Why should we expect the Risen Lord to be hungry? Because at the last supper, Jesus had sworn not to eat again until the reign of God. In Luke 22:15-18, Jesus said (translating literally): "With desire I desired to eat this Seder with you before my suffering, for I'm telling you that not no more never will I eat it until it is fulfilled in the kingdom of God." Neither will he drink wine again (22:18). Jesus has promised to fast until kingdom come; so if the Risen Lord is really Jesus, he is going to be pretty hungry.

But Luke associates hunger not only with the possibility of recognizing the Risen Lord but also with numerous teachings about resurrection in general. The little girl whom Jesus raises in Luke 8:49-56 comes back from the dead hungry; Jesus "ordered them to give her something to eat." At a dinner with the Pharisees, in Luke 14:1-14, Jesus says, "When you throw a dinner party, invite the poor, the crippled, the lame, the blind. In that case you are to be congratulated, since they cannot repay you. You will be repaid *at the resurrection* of the just." In the parable of the Prodigal Son, Luke 15:11-32, it is famine and the resultant hunger that drive the son to resolve, *"I'll rise and go to my father."* The father gives orders for a feast, saying to the servants, *"This son of mine was dead, and has come back to life,"* and to the brother, "This brother of yours was dead, and has come back to life." Hunger and resurrection are themes woven through the parable of the Rich Man and Lazarus in Luke 16:19-31. The rich man feasts, while Lazarus is hungry and wretched. Both die, and their situations are reversed. The rich man asks that Lazarus be sent back from the dead to warn his brothers. (It is interesting that Lazarus also is the name of the man whom Jesus calls back from the dead in John 11.)

The implication seems to be that the possibility of understanding resurrection comes through hunger: either one's own hunger or the hunger of another if one is able to recognize and alleviate it. Small wonder that women became resurrection witnesses, since, then as now, women often went hungry and alleviating hunger was largely women's work. In Acts 7:55-56, it is the soup-line worker Stephen (see Acts 6:1-5) who, "full of the Holy Spirit, was staring up into the sky and saw God's glory, and Jesus

standing at the right hand of God." No one in the New Testament understands resurrection better, or speaks of it more eloquently, than this man
whose daily job was to distribute food to widows.

There are interesting contrasts to be noted here with the Twelve, who
say in Acts 6:2 that "it wouldn't be appropriate for us to neglect God's word
to wait on tables," and also with Paul. In Acts 9:3-9, Saul is stunned by a
light and a voice and asks, "Who are you, Lord?" but receives an answer
that leaves him blind. "And for three days he couldn't see, and didn't eat or
drink anything." After Ananias visited him, Saul "got up and was baptized, and had a meal and got his strength back," Acts 9:18-19. In 1
Corinthians 11, Paul says that failure to recognize the hungers of community members is failure to discern the body of Christ. An issue that dogged
Paul's ministry was whether a preacher could claim to be an apostle, that is,
to have seen the Lord, without sharing the sustenance of the community.

For Luke, who was a great admirer of Paul, recognition of the Risen
Lord is possible only within a community that knows both how to be hungry and how to feed the hungry. Stories about empty tombs simply have
no efficacy, except within such a community. Luke's point seems to har-
monize with Matthew's, although it is not identical. As we saw above,
Matthew asserts that recognition of the Risen Lord is possible only within
a community that knows and obeys the official version of Jesus' ethical
instructions. Claims to speak "in Jesus' name" have no efficacy, except
within such a community.

In summary, if we may presume that the communities of Luke and
Matthew had a praxis or know-how of recognizing the Risen Lord, then it
should come as no shock to find that these texts are designed for passing
on that practical wisdom. The pattern that they establish becomes normative for teachers who seek to introduce people to the possibility of resurrection. The texts make this self-defeating assertion: Words cannot deliver
understanding. Access to the Risen Lord is opened through teaching that
both forms a community sensitive to the needs of the poor and transpires
within such a community. This teaching is rooted not only in formal theological reflection on the very possibility of gaining access to the Risen
Lord but also in action on behalf of the poor undertaken because the
teachers themselves want to see Jesus.

The Eyes Brimming Full

Matthew's and Luke's Easter stories have corroborated the claim made for
Jailhouse John in chapter 3: access to Jesus is conditioned by practices

responding to human need. Knowledge of the Risen Lord cannot be theoretical, detached, and visual. The eyes do not connect with Jesus, apart from practices addressing hunger and injustice. The tradition of resurrection appearances was not originally intended to stand apart from a community that fed the hungry and observed the laws of justice.

To conclude this chapter about laying eyes on Jesus, we recall that the Easter narratives in Matthew and Luke are relatively late compositions. They focus on "events" of appearance and discovery that had taken narrative shape well before the inscription of the texts that we have been examining. When was resurrection first associated with *visible* proofs like apparitions and bodiless tombs? The question should be approached with full awareness of the ethnic, gender, and economic interfaces being negotiated in first-century Palestine.

The very notion of a Risen Jesus who *appears* and displays himself for viewing is an idea that is more significant to Christians of Greek culture than to Galilean villagers like the alleged eyewitnesses at the tomb, those Marys. Luke's "appearance" stories backfire ingeniously: the Emmaus tale is actually a *dis*appearance story, while the Jerusalem apparition is not credited until it eats. At Matthew's Last Judgment, the just are vindicated on account of *not* seeing that it was Jesus whom they cared for. This resilient strand asserting the *in*visibility of the Risen Lord is intriguing. It may be an indication that a submerged tradition of *hearing* resurrection proofs now lies beneath the Greek texts, with their cultural and class bias toward what can be seen.

There may be one other indication in the empty tomb stories we have that would help to reconstruct the terms in which claims about the fate of Jesus might possibly have been circulating before crossing the gender, culture, and class frontier between Jesus' aunts and Luke. It consists in one little detail: that the women at the tomb were observing the customs of mourning. They were weeping for Jesus. Their eyes were full of tears when the realization hit them that Jesus was not in the grave. For the poor, for widows, for a colonized nation, the eyes are the organs that register pain. The Marys were using their eyes in that graveyard, but not like Greeks. They "saw" Jesus through tears.

The connection between tears and conquering death is made explicit elsewhere in the gospel tradition. "Jesus cried" before raising Lazarus (John 11:35). Mourning also figures importantly in one of the texts cited by Crossan in his discussion of claims about Jesus circulating before (and alongside) the appearance and empty tomb stories recorded in the canonical Gospels. Crossan has assembled evidence in New Testament texts of an early passion-parousia scheme that interpreted the sufferings of Jesus as leading directly into his triumphant return—without thematizing any intervening stages of burial, resurrection, or enthronement. The Hebrew texts that would inspire such an interpretation of Jesus' fate include Zech. 12:10:

> I will pour out on the House of David and the inhabitants of Jerusalem a spirit of compassion and supplication, so that, when they look on him whom they have pierced, they shall mourn for him, as one mourns for an only child, and weep bitterly over him as one weeps over a first-born son.[11]

If such a text was particularly meaningful within the Jesus movements immediately after Calvary, we can guess why. The community was grief-stricken, the women were wailing. It was awful; and if you haven't lost someone you love to a violent death, then you can't even begin to understand what it was like. Sixty years afterward, the churches had four sanitized little stories about a trip to a garden and a lovely surprise. But it wasn't like that when it happened. Grief may also be a precondition for resurrection, and tears for permitting the eyes to see.

Thus the words of the tradition—the New Testament canon—turn out to be words intending to inspire and partner with certain kinds of action. As texts, they "refer" to the mutual support of word and deed in their own immediate past, at the same time that they intend themselves to achieve their own meaning through deeds that must accompany their hearing. It would be a misconception to regard the Gospel words as referring, after the fact, to some event separate and self-contained that happened independently of those words and that subsists apart from them somewhere in the human past. They are, rather, words about the possibility of truth that can open under certain conditions, not all of which are verbal.

Tears for victims and action on their behalf are not the outcomes of resurrection faith but the preconditions for it. Talk about resurrection is literally meaningless in the absence of such action. This raises the serious question of what it takes to speak correctly today about resurrection, that is, to mean what the tradition has meant by the term. If talk about resurrection is attempted in a classroom, or even in a pulpit, its power for truth depends on the congregation's explicit and deliberate efforts to care for the poor and share their grief.

---

11. See Crossan, *The Historical Jesus*, 376–78. Crossan finds traces of the passion-parousia tradition in the *Epistle of Barnabas* 7; Matt. 24:30; John 19:34-37; and Rev. 1:7, 13.

This is not to say that a community that shelters the needy and grieves for the disappeared will always speak correctly or intelligibly about the Risen Lord. Criteria of sense and intelligibility must be observed by all Christians who speak and wish to be understood in the late twentieth century. But by the same token, the praxis criteria identified by Luke and Matthew must also be observed by philosophical theologians who intend their speech to be heard within the Christian tradition. Theology, even at its most academic, is resurrection talk. The ministries of the word are necessary, but not sufficient, to the continuing possibility of recognizing the availability of the Risen Lord. Actions of justice not only transform human need into well-being; they also transform words about resurrection into understanding of the identity of Jesus.

5
Son of God's Slavewoman

WITH THIS chapter, the focus of the inductive case studies shifts from bodily realities to textual ones, from issues of access to issues of identification. The three studies presented so far all have had to do with "access" to Jesus through bodily practices, or disciplines. In chapter 2, a saying about entering God's kingdom was traced as it developed into prescriptions for approaches to Jesus. We saw how the option of a Christian practice of paideia ultimately was rejected and how, in the course of that rejection, the kingdom of God was displaced by Jesus' body as the magnet drawing all things to itself. In chapter 3, a teacher incarnating the heavenly *bat qôl* sent disciples on their way to the Lord. We saw how teaching practices were designed to accomplish that spatially imagined objective. In chapter 4, compassionate response to human bodily needs was established as canonical precondition for whatever it might be that the early churches meant by "seeing the Lord." We found that the stories of the resurrection narratively deconstruct narrative itself, for they tell how words alone lack efficacy to come true.

These studies were addressing "how" questions. That is, they investigated the emerging praxes that were offering access to the body of the Risen Lord. It is time now to work from the other direction: to switch over to a consideration of the identity of that Lord to whom access is provided. This engages the "who" question, which is not at all independent of the "how" questions that we have been examining. The two kinds of issues are more like two sides of a coin. The practices of approaching "Jesus" contribute to the definition of who this "Jesus" is whom one is approaching, just as the identity of the Lord is already in some ways presupposed and encoded within the practices through which the church grasps him. Thus we are trying a different approach to understanding resurrection as we turn our attention now away from the accessing and toward the accessed.

Ekklēsia Poiētikē

If canonical bodily practices make contact, the one whom they contact is known to be "Jesus" thanks to canonical textual practices, that is, thanks to ecclesial poiesis. The availability of Jesus' body is for the sake of copying. He is given over in order to become the Christ, and, having become the Christ, in order to anoint others with his christological identity. Jesus' body is written onto what it "originally" was not: the hungry little ones, the food that nourishes them, the church itself.

In this and the next two chapters, three more studies will be presented. Their common focus is the identification of Jesus, that is, the strategies for ascribing identity to him. The early churches' recognition of the Risen Lord was a work of poietic imagination that progressively redesigned the bodily reality of Jesus of Nazareth. "Jesus" was not manufactured out of whole cloth. No, there was a quilting, through which God saved the ruined body of the Crucified, piecing it into a completely new pattern providing for the shelter and reproduction of the Christian community. This poiesis still can be observed at work within the materials presenting themselves for our text-archaeological inspection.

Was Jesus God's messiah and son? What would have been wagered in the claim to such an identity? Jesus' legitimacy on both counts, as christ and as son, appears to have been contested vigorously from Calvary onward. Factions within the Jesus movements legitimated Jesus in different ways. The arena in which those struggles are staged permanently is provided by the Gospels, with their narrative enframing of Jesus' career. These finely wrought fictions afford us glimpses of the negotiation of the identity of Jesus during the lifetimes of those who had known him. We discover that to portray Jesus, to tell stories about Jesus, is at the same time to renegotiate one's own identity and fate. "Meeting the Lord" is at the same time confronting oneself—which is the only way in which it can be a genuine meeting of the Lord. The recognition always is mutual, or not at all. Our sources indicate that this has been the experience of the church ever since Calvary.

Thus in the Gospels, certifying Jesus' identity is always the hidden agendum, even when the topic at hand seems to be discipleship or servanthood or the worship of the one God. To define the disciple is to define the master. The poietic strokes that sketch the profile of the ideal Christian are also sketching the Christ.

To say that this sketching is fictional and poietic is to set it in the very highest esteem. Poiesis is a productive kind of knowing. Where *theōria* requires detachment, poiesis is engaged and engaging. If our ancestors in faith had wanted to give us "the facts," cold and complete information, they would have provided us with histories. Among them were writers at least as competent as Suetonius, Josephus, or Tacitus. Instead, they sought to provide for the completion of a reality that still remained incomplete for them and remains so now within our own history. The catechesis that they left is meant to replicate a Christic pattern within each Christian, and this can be done only through the coordination of theoretical information with praxis and poiesis. The poietic legacy of resurrection is a miraculous gift; and the better one understands its nature, the more grateful one becomes.

In the following studies, then, I am not looking for "the historical Jesus." I am interested instead in what might be termed "the Jesus of literary history."[1] But no effective method is available to us today by which to distinguish the "Jesus" from the "literary history." It is precisely the poietic events of the prolific literary history that condition the possibility of my knowing any "Jesus." To some degree at least, then, the poiesis is intrinsic to who Jesus is. In other words, the Risen Lord spreads himself in bread and wine and oil and water, and the bodies of the people who need them. It was always in him to do this: to extend and share and replicate himself in this way, to get around the limitations of time and space and culture. That is what he is like. He is God's copy. He is that of God which copies and that through which all creation comes to be. The Alexandrian synagogue called God *patēr kai poiētēs*, "father and maker." Our Greco-Jewish forebears in the earliest churches saw Jesus as the poiesis of that poietic Father.

Alexandrian traditions of interpretation are known to us from the works of Philo, who was born some two decades before Jesus and died after 40 C.E. Although scholars generally treat Philo as an individual author, he did not invent all the scriptural interpretations and philosophical arguments that he transmits. He is best regarded as the spokesman for the Alexandrian synagogue's traditions of exegesis, traditions that were several centuries old when he was born. It is plausible to suppose that opinions and approaches characteristic of Philo's texts were familiar to educated Greek-reading Jews throughout the Roman Empire, including those in Palestine.

---

1. "The Jesus of literary history" is Bruce Chilton's phrase. See Chilton, *Profiles of a Rabbi*, 161.

Thus an Alexandrian, Septuagint-reading Judaism was a viable form of religious life all around the Mediterranean Sea, in hellenized cities such as Rome, Caesarea, Sepphoris, Tiberias, and even Jerusalem.

As we have seen, in Palestine before the tragedy of 70 C.E. there were three language groups: Jewish, but with contrasting customs for their teaching and reading. Jesus traditions filtered through each of them—even the Hebrew, as this chapter argues—and all of them took a hand in shaping the poiesis of Jesus. Because the New Testament canon is entirely Greek, however, this fact is obscured and too often discounted. Yet to understand the canon, we have to understand the Christians and the Christianity that predated the canon. Those people wrote the Gospels. But first they produced and performed them.

As an example of how all three cultural groups worked on the poiesis of Jesus' identity, in this chapter we examine the story of the annunciation in some detail. There is a great deal of information in the texts that bear this story to us. Those texts tell about what happened to Mary, but they also will tell about what happened to themselves as texts during their transmissional career—if we know how to ask them the right questions. The story of *the story of* the annunciation can be a window into the imaginations and the theological struggles of the people who have handed faith down to us. Perhaps it can even be a window into the heart of Mary herself: not just the "literary-historical" Mary but the flesh-and-blood woman. But there is work to do first.

I believe that the right question to ask about the annunciation is this: Who were telling Mary stories, and when, and why? We can proceed on the premise that the tellers were members of Jesus movements. The telling, as an oral performance, was also a varying. It took place, on a significantly wide scale, after Calvary and on into the middle of the second century at least. The general reason for the telling was to explore and clarify something about the identity and origin of Jesus. Mary's fictional function was that of a mirror for Jesus.

One must keep in mind the trilingual and tricultural fabric of Palestinian Judaism while examining key concepts that were in play during the transmission of this story. Each cultural subgroup differed not only in custom and language but also in the contours of its social construction of certain realities such as gender and labor. This consideration is quite pertinent here, inasmuch as our story is about a young woman's assenting to be a mother and a slave. If Mary said yes, in what language did she say it? In what language did God propose?

The Semitic languages differ from Greek in much more than vocabulary. Nevertheless a comparative study of a few terms in the vocabulary of gender and work can greatly illuminate how they functioned to shape the different realities that people's bodies inhabited. The Hebrew of the Torah reflects the society whose laws, customs, and insights are embedded in the sacred text. As is well known, the forebears of that society experienced a nomadic period and a period of forced labor in Egypt before settling down to an agrarian lifestyle in Palestine and embracing urbanism. Throughout those changes, the social structure remained patriarchal.[2]

Patriarchy for the ancient Hebrews meant more than second-class political and economic status for women. In the early period, before the monarchy, it meant that one male was the owner of an extended family that included wives, concubines, sons and their wives, several categories of dependent relatives, slaves, resident aliens, assorted other workers, priests, livestock, with all their implements of life support and of war. This entailed a kinship and status system that was functional within that social ecology, but that is difficult for Western people today even to imagine.

The Hebrew word for work also meant worship. The experience of escaping bondage in Egypt was at once an economic and a religious watershed. The law code of Sinai delimited work and worship in one stroke. The regulation of work by the Sabbath was intrinsically tied to the worship, or "service," of the only God there is, the God who frees slaves. Ancient sabbatical legislation provided that a Hebrew male who was bought as a slave must go free in the seventh year.

The verbal form of "work" is *ʿābad*. In its various moods it can mean to work, to till, to cultivate, to be a slave, to serve or worship, to perform rites for. With different vowels, the same root gives us the noun *ʿebed*, which means a male slave, a servant, a trustee. This word can also be used as a polite term of self-abasement: "I am your servant, sir!" When combined with the name of a god, it becomes the technical term designating someone who adheres to the religion of that god. The Hebrew conception of religion entails a lifestyle pervading all one's activities, not just the liturgical ones. For cultic service at the altar, there was a specialized term, *šārēt*; and for the bodily gesture of ritual prostration, *šāḥah*. But the reality of being the slave of the Lord was not contained in a cultic space or sacred gesture. It pervaded all places and all bodily activities.

Judging from the ways in which the term actually was used, the reality of male slavery in the midst of Israel ranged from miserable dirty work, to responsible stewardship, to vassalage toward the local strongman, to covenant faithfulness toward God. A man could take pride in

2. For an account of women's participation in the early life of the people of Israel, when the Hebrew way of life emerged as an alternative to urbanism, see Carol Meyers, *Discovering Eve: Ancient Israelite Women in Context* (New York: Oxford University Press, 1988).

being the ʿebed yhwh, for it meant that he and God were in a relationship in which both sides would fulfill certain obligations. Compared to being a slave in Egypt, that was a pretty good deal. Even the most miserable ʿebed in the extended patriarchal household had certain rights protected by the law of Israel.

It is grammatically possible to form a feminine noun from the root ʿbd, to indicate a female slave. That form, however, occurs nowhere in the Hebrew Bible. The reality of slavery was so different for women that a completely different vocabulary evolved for talking about it. In fact, there were two terms for female slaves that were used interchangeably: ʾāmāh and šipḥāh. These words both mean a female slave, an unfree woman of the household. One or the other of them also is used in the protocol of polite self-abasement: "Your servant, sir!"

The defining feature of female slavery was being bodily available to serve the physical requirements of the males of the household, subject to certain taboos. Thus, depending upon her age and the ages of the needy males, the ʾāmāh would be used as wet nurse, concubine, breeder, cook, laundress, seamstress, or charwoman. She was sexually available from menarche to grave. The comparable term in the vocabulary of American slavery is "mammy."[3]

Because there was no other word, no other reality, a woman speaking respectfully to a man could not help asserting her somatic availability for him if she pronounced the formula of courtesy, "Your servant, sir!" It is small wonder that women did not usually speak to strangers![4] Small wonder, too, that the Hebrew Bible so seldom casts a woman in the relationship of servant to the Lord, given what female servitude implied. Women are termed God's slaves only in rare instances, but those instances are highly significant for understanding Mary's story: (1) Hannah calls

3. Jacqueline Grant has shown that the experience of domestic service by African-American women gives them a different sensibility and a different agenda than white American feminist theologians. I was greatly enlightened by her conversation with the Women's Theology Seminar at the 1991 meeting of the Catholic Theological Society of America. See Grant's dissertation, *White Women's Christ and Black Women's Jesus: Feminist Christology and Womanist Response* (Atlanta: Scholars Press, 1989). For an important discussion related to this issue, see Clarice J. Martin, "Womanist Interpretation of the New Testament: The Quest for Holistic and Inclusive Translation and Interpretation," *Journal of Feminist Studies in Religion* 6 (1990): 41–61. See also the responses by Jane Schaberg and others.

4. The story of Abigail, who within days of addressing David as his servant found herself enrolled in his harem, was instructive. Compare, however, the tale of Judith. Although the Hebrew original of the story now is lost, the Greek at Judith 11:5 indicates that Judith's suggestive switch to the term denoting a sexually available slave was a key element in her strategy for tricking Holofernes.

herself God's servant while praying in the sanctuary at Bethel, 1 Samuel 1–2. (2) The psalmist calls himself "your *'ebed*, son of your *'āmāh*" in Ps. 86:16 and Ps. 116:16; the former instance is a request for salvation, and the latter is thanks for having been set free.[5] (3) The prophet Joel envisions a day on which God's spirit will be poured out upon maidservants and menservants alike.

One more Hebrew term completes the conceptual background for Mary's story. The verb *'ānah* means to bend down, to stoop, to be wretched, to submit. The flexibility of the mood structure in Hebrew lets forms of the same root also mean to humiliate someone, to make someone wretched, to overpower, to violate, to rape. In the very ancient legislation of Exod. 21:10, however, there is another, curious use of the same term.[6] If someone buys a Hebrew as a concubine, it says, and then later takes another woman to wife, he cannot deny the first her right to marital intercourse with him, that is, to motherhood and children. In this text, *'ōnah* is the slave wife's right, protected by divine law. Hannah's appeal to the Lord for a son seems to be making its case on the basis of that law. The *'āmāh* of the Lord demands from her Lord what is her right: impregnation and motherhood.

Such an interpretation is supported by an additional consideration. Lexicons list a seemingly unrelated meaning for the root *'nh*: response, testimony, entreaty to a god, answering to judgment. In that sense, the word is used to describe the ritual taunts exchanged by warriors, or antiphonal response in a liturgical context, or even mutual indictment in a judicial context. But perhaps this is not really a separate meaning after all. The word encodes the tension of a back-and-forth provocation, a mutual arousal. It presumes two parties locked into a relationship that, although it may be unequal, still defines them both. In Israel's imagination, the poor by their very existence provoked God to action and demanded a response from other people. Human need incited God to act like God and Israelites to act like Israelites. Thus Hebrew prayer so often simply asked God to look upon, to notice, to remember the condition of the people. Given the constitutive relationship of the covenant, God could not "notice" without being driven

5. In Psalm 113, which begins the collection known as the Hallel, women are placed among two categories of servants whom God has helped: the poor who are raised up from dust and the barren who are given homes and children. In Ps. 123:2, "As the eyes of slaves look to the hand of their master, as the eyes of a maid look to the hand of her mistress, so our eyes look to the Lord our God."

6. Philologists may assert that these are simply two ranges of meaning, or conceal the sexual implications (like Francis Brown, S. R. Driver, and Charles A. Briggs, editors of *A Hebrew and English Lexicon of the Old Testament* [Oxford: Clarendon Press, 1955]). This obfuscation is unjustified and should be questioned.

to act, so to speak. In the same sense, then, this root ʿ*nh* encodes the construction of gender relations: womanhood incites manhood, and manhood incites womanhood. Perhaps humiliation for one party entered the picture only later.

The ambiguity of women's status within Israelite patriarchy is poignantly conveyed by the complex meanings of this word ʿ*ānah*. To be overpowered and humiliated was the essence of slavery, yet it was also woman's most basic right, guaranteed by a law so solemn that a woman, if denied that right, could bring suit against God himself (as Hannah did). Perhaps this is a "double" meaning only to our Western sensibilities. More likely, Hannah was not the only Israelite who appreciated the stunning irony of the way her language worked. In any event, as we shall see, Greek proved unequal to the challenge of combining both meanings in a single concept.

Boys and Girls

If the gender and labor system of ancient Israel seems alien to us, it must have seemed almost as strange to the Greco-Jews of classical antiquity. Alexandria's scholars no longer were herding sheep and keeping harems. Their sophisticated urban civilization also depended on slavery, but slavery for them was a vastly different institution than it had been for their desert-wandering forebears. In earlier chapters, we saw something of how those scholars accomplished a major philosophical reconstruction of the Jewish Scriptures as they translated them into Greek. Now we will see that translation had to be cultural as well as philosophical.

To bring the Scripture into Greek, the Septuagint scholars had to have a thorough and subtle understanding of the gender and labor systems of the language in which the texts originated as well as the language into which they were being transplanted. They also had to devise some conventions of equivalence between sets of terms—even though the conventions would be followed with some of the biblical books more closely than with others, and never mechanically. Perhaps the scholars drew up an official lexicon to coordinate their work; if so, it no longer survives. We can reconstruct what the conventions were, however, because we have good approximations of the Hebrew texts from which the scholars were working as well as the Greek texts they produced.

What slavery meant among the Greeks is encoded by their vocabulary. Greek is quite amply equipped with terminology for the management of all kinds of service and all kinds of workers. The basic term for male slave is *doulos,* and the term for female slave is *doulē,* both of which come from the same root. Among the Greeks, male slaves as well as females were sexually available to their masters.

The terms *doulos* and *doulē* always describe people whose service was not voluntary. Because slaves were unfree, the Greeks regarded them as subhuman. In fact, by the close of the classical period any labor at all was deemed to be beneath the dignity of the free Greek male. Yet the term *doulos* could still be applied to quite a classy personage—for example, the prince of a vassal state or a tutor exquisitely trained in literature and philosophy so that he could instruct the sons of his master. Slavery need not be permanent; although the Greeks had no equivalent to the sabbatical year of release, enterprising slaves could work, earn, save, and buy freedom for themselves and their families.

Another term that meant slave was *pais*. The same form can be either masculine or feminine, depending on its definite article. The basic meaning of *pais* is "child." The term can also mean son or daughter, although there are also special terms for these. Thus someone described as *pais* could be either one's own child or one's slave, or both. Some of the slave children born into a household were fathered by the master, although not necessarily acknowledged by him. The fully grown male slave was still a "boy," *pais*, because he did not enjoy full adult rights of self-determination, and in that he resembled children. Moreover, boys and girls were equally sexually available to the master, so one word could cover both until at least the time the boy attained manhood—although for the Greeks a male slave never attained full manhood.[7] Thus *pais* encodes a threefold ambiguity. Or rather, this one concept expresses three subordinations accomplished in one thought for the Greeks: adulthood over childhood, freedom over servitude, and sexual initiative over sexual vulnerability.

There is a diminutive form of *pais* that also can indicate servitude and is gender-specific. A boy can be called a *paidiskos*, meaning "lad." A girl is a *paidiskē*, "little girl." A *paidiskē* also could be a young female slave or courtesan, or a lady's maid.

Faced with this complex picture, some parts of which were morally repugnant to them, the Septuagint translators seem to have devised guidelines something like this. *Pais* and its diminutive forms would be used to translate *ʿebed*, *ʾāmāh*, and *šipḥāh* when the situation was one of private, household service. But *doulos* and *doulē* would translate the same

---

7. Peter Brown writes that it was considered virtuous of a man to confine his sexual activities to the members of his household: wife, concubine, and/or slaves. He cites the views of Lactantius and Musonius Rufus. See Peter Brown, *The Body and Society: Men, Women, and Sexual Renunciation in Early Christianity* (New York: Columbia University Press, 1988).

Hebrew words when used in a situation of public service or in recognition of some public status. For example, the many cases in the Hebrew text when men and even women make formal speeches to a king, a priest, or a potentate of some kind all would be translated with forms of *doulos* and *doulē.*

This decision produced something of an egalitarian tone in the Greek biblical text. Female protagonists as well as male ones now could refer to themselves in polite address as "your servant" without implying any particular degree of sexual availability. Jews who read only the Greek text could not discern as readily that slavery for women among their ancestors had been a different experience from slavery for men.

More important, the Septuagint translators increased the number of instances in which women are called servants of God. At Isa. 56:3-7, God is promising that foreigners and eunuchs who join themselves to the covenant really will remain part of the people of Israel. This text must have been extremely important to the many admirers of Judaism who sought various degrees of affiliation with the synagogue in a metropolis like Alexandria. The Hebrew text says that eunuchs who hold fast to the covenant will be given a name that will never be "cut off," while foreigners who join themselves to the Lord as servants (masculine plural of *'ebed*) will be accepted in God's house, which is to become a house of prayer for all nations. The Septuagint adjustments of this passage are quite tactful. The pun about having something cut off is itself excised; instead, the Septuagint has *ouk ekleipsei,* "will not be left out."

As for service, the Hebrew masculine plural term for servants of God is translated inclusively as *doulous kai doulas,* "male slaves and female slaves."[8] In the Greek Bible, then, Hannah's bold claim to status as a servant of the Lord now is ratified in two prophetic promises about God's plans for the future: Joel's glimpse of an outgushing of divine spirit upon women and Isaiah's vision of the Temple swarming with foreigners, eunuchs, and mammies.

The ingenuity of the Septuagint scholars was impressive but not unbounded. They found no Greek term that adequately captured the logic supporting Hannah's legal claim upon God: that the servant's condition indicted the master and that the process of becoming a mother was paradoxically both a humiliation and a right. In Hannah's story, therefore, they used the term *tapeinoō,* which means to lower, to abase, to discourage, and its cognate *tapeinōsis,* which means humility or a humbling. This casts Hannah in an entirely new light. She is "humiliated" simply because her husband's other wife is making fun of her for being childless. The Greek

8. In comparison, the targum retains the masculine plural.

retains no intimation that she has grounds to demand a pregnancy as her legal right from her Lord, because there is no longer a verbal link to the legislation of Exod. 21:10, concerning impregnation.

At Exod. 21:10, the Septuagint translators chose a form of the word *homileō*, which means to encounter, to converse with, to keep company with, to instruct. The related noun *homilia* means social intercourse or instruction.[9] Somewhat incongruously, then, the Greek reader of the ancient Mosaic legislation is given to imagine that a tent-dwelling patriarch has been enjoined to entertain his out-of-favor concubine with polite small talk there amid the goats and cookfires. That was not the sort of good breeding that Moses had in mind—or Hannah either.

With all their euphemisms and their theological innovations, the scholars of the Septuagint showed a degree of cross-cultural, interracial understanding without parallel in antiquity. The targums do not compare in that regard. Of course in their case the challenge was not as great, for the targumic interpreters had less cultural distance to cover between the Hebrew text and the Aramaic hearers.

Comparative vocabulary study between Hebrew and Aramaic is less revealing than with Greek, because the languages have so many cognates. Yet the Aramaic voice of the targums also contributed distinctive shades of meaning as well as outright additions to the sacred text. One of the most significant must be considered now before we proceed to an examination of Mary's story. The Aramaic religious imagination was interested in the activity of God among the people, but at the same time there was concern to preserve the sense of divine holy transcendence. The targums therefore tend to adjust the Hebrew anthropomorphisms that attribute bodily parts or spatial location to the deity.[10] A mediating term is introduced, and this helps the *meturgeman* to avoid mentioning God directly.

The targums typically speak of the *Memra* of God and the *Shekhinah* of God. *Memra* means "word" and refers to God's commands as well as to Israel's response. The divine *Memra* suffuses the whole world.[11] *Shekhinah*

---

9. This is also the vocabulary given to Holofernes when he invites Judith to dinner: "It will be a disgrace if we let such a woman go without enjoying her company (*ouk homilēsantes autē*), for if we do not embrace her (*mē epispasōmetha*) she will laugh at us" (Judith 12:12).

10. See Chilton, *A Galilean Rabbi and His Bible*, 35–56; idem, *The Isaiah Targum*, Aramaic Bible, vol. 11, lv–lvii; and Daniel J. Harrington and Anthony J. Saldarini, trans., *Targum Jonathan of the Former Prophets*, Aramaic Bible, vol. 10 (Wilmington, Del.: Michael Glazier, 1987), 8–10.

11. There was a subtle theology behind the choice of such terminology, and it differed from targum to targum. For an analysis of the range of meaning of *Memra*, see Bruce D. Chilton, "Recent and Prospective Discussion of Memra," in *From Ancient Israel to Modern Judaism: Intellect in Quest of Understanding*, ed. Jacob Neusner et al., vol. 2, Brown Judaic Studies 173 (Atlanta: Scholars Press, 1989), 119–37.

means "dwelling" or "presence," especially as cultically located. The divine *Shekhinah* may be in the Temple or it may be in heaven awaiting restoration. Both *Memra* and *Shekhinah* are conceived of as the means by which God exercises power in the world.

The targums also show deference to the divine name by switching from active to passive voice constructions, and by other periphrastic devices. Daniel Harrington and Anthony Saldarini point out the distinctive use of the phrase "before the Lord" in the Aramaic translation.

> "From the Lord" becomes "from before the Lord" in numerous instances, and "to the Lord" becomes "before the Lord." . . . "Before" (*qdm*) has the connotation of "in the presence of" God or "from the presence of" God. It is used in varied constructions; for example, "the Lord heard the voice of a man" becomes "the prayer of a man was accepted before the Lord."[12]

Because the targums were recited in synagogue worship, they project an attitude of piety and they avoid anything that might breach decorum when recited aloud. Otherwise, the targums' pastoral concerns are different from those of the Septuagint translators. The *meturgeman* simply is not faced with the Alexandrian challenges: the gentile constituency who wanted a place within the covenant and the socially prominent women who wanted to stand within the assembly of the Jewish people. His challenge instead is to update the old stories in a way that makes "the kingdom of God" a plausible naming of the frustrating political and economic realities experienced in Palestinian village life.

The Story about Mary

In what language, then, did Mary say yes to God? Who was telling the Mary story, and when, and why? The Mary story comes down to us in two versions, which are the textual survivors of very many retellings during the first centuries C.E. The more familiar version is the one in Luke's Gospel, of which we will consider here two segments: Mary's Canticle, Luke 1:46-55, and the Dialogue with the Angel, Luke 1:26-38. The less familiar text is that of the *Infancy Gospel of James* 11:1-3. Both of the texts as we receive them are Greek. Luke dates from the late first century and the

---

12. See the introduction to Harrington and Saldarini, *Targum Jonathan of the Former Prophets*, 9.

Infancy Gospel of James is placed at the mid-second century, or possibly a few decades later. Both of these texts preserve much earlier traditions, which are what I propose to dig out of them.

The three language communities introduced above give us three possible answers to our question, Who was talking about Mary? In fact, I will show that Mary stories were told in all three languages. But I must begin the excavations at the surface of these texts, which is Greek. The Canticle of Mary will be examined first, because it displays a relatively simple compositional history and because the explanation of that history can in turn help us to understand the more complicated compositional careers of the two versions of the angelic dialogue.

The similarities between Mary's story and Hannah's story have long been recognized. Mary's Canticle expresses many of the same sentiments as Hannah's Canticle, 1 Sam. 2:1-10. Luke's Mary gets her vocabulary from Hannah, both from the Canticle and from Hannah's prayer at Shiloh, 1 Sam. 1:11. To be more specific, Luke lifts Mary's words from the Hannah *of the Septuagint*, not the Hebrew Hannah. One example can suffice to illustrate this.

The "humility" that the Lukan text imputes to Mary is the Septuagint version, which is simple lowliness without any resonance of problematic female fecundity as in the Hebrew. The Septuagint's Hannah has that same wimpy kind of humility; the Hebrew Hannah does not. This can be shown in the following way. The Hebrew Hannah uses different words for "lowliness" at 1 Sam. 1:11 and at 2:7. The first place has a form of *'ānah*, which as we saw above has that astonishing range of meanings—humbling, indicting, inciting, impregnating—upon which the whole story turns. The second place has another word altogether. When Hebrew Hannah sings that God "humbles and exalts," we must take *both* verbs, in their paradoxical opposition, as equivalent to the term with which Hannah has described herself in the earlier prayer: her *'ānah* or impregnation is at once both a pushing down and a lifting up. But Greek Hannah is able to say no such thing. The Septuagint uses *tapeinōsis* for Hannah's situation at 1 Sam. 1:11, then turns around and uses the same word for *one side of* the pair at 2:7, *tapeinoi*. This makes Hannah's status as slave-of-the-Lord, with all that that entails, into *the opposite of* exaltation: something that exaltation erases, instead of a permanent feature of it.

Luke's Mary takes over the phrasing of Greek Hannah's prayer, making two slight adjustments: in the person and tense of the verb, to show that something has been accomplished, and in the possessive adjective, from "your" to "his." Greek Hannah's politely fawning request, "if looking down you would look down upon the humility of your slave," becomes

Greek Mary's boast, "that he has looked down upon the humility of his slave." The vocabulary is identical. The only problem is, what has been lost in translation is the rationale for *why* Mary's situation should ever have been compared with Hannah's in the first place, as we shall see.

If we can rule out the Hebrew text of Hannah's story as a source for Mary's Canticle, can we also rule out the targum? No decisive answer can be given, because we no longer have access to the targum that was being recited at the time when Luke's Gospel was written down. The text of the targum that descends to us indicates that it was developed to counteract despair following Rome's destruction of the Temple in 70 C.E. Being a targum, it cannot have been made up in an afternoon; and it must have been recited for a while before being written down. Therefore this written version of 1 Samuel 1–2 in Aramaic that comes down to us is either contemporary with or later than the written form of Mary's Canticle.

Hannah's Canticle in the targum that survives has become a flight of "prophecy" giving advance notice of the history of Israel from the time of her boy Samuel down through the conquests of Greece and Rome. Verse 7 concludes with a creative flourish:

> So Jerusalem, which was like a barren woman, is to be filled with her exiled people. And Rome, which was filled with great numbers of people—her armies will cease to be; she will be desolate and destroyed.

Thus the extant targum has drafted Hannah as a political propagandist to address the disaster of its day. We do not know what other messages the targumic Hannah might have delivered before that national crisis, in other circumstances. She certainly seems flexible.[13]

Yet the malleability of the targumic traditions of Hannah is owing to the fact that they were composed and transmitted by oral performance. In comparison, the Lukan text of the Canticle has done little more than write Mary's name over words that belonged to the Hannah of the Septuagint. This relatively conservative rewriting is an indication that Greek Mary's Canticle, unlike Aramaic Hannah's Canticle-turned-prophecy, was

---

13. Compare, for example, the version of Hannah's canticle in the document known to us from medieval Latin manuscripts as Pseudo-Philo's *Biblical Antiquities*, but likely composed in Hebrew about the time of Jesus. Hannah sings: "Come to my voice, all you nations, and pay attention to my speech, all you kingdoms (52:3)." Her outlook on the international situation seems optimistic. See J. D. Harrington, "Pseudo-Philo: A New Translation and Introduction," in *The Old Testament Pseudepigrapha*, vol. 2, ed. James H. Charlesworth (Garden City, N.Y.: Doubleday, 1985), 297–377.

composed and transmitted graphically, that is, with the support of the technology of reading and writing.

In addition, something very interesting emerges when we consider that Mary's Canticle and Hannah's targumic prophecy were being produced poietically about the same time. There seems to have been a tug-of-war going on over Hannah. She could not serve two ideologies, at least not at the same time in the same language. If the Aramaic community needed her to prophesy that God would expel the Romans from Jerusalem, she could not also be a new Hannah named Mary for whom salvation already had been accomplished in a pregnancy. Aramaic Hannah was too busy coping with national disaster to sing her Canticle for Mary.

Was there, then, any Aramaic Mary? She would have to be a Mary without a Canticle, a Mary not designed as the new Hannah. We do find such a Mary in the *Infancy Gospel of James*. Here is the version of Mary's dialogue with the angel from that text, *Infancy Gospel of James* 11:1-3. The Greek word *angelos* means messenger.

> (1) And she [that is, Mary] took the waterjar and went out to fill it up with water. And all of a sudden a voice is saying, "Hello there, you lucky girl! The Lord is on your side. You are well spoken of among women." And Mary was looking around, right and left; where would this voice be coming from? And getting scared, she was going into her house, and having put down the waterjar, she took out the purple [that is, according to 10:1-2, some fiber that she had been commissioned to spin for the veil of the Temple] and she sat upon her chair and carded it.

> (2) And all of a sudden a messenger stood before her saying, "Don't be afraid, Mary, for you have gained a favor before the Master of all things. You will conceive from his word." But Mary, when she had heard, made up her mind, saying, "Me! I'm going to conceive from the Lord, the Living God, as every woman bears!"

> (3) And the messenger stood saying to her, "Not that way, Mary. For God's power will overshadow you, and therefore the holy thing being born will be called son of the Most High. And you will call his name Jesus, for he will save what is his from its sin." And Mary said, "Look at me, the Lord's slavewoman down before him! Let it happen for me the way you said it."[14]

---

14. This is my translation, from the critical edition based on Papyrus Bodmer 5, in Emile de Strycker, *La forme la plus ancienne du Protévangile de Jacques* (Brussels: Société des Bollandistes, 1961), 112–16. The Greek is streamlined and abbreviated. Even in this short excerpt, however, the reader can tell that the details about the actions of the characters sound very much like stage directions. For alternate translations, see Robert J. Miller, ed.,

This version, also called the *Protevangelium of James,* is Greek and comparatively late. The document from which it is taken synthesizes the information in the infancy narratives of Matthew and Luke and adds details about the amazing girlhood of Mary. (In fact, for this text it is Mary's *mother* who gets to play the new Hannah, giving rise to Christian traditions about "Saint Anne." Mary herself plays the new Samuel, a youthful hearer of mysterious voices.) The *Infancy Gospel of James* is shot through with juicy dialogue and raw emotion. It sounds like a soap opera, and one can easily read it as a dramatic script. I believe that the text as we have it may have been designed for presentation as a liturgical drama. In later times, passages of the *Protevangelium* were widely used as liturgical readings in the East, and its portrayal of Mary profoundly influenced Christian art and spirituality.[15] But scholars have discounted the value of this text as a historical source because of its obvious dependence on Matthew and Luke.

Yet that dependence is only partial. There are elements here that cannot have come from Matthew or Luke at all. The *Protevangelium's* version of the Angelic Dialogue, which concerns us here, is not a simple rewrite and embellishment of Luke's. There is alien material. This material seems quite old, and it is definitely Semitic. It predates the Greek text in which we find it, and perhaps it even predates our version of Luke. At the very least, this material suggests a telling of the Mary story by Aramaic speakers at some time before the *Protevangelium* was composed.

Two aspects of the *Infancy Gospel of James's* Angelic Dialogue text can be explained only by the story's having lived for a while among either the Aramaic or the Hebrew language community, or both.

1. Before the message comes to Mary as a messenger or "angel," it comes as a *bat qôl.* In chapter 3 we saw that contemporary rabbinic stories preserved in the Mishnah are familiar with this kind of disembodied divine communication. In an age that no longer had prophets, the *bat qôl* seems to have taken over what had been prophecy's narrative function in stories that called for the introduction of a revelation or a special insight. However, Mary's *bat qôl* is rather more incisive than the rabbinic ones,

---

The Complete Gospels (Sonoma, Calif.: Polebridge Press, 1992), or Ron Cameron, ed., *The Other Gospels: Non-Canonical Gospel Texts* (Philadelphia: Westminster Press, 1982), both with introductions to the text.

15. The best lines in the play belong to Jesus' grandmother, when at a dinner party, after nursing the infant Mary, she crows, "Anna gives suck! Hearken you twelve tribes of Israel, Anna gives suck!" (*Infancy Gospel of James* 6:13). It must have brought the house down. Peter Brown suggests that the Protevangelium depiction of Mary's sheltered childhood within an enclosed sacred space became the model of Christian life for women from the fourth century onward. See Brown, *The Body and Society,* 273.

which tended to speak in riddles and to no one in particular. The *bat qôl* in the Mary story perhaps bears the marks of some dramatic license. Nevertheless it does resemble the more conventional *bat qôl* from the stories about Jesus' baptism in one important respect: it gives definition to the hearer's character, disclosing something about the hearer's own identity. Both voicings become more intelligible when considered in the context of the popular piety in first-century Palestine. The curious redundancy of having both a *bat qôl* and a messenger in the Mary story may be an artifact of the fusing of two traditions, or it may be an adaptation to help the story cross the cultural front between village and metropolis.

2. The references to the deity in *Infancy Gospel of James* 11:1-3 are characteristic of the pious periphrastic constructions of Hebrew, but more especially of Aramaic. Although some of these constructions also persist in the Lukan text, they are not typically Greek. Several of the divine epithets fit as easily into a Hebrew milieu as into Aramaic: the Master of all things, the Lord, the Living God, the Most High. But several are especially characteristic of the targumic periphrastic reconstrual of contact with the divine: the *Memra*, action by "God's power" instead of directly by God, Mary's favor "before" the divine Master, Mary's slavery "before" the Lord.[16]

These considerations strongly indicate, without conclusively proving, that a version of the Angelic Dialogue was repeated, and of course therefore shaped, within Aramaic-speaking communities in which the conventions of meturgemanic recitation were operative. However, the story cannot have *originated* within an Aramaic community, as we shall presently see.

Thus far, one possible career of the *Infancy Gospel of James's* story of the Angelic Dialogue has been ruled out. We *cannot* have the sequence LXX → Luke → *Infancy Gospel of James*, that is, a Lukan text concocted directly from Septuagint materials and subsequently undergoing targumic rewording before being reduced to Greek text again in the *Infancy Gospel of James*. That scenario is undermined by the presence of translated Semitic expressions already in Luke's text and especially by the presence in the *Infancy Gospel of*

---

16. A third feature of the text that suggests an Aramaic background is its naming of Jesus. "Salvation" and the name *Yēšûaʿ* were thought in the first century to have come from the same Hebrew root *yšʿ*, and the connection would have been plain in Aramaic as well. However, the Greek word for salvation, *soterios*, is not similarly related to the Greek for Jesus' name, *Iēsous*. The detail about the derivation of Jesus' name therefore would not have been invented by a Greek-speaking community; more likely, such a detail was carried in an earlier story but was dropped by the Greeks, whose traditions Luke's text represents. But see Matt. 1:21. Jesus pronounced his own name "Yesh-oo." For discussion of the derivation of the name, see Joseph A. Fitzmyer, *The Gospel According to Luke (I—IX): Introduction, Translation, and Notes,* Anchor Bible (Garden City, N.Y.: Doubleday & Co., 1981), 347; and Meier, *A Marginal Jew,* 1:205–8 and 231–33.

James of the *bat qôl* and the etymology of Jesus' name, both of which would require more than a *meturgeman's* skill to introduce them into the Lukan text. (Besides, the *meturgeman* translated Hebrew, not Greek.)

The annunciation story was not told first in Greek. Whatever Mary called herself, it was not *hē doulē kyriou*. Whoever styled Mary as the new Hannah cannot have done so on the basis of the Septuagint's Hannah alone. Greek Hannah has nothing to recommend her as a prototype of the young girl in Galilee. Greek Hannah's "humiliation" is merely her childlessness within her husband's house. Mary's case was not at all parallel: either she was childless in her father's house, which was honor, not humiliation, or she was pregnant in her father's house, which makes her shame doubly unlike Hannah's.[17] Whoever matched Mary's case to Hannah's had to have known about the manifold meanings of *ʿānah* in Hebrew: to be brought low, to be impregnated, to incite, all involving what an *ʾāmāh* had a legal right to expect from the one whom she served. The Lukan Canticle of Mary may indeed have been composed directly from the Septuagint— but only in the wake of a *prior* assimilation of Mary to Hannah, which cannot have been made on the basis of the Septuagint.

Like the Septuagint, the targums too lose sight of the thick connotation of *ʿānah*. They use different words at 1 Sam. 1:11 (Hannah's prayer at Bethel) and Exod. 21:10 (legislation about slave wives). In the targums it is no longer possible to find the logical link on the basis of which Mary's situation and Hannah's situation might plausibly be compared. Therefore the foregoing objection against a Greek origination also counts against an Aramaic origination. Or if you will, the *bat qôl* did not talk to the daughter of Abraham in Aramaic either.

One further consideration points—conclusively, I believe—toward a Hebrew origination. Besides the vocabulary of *ʿānah* and *ʾāmāh,* something more was required for associating Mary with Hannah. What is going on with this juxtaposition is not a mere literary allusion. It is a legal case, argued in detail. To connect Mary and Hannah with the hinge of "humiliation," and to pull all the corroborating parallels into line, there had to be someone with a legal mind and the know-how to extract and collate details from relevant texts. Moreover, a legal case always is made on the basis of some problem, as a plausible account of "the facts," for the purpose of establishing the legitimacy of a claim. No one goes to that much trouble just for the fun of it; something important was at stake. Interpreting

---

17. For a statement of this either/or situation, see Sir. 42:9-10. In that text, dated to about 180 B.C.E., the great patriarchal phobia is that a daughter will either conceive in her father's house or remain barren in her husband's house.

Mary's predicament according to the precedent of Hannah served some interest. As we shall see, that interest was the legitimation of Jesus. The scholarly and legal competences required to link Mary's case and Hannah's case were available in first-century Palestine: in the scholarly Hebrew-speaking community, and nowhere else.

The Legal Brief

We no longer have the brief presenting the Hebrew legal case for Jesus' legitimacy and divine sonship. We have only narrative texts, which were written down much later. But as I have indicated, the texts that we do have cannot have appeared through a process of Greek literary composition or through targumic expansion. First the connection between Mary and Hannah had to be plausibly established, through legal argument. I propose to reconstruct some elements of that argument, although the reader will of course recognize the highly hypothetical character of this experiment.

This case was put together after Calvary. The occasion for it was the need to legitimate someone who had become increasingly interesting to at least a segment of the tannaitic community. This individual was the subject of haggadoth and halakhoth that were raising eyebrows in Sepphoris and Jerusalem. Although some called him Teacher, he had neglected to establish teaching credentials, and according to reports his teachings were disrespectful of traditions, even flippant in a Cynic sort of way. The rabbis used to regard impudence in a son as the sure indication that he was the offspring of adultery or of a menstruating woman, or both.[18]

The problem of the pregnancy that was Jesus had been solved once before. As Jane Schaberg reconstructs the events, the problem was not unusual in the history of the world, although its solution in this instance had been most extraordinary. The girl Mary was the victim of violence; nevertheless a way was found by God through Joseph to settle her respectably into a proper Jewish home.[19]

18. See the astonishing story in *Kallah* 51a, cited in Jane Schaberg, *The Illegitimacy of Jesus: A Feminist Theological Interpretation of the Infancy Narratives* (San Francisco: Harper & Row, 1987), 171–72, and her interpretive discussion.

19. See the careful scholarly analysis of the evidence in Schaberg, *The Illegitimacy of Jesus.* Schaberg maintains that in some way, God secured Mary's courageously trusting consent to Jesus' conception beforehand, just as God would obtain Jesus' consent to his agony and death at Gethsemane. For a cross-cultural look at the definition of illegitimacy, see Jenny Teichman, *Illegitimacy: An Examination of Bastardy* (Ithaca, N.Y.: Cornell University Press, 1982). Because different castes in Israel had different definitions of permissible marriage partners, there were various degrees of illegitimate birth.

Schaberg meticulously combs through the infancy narratives of Matthew and Luke for indications that a tradition about a conception through violence was being transmitted, particularly by women, before these texts were composed. Schaberg suggests that Matthew and Luke knew this tradition and, although they camouflage it each in his own way, they fully intend to pass it on. Luke's annunciation narrative in her view anticipates the resurrection and reprises its theology; both before Jesus' birth and after his death, God intervenes to turn a disaster into fulfillment of a divine plan. (Schaberg builds her argument on allusions in the Gospels to the legislation of Deut. 22:23-27, the law concerning the rape of a betrothed virgin.) One critic of Schaberg says that the thesis of Jesus' illegitimacy "causes shock in the pious and glee in the impious," but he has inverted its import.[20] Rather, the pious should rejoice that God can bring a messiah out of a rape, just as they rejoice that God brings the Risen Lord out of a crucifixion. The impious who laugh at the passion and death of Jesus are the ones who snicker at Mary's suffering.

I would add to Shaberg's account the following historical details. The city of Sepphoris, which is an hour's walk from Nazareth and which dominated the affairs of the surrounding villages during the first century, was destroyed and burned by the legion of Varus in the year 4 B.C.E. The burn layer of that event was found in recent excavations of the ruin and can be seen there today.[21] When imperial legions burned cities, they murdered citizens, plundered property, and raped whomever they could catch inside the walls or in the countryside around. Mary's tragedy can be placed as part of a general calamity that befell her home in the year when Jesus was conceived.

Soon after its sacking, Sepphoris was rebuilt on a grander scale than ever by Herod Antipas during Jesus' youth. Its cultural and economic life

20. Meier, *A Marginal Jew,* 222. Schaberg makes her case in chapters on "Matthew's Account of Jesus' Origin" and "Luke's Account." Another chapter treats the corroborating texts in the post-gospel traditions. Meier quarrels with the corroborating texts but declines to attend to the exegetical arguments from Matthew and Luke, where the principal thesis is supported. Instead of considering the data and presenting a better interpretation, Meier ridicules Schaberg's effort: "She tries to bolster her strange position with a tour de force of exegetical expertise. . . . A great deal of learning is wasted on a quixotic project" (p. 246 n. 78). The tenor of this *ad hominem* criticism may indicate that Meier finds the question of Jesus' status rather too difficult to examine in so logical a manner as Schaberg's.

21. Sepphoris, or Zippori, was continuously occupied from antiquity until 1948, when its leadership made their second great political mistake in opposing the Israeli army. Now the Arab town has been leveled and the hillsides reforested, which is why the site is available for excavation by archaeologists.

was reestablished, to the extent that the Jews of Sepphoris would be able to take in and resettle some of the priestly refugees from the destruction of the Jerusalem Temple in 70 C.E. At that time, there were still old folks in the neighborhood who recalled the atrocities that attended the destruction of Sepphoris and the tragic price paid by women and children for the political mistakes of its former administration. They remembered Mary, and they remembered where Jesus came from.

Who, then, was Mary? Must she be imagined as an ignorant villager, or can she have come from one of the learned families of Sepphoris? Was Jesus' maternal grandfather a lawyer or a teacher or perhaps a correspondent of Philo—and did the boy learn his Hebrew letters at his grandfather's feet? Although it was a multicultural city, Sepphoris is mentioned often in the rabbinic literature as a city of synagogues, a center of learning, whose cultic purity was above reproach. In Sepphoris was the archive for marriage contracts that supported the genealogical research required for the arrangement of important marriages.[22] Sepphoris had two aqueducts, giant waterwheels lifting water to hilltop mansions, wide colonnaded avenues, two extensive markets, and a system of courts. Therefore it had lawyers.

Mary's pregnancy became a problem for the second time after Calvary, as questions were raised concerning Jesus' legal status. The case about Mary was made for the purpose of identifying and certifying Jesus. Mary was an old woman when it was filed, if indeed she was still on this earth at all. I suggest that the brief was compiled sometime before 70 C.E., because soon after the destruction of the Temple the figure of Hannah would be co-opted for another purpose in the Aramaic-speaking community, as we have seen.

Why was the Hannah story chosen as the legal precedent for legitimating Jesus? How effective a case can be made on that precedent? The concept of *'ānah* grounds Hannah's petition at Bethel upon the law about maternal rights in Exod. 21:10. We have seen that this term, describing the humiliation-cum-exaltation of the mother-to-be, also connotes a legal process of summons and reply. Hannah knows Torah, and Hannah's prayer fulfills the conditions of a proper legal petition. Thus it can be cited as a precedent for Mary's case. Here is an outline of the argument that a Hannah-Mary comparison makes possible.

---

22. In light of that, the Lukan and Matthean ancestor lists are a little less implausible. See Stuart S. Miller, *Studies in the History and Traditions of Sepphoris* (Leiden: E. J. Brill, 1984).

WHEREAS in view of Exod. 21:10 a slavewoman has a legal right to offspring from her master; and

WHEREAS it is permitted to call a woman the slave of God, according to precedents set (1) in Torah, by implication, because of Hannah's successful citation of Exod. 21:10 in her petition at Bethel, (2) in the Prophets, by Hannah at 1 Sam. 1:11 as well as by Joel's vision at Joel 3:2, and (3) in the Holy Writings, by Ps. 116:16 and 86:16; and

WHEREAS the son born out of the granting of a slavewoman's petition to her divine master may, like Samuel, function as a prophet and judge, so that God can speak and govern Israel through such a man; and

WHEREAS Mary was God's slave; and

WHEREAS Mary in prayerful petition invoked her rights as God's slavewoman under Exod. 21:10 as interpreted in 1 Sam. 1:11; and

WHEREAS God is faithful to his covenant with his slaves;

> THEREFORE Mary's son Jesus came into her womb according to the law of Exod. 21:10; and

> THEREFORE no legal impediment hinders Jesus from functioning in Israel as a prophet, priest, or judge; and there is no offense to Torah in claiming that God speaks and delivers judgment through Jesus.

WHEREAS Samuel was born to Hannah through her invoking of her slave rights under Exod. 21:10; and

WHEREAS Samuel has status as God's slave son because he is the son of God's slavewoman, according to Psalms 86 and 116; and

WHEREAS Samuel's status as God's slave son makes his biological begetting by Elkanah legally irrelevant; and

WHEREAS a woman in Israel is entitled to invoke Exod. 21:10 in declaring herself to be God's slave; and

WHEREAS Mary, a woman of Israel, did declare herself to be God's slave, and did invoke Exod. 21:10 in prayer to God; and

WHEREAS Jesus was born to God's slavewoman Mary after that prayer;

> THEREFORE Jesus was the slave son of God; and

> THEREFORE Jesus' status as God's slave son makes the circumstances of his biological begetting legally irrelevant.

WHEREAS God's slave receives certain promises in Isaiah 42–55; and

WHEREAS God's slave has a right to petition for divine salvation, according to the precedents of Psalms 86 and 116; and

WHEREAS Jesus was God's slave son;

> THEREFORE Jesus was legally entitled to call upon God to fulfill the divine promises concerning God's slave in the Psalms and in Isaiah.

WHEREAS it was at the northern shrine of Bethel, not Zion, that Hannah brought her petition before God; and

WHEREAS the son granted to her through that petition, Samuel, became the one to anoint David; and

WHEREAS without Samuel, there would have been no David, and no City of David;

> THEREFORE Samuel's authority is greater than David's; and

> THEREFORE Jerusalem is not the final authority in interpreting the Davidic tradition; and

> THEREFORE a northern court has the competence to review judgments rendered in Jerusalem.

WHEREAS in Hannah's case the original judgment of the religious authority, which took Hannah for a daughter of perdition (1 Sam. 1:16), was reversed, and Hannah was acknowledged to be pious and obedient; and

WHEREAS the outpouring of God's Spirit upon women is foreseen in Joel 2:29; and

WHEREAS Mary's family put forth the claim that Mary was overpowered by God's Spirit; and

WHEREAS there is no evidence that Mary or Mary's son acted in a way inconsistent with the presence of God's Spirit;

> THEREFORE it would contradict the Prophet to hold that a woman categorically cannot be overpowered by God's Spirit; and

> THEREFORE the presumption must be in favor of the woman's claim, based on Joel 3:2, unless conclusive evidence to the contrary is presented; and

> THEREFORE in the absence of such evidence, insufficient legal grounds exist for a finding against Mary's claim about the conception of Jesus; and

> THEREFORE the finding against Jesus by the Jerusalem Sanhedrin should be overturned.

Oral arguments supporting this brief could have cited further resemblances between Jesus and Samuel. For example, Hannah dedicated her son to God as a "nazirite," one whose head would not be shaved (Numbers 6). Jesus too was dedicated to God's service and was known as a Nazarene, or man from Nazareth. Like Samuel, Jesus attuned his ears to the voice of God and prayed as Samuel did: "Speak, for your slave is listening" (1 Sam. 3:10). On the other hand, a variation on some of the legal points is suggested by the version of the Mary story that comes to us in the *Infancy Gospel of James*. There the parallel is drawn between Hannah and Mary's *mother*, so that it is Mary herself who is cast as the new Samuel. On that line of reasoning, it is

Mary who gains entitlement to hear voices in the night and to identify and anoint Davidic figures, as Samuel did.

This reconstruction of an ancient legal case has only the indirect textual and archaeological support that I have cited in presenting it. My hypothesis is that, even if the case itself was never formally presented and heard, nevertheless this kind of legal analysis must underlie the narratives of the annunciation that come down to us.

It seems clear that some highly trained and legally astute Hebrew scholars involved themselves in the debates about Jesus at a very early date. It is not implausible to place them as members of Jesus' own family, his maternal cousins.[23] Perhaps the cousins were supported by the now-grown sons of Jesus' boyhood friends, who may also have been well connected in the scholarly community of Sepphoris. We do know that a few decades later, the same rabbinic circle in Sepphoris would be vigorously debating with, and about, certain individuals whom the Mishnah calls the *minim*, that is, "ex's" or heretics.[24] The *minim* were adepts at Hebrew letters, and in some sense they were insiders to the life of the rabbinic community—at least in their own estimation. But the majority of the community, or at least those members of it whose stories come down to us in the mishnaic texts, saw things very differently. History shows that rabbinic Judaism and the Jesus movements parted ways. We can only surmise that Jesus' cousins lost the case.

On the other hand, their legal struggle made a major contribution toward theorizing the identity of Jesus. In the next chapter, we will examine another struggle. That one took place between Grecophones and teachers like the *Tannaim* of Sepphoris who were at least bilingual in Greek and Hebrew.

23. Burton Mack surmises that one of the identifiable factions among the various Jesus movements in the first century, and later, was "the family of Jesus," a group led by James the brother of Jesus, one of the pillars of the community invoking Jesus' name in Jerusalem. Because James is associated with the *Protevangelium*, that document apparently was supposed to be the family's version of Mary's story. Mack suggests that "the people in the Q tradition may actually have had a little tussle with Jesus' family and friends over rights to claim his authority." See Mack, *Myth of Innocence*, 90.

24. The Talmud (Šabbat 116a) indicates that the rabbis were familiar enough with the Gospel as a text to make clever though disparaging plays on the Greek word *evangelion* by calling it, in Hebrew, *ʿaven gilyon*, "the falsehood of paper," and *ʿavon gilyon*, "the sin of paper." The latter pun is attributed to Rabbi Johanon, who was a younger contemporary of Jesus; however Frederic Manns dates these inside jokes to the beginning of the second century. See Frederic Manns, "An Important Jewish-Christian Center: Sepphoris," in *Essais sur le judéo-christianisme*, Studium Biblicum Franciscanum, Analecta 12 (Jerusalem: Franciscan Printing Press, 1977), 165–190; trans. James F. Strange and privately circulated for the University of South Florida Excavations at Sepphoris, 1987.

6

Hearing in Israel

THE INVESTIGATION of the poiesis of Jesus continues in this chapter as we sift through further evidence pertaining to the precanonical churches' imaginations of who he was. We have reviewed indications that those imaginations did their work in legal and in liturgical contexts as well as catechetical ones. Statements of fact about Jesus seem typically to have followed upon aesthetic intuitions, particularly those rooted in experiences of profound prayer. If you will, the "cold facts" and the "warm images" ran into the formative gospel traditions in alternating streams.

In chapter 5, I proposed that much poietic water had flowed under the bridge ahead of Luke's historicizing account of Jesus' conception, and even more flowed after it. Before the story took its Lukan shape, it had been an imaginative liturgical, perhaps meturgemanic, rendition expanding the Hannah story. Before that, there was a coldly logical legal core. Before that, there was Mary's anguished and perhaps wordless plea to God as a daughter of Israel in need. But the oral stream could not be frozen solid by Luke's text itself. After Luke, we found that poietic variance continued, with the story warming up again as it rejoined the flow of the living liturgy and contributed to the full-blown liturgical drama of the Mary story, reflected today for us in the *Protevangelium of James*.

Identifying Jesus, therefore, was both a liturgical and a doctrinal undertaking. The doctrinal side is the more familiar to us because it presents itself as the "content" of the Gospel texts that come down to us. Yet there is a certain dimensionality, a depth of field, that also presents itself in those texts. They *are* histories, but they also *have* histories. Our investigation seeks to explore that depth dimension by excavating layers of the prehistory of the gospel tradition. Thus in the preceding chapter I reconstructed a "legal case" concerning what happened to Mary. The "case" was not equivalent to Luke's annunciation narrative, nor to the somewhat different narrative in the *Protevangelium of James*. Rather, I argued that some such legal interpretation had to lie somewhere in the prehistory beneath both of the texts, given what we know about the cultures, languages, and history of first-century Palestine.

The present chapter investigates another story, the temptation narrative from Matthew and Luke, using a similar line of inquiry. This story also comes to us in two versions, although this time both are canonical and they are nearly identical. Once again we have a story that shows the marks of a "cool" or academic transmission by way of legal argument and scholarly debate as well as a "warm" or imaginative transmission in relation to liturgical performances and perhaps even public dramatization. Once again the cross-cultural perspective is indispensable to unlocking the conceptual negotiations and the competing portraitures at play in the production of the texts as we receive them.[1]

The poiesis of Jesus may be regarded as a gift from the earliest churches, from people who knew how to recognize the Lord. We are not dealing here with deception, with political self-interest, with free artistic fancy, or with an "anything goes" attitude of pragmatic relativism. We are instead taking the Gospels at their word: *that* their word alone is insufficient to bring anyone into position to "see the Lord" and that something else is needed. Therefore we are seeking to recover praxis and poiesis alongside the *theōria* or official statement about who Jesus is.

We are recovering these practices right out of the canon, which is to say that what is recovered is canonical as long as the method of recovery is sound. This suggests an expansion of what is meant theologically by the canonicity of the New Testament: the canon is not merely a set of texts but a repertoire of textual practices as well. Here the objection might be put forward that text can be inspired, while interpretation can at best be authoritative. I would respond that the alleged status of any text as inspired is moot unless the text can be read. Furthermore, any reading of a text

---

1. There is an implicit theology of revelation at work within the metaphor of descent in the customary phrase "the texts that have come down to us." It pictures them as having dropped out of heaven, clean and whole and crisp as snow, into our present world. In comparison, I am saying that texts have "come up to us" out of our past, that is, out of the ground composed by the ashes of our ancestors. They are dusty, cracked, alien, difficult to decipher; yet they are what civilization is built upon.

already is an interpretation. Even a conventional historical reading of the Gospels still entails some method of interpretation. The "archaeological" reading to find the texts' prehistory that I have undertaken differs from ordinary reading not in kind but only in degree. The New Testament's Gospel texts are themselves readings of other texts, and in this they encode practices of interpretation as well as "facts." If two texts are deemed to be inspired, and also are related to each other, then surely the poiesis that relates them must in some sense itself be spirit-driven as well.

More Cultural Vocabulary

With the Mary story, it was essential to keep track of the cultural construction of two realities: gender and work. With the story of the temptation, the reality of work continues to be a contested territory. In addition, we will now be tracking the meanings of a cluster of terms that have to do with knowing: hear, see, write, teach, and name. This time the poiesis seems to involve only two of the three language groups: Hebrew scholars and Greeks—although these Greeks are a much more proletarian lot than the Alexandrians. Their Bible is the Septuagint, but they seem to be reading it as people would who must worry about where their next meal is coming from. As for the Hebrew scholars, they resemble Sadducees in that they appear connected with the intellectual, liturgical, and legal traditions of the Jerusalem Temple. This time we will begin with Greek terms and work back into the Hebrew.

The words for slave, *doulos* and *doulē,* were encountered in chapter 5. The verb related to them is *douleuō,* which means simply to be a slave, to be subject to someone, to serve without pay. The noun *douleia* means uncompensated work, in the sense of bondage or slavery. In contrast, the verb *latreuō* means to work for pay (although occasionally it is used of slave labor as well). The related noun is *latreia,* meaning hired labor. It is interesting that this is the term used for worship or service to the gods. Either *douleia* or *latreia* is used by the Septuagint to translate the principal Hebrew term for divine service, ʿ*abōdāh.* This does not exhaust the Greek vocabulary of labor, by any means.

Related to work in the Septuagint is a cluster of terms that signal physical submission, the prostration of the body before one's social or economic superior. *Proskyneō* means to prostrate oneself before someone in respect, appeasement, or supplication. This term can also mean to worship or to mollify the gods, and in the form *proskynētēs* it means a worshiper. The Septuagint ordinarily uses it to indicate a bodily posture of obeisance toward God, as if toward a secular potentate. *Piptō* means to fall or to fall down. With the prefix, *propiptō* means to throw oneself forward or to rush forward. The use of these terms is not restricted to religious contexts.

The verb for seeing in Greek is *horaō*, and it is extremely interesting. It encodes the Greek cultural experience of what it means to know. *Horaō* is quite an irregular verb, and its principal parts have different stems. From this verb comes the word that means a gaze from afar: *theōria*. From another form of the verb to see comes the noun *eidos*, which means the shape of something that is visible. The Greek philosophers used *eidos* to designate that aspect of a thing which can be known by the human mind, its essence. It gives us our word "idea." An *eidōlon* is a vision, a fancy, a ghost, or a portrait; the Septuagint uses this term for false gods, and it gives us the English word "idol." The form for the perfect tense of the verb "to see," *oida*, literally "I have seen," is used as a virtual present-tense construction, "I know." The Greeks understood that there were cognitive components to other activities besides seeing; nevertheless they accorded to theoretical knowledge the most important status at the expense of the other kinds.

In comparison, Hebrew terminology encodes quite a different cultural experience. "To know" in Hebrew is *yāda'*. All of the meanings of this root connote engagement or contact of some kind: to notice, to find out, to recognize, to care about, to become acquainted with, to have sexual intercourse with, to choose, to understand, to reveal oneself, to know oneself, to inform, to announce, to be brought into awareness. While that constellation of meanings is not unfamiliar to English speakers, we tend to relegate such knower-involved activities to second place epistemologically behind "seeing." That is because the English language has been heavily influenced by the Greek philosophical vocabulary of the visual, so that our terms for looking also function as terms for knowing—for example, insight, idea, evidence, appear, see, clarify, specify. Yet an older, preliterate experience of knowing that is not seated in the eyes is still encoded in the English word "know" and in its cognates: ken and cunning, as in Greek: *gnōsis*, a seeking to know; *gnōmē*, the judgment or mind; and *gignōskō*, to understand. This older experience is preliterate. That is, it predates the visual bias that was introduced when people who could read began to think of themselves as having a monopoly on knowing.

With Hebrew, the most reliable organs for intaking knowledge are not the eyes but the ears, which are thought to be direct channels into the heart. To hear is *šāma'*, with a range of meanings including to listen to, to heed, to obey, to understand, to be heard, to make oneself heard, to announce, to summon, to become obedient. These relations characterize the important transactions among people, and especially between people and

God. Prophets recount visions of God (as in Isa. 6:1-10 or Amos 9:1), and liturgists associate righteousness with a glimpse of God (as in Pss. 11:7 and 17:15). Yet even in such instances, the kind of "perception" intended by the metaphor of vision must be determined by the context. Moreover, the Torah relegates the visions and dreams of prophets to second place, when compared with the verbal revelation given to Moses, the Torah itself. In Num. 12:6-8, God and Moses speak "mouth to mouth."[2]

In Exodus 33–34, the account of the divine lawgiving at Sinai says that God "used to speak to Moses face to face" (Exod. 33:11), and promised to grant Moses' request to show him the divine *kābôd*, or glory (Exod. 33:18-19). God's promise to "make all my goodness pass before you" is fulfilled in the dictation of the covenant commandments to Moses (Exod. 34:1-28). In Torah, then, the metaphor of "seeing God" is deflected from its literal sense of perception at a distance with the eyes and made to cover the observance of ethical and cultic directives. For subsequent rabbinic interpreters, the expression "to greet the face of the *Shekinah*" came to include prayer, study of Torah, pilgrimage to the Temple, and almsgiving to people in need.[3]

Thus in Torah, God is heard, not seen; and to "see" God, one observes the commandments of righteousness. Yet it is interesting that by the first century God's name or *šēm* is seen, although never heard except for a rare liturgical whisper. That is, the tetragrammaton—the four-letter divine name, *yhwh*—may be read with the eyes after it has been inscribed on a scroll, but never pronounced.

The concept of formal learning or instruction in Hebrew is expressed with a form of the root *yrh*. In some of its patterns or moods, this root means to toss, to throw, to shoot. Another pattern yields the meanings to water, to give to drink, or to be given to drink. In yet a third pattern, we get the technical pedagogical meaning of to teach, to instruct. This is the root that gives us the term *tôrāh*, instruction. Torah was not originally written down and visible; it was, according to a vivid metaphor, pitched or showered. Ancient Hebrew is ambivalent about writing. It encodes no particular fondness for that which is written or scratched onto scrolls, the Scripture. On one hand, Moses supposedly received the commands of God impressed into tablets of stone. On the other hand, the Hebrew word

---

2. For a thorough philological exposition, see Wilhelm Michaelis, *"horaō," Theological Dictionary of the New Testament*, esp. 328–34. Michaelis believes that a second negation has been dropped in the manuscript tradition at Num. 12:8 and that the restored text should read: "With him I speak mouth to mouth, and neither by visions nor by riddles," in order to match the thought of v. 6.

3. See Michaelis, *"horaō,"* 340.

for alien gods is *pesel,* literally a carved thing, from a root meaning to hew or dress rock. The Hebrew "scratched-out thing" becomes the "idol" or visualized thing of the Septuagint.

In light of the range of meaning of the root *yrh,* which embraces both instruction and being given to drink, it is intriguing to discover how Hebrew expresses physical obeisance. Several terms can mean both to bow in worship and to bend over a spring to drink. *Kāra'* means to crouch, to bear down in childbirth, to kneel in prayer, to bring low, to make kneel. The root *šḥḥ* means to stoop, to crouch, or to bring down. Another root, nearly identical, is *šḥh,* meaning to bow down or to be weighted down; this term often is used in cases of bowing to God or to a thing as if it were a god. None of these terms is used exclusively for worship. In fact, they denote physical postures that can be ascribed to people and animals alike. There is a more technical term, *šārēt,* to describe the cultic duties performed at the altar by a priest while the people are bowing. Both roots, *šrt* and *šḥḥ* (worship and stooping) would together comprise an expression for the cultic component of the all-pervasive activity of *'ăbōdāh:* service of the Lord.

These few terms from the conceptual vocabularies of two language communities, the Hebrew and the Greek, open the door to a line of questioning about the Gospel narratives of Jesus' temptation in the desert. The story's surface configuration, so to speak, is historical; that is, it purports to be reporting an event. As with the Mary story, however, this dialogue between a human being and an angelic being is a dramatic device for arguing a certain case, a certain configuration or construal of the "facts."

This story, like all stories, is an artifact: a built thing. Its generic architecture seems to have undergone renovation several times. The present shape of it is historical narrative, notwithstanding the supernatural details. Previously, as I will argue, it may well have been the script for a satirical dramatic dialogue. Before that, it was a judicial procedure in which one of the language communities discredited or excluded the other in some significant way. Before that, it was a debate ongoing between two factions within one community.

We cannot say how many of these generic permutations may have been written up as text. *Maybe* it all happened on paper, as follows:

1. Citations from the Septuagint and from the Holy Writings were jotted down for the debate;
2. Notes from the debate provided a documentary source for the legal briefs used in the inquest;
3. The briefs were rewritten as a script;
4. The script was revised as a story;

5. That story was written into the third recension of the hypothetical document Q;

6. Q begat Luke and Matthew out of Mark.

On the other hand, maybe there was no paper trail at all. Maybe the stages of genric evolution through successive recitations of this material were not nearly so clear-cut and discrete as I will sketch them below. Nevertheless the performances of this story undoubtedly entailed reimaginings of the identity of Jesus. It is that progressive poiesis that I am seeking to uncover. As before, our investigation will begin at the canonical surface of the story and work down into its past.

Temptation, Trial, Inquest, or Drama?

The story of Jesus' temptation in the desert is a long-standing puzzle for New Testament scholarship.[4] The rhetorical logic of the devil's three challenges and Jesus' three replies has eluded explanation. Moreover, the relationship of this pericope to the rest of the Sayings Source has remained unaccounted for, although it is the longest narrative segment and the only real dialogue in Q.

The story on its surface can be read as an encounter between Jesus and a nonhuman figure who dares him to three foolish deeds: wasting a miracle, leaping off a building, and idolatry. Since the Jesus character responds to each challenge with a pious quotation from Deuteronomy, the story might be taken simply as a dominical example of how to vanquish evil. Yet the historical Jesus is not speaking in this story, and still less any historical devil. If there is some factual core both presented and camouflaged in Q 4, what sort of core might it be?[5] My hypothesis is that these two dramatic characters, "Jesus" and "the devil," are representing the opposing arguments of two groups that once contended for a piece of conceptual territory comprised of theological axioms, economic relations, and paidaic practices.

The substance of the two opposing positions can be recovered by juxtaposing the texts that "Jesus" and "the devil" cite as authorities. Jesus is quoting Moses' homily from Deuteronomy, while the devil is quoting

---

4. See Kloppenborg, *The Formation of Q*, 246–62, for a review of the literature.

5. For summaries of strategies to tease out the historical core, see Rudolf Bultmann, *History of the Synoptic Tradition*, trans. John Marsh, rev. ed. (New York: Harper & Row, 1963), 254–57; and Fitzmyer, *The Gospel According to Luke (I—IX)*, 506–20.

Psalms. The source texts of the debate support a reconstruction of the contested issues as well as a profiling of the opposing parties.

This story is placed in Q incongruously between the words of John and the words of Jesus.[6] John Kloppenborg's thesis is that the story was added in the third and final recension of Q as a document. He argues persuasively that the earliest version of Q, the core around which the document would coalesce, consisted of six sapiential speeches or sayings collections. A second recension reshaped those collections by the addition of polemical material, producing a *chreia* collection designed for use in rhetorical composition. As a compendium of *chreia*, Q would have been a Greek text meant to support polemical oral performance.

One may assume that somebody, some constituency, was using Q in just that way. The reason for a *third* recension should be sought in the midst of the practices of that constituency. It appears that the Q folk had distinctive class-based teaching practices that differed markedly from those of other teachers within their society. Those practices were deemed deficient by some other teaching constituency and attracted its criticism.

That other constituency seems to have been more powerful than the Q sages, if we can rely on indications in the story that comes down to us. Caricatured as the devil, the opponents of the Q sages have the authority to transport people to the hill country, to hale them up to the Temple. Were there actual confrontations between the sages of a Jesus school and that other authoritative constituency? If so, how often, and of what character, and with what results? If not, did the Q sages wish for such a debate and fantasize how they would win it?

Of course we do not have a transcript of any such proceedings. However, the Q school seems to have left their own version of the trial-that-might-have-been, in the form of the dramatic debate staged between their Jesus and their devil. This fantasy has been produced and directed by the rhetors of the Q circle. They did the casting, so the devil portrays the arguments of their opponents, while Jesus speaks for the good guys, the Q teachers themselves. The staging is theatrical, the language is Greek, and the medium of expression is oratorical debate.[7]

---

6. The text of Q is handily presented in John S. Kloppenborg et al., *Q Thomas Reader* (Sonoma, Calif.: Polebridge Press, 1990), which supplies a hypothetical incipit, "These are the words of Jesus and John." The "Introduction" to the *Reader* summarizes the evolution of scholarship on the Sayings Source and gives bibliography. The argument for historical layering in Q is meticulously constructed by Kloppenborg in *The Formation of Q*, 102–245. In Miller, *The Complete Gospels*, Q appears in parallel columns displaying the Matthean and Lukan versions.

7. A theater in the ancient world would have a three-level *proskenion* building designed for representation of events occurring among human beings on earth, above the earth in the

Methodological Stipulations

James M. Robinson identified the genre of Q as *logoi sophōn*, "sayings of the sages." Kloppenborg refines this assessment. He suggests that the earliest version of Q was indeed sapiential instruction but that the second recension moved the document toward the genre of the *chreia* collection. That is, Q was remolded for polemical rhetorical use.[8] It is possible that the earliest layer was not Greek at all but Aramaic and was a kind of halakhic recitation: not a written text but a repertoire of oral performance. Kloppenborg, while he argues that Q as known to Luke and Matthew must have been a Greek text, still comments as follows:

> No one would seriously dispute that Q was formulated in proximity to
> a Semitic-speaking area, under the influence of the Semitizing Greek
> of the Septuagint, and in part, from orally transmitted sayings which
> had their origin in Aramaic-speaking circles.[9]

Halakhic Q would have been delivered in the schoolroom or *bêt midrāš* of the synagogue.[10] Its reciters (all of them men) would have been those whom the Greek Jesus people (men and women) would later remember nostalgically as traveling prophets. This practice came to a close when the Jesus sages wore out their welcome in the village synagogues.

The second recension of Q may then have entailed not just addition of new material but translation into *koinē* Greek. The Q speakers using the second recension did not simply read selections aloud; rather, they employed standard rhetorical practices in producing oratorical expansions of the words of Jesus. Like the Aramaic targums their addresses were creative productions, although in Greek the principles governing expansion

---

realm of the gods, or below the earth. The drama of Jesus' threefold temptation, with its startling scene changes, could easily be staged in such a structure. Palestine had such theaters in the first century. See Richard A. Batey, "Jesus and the Theater," *New Testament Studies* 30 (1984): 563–74. It is likely that provincial theaters featured mime shows and oratorical recitals, if not the classic tragedies. Theatrical performances also were staged at formal banquets.

8. See James M. Robinson, "LOGOI SOPHON: On the Gattung of Q," in James M. Robinson and Helmut Koester, *Trajectories through Early Christianity* (Philadelphia: Fortress Press, 1971), 71–113. See also Kloppenborg, *The Formation of Q*, 317–28.

9. See Kloppenborg, *The Formation of Q*, 64. On the preceding pages he painstakingly lays out the evidence for his conclusion that the text was written down in Greek, however.

10. Bruce Chilton argues that a halakhah of Jesus is more plausible than a written document Q. See Chilton, *Profiles of a Rabbi*, 174. Chilton also discusses *mishnah* of Jesus in *The Temple of Jesus: His Sacrificial Program Within a Cultural History of Sacrifice* (University Park, Pa.: Pennsylvania State University, 1992).

were different. Such orations would occur elsewhere than in the Aramaic synagogues and likely now beyond Palestine itself.

In first-century Galilee, Syria, and Asia Minor, rhetorical productions may be placed in the market squares of the towns and cities, in the basilical synagogues of Greco-Jewish communities, in the dining halls of great houses, or even in the theaters. Thus at least some of those Q rhetors were coming up in the world, out of the village courtyards and into the public arena.[11] This development may be reflected in the third recension of Q, with the formal debate between Jesus and the devil. It mirrors the creative work of someone whom we can hardly avoid calling a satirist, a dramatist, a playwright.[12]

This complicates the task of historical reconstruction. In order to get at the nonfictional confrontation of two ideologies, we have to work through the fictional dramatization of their positions. We have to "suspend disbelief" in the dramatic sense and play along with the premise of the debate.

The story as we have it cannot be a complete script; it is too short. For that matter, neither could any of the sayings recorded elsewhere in Q be a complete teaching. Those sayings, as *chreiai*, were something like sound bites. They were meant to be skillfully expanded in oral performance and adapted to circumstances. Therefore it is plausible that the script of Q 4:1-13 is meant to be orally expanded in performance as well. How would that have been done? In the case of *chreiai*, we know the procedures for expansion, thanks to classical sources.[13] Perhaps similar procedures were supposed to be applied to the lines of "Jesus" and "the devil."

On the other hand, perhaps the scriptural sound bites in Q 4 call for a different sort of expansion altogether. Perhaps they direct the orator back to the source documents from which they were excerpted: the

---

11. Some of the Aramaic sages of Jesus may of course have continued their more traditional practice of circulating among villages and speaking to small groups gathered in homes. Indeed, this practice would be among the things defended in the debate.

12. It is interesting that *didaskalos*, "teacher," in classical Greek could also refer to the chorus master who conducted the theatrical presentation of a poetic composition that often was his own. The verb *didaskō*, "to teach," could also mean to perform or to execute. According to Karl Heinrich Rengstorf, however, this usage had disappeared in Hellenistic Greek. Yet the verb retained a histrionic sense well into the common era, and in nonliterary usage it could mean to demonstrate or to prove. See Rengstorf, *"didaskō," Theological Dictionary of the New Testament*. This puts an interesting spin on the title *didaskalos*, master or teacher, by which Jesus may (or may not) be addressed in Q 12:13. (There is as yet no consensus on whether the term is Q or Lukan in this incident, in which Jesus is asked to settle a dispute.)

13. See Mack, *Myth of Innocence*, 179–92; and Mack and Robbins, *Patterns of Persuasion*. On the interplay between social factors and the processes of text formation, I have also been enlightened by Kelber, *The Oral and the Written Gospel*.

Psalms and Deuteronomy. Perhaps the "complete script" had to be read out of those sources. The quotes as we have them are condensations of the passages from which they have been taken. This premise makes possible an attractive historical reconstruction. By looking at the citations in context, one can reconstruct the script of the fictionalized debate, and with that script one can illuminate the historical points of contention between the two groups of teachers.

But a problem immediately arises. Of the six speeches in the story, only four seem to contain quotations. The first and third speeches of the devil are not quotations. At least, they are not quotations *from the Septuagint.* I will argue below that the devil speeches nevertheless reflect *Hebrew* psalm texts.

The devil character thinks Hebrew, as it were, for he advances offers whose terms reflect psalmic messianic and liturgical theology. However, the Jesus character systematically misconstrues those offers by transposing them into Greek. This solution suggests itself when one tries to puzzle out the rhetorical flow of the exchange, that is, to find some sense in which one character's reply can function as an answer to the other character's challenge. Between the opponents there are clear cultural differences touching both the method of argumentation and the connotations of the words that fly back and forth.

This suggests that, while the script is wholly Greek, the historical conflict underlying it was bilingual and bicultural. At issue in that dispute were the following:

> *divine sonship:* its nature, and the right to claim it
> *living well:* managing goods, services, and economic class relations
> *orthodoxy:* whether reading or speaking is more authoritative
> *knowledge of God:* who knows God, and who forgets God
> *salvation:* is it available now, or displaced to the past and future
> *destruction:* who is going to be wiped out (in retrospect), and why

Judaism offered a range of options on each of these issues. The Q speakers made different choices from those of their opponents, and those choices amounted to a distinctive and eventually canonical poiesis of Jesus.

In the remainder of this chapter we will reconstruct the moves made in the dramatized debate of Q 4, and we will infer the ideologies and practices that motivate them. A brief preview of the opposed sides will serve to introduce the more detailed presentation that follows. In my hypothetical reconstruction, the devil stands for a community with certain distinctive teachings and teaching practices that are at odds with those of the Q rhetors. We do not know what these people called themselves. I will call them the Professors of the Name, for they seem to champion the privileged figure of Psalm 91 who is said to know the name of the Lord: *Yahweh* (v. 14).

These Professors seem to have the authority to examine and try the practices and the message of the Q speakers, while the latter are struggling to renegotiate that claim to authority. The Professors look very much like Sadducees, who were aristocratic scholars based at the Jerusalem Temple, with a liturgical theology and a teaching tradition emphasizing the Torah as Scripture and popularly recognized as authoritative. The Sadducees had colleagues in Sepphoris. While the Pharisaic tradition would eclipse them after 70 C.E., nevertheless they contributed their teaching traditions into the rabbinic Judaism aborning at Sepphoris and especially at the academic center of Jamnia, which they would found after the Temple's destruction in 70 C.E. (I refrain from the claim that the Professors of the Name *are* the Sadducees, because I want to keep in view the fact that I am reconstructing a hypothetical school indirectly, out of Christian texts, rather than profiling them directly from less biased historical sources. In addition, the Professors have a revisionist approach to Mosaic law that is not attested among the Sadducees as orthodox sources portray them.)

Like the Sadducees, my Professors of the Name are reading Hebrew texts, and they understand certain important biblical terms without the nuances introduced in the Alexandrian Greek translation. They stand within a sapiential tradition, so that for them the orthodox interpretation of Torah is found in the psalms of the Temple liturgy rather than in the practical applications to everyday life devised by the lay Pharisees. These Professors of the Name may well be in dialogue with the Tannaim, the rabbinic sages of the first century whose work comes down to us in the Mishnah. One might call them "establishment" types. They enjoy a comfortable standard of living, and they have aristocratic views about the political profile of God's anointed one, the messiah.

Those views would exert a certain political poietic pressure upon the malleable haggadah of any putative messiah such as Jesus of Nazareth, but a pressure that would not carry it beyond the pale of viable rabbinic opinion and into the sort of extravagant portrayal that the Q speakers were projecting. The learned Professors of the Name are quite interested in the credentialing of messiahs. The Anointed must be a "son" in the sense of an authorized exegete of God's instruction.

In other words, the poiesis of Jesus suggested by the Professors of the Name may represent an option for a Jewish Christianity that, at the time of

the debate, had not yet been foreclosed. We are focusing on relations between the Professors of the Name and the Q speakers at a point in their history when lines of communication between the two groups are still open,
that is, well before the composition of the temptation satire. Indeed, at this
point the established Professors are still using the tactics of persuasion in
an attempt to enlist the Q teachers' support for their own agenda.

Like the Professors of the Name, the Q speakers are concerned about
what divine sonship means. They claim sonship for Jesus—not because Jesus *brings* special instruction but because he has *received* God's instruction
as one receives instruction from a father. The Q sages can read, but they
pour their best energies into speaking and hearing. They are professors
not of the *Šēm* but of the *Šᵉmaʿ*, the "Hear-O-Israel," Deut. 6:4. Adherents
of the Q school are less materially secure than the Professors of the Name.
Hunger is a real factor in their lives. They do their teaching not at seminar
tables or sitting in the *bêt midrās* but on the roads and in the cramped
courtyards of their little houses, finding in Deut. 6:7 a warrant for this
distinctive practice.

The Jesus of the Q speakers is God's son simply because he is the best
hearer of the *Akoue Israēl*, Deut. 6:4. They portray him as the one who loves
God with all his mind, soul, and strength. That is precisely why their
Jesus is the one who speaks for God. He is the voice of God, God's son. He
quotes the Book of the Law: Deuteronomy, the *logoi* that Moses spoke to all
Israel. Through intensive hearing, the Mosaic words have become Jesus'
very own words. But the Q sages' Jesus also obeys the law, pursues righteousness instead of possessions, and enters into life.

As the dispute between the two groups of teachers comes to a full boil,
it focuses itself into a summary exchange of accusations. The Professors of
the Name charge that the Q sages *do not know the name of God*, whose proper
name, *yhwh*, can be seen in the sacred text but never pronounced or heard.
The Q speakers countercharge that the Professors of the Name for their part
cannot hear God because their possessions have made them forget the basic
prerequisite: to love God and obey God.

While most interpreters of the Synoptic Gospels tradition believe
that Q existed as a discrete document, no manuscript comes down to us.
Only the portions included in Matthew's and Luke's Gospels are available
for analysis. Q material is cited by its versification in Luke. Therefore our
story, Q 4:1-13, equals Luke 4:1-13; the parallel is Matt. 4:1-11. The sayings
come in different order in the two versions, but the Matthean order is
likely the older and so it will be followed here. There is remarkable verbal
agreement between the two versions. It is plausible that the common
words are those which appeared in the source document, and they are

shown in Figure 3 in capital letters. The passages that I will use in expanding the script of the debate are given in parentheses.[14]

First Devil Speech, Q 4:3

A. *Expanding the Script.* Right away we are facing the problem of finding a background text when Q 4:3 is not a direct quotation. What warrants my hunt for a biblical citation when none is found in the text? My premise is that the Q playwright has rewritten the historic positions with the intention of making the opponents' proposals seem outrageous. The satirist intended to camouflage the reasonableness of the opponents' proposals as well as the scriptural precedent for them. Yet the playwright did not want to make the devil's positions so strange that the audience could not figure out the identity of the devil. Therefore the camouflage is deliberately thin. The artful challenge of the satirist confronts the reader even today: "Guess who this devil is!" How shall we proceed to make our educated guess? Some criteria suggest themselves:

1. The text we are looking for should feature some words or concepts that actually appear in Q 4:1-3.
2. The text should be suited to set in motion the dramatic action of the debate.
3. The text should be one that could plausibly provoke the specific reply of Q 4:4, as expanded by Deuteronomy 8.
4. The text should fight for the same turf that is being claimed by Deuteronomy 5–8, which the other side is going to be citing.
5. The text should have some affinity with the material from which comes the only biblical quote that the Q playwright has allowed his devil, Psalm 91.

(In other words, Q 4:1-13 gives us four of the six pieces of a jigsaw puzzle. We will know when we have found the other two pieces, because their knobs will fit the notches and their notches will fit the knobs of the original four.)

By these criteria, Psalm 50 is a good candidate for the missing background text of the first devil speech, as the following considerations show.

---

14. This text is taken from the *Q Thomas Reader,* which prints the common words in boldface type instead of capitalizing them. The parenthetical matter is of course my own.

Figure 3.   Script of the Debate at Q4

(1) JESUS WAS LED up into THE WILDERNESS by THE SPIRIT to be TEMPTED BY THE DEVIL. (2) AND since he had fasted FORTY DAYS and forty nights, afterward HE WAS HUNGRY.

(3) And approaching, the tempter SAID TO HIM, "IF YOU ARE THE SON OF GOD, TELL THESE STONES TO BECOME LOAves OF BREAD."
   (abridgment of Psalms 50 and 132?)

(4) But he ANSWERED, "IT IS WRITTEN, 'NO ONE CAN LIVE BY BREAD ALONE . . . . '"
   (abridgment of Deuteronomy 8)

(9) Then the devil took HIM TO the holy city, AND SET him ON THE PINNACLE OF THE TEMPLE, AND SAID TO HIM, "IF YOU ARE THE SON OF GOD, THROW YOURSELF DOWN;

(10) FOR IT IS WRITTEN, 'HE WILL GIVE HIS ANGELS CHARGE OF YOU,'

(11) AND 'ON THEIR HANDS THEY WILL BEAR YOU UP, LEST YOU STRIKE YOUR FOOT AGAINST A STONE.'"
   (abridgment of Psalm 91; also 48?)

(12) JESUS said TO HIM, "Again it is written, 'YOU SHALL NOT TEMPT THE LORD YOUR GOD.'"
   (abridgment of Deuteronomy 6)

(5) Again the devil took HIM to a very high mountain, and SHOWED HIM ALL THE KINGDOMS OF THE world AND THEIR GLORY;

(6) AND he SAID TO HIM, "All these I WILL GIVE YOU, (7) IF YOU will fall down and WORSHIP ME."
   (abridgment of Psalm 72?)

(8) Then JESUS said to HIM, "Depart Satan! for IT IS WRITTEN, 'YOU SHALL WORSHIP THE LORD YOUR GOD AND HIM ALONE SHALL YOU SERVE.'"
   (abridgment of Deuteronomy 5)

(13) Then THE DEVIL left him, and behold, angels came and were serving him.

1. Psalm 50 mentions hunger and divinity in the same breath, although as incompatible. Its setting is a cosmic trial, with a summons, testimony, and a challenge to present credentials, for in v. 16 the judge demands, "What right have you to recite my laws?" Both divine hunger and the demand for evidence are also features of Q 4:3.

2. Psalm 50 would set the stage nicely for an inquest. Verses 16-22 make a feisty opening sally against deviant teachers: "You hate my instruction. . . . You use your mouth for evil. . . . You speak continually against your brother."

3. Psalm 50 maps some specific issues that the response produced by Q 4:4 with Deuteronomy 8 is going to try to reconfigure. Psalm 50:16's "What right have you to recite my laws?" sets up Deut. 8:6's answer: It was Moses who told us to keep the commands of the Lord. Psalm 50:10-11's claim that sacrifice is no big deal because God owns the animals anyway is answered by Deut. 8:7, 10, 13, where God has given animals, produce, and land to the people expecting obedience in return. Psalm 50:5's mention of covenant by sacrifice is countered by Deut. 8:1, 18, where covenant is linked to God's oath and human obedience. Psalm 50:12's negative statement about divine hunger opens up the vitally important question of the function of hunger. In Deut. 8:3 hunger is caused by God for a pedagogical purpose, while in Deut. 8:10 the absence of hunger brings the danger of forgetfulness.

4. Psalm 50 does indeed extend its claims over the same conceptual territory covered by Moses' homily. The list of charges in vv. 16-20 reprises the Decalogue: blasphemy, stealing, adultery, lying, disloyalty to one's family. Verse 7 has a *šᵉmaʿ*, although it is spoken by God instead of by Moses. In addition, the common themes of law, instruction, covenant, agricultural ownership, deliverance, and destruction are introduced.

5. Both Psalm 50 and the one quotation actually found in the devil speeches, Psalm 91, are the same sort of literature: cultic psalms. Both conclude with a divine promise to show someone salvation.

B. *Substance of the First Proposition.* If Psalm 50 gives us the general terms of the dispute between the Q folk and the People of the Name, still we need to decipher the specific offer being made in the first devil speech. What is encoded in its four terms: devil/tempter, son of God, stones, and bread?

The second pair, stones and bread, reminds us to consider the social location of those on either side of the debate. The first pair, devil and divine son, reminds us that teachers who quote psalms are constituents of the sapiential tradition. As readers of the Holy Writings, the Professors of the Name are familiar with a scenario in which a just man is tempted by Satan. In Job 1:6, Satan appears among the "sons of God," *bᵉnê hā-ʾelōhîm,* to accuse and try Job.[15] In Q 4, the tempter himself therefore has some claim to the title "son of God" that he dangles before Jesus. In view of the poverty of the landless "people of the land" in prosperous Galilee, the devil's request is exquisitely mocking.[16] The Q speakers seem to the privileged class to be indecorously preoccupied with food, because they have trouble feeding themselves. But Jesus is asked to do what the Q folk do well: talk. He is invited to work his mouth to work a marvel, and a trivial one at that: *tell* these stones to transubstantiate. The ability to provide bread for the poor of Zion is a messianic credential in the psalmic liturgical theology, for example, in Psalm 132.

But there is more to the first proposal of the devil than a request for a nature miracle. Stones in Deut. 5:22 are the original tablets upon which God wrote the commandments after first speaking them. Precisely because of those "stones" (that is, those commandments), the land is supposed to be a place where "bread will not be scarce," according to the ideology advanced by the Q speakers, Deut. 8:9. Yet as both sides know, bread is indeed scarce for growing numbers of Galileans. So the devil's first taunt points to the proven impracticality of bringing economic prosperity out of the stones of the Deuteronomic economic program. This is a bid to discredit the Mosaic version of the covenant as outdated and impractical. Stones do not turn into bread, and the antique commandments alone are not working to bring prosperity to the people.

The Professors of the Name have another agenda. Bread is to be provided through Zion, not Horeb, according to Psalm 132. The alternative to "bread from stones" is their plan for messianic salvation with its economic basis in a system of international trade and class stratification, as we shall see. It is interesting that salvation is the *yēšaʿ* promised in the last lines of Psalm 50 and Psalm 91 (and that term evokes the popular etymology of the name of Jesus).

First Jesus Speech, Q 4:4

A. *Expanding the Script.* Because Q 4:4 is clearly a quotation of Deut. 8:3, we have no difficulty finding the background text with which to expand the Jesus character's reply to the devil's first proposal. There is a decision to

15. These sons of God become *angeloi* in the Septuagint, so the Grecophone Q folk might not perceive the irony of having a son of God examine a son of God even if they recognized the propriety of the prosecutorial role for the devil.

16. For a perspective on economic developments in first-century Galilee, see Freyne, *Galilee, Jesus, and the Gospels* (see chap. 1, n. 7), esp. 155–67. For the opinion that poverty among the Q people was voluntary, see Kloppenborg, *The Formation of Q*, 240.

be made, however, about how much of Moses' homily to use. In the first century, there was no "eighth chapter" of Deuteronomy, for versification is a modern innovation. What we today call Deuteronomy 5 through 8 was transmitted as one long discourse, a discourse extending onward for many more "chapters." Yet because the discourse is repetitious and somewhat rambling, at least by Western literary conventions, there is little danger of losing a contextual nuance or a turn of argument by slicing off verses from the top or bottom of a passage. Therefore for convenience we may as well follow the customary chapter boundaries in identifying the context of the quotation.

B. *Substance of the Rejection of the First Proposition.* The words that appear in Q 4:4 assert that bread is insufficient to support life. If I am correct about the terms of the devil's proposal, then this response makes its move by seizing upon the proffer of "messianic salvation" and reconfiguring it as "life." The viability of the opponent's agenda is not disputed: sure, it might bring bread, but bread is not enough.

When the scant wording of Q 4:4 is expanded with Deuteronomy 8, the contours of the Q folk's position emerge. The Jesus character faces off against the tradition of Temple liturgical theology by quoting a teaching from the Torah, in a bid to take back the conceptual turf for the Q speakers. Hunger in Deuteronomy 8 is by no means an embarrassing disconfirmation of the covenant's validity. On the contrary, hunger is actually God's way of overcoming ignorance and announcing the source of human life. In v. 3: God made you humble and made you hungry and made you eat, so as to make you know the teaching cited by "Jesus" in Q 4:4: not on bread alone does a human being live, but on every word coming out of God's mouth does a human being live. The good land and its produce are God's gifts in vv. 10 and 18. But a comfortable lifestyle and the ending of hunger entail in vv. 10-17 the danger of forgetting God and the desert experience. Professors, please note.

The hearer of v. 5 is told to know by heart that God is teaching him just as a person teaches a son. Thus the Q folk's answer to the challenge of divine sonship is that being God's son means being taught by God, even if this means being made hungry by God. If the Professors of the Name have cited Ps. 50:12 to indicate that a hungry Jesus ipso facto can have nothing to do with divinity, then the Q speakers can countercite with Deut. 8:3, 5 to indicate that a hungry Jesus actually is someone prepared to listen to God and thus come to know how to live.

Also contested in the first Jesus speech are the proper conditions for knowledge. The good guys favor hearing and speaking, while their opponents favor seeing and especially the visual activity of reading. These preferences are even more striking when one considers that they run contrary to the biases inherent in the languages that the two sides use. Greek construes knowing as a visual experience; yet the Q speakers fasten upon the Deuteronomic *akoue* of the Septuagint. Hebrew, on the other hand, favors hearing and speaking, yet the Professors seem to be subordinating the *šᵉmaʿ yiśrāʾēl* of Deuteronomy and the *ʾāmar yhwh* of the Prophets to the psalmic *rāʾāh bᵉyēšaʿ*: "show salvation." Why would that be? Perhaps the difference between the so-called Greek and Hebrew mentality is really less than the difference between full literacy and the marginally literate or oral mentality.[17] The Professors of the Name, as we reconstruct them, must be highly literate and skilled in the reading and interpretation of written texts.

The Q sages are highly skilled at oration, but they cannot claim to share the authoritative text literacy of the Temple faculty. In the strategy of the debate, therefore, the Q folk want to assert that, contrary to appearances, it is their opponents who are ignorant and unknowing. They seize upon Deut. 8:3 to impugn the knowledge of the opponents and their fathers to boot. There and at v. 16, manna is called something your fathers did not see (for *yādaʿ*, the Septuagint has *horaō*). But the *coup de grâce* of the first reply is delivered in the last two verses of Deuteronomy 8:

> If you ever forget the Lord your God and follow other gods and worship and bow down to them (*lutreuō, proskyneō*), I testify against you today that you will surely be destroyed. Like the nations the Lord destroyed before you, so you will be destroyed for not hearing the voice of the Lord your God (*ēkusate tēs phōnēs kyriou* = *tišmᵉʿûn bᵉqôl yhwh*).

What hastens destruction is failure to hear.

The "Jesus" of the good guys obviously isn't the well-fed messiah of those literati, the Professors of the Name. He has resisted their charges, redefined sonship and knowledge, and raised the stakes of the debate by introducing the key themes of life and idolatry. Life is the promised result of hearing God's word, as in Deut. 8:1 and 3. Too much bread leads to forgetfulness, and that leads to bowing down to other gods, and *that* leads to destruction on account of failure to hear the Lord.

---

17. Literacy and orality are discussed in depth by Walter J. Ong, *Orality and Literacy: The Technologizing of the Word* (London: Methuen, 1982). The perceptual difference will have implications for subsequent Christian claims about how Jesus is recognized after Calvary: by his words or by sight? Oral people want to hear him, but literate people want to see him.

Second Devil Speech, Q 4:9-11

A. *Expanding the Script.* Once again we can easily identify a background text for this speech, since the devil quotes Psalm 91 directly. Psalm 48 also can help by casting a spotlight on the symbolism of the Temple's architectural features for the liturgical theology of Zion.

Act 2 opens with a change of scene, signaling a change of venue. The protagonists, or litigants, are transported to the holy city, the mountain of God, "beautiful in elevation" according to Ps. 48:1. Pilgrims attending the Temple liturgies were enjoined to "walk about Zion, go round about her, number her towers, consider well her ramparts, go through her citadels," Ps. 48:12-13.

B. *Substance of the Second Proposition.* In this impressive setting, the devil lays out his second proposal with the same premise as the first: "if you are the son of God." The suggestion that follows is bizarre. On the surface, it makes little sense other than as a gross and egotistical demonstration of exemption from the law of gravity. One has to turn to the background texts to get the sense of the proposition and understand its logical place within the oratorical exchange.

In the first Jesus speech, the ante was raised as new concepts were brought into play: prosperity versus life, ignorance versus instruction, destruction versus salvation, seeing versus hearing. Now Psalm 91 provides the devil with the wherewithal to match this ante and raise it, while countering the dangerous insinuation of bowing down to other gods, Deut. 8:19. The devil's rhetorical strategy is to retrieve the disputed concepts from the Greek of the Septuagint and reposition them in the Hebrew to renegotiate their configuration. As this strategy rises to the challenge posed by the Jesus character's citation of Torah against the liturgical tradition, it reasserts the viability of the latter and the need for it within a formal literate study of Torah itself.

Psalm 91 is a sustained assurance that the one who dwells in the shelter of the Most High will be protected from destruction. In the last verse God says, "With long life I will satisfy him, and let him see my salvation." God will tell the angels to guard you, v. 11. Moreover, you will observe with your eyes and see the destruction of the wicked, v. 8. Far from forgetting God, the favored one of Psalm 91 knows the name of God in v. 14, and of course that name in first-century Hebrew is no longer a sound but a text only, *yhwh*.

For the Professors of the Name, the honor and prosperity and long life of the favored one are owing to knowledge of God. This citation of Psalm 91 has shifted the venue up to the Jerusalem Temple: the mountain refuge of the High God. In that place the favored one "stays": *yāšab*. This verb means to sit, and in rabbinic usage it means to study; hence, "yeshiva," the place to sit and study.

What one studies is Torah, which means instruction. The Septuagint translators rendered *tôrāh* with *nomos*, "law," but that term loses the connotation of learning and several other nuances carried by the Hebrew term. The term *tôrāh* is derived from the root meaning to instruct, *yrh*. This word has a rich metaphorical aura, as we saw above. The lexicon gives clusters of meanings: (1) to throw, as in throwing stones; or to shoot, as in shooting arrows; or to erect, as in raising a heap of stones or laying a cornerstone; (2) to give to drink, or to be given to drink one's fill; (3) to instruct or teach. Thus in Hebrew, instruction or *tôrāh* has the feel of something that has been thrown or pitched at the people. It is heavy, and it accumulates like stones. It is also something wet and thirst-quenching, like rain. These textures are lost in the Septuagint's *nomos*.

The devil's second dare is an ingenious inside joke for those who read Hebrew. The devil grabs the ball of Torah that has been tossed into play by the first Jesus speech. That first response of the Q sages has amounted to the claim that Jesus heard God's instruction, and therefore spoke God's instruction, and therefore *was* God's instruction. Fine, says the prosecutor. So you want to play *tôrāh*; that's my game too. Step right up and take a seat in the *yeshiva*. Let's study. You be the *tôrāh*. Go ahead and throw yourself down; pitch your halakhah. On the other hand, if our *tôrāh* is the Torah and you are just an ignorant fool, then what you throw down will smash when it hits that which God has thrown down (literally, *tôrāh*), and which we have caught and built up into these stone walls, these Temple parapets which, unlike your own pathetic self, really mean something.

Second Jesus Speech, Q 4:12

A. *Expanding the Text.* The direct quotation in Q 4:12 points us toward the material in the sixth chapter of Deuteronomy. As before, the arbitrary modern boundaries of this chapter are not significant.

B. *Substance of the Rejection of the Second Proposition.* It looks as though the Jesus character doesn't want to play by the rules of the opponents. But what rhetorical move is being made with this terse reply? Does Q 4:12 imply that the devil is tempting God in the person of Jesus? Or is Jesus conceding that the promises of God may not be as trustworthy as they appear? Neither seems plausible, for the Q folk have not claimed that Jesus is God; and if they go soft now on the promises of God, they blow their whole case.

Thus another interpretation seems more tenable. The Jesus character is pointing out that what may seem feasible according to the opponents' reading of the Psalms actually is forbidden in the Torah itself. The focus is on the relative authority of two teachings and two ways of teaching.

How does Deuteronomy 6 flesh out this dispute? The sarcasm of the second devil speech has left the Professors chortling, but some people don't appreciate the joke. The Q speakers frame their reply without humor, but they do address the key points raised by their opponents: orthodoxy, the nature of instruction, the love of God, the prolonging of life, and the question of just whose hands or hearts have caught the Torah.

The devil has cited God's promise in Ps. 91:14-15: "Because he loves me I will deliver him; I will protect him *because he knows my name.*" The Jesus character counters with a citation that equates loving God with hearing and obeying God's commands rather than knowing God's name. In Deuteronomy 6, hearing means receiving God's commands into the body as well as the mind. The pairing of *kardia* with *psychē* in v. 6 is a Septuagint innovation; the Hebrew has only *lēbāb.* The heart/mind pairing nicely parallels the hand/eye pairing of v. 8, where the commands of the Lord are to bind both one's hands and one's eyes. The eye, *ophthalmos,* is the organ of seeing; *idein,* the activity through which ideas enter the mind (at least in Greek). Thus, knowing and doing are to be bound alike by God's commands.

Here we have an argument that can be made through the Greek of the Septuagint but not through the Hebrew. The *psychē* of v. 6 had no Hebrew original, while the *psychē* of v. 5 stands for *nepeš* and the *ophthalmos* of v. 8 stands for *ʿāyin.* Neither *nepeš* nor *ʿāyin* has any particular affinity with "ideas" in the Greek sense.

For the Q speakers, Deuteronomy 6 is the real pinnacle of the Temple, the high point of the instruction that God gives to Israel. They make the case that knowing is doing; moreover, both are prompted by hearing. The sequence of the command verbs in Deut. 6:4-9 is significant: *akouō, agapaō, probibazō, laleō, aphaptō, graphō.* "Listen, love, promote, talk about, fasten upon"—and then "write," which comes last. The Hear-O-Israel, vv. 4-9, is to resound throughout daily life. This saying is the true guardian for the door and the gate; thus protected, who would need the angels of Ps. 91:11-12 for a bodyguard?

What the Q speakers hear in Deut. 6:13 is a manumission from servitude. "Fear the Lord your God and work for him only." The Septuagint translation of *ʿābad* here is *latreuō.* The basic meaning of this verb is to work for pay, as hired labor, even though the next verse specifies that what is proscribed here is hiring oneself out to strange gods. Yet the term *latreuō* in Deut. 6:13 is not paired with *proskyneō* as in the formula of Deut. 8:19 and 5:9; and the context of Deut. 6:10-12 emphasizes freedom from manual labor.

The favored one of Psalm 91 has been promised long life for loving God and knowing God's name. By contrast, those to whom Deut. 6:2 promises lengthened life are those who obey God's commands. In 6:24, obedience brings prosperity and continuing life. The righteous one is still living today.

Thus the stakes of the debate have been redefined. The payoff for knowledge in Psalm 91 was protection, honor, and long life; these together amounted to salvation. The payoff for obedience here in Deuteronomy 6 is significantly different: prosperity, the takeover of land, freedom from service to anyone but the Lord (6:13), the vanquishing of enemies, and being continuously kept alive. Perhaps this scenario is what the Q speakers pray and hope for; it seems to imply something of a political program. The configuration of salvation along these particular lines could very well be what first attracted the opposition of the authoritative Professors of the Name.

The second Jesus speech has also challenged the prosecuting devil with several new terms: righteousness, the interests of the landless poor, the propriety of servitude, the character of everlasting life, and international relations. The Q speakers' version of sonship has been reinforced: the son is the one who receives instruction in Deut. 6:7 and 20. The Q version of living well has been reasserted: doing good leads into prosperity, while possessions lead into forgetfulness and the service of someone other than the Lord.

Third Devil Speech, Q 4:5-7

A. *Expanding the Script.* We have now come to the other spot where I must go fishing for a background text, because Q 4:5-7 has no direct quotation. Criteria like the ones used above will be helpful:

1. The text we are looking for should feature some words or concepts that actually appear in Q 4:5-7.
2. The text should be suited to provide the finale, the devil's best hand, a hat trick if possible.
3. The text should be one that could plausibly frame a reply for what has gone before, Q 4:12/Deuteronomy 6; and at the same time/it should provoke the specific response of Q 4:8/Deuteronomy 5.
4. The text should have some affinity with the kind of literature that the devil does quote, Psalm 91.

By these criteria, the Septuagint's Psalm 72 is a good candidate for the veiled background text of the third devil speech.

1. In Q 4:5-7 we have a mountain, kingdoms of the world, glory, giving, obeisance, and service. Psalm 72 has identical terms or close cognates: *orē* in v. 3; *basileus* in vv. 1, 10, 11; *doxēs* in v. 19; *dōra* in v. 10; *propesountai* in v. 9; and *proskynēsousin* and *douleusosin* in v. 11. Both texts link obeisance with immense wealth (although in the psalm, obeisance is not the quid pro quo).

2. Psalm 72 gives the devil quite a trump card. It unveils an economic program and produces the royal son himself, the messiah, the star of the show. But its most stunning coup is not visible in the Septuagint. The Hebrew of Ps. 72:11 says that the royal son will be entitled to receive what is formulaically forbidden toward any but God in Deut. 5:9 and 8:19: *šḥh* and *'bd*, or bowing down and service.[18] This formula is rendered in the Septuagint with *proskyneō . . . douleuō* at Ps. 72:11, but with forms of *proskyneō . . . latreuō* at Deut. 5:9 and 8:19. Moreover, in Ps. 72:9 the royal son gets still another kind of obeisance, *kr'*. So the devil has quite a bit of maneuvering room in framing his demands for service, but at the same time he is rhetorically vulnerable to having his offer misconstrued by way of the Septuagint.

3. Psalm 72 makes a nice follow-up to the second Jesus speech and Deuteronomy 6, with which it shares several themes. The psalm's first verse picks up *ṣedāqāh*, righteousness, from the last verse of Deuteronomy 6 and attributes it to the royal son. This also supplies a mention of sonship to match those of the other two devil speeches, Q 4:3 and 9 (although here the devil wants to play the role of son himself). Like Deuteronomy, Psalm 72 has an economic plan; and like Deuteronomy 6, that plan promises prosperity without work. Both texts have inquiring sons: the one in Deut. 6:20 asks about the meaning of the commandments, while the one in Psalm 72 is a judge. Both texts deal with foreigners, national enemies, long life, destruction, servitude, and the needy.

4. Psalm 72 also makes a nice foil for what follows: Q 4:8/Deuteronomy 5. The fruitful mountains of Ps. 72:3, 16 give way to Horeb in Deuteronomy 5. The psalm's offer of prosperity from world trade sets up the rhetorical foil for Deut. 5:21's prohibition of coveting goods. The psalm's promise to combat oppression, 72:4, 12, 14, leads into the reminder in Deut. 5:6 and 15 that God has already ended oppression. The psalm's concern with land in 72:8-10 and 16 can be answered by Deut. 5:32's promise of land ownership. The foreign services of Ps. 72:10-11 set us up for the limitation of domestic service

---

18. Benjamin Davidson derives *yištaḥawû* from the root *šḥh*; see Benjamin D. Davidson, *The Analytical Hebrew and Chaldee Lexicon* (London: S. Bagster and Sons, n.d.), 361.

in Deut. 5:13-14. The psalm associates longevity with the royal son in 72:5, 15, 17, and life is also the concern of Deut. 5:3, 16, 24-26, and 32. The psalm's blessings on the name of the royal son in 72:17 and the name of God in 72:19 are echoed by Deut. 5:11, which forbids misusing God's name.

5. Psalm 72 is a messianic promise like Psalm 91, which the devil has directly quoted in Q 4:10-11.

B. *Substance of the Third Proposition.* We have arrived at the bottom line. There are two parts to the deal that the devil offers: the demand is for service, but the payoff is to be economic prosperity. It is customary to construe this as an invitation to idolatry, because the Q playwright has used the reply of Jesus to frame it that way. But are there grounds for a more benign interpretation? Is the devil really asking for something that is categorically forbidden? That is to say, in the historical conflict lying behind the fiction of Q 4:1-13, were the opponents of the Q speakers really proposing something offensive to Israelite religion? The answer seems to depend on whether they were exegeting the Greek Pentateuch or doing liturgical theology in the tradition of the Hebrew psalms.

The script that comes down to us is Greek and uses the Septuagint terminology: *pesōn proskynēsēs moi:* "getting down do me obeisance" (Matt. 4:9). This recalls the prohibited *proskyneia + latreia* of Deut. 8:19 and 5:9 but also the *proskyneia + douleia* of Ps. 72:11. The former pair must be given only to God, and given freely, while the latter was for the messianic royal son and would be given under compulsion. But in comparison the Hebrew texts in all three places have the same plain old generic terms: *šḥh* and *'bd*, "bowing down" and "service." These verbs do not reserve any special bowing and service for God, and they do not distinguish between free service of God and involuntary service of human aristocrats.

In Psalm 72, those terms specify something to which the king's son is entitled. In 72:9, desert people bow down, *kr'*, to this aristocrat. In 72:11, all nations bow and serve him, *šḥh* and *'bd*. What is actually involved in this relationship? The term *'abōdāh* is the ordinary Hebrew word for labor, used, for example, in Deut. 5:13, which restricts work on the Sabbath. Of course the Septuagint has various translations for this all-purpose, no-nonsense, sweaty Hebrew verb. At Deut. 5:13, *'ābad* becomes *erdō.* At Deut. 5:9, *'ābad* becomes *latreuō,* connoting worship as a kind of paid labor. At Ps. 72:11, *'ābad* becomes *douleuō,* connoting political subjugation as a kind of slave labor.

If the devil's third proposal is based on an initiative that the Professors of the Name framed in Hebrew, then that initiative may have been something altogether different from an invitation to idolatry. If the Professors asked for *'bd*, they were asking for labor, which is what working people would do for landowning aristocrats. If they asked for *šḥh*, this too was what those in society's upper crust had a right to expect from their inferiors. But if they were asking for *kr'*, that is a more intriguing request. *Kr'*, accorded to the messianic royal son by the desert people in Ps. 72:9, means to crouch down, as an animal might do at a stream to drink. The watery context of 72:6 and 8 contrasts with the desert and dustiness of 72:9 where *kr'* occurs. Thus, bending to quench thirst is a plausible meaning of *kr'* in Psalm 72, and there is a connotational link to the "wetness" of the verb to teach, *yrh*. The one who is the object of *kr'* is the source of benefits, and he may be something of a teacher.

Perhaps, then, the Q folk are being invited to come in out of the Deuteronomic desert, bend down to drink from the stream of the liturgical theology of the Temple faculty, soak up proper modern-day Torah, and stop fomenting lower-class discontent with their quaint old Mosaic economic practices. This is the last, best, and most realistic offer from the Professors of the Name.

The plan for prosperity set forth in Psalm 72 entails an aristocratic administration based in the capital, through which wealth generated by international trade could trickle down to the ordinary people. Of course, this plan conveniently overlooks the fact that wealth actually is flowing in the opposite direction: from the Galilean countryside up to Jerusalem and to Hellenistic cities like Tiberias and Sepphoris. The messiah, whose mandate will be both divine and political, is supposed to defend the afflicted and put a stop to abuses so that this ideal hierarchical society can function smoothly. He will save the poor, 72:4 and 12-14. He "will rule from sea to sea and from the River to the ends of the earth. . . . The kings of Tarshish and of distant shores will bring tribute to him; the kings of Sheba and Seba will present him gifts," 72:8 and 10. And a thousand points of light will glimmer.

This is a dream dreamed in Jerusalem, not in Galilee. To share it with Jesus, the devil has to transport him up to a mountain. In Ps. 72:3 prosperity comes from the mountains—not the mountain of Deuteronomy where Moses spoke but the mountain of Zion and the hill country of Judea, where the aristocracy are based. This interpretation fits historical conditions of first-century Galilee, in which imperial and religious taxation was making the rich richer and the poor poorer.

That gives us the context for the devil's final challenge to Jesus. In his third initiative, the devil is promising to act like the magnanimous royal administrator of Psalm 72 and pass on what he gleans from the kingdoms of the world. This time the People of the Name try giving the Q folk an insider's perspective. They are invited to take in the mountain view, to see how things look from the better neighborhoods. A picture is painted for them in which they are shown how the wealth of the world's kingdoms can be shared if only the Q folk will stop griping about the economic status quo. According to the cheery vision of the Professors of the Name, the common people should serve and the elite should rule. Service to the landed gentry and an updating of Deuteronomy are the strings that they would attach to the people's hope of prosperity.

Third Jesus Speech, Q 4:8

A. *Expanding the Script.* The paraphrase of Deut. 5:9 by Q 4:8 indicates the text that should be used to sketch in the details of the Q folk's response to their opponents' bottom-line offer.

B. *Substance of the Rejection of the Third Proposition.* Jesus says no way. He recites the Decalogue to indicate that the Q folk have already cut a deal on another mountain, Horeb. As for the Name, "You shall not misuse the name of the Lord," Deut. 5:11. As for teachings, the Q speakers are taught by Moses, Deut. 5:1 and 31. As for labor, God has placed limits on the work that can be extracted from working men and women, Deut. 5:13-15. As for ancestral customs, "It was not with our fathers that the Lord made this covenant, but with us," Deut. 5:3. As for long life, *lalesei ho theos pros anthrōpon kai zēsetai:* "God can speak to a human being and the person can go on living," Deut. 5:24.

Voice and hearing are the favored means of divine communication in this passage. "Hear, O Israel, . . . the Lord spoke with you face to face," Deut. 5:1 and 4. God proclaimed the commandments in a loud voice and in deep darkness before writing them on stone, Deut. 5:22; you heard the voice out of the darkness, Deut. 5:23.

Moreover, the Greek of the Septuagint at Deut. 5:8 gives the Q folk the word idol, *eidōlon,* where the Hebrew has *pesel,* literally a carved thing. *Eidōlon* comes from the word for seeing and is thus tied into the realm of visually biased intellectual knowing. The idol is a shape that can be seen. The design of the tetragrammaton, which is scratched onto a surface so that it can be seen, falls well within the definition of an *eidōlon.* If the Temple faculty think that only they, as Hebrew readers, can know the Name that is written and seen but never pronounced or heard, well then the Q folk, who have heard the voice of God booming out of blackness, respond that the visible *yhwh* is no less an idol than any other shape a man might carve.[19]

---

19. These arguments are coherent with those remembered in talmudic discussions of contention between the Tannaim and *minim* (excommunicants) over scrolls and the divine name. See *Šabbat* 115a–116b.

Having handily classified the liturgical scholars as idolators, the Q speakers' spokesman cites the teachings of Moses to prove that what the opponents have proposed is forbidden. But has the Jesus character correctly construed the proposal, or is this some clever rhetorical sleight-of-hand? Jesus' citation is a paraphrase of Deut. 5:9. He says that *proskyneia* and *latreia* are required toward God. Now what the Septuagint actually has said is that *proskyneia* and *latreia* are forbidden in regard to idols. Moreover, the other side has not asked for *proskyneia* and *latreia*, but only *pesōn proskynhsēs* (in Q's rendition) or perhaps simply *ʿbd* and *šḥh* or *krʿ* (in my reconstruction of the terms of the psalmic liturgical theology). The proposal was eminently reasonable. But the playwright has taken full advantage of the Septuagint terminology to make it appear outrageous.

The Q folk in their final response have scored points by switching contexts and switching languages. This is a canny rhetorical move, although it violates the etiquette of sapiential exegesis. The devil concludes that he cannot work with Jesus and leaves in frustration. Not only the content but also the method of the Q speakers' argumentation exasperates the Professors of the Name.

Placing the Inquest

In conducting this excavation of the text of the temptation narrative, I found it expedient to stipulate some assumptions about the socioeconomic identity of the Q folk and their opponents before producing the textual evidence that supported those assumptions. But now, with the evidence in full view, I can state more confidently what the evidence suggests.

The devil's citations, although partly camouflaged by a satirist, indicate a logic founded on reading Hebrew texts and interpreting them by established hermeneutical principles. They also reflect a privileged economic status, a realistic political savvy, and a felt responsibility for the welfare of all social classes. This devil is a learned and leisured aristocrat. He has a benevolent but patronizing attitude toward the people of the land. His ideology is Davidic, Judean, sacerdotal, liturgical, and collaborationist.

Jesus' citations employ rhetorical logic and the quick verbal moves by which a debater seizes advantage in oral combat. They also reflect the tenuous economic status of the mobile artisan class and the anxieties of the landless poor. This Jesus is a grassroots spokesman and a peasant. He does not disdain the people of the land, and he lobbies to return land to the people. His ideology is Mosaic and he takes a dim view of Zion.

Citations on both sides of the debate repeatedly bring up the ominous topic of destruction. The Q speakers and the liturgical theologians exchange warnings about practices that must bring on annihilation. This suggests a historical placing of this story in relation to the calamity of 70 C.E. The stylized drama that comes down to us in Q may have been composed just after the fall of Jerusalem, contemporaneous with the production of Mark's Gospel.

This helps us to decide whether the inquest behind the fiction of Q 4:1-13 was a historical event or a fantasy of the Q sages (assuming that it is more than my own fantasy). It is now clear that there cannot have been an actual inquest, because there is no possible historical placing of the materials that our investigation has disclosed. In an inquest occurring *before* the Jewish uprising of 66–74 C.E., the arguments would not have carried such an ominous undertone of threatening destruction. In an inquest occurring *during* the uprising, it would no longer make sense to cite the psalmic promises of messianic prosperity. In an inquest occurring *after* the destruction of Jerusalem, there could have been no summons to the Temple, no optimistic view from the mountain of Zion. Therefore the inquest took place in the poietic imagination of the Q rhetors after 70 C.E., when the Professors of the Name had graver matters on their minds.

The inquest was fantasy. Yet the lively contention between the Q speakers and their opponents was quite real, and it significantly shapes the Gospel that we have received. But was there actually an oratorical replay of the dispute after the tragedy of 70 C.E. smothered the real thing? It is plausible to suppose that such a theatrical production was indeed staged at least once, by expanding the skeleton script that is found in Q 4:1-13 along the lines that I have suggested. Ironically, if this strategy generated a liturgical drama, then Christianity thus launched a liturgical poiesis of Jesus in place of the Temple liturgical theology now annihilated.

The starkest contrast between the citations of the devil and those of Jesus has to do with the means of perception that are engaged for revelation, teaching, and learning. The devil represents those who favor seeing and showing. Jesus represents those who favor hearing and speaking. The whole debate revolves around salvation: Is it *yešû'āh*, something that we see because we are shown; or is it, *Yēšûa*—*Iēsous*—someone whom we hear because he has listened to God? The victory of the Q speakers, which if truth be told was won by default and not on the merits of their case, turned the tide of Christian teaching in favor of the way of hearing.[20] The final recension of Q displays this story like a pennant flying over the

---

20. This is corroborated by another feature of the Gospels that was noted above: the displacement of paideia terminology with the terminology of hearing and discipling. Yet the tide would turn again with Mark's literary masterpiece.

opening of the words of Jesus. It becomes the new mezuzah on the Gospel's doorpost, encapsulating the prescribed praxis for reading the sayings that live within.[21]

The theme of life—living well, living long, and living continuously until today—is a crescendo that builds throughout the debate. Here is the budding of a resurrection theology. Q has neither a crucifixion nor an empty tomb, and certainly no claims that the living Jesus has been *seen* after Calvary. But as a collection of sayings purportedly from Jesus and meant to be performed on his behalf, Q implicitly claims that the living Jesus is *heard* beyond his natural lifetime and out of mouths other than his own. This claim is counterintuitive and needs to be legitimated. The compilation of promises of life that we have traced throughout the decertification debate is the beginning of that legitimation.

21. At Deut. 6:9, *Targum Onqelos* reads: "and you should inscribe them in Mezuzot and affix them on the doorposts of your houses and of your gates." See Bernard Grossfeld, trans., *The Targum Onqelos to Deuteronomy*, Aramaic Bible, vol. 9 (Wilmington, Del.: Michael Glazier, 1988).

7

Grooming Messiah for Death

THE TEMPTATION narrative at the opening of the Sayings Collection advertises the victory of Deuteronomic hortatory practices over psalmic liturgical practices in the struggle for the identity of Jesus. As chapter 6 argued, the Q material in Matthew and Luke consists of sayings of the Lord that were supposed to be recited, expanded rhetorically, and applied homiletically to changing circumstances. They were *not* supposed to be gazed upon with the eyes or studied textually. How curious, then, that we now see these sayings cut, dried, and mounted on the pages of texts called Luke and Matthew.

The victory of the *Š^ema‘*, in Q's Temptation Play, was short-lived. It would seem that the Q speakers won their war against the text scholars only temporarily. It was only a matter of time until the productive practices of the older culture would be adopted by the newer one, gradually becoming indispensable. So the Sayings of Jesus get written down. Mark the author succeeds where Q's devil failed—at least, on two out of the three proposals. Mark's Jesus offers a *pesel*, an "engraving" or scripture, as bread, and in doing so he pitches himself as *tôrāh*, "instruction." This homage to the written word is the unavoidable price that must be paid for the continuing mutual availability between the Risen Lord and the church. Jesus must be packaged. But the package must be carefully constructed so that it can alternately contain him and let him out. In short, those are the specs for the construction of a narrative gospel. That is what the canonical Gospels are designed to do.

The Gospel text works like the tomb where Jesus was laid after Calvary. It receives the physical result of the crucifixion. It closes over the dead body and ensures its silence henceforth. But then the textual tomb is smashed open again. The stone where Jesus was laid is broken. This fractured tombstone becomes the cornerstone of the church.

The architectural practice, as it were, that accomplishes the building of this church—this ecclesial availability of and to Jesus—is a poiesis: a creatively constructive enterprise. The Gospel text called Mark is one of its blueprints, although the author "Mark" was only one of many textual technicians whose productive labor shaped that text.

The Markan narrative of the passion, death, and resurrection is a structure built with four broken cornerstones: (1) the little *alabastron* crushed for Jesus' messianic anointing at Mark 14:3; (2) the loaf broken at Mark 14:22; (3) the body violated at Mark 15:15-25; and (4) the tombstone dislodged at Mark 16:4. Vial, loaf, body, tomb: Mark did not quarry these "stones" directly from the bedrock of history so called. Rather, like most builders in the ancient Near East, he scavenged blocks that had been used already in earlier structures. All of his stories were previously told. Switching metaphors, one could also say that Mark snipped and cut his fabric from the webwork of Jesus stories continually being spun out in the oral performances of the Jesus movements known to him. He may also have pieced in some patches cut from earlier texts. The design is Mark's; the material comes from many hands and mouths.

How, then, does Mark style Jesus the messiah? This Gospel establishes and stabilizes a version of Jesus that first was produced by someone else. Its inventor was the woman who is credited in Mark 14:9. That verse serves as both a citation attributing credit and an assurance that the information is authoritative because of its source. The anointing of Jesus is the mimetic inscription of his christological identity upon his body as a destining for death. The anointing was an event of ecclesial poiesis occurring after Calvary. The woman's poiesis of Jesus as anointed-for-death is "her memory": that is, the distinctive memory or version of Jesus that is her gift to the church. Mark's text conveys the sense that the woman's work made a messiah out of Jesus:

(14:6) *Iēsous eipen* . . .	Jesus said . . .
kalon ergon ērgasato en emoi . . .	She has made a good work out of me.
ho eschen epoiēsen	She has given shape to the way things are going.

(14:8) *proelaben*
  myrisai to sōma mou
  eis ton entaphiasmon
	She has gotten a head start on
	    anointing my body
	    toward burial.

(14:9) *amēn de legō humin*   So I swear to you,

hopou ean kērychthē to euangelion   wherever the gospel is announced
  eis holon ton kosmon   into the whole world

kai ho epoiēsen autē   also what she wrought
  lalēthēsetai   will be talked about
eis mnēmosynon autēs.   in her memory.

Her memory is her "take," her version of what was happening with Jesus. In the phrase *mnēmosynon autēs*, the possessive "her" has been interpreted by Elisabeth Schüssler Fiorenza and others as an *objective* genitive.[1] That reading makes the story of the anointing a story in which the woman is the one who should be remembered. I would instead interpret the "her" as a *subjective* genitive, so that the anointing is the woman's poiesis: what she has made out of Jesus, her memory of him.[2] Her work is what will be remembered. Out of all possible versions of Jesus, it is *her* memory, *her* poiesis, that becomes the gospel. This woman was a spinner of Jesus stories, and in turn she was spun into the recitation of the stories by subsequent tellers, among whom was Mark.

It is beside the point to try to assign a name or an individual authorial identity to "her." Quite likely, "she" was a "them"—but, very significantly, a feminine them. Their naming praxis, not their names, is the important thing. The tableau recounted by Mark is an event constructed out of a practice.[3] The story artfully places Jesus among diners whose company cannot have convened until after his death, and it places in Jesus' own mouth the decisive approval of an interpretation of his fate that has been under discussion by the diners.

The *symposion* was a social institution among whose principal functions were the maintenance of upper-class personal alliances and the

1. Hence the title of Elisabeth Schüssler Fiorenza's recovery of the memories about the activities of early Christian women, *In Memory of Her: A Feminist Theological Reconstruction of Christian Origins* (New York: Crossroad, 1984).

2. *En* plus the dative indicates the raw material out of which something has been constructed, and also the instrumentality through which it was accomplished. *En emoi* here compares with the Pauline expression *en Christō*; see also Matt. 9:34 and parallels. John Dominic Crossan suggests in passing that Mark 14:9 can be interpreted as an oblique signature of the author. See Crossan, *The Historical Jesus*, 416.

3. Representing a familiar process with a paradigmatic but invented event was a technique whose results are detectable in several places in the Gospel narratives. John Dominic Crossan proposes this kind of genesis for stories about meals of bread and fish, e.g. See Crossan, *The Historical Jesus*, 331, 396.

memorializing of heroic deeds and virtues through poetic recitation.[4] The *symposion* was one among several types of formal banquets, and it involved lengthy discussion among a circle of intimates (*hetairoi*) who reciprocated hospitality on a regular basis. Among elite hellenized Jews the custom can easily have fused with that of the voluntary pious association or *ḥaburah*, but would have imported class exclusivity into the latter. Jesus did not attend *symposia* before Calvary. Nevertheless Mark's vocabulary associates the so-called anointing of Jesus with such a situation: reclining (*katakeimenou*, 14:3), poietic performance (*kalon ergon . . . epoiēsen*, 14:3, 6, 8), memory (*mnēmosynon*, 14:9), pledging faith (*pistikēs*, 14:3), and intense discussion (*aganaktountes, lalēthēsetai*, 14:4, 9).

This suggests a *symposion* where Jesus' death is the focus of the artistic performance and the conversation. A women's histrionic work has proposed to the symposiasts that Jesus died obediently, faithfully, divinely, and freely. The script with this reading of Jesus' death is no longer available to us. We do not know whether it was a pantomime (as the story suggests), a drama, an epigram or lyric, an epitaph, or another of the performance genres culturally attested for banquets in the Greco-Roman period. But we are given to understand that this interpretation of Jesus' stance toward his own death caused consternation amid the assembled company. There are divergent explanations of why. Luke mentions horror at the touch of a sinful woman; the other Gospels cite neglect of charitable obligations. This divergence indicates that the canonical accounts all branched off from an earlier story of an anointing.[5] That earlier story, I suggest, was itself the precipitate of a prior practice of women's talking and teaching about Jesus in the years immediately following his death.

This practice grew out of the grieving customs of elite hellenized Jewish women in the city of Jerusalem. It can be recovered historically as the prehistory of the Gospels: a clustering of teaching procedures and themes associated with the constituency who were identifying Jesus as messiah anointed for death yet not claimed by it. Thus we may imagine a

---

4. See Wolfgang Rösler, "*Mnemosyne* in the *Symposion*," 230–37, in *Sympotica: A Symposium on the* Symposion, ed. Oswyn Murray (Oxford: Clarendon Press, 1990).

5. See Burton L. Mack, "The Anointing of Jesus: Elaboration within a Chreia," 85–106, in Mack and Robbins, *Patterns of Persuasion in the Gospels*. Mack suggests that an earlier challenge/response pair has been displaced with different objections in Mark and Luke. In my view, the underlying objection to the anointing was the disciples' protest that the messiah should not have to die.

Figure 4. Compositional History of the Anointing

A	The disaster at Calvary becomes known.

B	Hellenized Jewish women gather in a *gynaikōn* to grieve over Jesus. They come to accept his death as meaningful and deliberate. They synthesize a coherent account of his identity.

C	This women's christological interpretation of Jesus' career and fate is presented to members of a *symposion/ḥaburah*. It is discussed and debated, and found to be convincing.

D	The consensus of that *symposion/ḥaburah* is expressed in a dramatic composition that portrays Jesus as agreeing to die, notwithstanding the objections of his companions. In the play, Jesus pledges his fidelity by allowing the *myron pistikon* to be poured over his head.	the messiah shouldn't die —— BUT —— I must die because . . . ?

E	This dramatization is presented for other *symposia/ḥaburot,* and it succeeds in establishing the notion of Jesus as slain messiah. But various objections now are raised against the woman's role. So Jesus is given new lines to answer those objections.

F	The anointing stories, featuring various objections and replies, circulate orally in several versions beyond the *symposia/ḥaburot* where originally performed. These versions are available to the writers of the Gospels:

you should have helped the poor —— BUT —— you always have them but not me	this woman is a sinner —— BUT —— great forgiveness evokes great love	other challenges . . . ? —— BUT —— other responses . . . ?

G	**Mark,** where the last supper copies the breaking but adds the note of vicarious bloodshed.	**Matthew,** where the last supper copies the breaking but connects vicarious bloodshed to forgiveness of sins.	**John,** where the last supper copies the foot bath, great love, impending departure.	**Luke,** where the last supper copies the remembrance but transposes it to vicarious bloodshed. (Anointing is detached from crucifixion.)

compositional history for Mark 14:3-9 with the seven stages suggested in Figure 4.

Mark mortars the story into his novel argument that the death of Jesus was a sacrifice; however, the salvific sacrificial motif is a secondary interpretation of christhood. What founds the canonical gospel tradition is the poiesis of women. We can hear them at work in a skein of stories going the rounds of the Greek-speaking Jesus communities toward the middle of the first century.

Grooming Jesus for Resurrection

To get at these stories, one must reach back into an oral practice, but at this distance in time that means reaching through the texts, that is, through the several versions in which the stories have been written down. (In terms of the compositional history in Figure 4, one works through the written texts at level G in hopes of finding levels C and B, where women's perceptions of Jesus were first formulated and presented to a wider circle.) The skein of stories is tangled. Any strand selected inevitably will be tied to another and another, so that eventually some will have to be snipped off in order to get a bundle of manageable size to examine.[6]

My attempt to isolate the traditions about the woman who anoints Jesus yields nine texts from the canonical Gospels. (These are listed in Figure 5.) The first four are "parallels," that is, they are recognized by modern scholars as being a set of stories about "the same event" with some kind of literary dependence among them. This set goes by the title "The Anointing at Bethany." The ubiquity of the story is remarkable in itself. Each of our four canonical Gospels has a version: Matt. 26:6-13; Mark 14:3-9; Luke 7:36-50; and John 12:1-8. Moreover, the woman who anoints Jesus is quite a flexible character. Mark's anointer breaks her vial to pour the contents on Jesus' head. Matthew's simply pours the vial over Jesus' head. Luke's anointer is identified as a sinner, and she pours her vial over Jesus' feet after weeping upon them and wiping them with her

---

6. E.g., the *Secret Gospel of Mark* also preserves a story in which a woman is rebuked for approaching Jesus and her brother then is raised from the dead. These features would qualify the story to be considered alongside the stories included in the comparative analysis to be presented here.

hair. John's anointer has become Mary of Bethany, Jesus' pupil, and she too anoints only the feet and wipes them with her hair.

Because the tradition of the anointing known to John identifies the anointer as Mary of Bethany, a fifth story can be pulled out of the skein: Luke 10:38-42, "Mary and Martha." There is no recognized textual "parallel" for that story. However, it does share some details with the Lukan and Johannine versions of the anointing: for example, Jesus' defense of Mary's initiative as "a good thing"; Mary's silent eloquence; and Mary's association with the feet of Jesus.

John's tradition connects yet another thread to the anointing with the name of Lazarus, who is said to be present at the table when Mary goes after Jesus' feet. This and other similarities pull out two more stories. "The Raising of Lazarus" in John 11:1-44 has the same characters present as at Bethany for the anointing. "The Parable of the Rich Man and Lazarus" in Luke 16:19-31 has interesting resonances with the anointing and/or with "The Raising of Lazarus": for example, surviving the grave, a dining room setting, and oral contact with someone hairy: a dog or a dog-like woman with undone hair.

Finally, the dogs and the snatching of table crumbs from the Lazarus parable now tug out yet another strand, the two parallel versions of "The Syrophoenician Woman," Matt. 15:21-28 and Mark 7:24-30. She is also someone who despite a rebuff successfully defends her access to "the table" where Jesus' power is available.

In summary, then, these nine passages comprise five interrelated stories, as "parallels" usually are reckoned. They can be consolidated further into three themes: (1) grooming Jesus: the care and feeding of the messianic teacher; (2) the bitch under the table; (3) surviving the grave. Figure 5 shows how these stories are related to one another. The distribution of thirty selected narrative elements in the nine passages shows significant similarities across the three themes as well as significant divergences within each. The chart presumes no *literary* dependence between any two versions, such that one would be a rewrite of the other. Rather, it assumes that these nine are a sample of the possibilities for combining the elements in a constantly adapting oral repertoire.

A thoughtful examination of Figure 5 will suggest numerous intriguing approaches to the theories, imaginative associations, and practices current among early Christian communities. Only two lines of inquiry will be pursued here: the distinctive Lukan management of the anointing of Jesus and the role of Jesus' messianic grooming within the Markan architecture of the passion, death, and resurrection of a Christ.

THEMES	TRADITIONAL TITLES	TEXTS			
		Mt	Mk	Lk	Jn
Grooming Jesus: the care and feeding of the messianic teacher	"The Anointing at Bethany" "Mary and Martha"	26:6-13	14:3-9	7:36-50 10:38-42	12:1-8
The bitch under the table	"The Syrophoenician Woman"	15:21-28	7:24-30		
Surviving the grave	"The Raising of Lazarus" "Parable of Rich Man and Lazarus"			16:19-31	11:1-45

What Luke Makes of the Anointing

Luke has undeservedly enjoyed a reputation as a woman-friendly author because his text seems to address women directly rather often, because it preserves the Mary story, because it mentions women accompanying and supporting Jesus' road show (Luke 8:1-3), and because Luke's second volume, the Acts of the Apostles, places women among the disciples praying before Pentecost (Acts 2:14). Yet Figure 5 discloses that there is something suspicious about Luke and women, when compared with other treatments of these traditions.

The Syrophoenician woman turns up missing in Luke. This is surprising, given that her story makes such a point of defending the place of Gentiles in the Jesus movement, a cause fundamental to the Lukan agenda.[7] Why doesn't Luke make use of this handy material? Perhaps the

7. Since Luke leaves out a large block of Mark's text containing the story, Mark 6:45–8:26, it might be argued that the omission had nothing to do with the shameless

	1	2	3	4	5	6	7	8	9	10	11	12	13	14	15	16	17	18	19	20	21	22	23	24	25	26	27	28	29	30
1 = life beyond the grave																														
2 = faith; persuasion																														
3 = teacher, teaching, learner, prophet, warning																														
4 = outlaw woman																														
5 = burial, walling off, gates, chasms																														
6 = breaking of rock: "alabastron," tombstone																														
7 = anointing or christ-naming by a woman																														
8 = reproach or hassle for a woman																														
9 = objection to an impropriety																														
10 = defense of allocation of a good thing or portion																														
11 = table																														
12 = scraps that fall from table																														
13 = the poor																														
14 = extravagance, calculation, comparison																														
15 = repartee with Jesus																														
16 = silent eloquence of a key character																														
17 = hairy things: unbound hair, stray dogs, house dogs																														
18 = unbinding, forgiveness																														
19 = weeping, tears, saliva																														
20 = kissing, licking																														
21 = feet of Jesus																														
22 = head of Jesus																														
23 = rotting flesh, sores, a leper																														
24 = intimacy while reclining																														
25 = a house																														
26 = "Martha"																														
27 = "Mary"																														
28 = "Lazarus"																														
29 = "Jesus"																														
30 = "Bethany"																														

(The grid of data marks associated with the above numbered categories appears in the original as rows of X's arranged in three blocks.)

	1	2	3	4	5	6	7	8	9	10	11	12	13	14	15	16	17	18	19	20	21	22	23	24	25	26	27	28	29	30
		X		X		X	X	X	X			X	X		X		X						X	X		X				X	X
	X			X	X	X	X	X	X			X	X		X		X						X	X	X	X				X	X
		X	X	X			X			X	X	X			X		X	X	X	X	X	X	X		X	X				X
	X	X	X			X		X	X		X			X	X		X	X				X			X	X	X	X	X	X
		X								X	X				X	X						X			X	X	X	X		
		X	X	X					X	X	X	X	X			X		X				X							X	
		X							X	X	X	X	X			X		X				X			X					
	X	X	X			X	X	X		X					X	X			X	X		X		X	X	X	X	X	X	X
	X		X		X	X			X	X	X	X	X	X			X			X	X			X	X	X			X	

story is untellable amid Luke's community because his gentile women colleagues would be offended by Jesus' insult: "It isn't good to take bread out of children's mouths and throw it to the dogs."[8] Were there, then, no women among the Greek readers of Mark and Matthew? Or were they less in control of purse strings? Or were they less easily offended by being likened to bitches?

Perhaps the logic of the insult itself can provide a clue. The wisecrack is quite Greek. It originates with someone who knows the range of misogynist slurs available in Greek culture (and who probably wasn't Jesus of Nazareth). Now Hebrew and Aramaic imaginations also were well equipped with epithets to ridicule women, such as the dripping roof, the

woman begging at Jesus' feet. On the other hand, perhaps the story of this woman tainted the material around it, in Luke's estimation. A common factor in the excised material is its tendency to offend or disgust readers of a certain sophistication.

8. Literally, whelps or puppies: canine sucklings. Since the Syrophoenician woman was asking for something for her own child, the dominical analogy makes her the bitch.

whore, the moth, the bear, and the temptress;[9] but "bitch" was not among them. It was the Greeks who gave us that curious epithet. The ancient poet Simonides (whose work was written for recitation at *symposia*), enumerating the different kinds of beasts that women were divinely created to resemble, wrote this:

> Another he made from a bitch, vicious, own daughter of her mother, who wants to hear everything and know everything. She peers everywhere and strays everywhere, always yapping. . . . A man cannot stop her by threatening, nor by losing his temper and knocking out her teeth with a stone, nor with honeyed words, not even if she is sitting with friends, but ceaselessly she keeps up a barking you can do nothing with.[10]

The behaviors that this poem ascribes to the man are of course shameful: violence, anger, deception. However, the behaviors ascribed to the dog are not so bad: persistence, curiosity, initiative, wanting to hear and know everything. Used as an epithet, *kyōn* imputes shamelessness and audacity.[11] The English word "bitch" simply means a mature female dog, and it is not a curse word in rural America. As it happens, there were women in Hellenistic society who did not mind being compared to bitches. In fact, they took it as a compliment. They were Cynic philosophers.

The Cynics were popular wandering philosophers of the Hellenistic era. The more flamboyant among them went out of their way to violate social conventions, which they considered unnatural. Their name comes from *kyōn*, dog, because their contemporaries described their obnoxious deportment as canine. Rhetorical practices characteristic of the Cynic school are in evidence in the texts of the Synoptic Gospels, as was noted in an earlier chapter. That would indicate Cynic influence, at least indirectly, in the compositional process. Some people who found the

---

9. See Prov. 20:13; Sir. 9:1-9; 25:15-17.

10. Translated by Hugh Lloyd-Jones. Greek text and translation appear in *Females of the Species: Semonides on Women* (Parkridge, N.J.: Noyes Press, 1975).

11. The noun *kyōn* has the same form for masculine and feminine gender, so its definite article, *ho* or *hē*, determines whether it should be translated "male dog" or "bitch." Moreover, this form *kyōn* is also the (masculine) present participle of the verb *kyō*, meaning to be pregnant and to carry in the womb. In Greek a participle can stand alone as a substantive, to mean "someone who is pregnant, expectant mother." So the very structure of the language tends to disparage motherhood as a dog-like condition.

Cynic style appealing must also have found something to like in the Jesus *chreiai*, and they were attracted to the Jesus movement. A Cynic
Christian constituency was active in early Christianity—perhaps con-
troversially so. The Syrophoenician woman in Mark and Matthew
sounds very much like one of them.

This suggests another motive for Luke's dispensing with that
story. Far from fearing to insult the women of his community, *Luke may
have wished to avoid encouraging them.* Bitch-Cynicism was flourishing
among the Jesus movements. It was common enough, and creditable
enough, so that dominical approval of it turns up in two of the four
canonical Gospels. What was its agenda? According to the stories we
have, Christian Bitch-Cynicism was a friendly and witty assault upon
the table, which succeeded in winning a share of the heirs' food for the
Bitch-Christians and their offspring. According to the stories we *don't*
have, Christian Bitch-Cynicism also was, in the eyes of some other teachers, a shocking, dangerous, improper, and thoroughly unacceptable
movement. Opponents arose to defend the table and the teaching from
the Bitch-Christians.

Textually, this defense was made in two moves: conveniently forgetting to tell the story of the Syrophoenician woman and moving the
women characters in other stories away from the table, the cross, and the
capacity for christological poiesis. In Luke's tradition, the story of the Syrophoenician Bitch-Cynic is not just ignored but counteracted by means of
two other special Lukan stories: "Mary and Martha" and "The Parable of
the Rich Man and Lazarus." A comparison of the structures of the latter
stories with that of the Syrophoenician is revealing. Both of the special
Lukan stories are about lines of demarcation that must not be crossed.
Each ratifies "a portion" as it has been allotted in the status quo. On one
hand, the rich man in torment wants someone to traverse the great chasm
between himself and Lazarus after death, just as in life table crumbs could
have been tossed across the social barrier. But Father Abraham forbids it.
On the other hand, Martha wants some help with the serving from her
inactive and silent sister, but Luke's Jesus declines to allow that portion to
be taken from that lady. These two Lukan stories are sympathetic to privilege (albeit, in the case of Lazarus, ironically so). In contrast, the Syrophoenician Bitch-Cynic succeeds where the rich man and Martha fail.
She crosses the chasm, thanks to her own wits, and she gets herself that
portion she has begged for.

Luke wants none of this dominical precedent for ecclesial reapportion-
ment. He politely neglects to remember the names of women standing at the

cross (Luke 23:49).[12] He remarks that women's words about resurrection seemed of course like nonsense (Luke 24:11). In the same spirit, the Lukan tradition reworks the story of the woman's anointing that sent Jesus on his way to Calvary. In Luke's Gospel the story of the anointing is in no sense a messianic identification. It is detached from the passion sequence and removed from Bethany. In Luke's telling, only the feet are anointed. The motive is not "for burial" but for great love and, presumably, for great remorse. The anointer herself is redesigned as an extremely sensuous and emotional character. She cries all over Jesus' feet, wipes them with her unbound hair, and kisses them before slathering them with ointment.

Honed now to a Lukan point, the story illustrates forgiveness. Instead of the one who identifies the messiah, the woman now is a repentant offender who can be told, "Your sins are forgiven. . . . Go in peace"—but *do go*. Here we have the Lukan fantasy for a happy ending to the ecclesiastical careers of the Christian Bitch-Cynics and all troublesome females. Luke's tradition "converts" the prophetic messiah-designator into a sniveling bundle of emotion. It reconstructs the christological identification at Bethany as an acknowledgment of personal sin and a gesture of lowly physical service. Humble charity is the better part for women—emotional and loving and doggedly faithful as they are. Luke, reputed great champion of the egalitarian Spirit, has a glass ceiling after all. He follows the Pauline rule: accept their money and their service, but not their words.

Down Girl

The politics of the table was a significant formative influence on the gospel traditions. It is interesting that three of the themes invoked in the Lukan program for pushing women away from the table also turn up in John's text, right back there again at *the* table, the last supper narrative. John has foot washing as the great act of dominical teaching and self-revelation (John 13:3-17). John also has the dominical "new commandment: love one another" (John 13:34-35). At the Johannine table, love is the precondition for revelation of the identity of Jesus and the Father. Third, John has the gift of peace given at the table (John 14:27). (Power to forgive sin, however, is not

12. In Greek etiquette, a gentleman would mention the names of women in public only if he wanted to deliver a severe insult to their male relatives among his peers. (Funeral eulogies were the one exception.) See David M. Schaps, "The Woman Least Mentioned: Etiquette and Women's Names," *Classical Quarterly* 27 (1977): 323–30.

given until the evening of the day of the resurrection, John 20:22.) Even at Mark's and Matthew's table at Bethany, the suggestion that the messiah-designator should attend instead to charity is interjected between her poiesis and its ratification, although here the suggestion is overruled (Matt. 26:9, 11; Mark 14:5, 7).

The politics of the table was related, curiously, to the politics of hair. In both Luke's and John's versions of the anointing, Jesus' feet are wiped with the woman's hair, which must be unbound and flowing in order for that to happen. The customary Septuagint word for worship, adopted in the Gospels, is *proskyneō*. In that term the basic meaning of *kyneō*, to nuzzle or blow kisses toward, is modified with the prefix *pros*, indicating a prostration in order to kiss or to beg like dogs (*kynes*). We know how unsettling it was for someone like Paul of Tarsus to see women with loose hair at worship.[13] Yet much more is at stake here than a matter of decorum, custom, or taste. In the anointing story, a clue comes from the terminological variation between "pouring upon the head," in Mark's and Matthew's versions, and "smearing the feet," in Luke's and John's versions. With the former, the woman stands over Jesus and drizzles ointment into Jesus' hair; in the latter, she crouches and uses her own hair to absorb the ointment and the tears.

When Mark's text says that the woman "poured" the sweet ointment on Jesus' head (*katecheen autou tēs kephalēs*), it does not use the expected verb *myrizō* to indicate that she rubbed, daubed, or smeared him with it. (This verb will be used later in Jesus' interpretation of the pouring as anointing: *myrisai* in Mark 14:8.) Yet in fact there was a custom among the Greeks according to which a woman threw something sweet over someone else's head. Mark's text alludes to that custom with the verb *katacheō*. *Katachysmata* (literally, "things dropped") means dessert food, sweet spicy treats, goodies. But the term also signifies the domestic ritual through which the senior wife would welcome a newcomer to her household. Standing before the hearth, the matron would toss a handful of sweets over the head of a new daughter-in-law or a slave newly purchased (that is, a slave of non-Greek ethnicity perhaps captured in war). This gesture asserted the matron's authority over the bride or the slave[14] and at the same

---

13. See 1 Cor. 11:4-16. Peter Brown points out that flowing female hair continued to trouble Tertullian. See Brown, *The Body and Society*, 80–81.

14. Their status is remarkably alike, since both bride and slave are from outside the kin group and therefore owe their labor to the kin group but are denied the free use of the fruits of their own labor. The young wife gradually acquires kin status as she gives birth to

time promised to fulfill the responsibility of providing for the needs of the new member of the household.[15]

The custom of the *katachysmata*, "shower," asserts the authority of the mature woman as head of her household. The authority, wealth, and largesse of elite women also could be expressed in municipal gifts together with public service or *leitourgia*. Civic offices entailed benefactions. An important bequest to a city was to provide for the needs of the *gymnasion*, especially olive oil.[16] The lady benefactors probably did not personally teach in the *gymnasion* or personally pour out the oil for the athletes, but their control of (olive) oil-producing estates is attested by their extravagant generosity. It is often noted that the public civic role of elite women in the Roman period departs from the earlier custom whereby women remained unnoticed and unmentioned. But perhaps this exception proves the rule. The Greco-Roman city, functioning as a vehicle of hellenization and then of cultural and political control across the empire, was reimagined as one large house.[17] A woman of the ruling class was therefore "at home" wherever she went in the public buildings to administer her household, the polis. However, elite women of

---

heirs, while the slave may earn freedom in various ways, e.g., by bearing a slave child to take her place or by going into business to earn her purchase price.

15. Eva Keuls misses the point of the ceremony when she says that a new bride was greeted with a shower of nuts; see Eva C. Keuls, *The Reign of the Phallus: Sexual Politics in Ancient Athens* (New York: Harper & Row, 1985), 6, 124, 127. Aristophanes (5–4 century B.C.E.) illustrates the custom. One of his characters, Karion's wife, wishes to present *katachysmata*, or "welcoming gifts," when her husband brings the god Plutus ("Wealth") home to dinner. (See *Plutus* 764–801.) This may look to us like the simple courtesy of a hostess; however, given the meaning of the custom, the wife is signaling her intent to place the wealth-giving god permanently in service in her household. In Athenaeus (ca. 200 C.E.), however, *katachysmata* appears with a more generic sense, "sprinklings," that is, condiments. (See Athenaeus, *Deipnosophistae* 2.76.15 and 9.61.10.) The word can also mean sauce or gravy. Yet this sort of pouring still signifies a seasoning, a change in status.

16. Mendora of the second-century C.E. Pisidian city of Sillyon reputedly supplied 220,000 denarii worth of oil for the *gymnasion*, according to Riet Van Bremen, "Women and Wealth," in Cameron and Kuhrt, *Images of Women in Antiquity* (see chap. 2, n. 18), 223. Van Bremen documents women as *gymnasiarchoi*. Historians have speculated that such offices were merely honorary in the case of elite women, but it is not clear that they were any less so in the case of elite men. However, Mary Lefkowitz argues that women did not participate in the processes of government; see "Influential Women," in Cameron and Kuhrt, *Images of Women in Antiquity*, 49–64.

17. This is the thesis of Van Bremen. Thus under the system of euergetism ("good-works-ism"), the elite woman's civic benefactions became *katachysmata*—goodies—by which she asserted her benevolent authority over the polis as her household and its people as her retainers.

slightly lower rank still remained secluded and unnamed, at least until after death.

The word for pouring in Mark 14:3 and Matt. 26:7, *katachein,* means "to shower down, to throw down," and in the middle voice "to let flow down," especially the hair.[18] One recalls that in Hebrew, "instruction" also was imagined as something thrown or rained down from above: *tôrāh.* Here the conceptual switch from flowing ointment/instruction to flowing hair is easily made with a switch from the active to the middle voice. One pours ointment; one lets one's hair flow. But the course of the woman's instruction is detoured and reversed narratively in Luke and John by positioning her body beneath Jesus', by deflecting her action from his head to his feet, and by diverting attention to the odd use of her hair as a scrub rag. Moreover, the generation of hair as a key narrative detail in the stories preserved by Luke and John is difficult to explain in any other way than as a diversion of the import of the *katachysmata*/cate-chesis of the messiah-maker, as she was known to Mark and Matthew. For the tradition preserved in Luke 7 and John 12, the unruly flowing hair is styled now no longer as authoritatively catechetical but as the badge of the sinner. This caricature serves to mock and discredit the prophetic women from whom had flowed a messianic anointing, a chris-tological teaching. That teaching is given to others—for example, to Peter after Pentecost. Yet even in her disheveled Lukan state, the anointing woman apparently was too important to leave out of the text. The founda-tional fact of her poiesis had to be dealt with, one way or another.

The Markan Architecture: Blueprints

Mark has dealt with the women's christological poiesis of Jesus by laying it as the cornerstone of his passion narrative. Their teaching about Jesus is *fashioned into an event* occurring during the career of Jesus. That "event" had already congealed in the performance tradition before Mark, and he appropriates it whole. In Mark's text, the woman teaches *even Jesus* who he is. She offers the first formulation of his identity that Mark's Jesus can accept. Moreover, Jesus will even mime her action later

---

18. *Katacheō* would also be a variant spelling of *katēcheō:* "to teach by word of mouth, to sound a thing in one's ears." Even in standard Attic spelling, the distinction between the two terms could be seen but not heard.

in the self-identifying *fractio panis* at the Seder table. As Mark's passion narrative designs things, the breaking of bread is a promise fulfilled in the breaking of Jesus' body on the cross, while the breaking of the alabaster flask is a prophecy fulfilled by the violation of the closure of the tomb. The ointment is called *pistikēs*, an adjective related to the terms for belief and rhetorical persuasion. *Pistis*, "faith," is also the term that denoted the loyalty of *symposium* companions to one another as well as the daring deeds that they would pledge themselves to do in confirmation of that bond.[19] In Mark's story, the anointing amidst a *symposion* challenged Jesus to die for *pistis*, and he accepted.

Somewhere in the past of Mark's text, women had made a good thing out of Jesus. Now in his turn the author of Mark also poietically produces another good message—*euangelion*—using the women's earlier poietic catechesis as his raw material. If Mark wrote his text about the year 70 C.E., then the "original" women's catechetical identification of Jesus lay some three decades behind him in his past. The edge of its originality had long since worn away. Yet the association of Jesus' messianic identity with an impropriety involving women was retained in versions of the anointing story that were available in the Christian repertoire for Mark to use as he would. Mark's text also preserves hints of matronly authority reinforced by economic and class status. The *myron* is originally a *katachysma*, a shower that seasons and redefines the status of its target. In Mark the *myron* reveals and enacts the christhood (anointedness) of Jesus at a point in the narrative when the christological characterization starts to escalate toward Calvary. But behind the Markan *myron* is some older discourse in which the memory of Jesus was refashioned to match the specifications for a christ who was not yet a self-immolating priest.

That christological, christogenic discourse was *katachysmata*, the gift of matrons. Its *Sitz im Leben* was the women's apartments or *gynaikōn* within elegant homes of certain hellenized Jews, where matrons met and mourned for Jesus and talked about him among themselves. This fits perfectly well with elite women's customs as known to us from secular sources (and would fit equally well with the religious customs of *ḥaburot* and sisterhood burial societies). In other words, it was the *gynaikōn* whose closed doors the Spirit first penetrated; and the first sight of a risen Christ came through women's tears.[20] Mark's story commemorates the consternation that greeted this

---

19. On *pistis* as conspiratorial pledge or dare, see Murray, *Sympotica;* 7, 153.

20. As Crossan has suggested, Scripture verses about weeping and looking upon a pierced animal were vehicles of protochristological reflection. Zechariah 12:10 is the focal verse. See Crossan, *The Historical Jesus,* 246, 376–79.

"shower" when it was brought out of the *gynaikōn*, into the *andrōn* (men's dining hall), and up to the table.

The Markan characterization of Jesus rides upon a prior redesign engineered by women who were both weepers and anointers. These women made something good out of Jesus. At first among themselves, and later more widely, these christifying women are teachers. Their discussions confect belief. The *myron* is called *pistikēs*, connoting both faith and persuasion. This *myron* induces belief (*peithō/pistis*), as distinguished from learning (*manthanō/ēpistēme*). The notion of "something thrown" makes a startling connection between the Greek and Hebrew sensibilities: Greek *katacheō* translates Hebrew *yārāh*, and *katachysma* translates *tôrāh*, "instruction." Thus the christ-making matrons' *katachysma* is identified with Torah.

Well in advance of Markan composition, then, there was a practice of women's constructive discussion among themselves, in which they grieved for Jesus and together re-remembered him. This was a rhetorical practice; it was *pistikos*, persuasive. In the midst of their gatherings was forged the distinctive understanding of Christic identity that would supply the infrastructure for Gospels. As yet, there was neither "last supper" nor "empty tomb." The circle of matrons met to mourn the untimely death of a beloved young man and to cherish their recollections of him. Weeping women tried to find some sense in their bereavement. They comforted one another with assurances that the dear departed had been enfolded in divine care, and they framed expectations of reunion and vindication.

The matrons' rhetoric crystallized the selection and application of Septuagint passages to Jesus, although it did not continue very long. Allusions to tortures and a rag lottery, first compiled by the grieving women, later entered the gospel tradition as details of the passion narrative. In Mark's narrative artifact, the identification of Jesus as death-destined anointed one has been loaded into an event sited at Bethany. The tableau functions both to inaugurate the passion and to encapsulate a series of teachings that have been discursively laid out in the text already. Mark's Jesus is identified as messiah in a stunning symbolic action that reveals teacher and disciple to one another and to themselves. That Gospel in pantomime "says," on behalf of the Markan disciple, what the broken bread will "say" for the messianic teacher: Here is my body. Take it, it's yours. The vial represents the woman's body, as the bread will represent Jesus' body. A little perfume vial worn around the neck on a cord was the emblem of the proper married woman in Greek society. Many of the ones that have been unearthed in the eastern Mediterranean region were made of glass. Illustrations painted on vases employ the *alabastron* as a symbol of the matron in her home.[21] To smash the emblem of one's matronly respectability would be a shocking and foolish gesture, if done in real life. It makes better sense as the climax of a pantomime performed to dramatize and reinterpret the meaning of a troubling prior event. The same may be said for the eucharist.

Mark's text, then, aligns two great blocks of early Christian masonry that may not have fit together before: messianic theory and eucharistic practice. This text has come up with a solution, a compromise, a synthesis. It builds a new house with rooms in it for the several Jesus factions, who had not been able to cohabitate otherwise.

The social synthesis at work in Mark's text has been the subject of escalating scholarly investigation. The major incongruence that Mark had to finesse, according to Burton Mack's reconstruction, lay between the Aramaic-Jewish and Greco-Jewish Jesus movements, on the one hand, and a Hellenistic Christ cult, on the other. The Christ cult was interpreting what happened to Jesus as a martyrdom, employing the Greek ideology of "the noble death," *mimesis,* and "losing one's life in order to save it."[22] They met for ritual meals to "remember" the death of Jesus, and they expected his cosmic return, but they (like Paul) did not have much use for his Sayings. On the other hand, the various Jesus movements were speaking the words of the living Jesus who died, without any theoretical consensus about how such a thing might be possible. They were also facing the fact that that practice was inexorably driving a wedge between them and their synagogue communities. Thus there were two general ways of "remembering" Jesus: cultically and catechetically.

Mark was familiar with the practices of both kinds of communities. He saw that cult and catechesis were like two boats, and the "Jesus" memory was tottering with one foot in each. As catechesis lost its moorings to the synagogues, the boats were starting to drift apart. The "Jesus" whom they kept precariously afloat was therefore in an increasingly dangerous position. Mark needed to build a dock.

---

21. For illustrations of these tiny vials, see Daremberg and Saglio, *Dictionnaire des antiquités grèques et romains* (Paris, 1877). For vase art, see Keuls, *The Reign of the Phallus.* The custom was known to Jewish scholars as well; see the Mishnah, *Šabbat* 6:3, *Kelim* 30:4, *Ketubot* 6:4; and the Talmud *Šabbat* 62a–b.

22. See Mack, *Myth of Innocence,* 277. I am citing Mack's position selectively here; his brilliant deduction deserves a careful reading on its own terms. Elizabeth A. Castelli explores *mimesis* in *Imitating Paul: A Discourse of Power.*

The passion narrative, from Bethany to Golgotha, is Mark's construction.[23] It is "mythic" in the sense that it makes a story or plot, *mythos*, out of what had been practices and poiesis. The practice of eucharistic feasting is sited narratively in an event of origin, "the last supper," while the poiesis of christological catechesis among women is sited narratively as an event of anointing, "at Bethany." Reconstructed as events, these things can be strung together in a sequence with the thread of time, and they can be tied onto a historical Jesus. Or rather, the historical Jesus can be tethered securely to them.

The Markan Architecture: Bricks

Mark's text, then, is a poiesis of Jesus in its own right—but one accomplished a generation or more after the women's christological identification and founded squarely upon the latter. We can now examine the surface of Mark's text for the beautifully crafted artifact that it is. But in order to focus on the surface contours of the Markan text (level G in Figure 4 above), one must allow the deeper generative structures to go out of focus. They recede beneath the literary work, taken now in its unity. As we put the Gospel of Mark back together again, we lose sight of elements of its prehistory such as messianic catechesis or the table-crashing agenda of Christian Bitch-Cynicism. But we catch sight of a breathtaking overall design. The Bethany pantomime and its three sequels function within that design as so-called presentational symbols. Their semantic is sudden, in comparison with the cumulative semantic of discursive communication.

The distinction between discursive and presentational symbolic function is a distinction between two ways in which meaning may be conveyed.[24] Discursive semantic is a linear, term-by-term arrangement of elements into relationships that gradually builds up a significant whole, a statement. Nondiscursive or presentational semantic is a simultaneous, all-at-once picturing of significant relation. Discursive symbols, like declarative sentences, can be reworded into other, equivalent discursive symbols

---

23. See Burton Mack's imagination of Mark leading a scholarly seminar seated in a study furnished with every kind of text *except* for "a copy of the passion narrative because there was none until he wrote it," in Mack, *Myth of Innocence*, 323–24.

24. The distinction was proposed by Susanne K. Langer in *Philosophy in a New Key: A Study in the Symbolism of Reason, Rite, and Art* (Cambridge: Harvard University Press, 1942; New York: Mentor, 1948).

or statements because they are composed of discrete, translatable units. But there can be no such exact translation of presentational symbols into discursive symbols—or even into other presentational symbols. The meaning of a painting does not translate either into a piece of sculpture or into a critical essay "about" its meaning.

The anointing at Bethany, in Mark's fiction, condenses the key elements that previously have been laid out in the text as components defining God's kingdom and the complementary roles of messiah and disciple within it.[25] The gesture collects these meanings like a lightning rod. They flash out with a crack as the vial snaps in Mark 14:3. The energy of this discharge has been built up from the juxtaposition of several important concepts that have occurred earlier in the narrative and have been linked to each other in interesting ways. A brief examination of six elements of this web of meanings will show how they form a network along which a charge of meaning has been made to gather.[26]

Gospel. Jesus' promise in Mark 14:9 that the woman's gesture henceforth must be part of the proclamation of the *euangelion* is the seventh and final time Mark uses this term. The narration opened as "the beginning of the gospel of Jesus Christ" (Mark 1:1). The term was soon linked with the idea of God's kingdom in 1:14-15, where the gospel is identified as the message that God's *basileia* is near. Later, the term appears in apposition with Jesus himself to delineate the demands of discipleship: in 8:35, the one who loses one's life for Jesus' sake and the gospel's will save it; and in 10:29, one who leaves family and farm for Jesus' sake and the gospel's will receive a hundredfold. Later still, the *euangelion* is interjected (13:10) into a prediction of the troubles of the end times, when the disciples will be put on trial and face censure for it (13:5-37).

---

25. What it means to be the christ, the anointed one or messiah, is at issue in Mark's Gospel. The thesis that, for Mark, Jesus' messianic identity is a secret was proposed in 1901 by William Wrede, *The Messianic Secret* (London: Clarke & Co., 1971). Wrede's work set the agenda for a good deal of Markan research in this century; for an excellent survey of that scholarly discussion, see Jack Dean Kingsbury, *The Christology of Mark's Gospel* (Philadelphia: Fortress Press, 1983), chap. 1. In Kingsbury's view, "The secret of Jesus' identity in Mark is not, characteristically, a 'messianic' secret but the secret that Jesus is the Son of God" (p. 21). Therefore, Kingsbury does not even treat the pericope under consideration here. Mark 14:3-9, with its insights into a woman's role in identifying Jesus, has been largely overlooked in studies of the meaning of messiahship. Even Elisabeth Schüssler Fiorenza has neglected to present exegesis of the passage from which she takes her title, *In Memory of Her.*

26. The following material reflects my collaborative research with Robert J. Miller in an earlier study; however, the interpretation offered here is in some respects incompatible with Miller's own rigorous historical-critical reading.

On this basis, Mark's final use of *euangelion,* in 14:9, reviews this network of meanings. The framing of the christological catechesis in the woman's gesture is "gospel" for several reasons. The gesture incurs the judgment and censure of bystanders as it makes its statement about the messiah. For Jesus' sake the woman has given up a costly possession, and possibly her family standing as well, since a woman who squandered wealth would face grave social consequences, perhaps even divorce. Moreover, the ointment in the vial presumably should be reserved for her own husband's comfort. The spontaneity of her act, its thoughtlessness of the future and its disregard for prudent use of riches, all match up with other similitudes that Mark's Jesus has used to describe God's kingdom, as we shall see.

"Gospel" is fraught with incongruencies. According to the Markan tableau, the woman *unknowingly* tells the good news of Jesus' christhood, and she tells it without using words. The reaction to this news makes it come true, in Mark's design. Upon hearing Jesus' pronouncement that the woman's prophetic act, which has linked christhood with death, is going to be told as the gospel, Judas goes off to deliver some good news of his own. He tells the chief priests that he is ready to betray Jesus and "when they heard, they were delighted" (14:11). On three other occasions Mark has already associated the glad hearing of the spoken word with a reception that is not genuine. In the parable of the Sower, people who, "whenever they listen to the message, right away they receive it happily" (4:16), nevertheless fall away in time of persecution. When Herod listened to the preaching of John "he was very confused, yet he listened to him eagerly" (6:20). When Jesus got the better of scholars in a duel of words concerning the relative status of David and the messiah, "a huge crowd would listen to him with delight" (12:37); yet the crowd later clamored for his crucifixion (15:13-14).

The Markan verdict is that spoken words may evoke a glad response, yet invariably it is one that is shallow and temporary and does not lead into the kingdom of God.

The Poor. The anointing woman incurs censure on grounds that what she wasted should have been sold so that the proceeds could be given to the poor (14:4-5). Mark has arranged for the justification of this censure by posting Jesus' own instructions concerning discipleship at 10:21, where the millionaire was told, "Sell whatever you have and give to the poor . . . and come, follow me." But at Bethany, Jesus approves this particular squandering of resources upon himself on grounds that (1) unlike the poor, he will not always be around (14:7); and (2) the act has a meaning in terms of his own fate (14:8). Mark offers the woman's antic as the first coherent interpretation of what that fate must be.

Christ. The woman's anointing indicates what it means to be "Christ," but the meaning emerges in her deed of anointing rather than in the term "anointed," *christos,* which does not occur in this story. In effect, her act itself says that Jesus is the Christ by anointing him, albeit in a most unconventional way. Earlier, Peter had declared that Jesus was Christ (8:29), but Jesus had forbidden him to tell anyone (8:30). Mark had Jesus immediately correct Peter's understanding of messiahship by teaching "that the son of Adam was destined to suffer a great deal" and that the disciple must pick up the cross and risk one's life (8:31-35). But in response to the woman's gesture, Jesus unconditionally affirms what she has acted out concerning the character of his christhood, by making her gesture constitutive of the gospel. Thereafter Mark has Jesus admit to the title of Christ in his trial before the Sanhedrin (14:61-62).

Destruction. The literal reading of 14:4 is, "Why has this destruction of ointment happened?"[27] *Apōleia* is usually translated "waste" or "loss" in this passage. While that translation is defensible, it hinders readers from noticing the resonance with Mark's earlier uses of the cognate verb *apollumi,* "to destroy." At 1:24, demons ask Jesus, "Have you come to destroy us?" At 2:22, both new wine and old wineskins are "destroyed." At 12:9, the owner of the vineyard comes to "destroy" its tenants. At 8:35, the one who strives to save his life will "destroy" it. In narrating the plans of Jesus' enemies (3:6 and 11:18), Mark uses "to destroy" instead of the more appropriate "to kill." Thus Mark verbally associates the violent fate of Jesus with the other instances of destruction catalyzed by the ministry of Jesus. It is high irony that the ointment that prepares Jesus for destruction/death should itself be designated as "destroyed."

Breaking. Related to destruction is Mark's use of "breaking." It connotes revelation and recognition that cannot be undone—in contrast to speech. For Mark, responses expressed in words tend to be short-lived. The woman's act, however, is irrevocable. Mark arranges to identify Jesus as Christ wordlessly, even unwittingly, with her breaking of a vial. The verb *syntribō* (14:3) usually is associated with divinely impelled action in the Septuagint. Mark has used it once before (5:4), describing what the demoniac did to his chains. That was the man whose demons identified Jesus as "son of the Most High God" (5:7). Mark's narrative abounds in verbs of tearing, splitting, snapping, and breaking—all in

---

27. The Scholars Version translation is being adjusted here to show the literal sense.

some way describing the arrival of God's kingdom. For example, the heavens are torn apart (*schizomenous*) at Jesus' baptism in 1:10, and the Temple veil is split (*eschisthē*) at his death in 15:38. New wine will burst (*rēxei*) old wineskins in 2:22, and a patch tears away (*schisma*) from old cloth in 2:21. The high priest rips (*diarēxas*) his clothes at Jesus' trial in 14:63. Moreover, bread is broken to feed the crowds in 6:41 (*kateklasen*) and in 8:6 (*eklasen*) and 8:19 (*eklasa*). In 14:22 the bread breaking is the prophetic and eschatological act of the eucharist.

Woman. The woman who breaks the vial in the Bethany pantomime has also broken custom by breaking in upon a group of men reclining for a formal dinner.[28] These transgressions associate her with the other women whom Mark mentions without naming—all of whom are in some way outside the law and therefore not "good" women. The woman with the hemorrhage in 5:25-34 was unclean because of her gynecological disorder, and in touching Jesus did what an unclean woman was not supposed to do. The Syrophoenician woman in 7:25-30 was a Gentile, and in arguing with Jesus did what no woman, Jew or Greek, was supposed to do. In 15:41 the disciples who witness Jesus' death include "many other women who had come up to Jerusalem in his company," that is, who left their family obligations and their homes in Galilee, in violation of both law and custom. Mark gives us the names of three of those women in 15:40, for the same three will find Jesus' tomb empty in 16:1-8.

The story of the anointing at Bethany, then, is integral to Mark's narrative, because it weaves together a number of important concepts. It juxtaposes all the pieces of the Markan picture of Jesus' mission: christhood is connected to death; the presently inbreaking kingdom of God demands a spontaneous and total divestiture of one's future security; the deeds of a silent rule breaker express the truth where words have failed. But the meaning achieved in this pericope is more than discursive. The

---

28. In polite Greek society, the *andrōn* or banquet hall of a house was inaccessible from the apartments of the women of the family. Women who attended banquets were kinless women, that is, women outside the social protections and constraints of the kinship system: actresses, prostitutes, slaves. By custom, women of good family kept to the *gynaikōn* until they had passed menopause. However, due to economic and political changes in the first century, it was becoming possible to construe the entire polis or city as the family home of a wealthy woman who adopted it, participated in civic administration, and took on the burden of financing prestigious public works. See Van Bremen, "Women and Wealth." For a detailed study, see Kathleen Corley, *Private Women, Public Meals: Social Conflict and Women in the Synoptic Gospels* (Peabody, Mass.: Hendrickson Publishers, 1993).

discursive discussion of it in the last few pages of analysis has but begun to plumb the meaning that is there. The concepts of discipleship, christhood, and kingdom of God are given meaning here by way of the presentational semantic of the prophetic gesture that the pericope merely recounts. The shattering of the alabaster jar assembles these diverse pieces into a glimpse of what the gospel *is*. It remains for Jesus, in his turn, to act it out.

The Silenced Proclaimer

The woman who anoints Jesus is a mysterious figure in Mark's Gospel, both anonymous and speechless on the surface of this text. She fits none of the character roles vital to Mark's narrative: she is neither disciple, opponent, supplicant, nor bystander. As a narrative figure, she is perhaps most like the only other person who performs a deed that is commended by Jesus: the widow of 12:41-44 who gave "her whole life" (*holon ton bion autēs*) to the Temple.[29] This widow, like the woman of 14:3-9, is in Mark's telling also anonymous, speechless, and unaware of the significance that Mark's Jesus attaches to her deed.

The woman of Mark 14 is unique in that hers is the only act of kindness done for Jesus in the whole Gospel.[30] Every other action in which others physically touch Jesus is either an attempt by the afflicted to grab his power of healing or an act of violence done by his enemies. From this perspective, it is significant that the text does not tell us that the woman touched Jesus. (In this, her action resembles the only other one performed for Jesus' benefit: his baptism by John.) It is characteristic Markan irony that this sole act of solicitude for Jesus is interpreted as a ritual that treats him like a dead man. A more bitter irony rides on the kiss of Judas. This sole act of affection bestowed on Jesus in Mark's text is in reality a deadly betrayal.

29. The Markan Jesus is extremely sparing in his praise of people. Only these two are commended for what they do. Only two others are commended for what they say: the woman healed of the flow of blood (Mark 5:34) and the Syrophoenician woman (Mark 7:29). (Perhaps in Mark 10:21 Jesus approves of the rich man's answer, but the disappointing conclusion of this pericope makes this doubtful.) Not once does Jesus ever commend the disciples. On the contrary, he frequently rebukes and upbraids them for their ignorance and hardness of heart.

30. Perhaps one should also count here the burial of Jesus by Joseph of Arimathea, one of those who voted for his death (Mark 14:53, 64; 15:43-46). But see the provision for the posthumous humiliation of executed criminals in Mishnah *Sanhedrin* 6:5.

Mark makes the woman's anointing of Jesus a nonverbal affirmation of his messiahship. The setting and circumstances of this "messianic installation" reflect the Markan emphasis on the hiddenness of Jesus' messianic identity. They also play out a complete reversal of the anointing ceremony proper to a Davidic successor. Jesus is anointed, not in the Temple, but in Bethany, in a so-called leper's house; not by the authorized clergy, but by a nameless woman; not to acclaim by the crowds, but to criticism by his companions; and not to a throne, but to a tomb.[31]

The woman symbolically proclaims Jesus the messiah; but Mark, in keeping with his theme of the hiddenness of Jesus' messiahship, has her do so silently and at a private home. Mark's text constrains the reader not to impute to this woman any understanding that messiahship and death are connected, prior to the superimposition of these fates by the presentational semantic of the anointing. The logic combining christhood and death is withheld until this synthesizing tableau. The novelty of the meaning wrought through the symbolic gesture is emphasized by the hostile response to it among Jesus' companions. Their response illustrates a failure to discern (or if discerning, to accept) the significance of this act. The disciples find it foolish, wasteful, and absurd. Mark plays out the motif of misunderstanding all through his narrative. Indeed, it is a central contention of his Gospel that Jesus' identity was not understood, even by his followers.

Mark therefore has his Jesus offer a narrative interpretation of the pantomime. It is Jesus who insists that *because he is messiah* he must die. His identity cannot be understood apart from the cross. When the woman anoints him, he does not say, "She has proclaimed me the Anointed One," but rather, "She anticipates in anointing my body for burial." This gesture is made to presuppose Jesus the crucified even as it identifies Jesus the messiah.

The woman's pantomime, in Mark's design, announces Jesus' sacred identity but does so in silence and in private, without her knowing what she was doing, among a hostile audience, and in a manner inextricably associated with Jesus' violent fate. As such, it is akin to the other proclamations of Jesus' identity in Mark. Peter has proclaimed Jesus the messiah, but without understanding what this will entail. Soldiers sarcastically will hail him as prophet (14:65) and king (15:17-19) while brutalizing him. His enemies will name him the messiah, but to taunt and mock him on

---

31. See Werner Kelber, *Mark's Story of Jesus* (Philadelphia: Fortress Press, 1979), 72.

the cross (15:32). The centurion, the one who supervises his execution, will announce to no one in particular that he was "God's son" (15:39). Jesus' only public disclosure of his identity will be at his trial, and it will lead instantly to the death sentence (14:61-64). In fact, the only ones who have understood who Jesus is and said so openly are the demons. Jesus has tried, not always successfully,[32] to silence them.

What Did They Know, and When Did They Know It?

Mark sandwiches the anointing tableau in between the brief notice that Jesus' enemies were seeking a way to seize him (14:1-2) and the equally terse report that Judas came forward and agreed to hand Jesus over to them (14:10-11). It is as if Mark had to get Jesus properly prepared for death before the actual plot against him could get under way. There is a tone of bitter irony in v. 11: Jesus' enemies "were delighted, and promised to pay" Judas. This is the only occurrence of *chairō*[33] and of *epangellomai* in Mark. The only rejoicing and the only promises in the Gospel come from his enemies as they plan his death.

The juxtaposition of Jesus-anointed-by-the-woman with Jesus-be-trayed-by-Judas illuminates an odd similarity between the woman and Judas. Mark's narrative declines to supply any motivation for either of their actions. The woman just happens to anoint Jesus; Judas just happens to betray him. Mark has not prepared for Judas' deed in the plotline of the story, and he offers no clue about its rationale. In fact, prior to 14:10, Judas has been mentioned only once, in 3:19 where the Twelve are introduced and Judas is identified as the traitor to be, *hos paredōken auton*. So, in 14:10 when Judas goes to the priests "to turn him over," the reader is not surprised that Judas does it but is baffled as to why.[34]

---

32. In Mark 1:24-25 and 3:11-12, Jesus orders the demons to be silent *after* they "shouted" his sacred identity. In 5:7 the demoniac was "shouting at the top of his voice" as he called Jesus "son of the most high God" *after* Jesus had tried to exorcise him.

33. A form of the verb *chairō* also is found in Mark 15:15, but there it is a cliché greeting ("hail") addressed mockingly to Jesus by the soldiers.

34. This lack of motive apparently bothered Matthew and Luke, for they both supplied an explanation. In Matthew (24:14-16), Judas bargains for money; in Luke (22:3-6), he is possessed by Satan. It is important to recognize that in Mark, money is not Judas' incentive. He is promised money by the priests, but only after he volunteers his cooperation.

On the surface of the plot, this absence of motivation is mysterious and opaque. A reader is unsatisfied when events of this proportion "just happen." From the perspective of the full Gospel narrative, however, the unmotivated quality of these deeds—the woman's and Judas'—coheres with Mark's narrative strategy and ideological program. Why does the woman anoint Jesus for messiahship/death? Ideologically, Jesus is anointed because his messianic status is revealed fully only in his death. Within the narrative line, she anoints him for burial beforehand because there will be no body to anoint when the women come to the tomb and also because such a proleptic enactment of his death is fitting at the beginning of the passion narrative. Jesus is commissioned for his destiny by this anointing, much the same as he was commissioned for his ministry by his baptism. Just as Mark has construed the baptism as a personal revelation to Jesus of his status, so now the anointing constitutes a consummating disclosure to Jesus of his fate.

Why does Judas betray Jesus? Again, to seek an answer in terms of the character of Judas' personal motivation can obscure one's view of Mark's ideological purpose. Judas betrays Jesus because Jesus must be betrayed. In 8:31 Jesus said that he "must" suffer many things and be abused by his enemies. In 9:31 he said that he will be "turned over" (*paradidotai*) to those who will kill him. In 10:33 he "will be turned over" (*paradothēsetai*) to the high priests and scribes, who will "turn him over" (*paradōsousin*) to the foreigners. So far these predictions describe Jesus' fate only in terms of what will happen to him. His role is entirely passive. In 10:45 the reader is told for the first time that Jesus has an active role in his own destiny: the Son of man has come "to give" (*dounai*) his life as a ransom.

Since 3:6 the reader has known that Jesus' enemies want to kill him. Just before the anointing pericope, Mark told the reader that they were actively seeking how to arrest (literally, "to take, seize") and kill him. The narrative forces are all deployed: it is the divine will that Jesus must die; his enemies want to "take" him; he intends to "give" himself. The only thing needed is for someone to hand Jesus over to his enemies. All these narrative lines intersect in the figure of Judas. Judas does what needs to be done. The wordplay is suggestive: Jesus has come to "give" (*didōmi*) his life, while Judas "gives over" (*paradidōmi*) Jesus to those who want to "take" him.

In this way Mark arranges things so that Judas (like the messiah-maker at Bethany) acts *as if* he understood the identity and destiny of Jesus. Peter named Jesus the Messiah but resisted the notion of his violent fate. It is grotesque and splendid irony that Judas, of all the disciples, does for Jesus what he needs to have done. This irony is amplified by the forced juxtaposition of the woman and Judas: two deeds with no narrative motivation, both of which help to accomplish the divinely mandated destiny for Jesus, both of which seem to "understand" the affinity of christ and cross, one of them an act of treachery by someone whose name has become infamous as the synonym for traitors, the other a "good work" by a nameless woman whose fame (and anonymity) is guaranteed by the proclamation of the Gospel.

Character Profile

Good news and personal response to it are one in the cameo of Mark 14:3-9. The woman with the alabaster jar both expresses the complete gospel and embodies the ideal evangelist needed for a gospel now sealed into a text. Mark has redefined her by juxtaposing her with Judas, the very antithesis of what a disciple should be. A comparison of the profiles of these two characters brings to light Mark's conception of the kingdom of God, in terms of one who accepts and propagates it versus one who does not accept it yet inadvertently advances it anyway.

The woman with the jar is nameless, while "Judas Iscariot" has two names plus a further identification as "one of the Twelve" (14:10). She is silent, while he speaks. She allows her symbolic action to speak for itself and speak truthfully, while his sign, the betraying kiss, is bent into a duplicit meaning by his words (14:44-45).

The woman's action appears spontaneous and impulsive, while Judas' is well planned and carefully executed. The woman does something extravagant; had she sold the perfume, she would have gotten money, but after wasting the perfume on Jesus, she likely faces divorce, disgrace, and a future of economic hardship. Judas, however, has done something rational in turning a troublemaker over to the authorities, and his payoff is to be silver. (The woman's anointing and Judas' betrayal are the only two instances in the Gospel where Mark reports that money was spent on Jesus.) Jesus commends the woman and says that her good work (*kalon ergon*) will be recounted "in memory of her" (14:9), but he says of his betrayer that "it would have been better for that man (*kalon autō*) had he never been born" (14:21).

Both Judas and the woman go where they should not go. He goes to Jesus' enemies (14:10), while she intrudes among Jesus' male friends. Both receive a promise. The priests promise Judas money (14:11), while Jesus promises the woman remembrance (14:9). Both Judas and the woman perform symbolic gestures that are intimate and extravagant. His kiss is effusive;[35] her perfume cost a year's pay. His gesture is proper, as a greeting of a male disciple for a teacher; hers is improper. But hers is genuine, while his is counterfeit. She "destroys" perfume, possibly a gift that someone had given to her; Judas hands Jesus over to those who would destroy him. She wastes the gift of perfume; he wastes Jesus, whose body so recently had been given to all of the Twelve (14:22-24).

Besides the anonymous woman and Judas, there is someone else in Mark 14 who disposes of something precious in a symbolic gesture that is reckless of the value at stake. Jesus himself gives away his body and blood in the eucharistic institution narrative of 14:22-24. Like the perfume, the blood is to be poured out. Like the betrayal and arrest, the body is to be taken. Mark has set up a parallel between the two symbolic givings: the alabaster vial and the eucharist. The breaking of the flask at Wednesday's[36] supper leads to the making of the deal between Judas and the authorities. Then the breaking of the bread at Thursday's supper leads to the taking of Jesus' body by the agents of the authorities, as Judas' deal is consummated.

Judas makes the deal after the incident of the anointing has shown that Jesus is destined for death. Then Judas goes through with the deal after the incident of the sharing of bread and cup has shown that whatever Jesus means by the kingdom of God lies on the other side of death (14:25). Both incidents have demonstrated the foolishness of Jesus' mission, and therefore the action that Judas takes is sensible. The linkage of these four elements of Mark 14—two symbolic gestures and two stages of betrayal— both interprets and achieves Jesus' christhood and therefore invites closer examination.

The parallels between the events at the last two suppers of Jesus' life are striking. At Bethany, the aromatic nard is pure and costly, and, like any gift, it represents the giver herself even though this personal identification

35. *Kataphileō* usually conveys an intensive meaning ("kiss tenderly") in contrast to the uncompounded *phileō* ("kiss"). In Mark 14:44-45, both forms occur. In describing his plan to kiss Jesus, Judas uses *phileō*, but when he actually kisses him, *kataphileō* underlines the perfidy of the act by connoting the affection with which he carried it out. Compare also Luke's use of *phileō* in the betrayal scene (Luke 22:47-48) and of the compound verb when the sinner woman kisses Jesus' feet (Luke 7:38), when the father greets his prodigal son (Luke 15:20), and when the Ephesian elders tearfully bid Paul farewell (Acts 20:37).

36. Because the chronology of Mark 11–16 is unclear, the specific days of these events cannot be determined from the narrative. What is certain is the sequence: the woman anoints Jesus; the next evening (Mark 14:12) he eats with his disciples; the next day (Mark 15:1) he dies. For a brief exposition of the problem in Markan chronology here, see Paul Achtemeier, *Mark* (Philadelphia: Fortress Press, 1975), 84–86.

is left implicit. At Jerusalem, the bread and the wine are common things that become precious when Jesus makes explicit their personal identification with their giver. At both dinners, the giving of the gifts is an effective sign whose apparent meaning is immediately fulfilled but whose ultimate meanings come true only later. The messianic anointing immediately grooms and cares for Jesus; later, its meaning as preparation for burial comes true. The eucharistic feeding immediately nourishes and strengthens the Twelve; later, its meaning as Jesus' consent to shed blood for them comes true. Both signs also are invested with a third meaning that can be fulfilled only in an eschatological time frame, that is, outside the events that Mark is recounting in the story. The anointing signals Jesus' christhood, and the eucharist points to "that day" when Jesus will drink new wine in the kingdom of God.

By contrast, Judas' sign achieves its entire effect in present time, when "the hour has come" (14:41). The meaning of this signal has been settled in the past time, relative to Mark's narrative: "now the betrayer had given them a signal" (14:44). This sign, the kiss, is executed in the narrative's present and immediately has its prearranged effect as Jesus is seized (14:45-46). The natural meaning of the kiss must be contravened for this to happen. Judas takes a short-term view of the situation, as it were. In 14:11, what he intends is an *eukairōs* (literally, good-timely or opportune) betrayal. But Jesus takes a long-term view of things. In taking the cup, he orients this gesture toward the eschatological future. Mark's Jesus imputes to the woman with the alabaster vial his own long-term view, although her gesture, like that of Judas, is also quite timely. As Jesus indicates, the poor are "always" (*pantote*) around and can be helped "whenever" (*hotan*); but his presence is temporary (*ou pantote*). The woman has seized the moment to do for him what must be done before much longer if it is to be done at all.

There is an "amen" oath by Jesus connected with each of these signs: the kiss, the anointing, and the eucharist. In 14:17, Jesus had said, "So help me, one of you eating with me is going to turn me in!" Judas' kiss fulfills this oath. In 14:9, "So help me, wherever the good news is announced in all the world, what she has done will also be told in memory of her." This oath is fulfilled for the reader who is encountering the woman's story embedded in the text of the passion narrative. In 14:25, "So help me, I certainly won't drink any of the fruit of the vine again until that day when I drink it for the first time in God's kingdom." This oath points forward, out of Mark's narrative and past the time of the narrative's reader, on beyond human events to an eschatological fulfillment. In the meantime—that is, outside the realtime projected by the narrative but within the time of the church—there are reenactments of Jesus' self-gift in the eucharistic ritual and reconstitutions of the Gospel by the self-gifts of ensuing generations of disciples subsequent to the anointing woman. It is these which prolong the trajectory of Mark's story toward the kingdom of God.

There is a fourth "amen" oath within Mark 14. In 14:30, Peter is told, "So help me, tonight before the rooster crows twice you will disown me three times." This oath, too, comes true within the narrative time of the fourteenth chapter. Mark knows that the reader knows that Peter's betrayal would be reversed outside the narrative time, in the realtime of the church. Peter's denial is made in mere words (14:66-72), which, as Mark has shown, seldom have irrevocable effects. It is the three nonverbal signs of Mark 14—the messianic grooming, the eucharist, and the kiss—that cannot be undone.

The signs of Mark 14 mean to nail down the related meanings of discipleship, christhood, the kingdom of God, and the Gospel itself. It seems that, for Mark, the *gospel* is neither a spoken message nor a written narrative. Rather, it is the symbolically expressive, and therefore contagious, dimension of a human being's total divestiture of her or his future in favor of the *kingdom of God*. For Jesus, this is *christhood:* he suffers and dies to inaugurate God's kingdom. For the evangelist, this is the imprudent giving over of her possessions and family ties, even of her name and her voice—in short, of everything that would ensure a personal future. One becomes part of the gospel by doing, not by saying. Jesus' words are consistently misunderstood in Mark's narrative; only his deeds effectively enact the gospel.

Discipleship means following Christ to death. The woman with the alabaster vial is the first, in Mark's telling, to express this fact. Her gesture is a proto-eucharist. The broken flask stands for her own broken future, but it also stands for the body of Jesus broken on the cross. She is voiceless as the smell of the nard is released and fills the room. He dies "letting go voice" (*apheis phōnēn*) and releases spirit (*exepneusen*). Mark's narrative puts the reader into the picture: at the table with the Twelve to receive bread and wine passively and without understanding; but also in the sandals of the woman who shatters her future for Jesus' sake and the gospel's. By itself, the eucharistic symbol risks cultivating well-fed disciples whose cross will be carried for them. But Mark sharpens the eucharistic symbol by juxtaposing broken bread with broken vial. It is not enough to share the body and blood of the Lord. Judas did as much. One must break one's own flask and pour out the contents, as did Jesus and the nameless woman who put it all together.

What Happened to Jesus' Body?

Mark's text is one of the things that happened to Jesus' body. At the same time, it is also *about* the things that happened to Jesus' body. Like all human bodies, Jesus' body was receptive to text. It was a vellum surface, a lambskin prepared for inscription. The torture and the execution of Jesus' body are at once the most decisive text it received and the one to which our access is most historically reliable. He really died, and he died horribly. Crucifixion was a tool of political terrorism effectively applied by the imperial administration. The Gospel stories mention scourging and humiliation; but sexual abuse by the Syrian mercenaries in the garrison also is quite likely. The Gospel stories mention a gentle enshrouding, a magnanimous laying out, and a loving tombside vigil; but a limed pit is much more probable. Like countless others of the "disappeared," Jesus was not important enough to trouble the governor with a trial or the death squad with returning the remains to the family. Lime eats the body quickly and hygienically. Therefore we find virtually no skeletal remains of the thousands crucified outside Jerusalem in the first century.

To groom Jesus for resurrection, the church could not ignore the reality that was crucifixion. The messianic eucharistic grooming had to be done *through* the realities of this crucifixion. It had to be a version or poiesis or *mimesis* of crucifixion. The sound of the catechesis and of the eucharist had to be a recognizable echo of the sound of the torture. When you hear the hammer strike and the victim scream, you have to hear the vial snap and the loaf tear. You have to hear all of them when you hear any of them. And that sound will also be the impossible sound of the tombstone creeping back. Your tombstone.

What is the reality of any of these sounds, such that they can be "the same"? Matter has no voice, and physical things do not get inside one another. The surfaces of mere bodies—bodies like Newtonian billiard balls, and nothing more—assert their integrity and withhold their inner reality from the access of other bodies. Pure bodies collide and bounce off of one another; otherwise they fracture one another, but then all you get is a proliferation of pebbles, just as impenetrable, keeping their insides to themselves.

Therefore, human bodies are not "pure" Newtonian bodies. Human bodies hear. They admit the internal influence of other bodies. Somehow the material flesh opens into meaning, intention, and consciousness. Consciousness opens out into physical expression. Voice is efficacious, although not as a physical cause. Text affects the reality of what it inscribes, although a pen cannot drive a nail.

No two physical bodies are the same. Mine is not the same as yours, and mine today is not even the same as mine yesterday or tomorrow. Recognition of sameness is an achievement of mind, accomplished through a textual artifact. You recognize your own sameness from day to day, in the midst of change, by means of the persistence of patterns: not only organic patterns but artifactual ones as well. Humans are endowed with a capacity to inscribe pattern as well as to express it. What is recognized in the intuition of sameness is not material identity but congruence of meaning.

What happened to Jesus' body? It became the textual site of the rupture of material impediments to the transhistorical availability of the human person who was Jesus of Nazareth. It was given, and it was taken. Often. Still.

Theories of Corporality, Textuality, and Humanity

8

Bodies Born and Grown

THE CULTURAL diversity of hellenized first-century Palestine has been the key premise behind the inductive studies pursued in the last six chapters. We discovered that semantic frontiers criss-crossed the social terrain of Eretz Israel. Realities such as work, servitude, knowing, learning, law, and nature were different experiences depending upon where one stood in the complex network of gender, racial, and economic relationships.

Yet this very recognition of radical diversity now must be addressed from another perspective as we turn to the task of consolidating, synthesizing, and interpreting the data that we have uncovered. On the one hand, we have unearthed some fascinating details about the early days of the churches. On the other hand, we realize that as investigators we ourselves do not in our century escape the kind of cultural determination that we have been documenting in the past. Our own understanding in the late twentieth century is inevitably located and defined in reference to the social frontiers that structure the societies in which we ourselves live and read. There is no possibility, then, of our discovering and embracing "the real, original, authentic truth" about anything in the past—knowledge that would escape the conditioning effects of the social location in which it occurs, the Western academic world of the late twentieth century. Thus we simply cannot know, absolutely and exhaustively, what the resurrection of Jesus means. We can know only what it could have meant for *people in a particular context* to claim that Jesus rose bodily from the dead. Or rather, we can approximate such knowledge on the basis of an analogy between their understanding and ours, by virtue of something that we most certainly do have in common despite all social differences.

What makes cross-cultural and historical understanding possible at all is the element that every human being shares, the human body. This consideration saves our investigation from foundering on the rocks of cultural relativism and shattering its findings into a pile of glittering trivia. We do have a solid starting point from which to begin the task of interpreting what people of other races, genders, classes, and eras have said and written: we all are bodies. Texts ultimately refer back to bodies, and we have pre-textual, precultural knowledge of what we bodies are and do. To be sure, one does not encounter the body in the raw abstract, with social interpretations peeled away. All of us bodies are culturally textured. Yet there is something stable that persists throughout the social versions that one always encounters. Something prior to the texturing subsists as the referent receiving meaning from the term "body" with its infinitely variable cultural entanglements. That is not to say that the body is impervious to the meanings it receives; far from it. The body is both fragile and resilient: vulnerable to meanings imposed upon it even as it pushes back against their onslaught.

Thus we today do have a basis for understanding what was meant in the first century by the claim that a certain political prisoner was brutally executed and then raised to life. This claim is being made about a human body like yours and mine. It concerns the capabilities, needs, wants, and vulnerabilities of the body. The claim remains tethered to these, no matter how high the theories fly. The claim of resurrection has to be about what the body is about: the rhythms of labor and rest, hunger and feast, sexuality and birth, building and dwelling. In principle, knowledge of some version of these simple bodily realities is unproblematically available to all human beings, albeit in a variety of distinctive cultural mediations. In actuality, that knowledge can be faulty or distorted. For example, in Western consumerist societies an obsessive concern for leisure may camouflage both the pains and the satisfactions of the work that supports it; or preoccupation with issues of sexuality may distort issues of reproduction such as the provision of support for mothers and children.

Knowing the body, then, is difficult. The task requires interpretive strategies. By the dawn of the twentieth century, three new theoretical options were rapidly unfolding as strategic reconceptions of traditional questions in epistemology and metaphysics (that is, questions of knowledge and reality). These major social interpretive traditions were materialist economic analysis, the psychoanalytic tradition, and pragmatism. These approaches profoundly shaped the theorizations of the social sciences that evolved later in the century.[1] Each of these traditions suggests an approach to the question of the fate of the human body. They will be considered in turn later in this chapter. The first task, however, is to clear the way for questioning and for the emergence of a sense of wonder about the body.

What Is Body?

In taking up the question of the body, the honest inquirer must face the question behind that question: How can there be any question about the body? Where would one stand to ask it, and where would one stand to propose an answer? Are human beings ever in a state of sufficient ignorance about our bodies to leave room for questioning? Or are we ever distanced enough from our bodies to claim disinterested objectivity for whatever answer might occur? You, as a reader of these lines, are already grasping them physically with eyes and hands, and so you scarcely need an introduction to the body that is even now actively engaged in your uptake of this discussion. Nor should any reader expect a definition of the body to settle its question once and for all—for of course you do much more than read with your body, and so you have firsthand familiarity with its mysterious delights and dangers. Yet definitions aplenty have been offered, even forcibly imposed, upon human bodies. There is a need to un-define the body. There is a need to loosen some of the conceptual bindings that secure the foundations of Western thought and therefore of Christian theologies of the body. The task of this chapter, then, is not to settle the question of the body but to question the ways in which the question of the body customarily has been arbitrarily and prematurely foreclosed, or perhaps never allowed to emerge at all.

How may one begin to unravel the conceptual swaddling of the human body? The cocoon that is Western culture fortunately is no seamless garment. Several loose threads are dangling handily from it—for example, the precariousness of the very project of definition itself. The human body too often is defined by opposition to something else—for example, "soul." This attempt at definition projects a binary pair, each of whose identities consists chiefly in its opposition to the other: the body is non-soul, soul is

---

1. For a time, theology was able to evade the epistemological and ontological challenges brought by these theories and took refuge in so-called personalism and new hermeneutics. Yet the term "person" may mask the fact that human beings are bodies who express every aspect of their knowing and loving with bodily media. For this reason I am avoiding the term "person" whenever possible, and I am insisting that "body" names the reality of the human being, soul and all.

non-body. Instead of describing the positive faculties of soul that would complement physical capabilities, one arbitrarily sunders human faculties into two exclusive and contrasting sets. By a similar logic, in other contexts the human body is opposed to those of animals, the "non-humans." This strategy of opposition loads positive value onto one of the pair, while the other receives a negative valuation. Thus soul is conceived to be more important than body; the human body is privileged over those of other animals. Yet there is something circular and tautologous about this way of defining. This strategy cannot fill in the particulars about what the body is. If we know only that the human body is "not the soul" and "not a monkey," we still do not know very much.

The binary definitional process described in the preceding paragraph asserts a relationship of "is not," and that assertion sets up, separates, and defines two entities. Another common approach to understanding the human body is through metaphors. The term "metaphor" denotes both a process of producing meaning and the product of that process. Metaphor, although it too begins with disjunction, works back in the other direction. Metaphor asserts a relationship of "is" between two nonidentical entities. That assertion overlays the two and imposes congruence. Metaphors are sometimes explicitly stated, but often they are implied. Metaphoric process is a kind of reading. In metaphor, one impresses certain elements of a field into a relation configured according to the contours of another relation, already known in another field. When those elements are "read" in this way, their field itself is warped to make them fit. The warp is the new meaning created by metaphor. The entities may have to be bent a little to achieve a fit. This bending, or assimilation of improper qualities, can be creative and functional, or destructive and dysfunctional, or ambiguous. Metaphoric process cannot be avoided, but one can and should be mindful of its side-effects.[2]

One metaphor for the human body that seems quite widespread across cultures is that of the artifact. Cosmogonic myths like those in the first two chapters of Genesis portray the human body as a made thing. God, the creator, fashioned the original models, and God designed the ways in which they would operate and reproduce. This is a beautiful truth but not a literal one. For, literally speaking, the body is not made. It grows.

2. For a survey of theories of metaphor and a constructive proposal, see Mary Gerhart and Allan Melvin Russell, *Metaphoric Process: The Creation of Scientific and Religious Understanding* (Fort Worth, Tex.: Texas Christian University Press, 1984). Where other theorists regard metaphor as a tool for expressing or describing what is already known, Gerhart and Russell show that metaphor as a thought process actually invents new knowledge (see esp. p. 108).

It grows itself according to a pattern that the body itself contains in its molecular structure. A metaphorical assertion, that the growing of the body "is" a being-made-by-God, makes a meaning. That meaning is an artifact, but the human body itself literally is not an artifact. (If the body were literally an artifact, perhaps it could not make such lovely artifacts as metaphors and myths.)

Other metaphors for the human body are quite familiar, for example, that of the machine. In medicine the body may be regarded as a complex of interrelated parts and systems. Each has its function. When function is impaired, one seeks to repair or replace the part. In industrial science also, the bodies of the workers are themselves counted to be part of the systems of production or the provision of services. On the other hand, the body may also be regarded as a product, as when one works on its shape through exercise and diet plans and then displays the result for the admiration of others. In Western philosophy, the body also has been regarded as a tool or instrument to be used in the accomplishment of purposes. One employs or inhabits the body, rides around in it like a vehicle, resides within it as in a house. One perfects the body as a medium of communication: dressing it for success, training it for assertiveness, grooming it so that it will enhance the messages that one wishes to convey.

These metaphors—machine, product, tool, vehicle—all alienate the body while disguising the fact of that alienation. That is, they make the tacit assertion that myself and my body are two distinct entities, with one controlling the other. There are some situations in which this fiction can be helpful; in other contexts, it can be a major hindrance to understanding the body. There is no escape from metaphor as a means of access to the body. Yet to be mindful of metaphors makes it possible to monitor their function and to suspend and replace them when appropriate.

Besides these two ways of thinking about the body—by metaphor and by definition of opposites—there is a third and very intriguing way. The body is the symbol of the person.[3] The "of" that connects symbol and person is a two-way street. The body *is* me, it lets me be me; but at the same time, I am more than the here-and-now body that just had breakfast and later today will go downtown on an errand. The "more than" is inherently undefinable; it is my future and my plans and my unpredictability—all that whose mode of being is to-be-not-yet. The human body is the

3. Karl Rahner has led contemporary Catholic theologians in the movement to explore the symbolic character of the body. Rahner proposes the metaphysical category of the "realsymbol," instantiated in the human body, whose self-projection can provide an analogue for the incarnation and the eucharist.

point of access both to the person and for the person to the world. The reader of these lines has access to the writer through her body, not directly but through what her body has done: the writing of these words. Both writer and readers, like all human beings, access their worlds through being physically present with those worlds. Our physical senses let us receive *what is* as the outcome of all that has been. At the same time our hands, arms, backs, and feet let us produce *what is not yet* out of what the worlds give us to work with. The body as symbol is placental hinge "between" material and transcendent reality, past and future.

Thus there are several significant characteristics of the unmade or organic symbol that is the human body. First, this symbol expresses a personal being, yet it is not, like a product, something other than the one whom it symbolizes. Second, this symbol provides for access: through it the person goes out into the world, and the world comes into the person. Third, this symbol is a partial and provisional expression and access. Fourth, this symbol is a means of production and reproduction, change and maintenance. Fifth, the body's productions also are symbols, but these secondary symbols are artifacts as well, and their nature should be distinguished from that of the nonartifactual protoplasmic personal symbolic beings who create them.

It is this distinction which is sometimes forgotten when one thinks about the human body through the metaphor of artifact. The origination of the human body is radically different from the making of artifacts. Artifacts, of whatever kind, cannot lay claim to our care and concern as the needs of human bodies do. Artifacts, after all, are replaceable. Human bodies are irreplaceable, in an absolute and fundamental sense. But why has it so often been possible to overlook this distinction between the body and made things? Is it because bodies seem to sit there along with the furniture like objects in the perceived world? Is it because of the economic habit of using other people's bodily labor to make ourselves more comfortable? Is it because we "read" bodies through their artifacts: their words, their clothing, their writings, their employments, their possessions; and because we read texts in which bodies have been read in that way? These questions flutter up, like moths from garments,[4] when one begins to unwind the conceptual shroud of text.

---

4. In the New American Bible translation, the author of the book of Sirach uses this simile to warn a father not to let a young daughter converse with married women, "for just as moths come from garments, so harm to women comes from women" (Sir. 42:13).

The Body-Text Continuum

The distinction between body and artifact is at the same time a relation, but an extremely complex one. Conceiving of this relation as a continuum rather than as a disjunction may be more helpful. At one end of the continuum would lie the human body without any of its symbolic expressions. Let us imagine it as perhaps a sleeping body, or one terminally ill, or a newborn baby. At the other end would lie a text completely alienated from the human hands of its writer. Let us imagine it as perhaps an ancient petroglyph, or a tablet impressed with forgotten characters, gathering dust on a museum shelf. Even beyond these real extremes, let us imagine two ideal points and call them "pure body" and "pure text," in which the level of communication is at absolute zero. These points exist only in imagination. Even the comatose body and the crumbling tablet communicate *something*, because one can still read out of them their basic symbolic nature: the one as a former or potential author, the other as evidence that there has been and may yet be again an author. What makes room for this reading, as it were, is time. Time is our habitual working knowledge of the dynamic relation between texts and bodies, bodies and texts. The human realities that we encounter in the world all register somewhere between the two extremes of pure bodiliness and pure textuality.

While the body itself is not an artifact, a made thing, artifacts do affect or remake the body. Elaine Scarry provides a phenomenology of this process in her work *The Body in Pain*.[5] In Scarry's account, the worker fabricates a product in two steps: by first imagining a potential reconfiguration of physical materials in correspondence to a bodily need (that is, by making up a fictional object) and, second, by actualizing that reconfiguration (that is, by making it real, material, nonfictional). Scarry terms this "projection." Projection comprises the two moments: making up plus making real. After projection, the product, in its turn, acts upon the worker's body (or someone else's) to alleviate the need. Scarry terms this "reciprocation."[6] The artifact is the site of both the projection and the reciprocation of human need. The human creative act travels or "arcs out," as it were, from the body to the artifact, and then back to the body again. Together these two movements constitute the interior structure of the artifact, according to Scarry's proposal.

---

5. See Elaine Scarry, *The Body in Pain: The Making and Unmaking of the World* (New York: Oxford University Press, 1985), esp. chap. 5, "The Interior Structure of the Artifact."
6. Scarry, *Body in Pain*, 280–81, 307.

Further, on the analogy of a simple machine, the work of reciprocation is many times greater than the work of projection. Therefore the projected or created aspect of the artifact tends to fade out of one's awareness
as the artifact is put to use to serve its purpose. But in certain special cases
the fading out of the projective moment is either arrested or accelerated.
For those artifacts that we call artworks, the act of projection is deliberately held in view by the affixing of a signature and by the enshrining of
the artwork in a museum, a theater, an electronic recording, or another
special time-suspending site. This distinguishes artworks from other
products. As Scarry writes:

> Artifacts that are purposely allowed to remain in the made-up stage—
> artifacts that are not only permitted but intended to be recognizable
> as fictitious—have pronounced signatures attached to them, signa-
> tures assuring that the first half of the arcing action will be remem-
> bered, whereas artifacts that are not intended to be self-announcingly
> fictitious usually have no such signature attached to them. When
> "Ode to Autumn" acts upon us, we know that it is actually John Keats
> who acts on us, whereas when with the same coming of autumn our
> coats begin to act on us, we do not overtly recognize that it is actually
> Mildred Keats (or any other specified coatmaker) who has reached out
> through the caritas of anonymous labor to make us warm.[7]

Yet even the winter coat retains details that, if one stops to examine them,
bespeak the origin of the coat from human hands: if not the International
Ladies' Garment Workers' Union (ILGWU) label, then at least the constructed character of the seams and buttonholes. On the other hand, the
moment of projection is erased and forgotten in the case of certain other
artifacts. Mores, folkways, political relationships, and the social configurations of gender, race, and class—although quite different from one another—all are that sort of artifact. They work more effectively to remake
human bodies, the more thoroughly the community forgets their artificial
character, their origin in human action.

How does it happen that we forget where these social conventions
have come from? Certainly the passage of time is a factor. But one also notices that two erasures must occur in tandem: the madeness of these social
realities is forgotten in the same stroke that erases the nonartifactual, unmade character of the human body itself. Thus it is human beings who appear as having been made, instead of the social definitions. But by whom
are people supposedly made? The need to specify a maker, cognitively

7. Scarry, *Body in Pain*, 311.

generated from the metaphor of body as artifact, motivates the construction of another artifact. Scarry terms God the Prime Artifact, continually in need of projection, whose projection by the human imagination also needs continually to be forgotten. The projection of God is part of the forgetting of the unmadeness of the human body. God, like other made-up entities, is made real by inflicting pain upon human bodies. Scarry reads within the Hebrew Scriptures a narrative tendency toward plots in which the people of Israel are punished repeatedly for attempting to endow their Divine Artifact with a body. God must be unmade and unmakable, impervious to the risks of bodily being. The body in its vulnerability is the proving ground for the distinction between divine maker and human product.

For Scarry, the Scripture positions God and humanity at the opposite ends of a weapon. Wounding serves as the antidote for doubting the independent reality of God. Unlike other artifacts, through which creative action arcs out from and then back again onto the human creators themselves, the weapon strikes out at someone other than its wielder because it has two ends. The two ends of the weapon—hilt and blade, trigger and barrel—locate a wounder in relation to a wounded and then transfer power between them. In the case of the Prime Artifact, the wound*ed*, humanity, is woundable because it is embodied. The wound*er* is not woundable; that is, he has no body. God instead is pure voice. Voice is the prerogative of the bodyless God. Human appropriations of voice are always punished as attempts to act upon God, who must remain the unaffected affector of human bodily being as well as its uneffected effector.

The opposition of voice and body gives Scarry a subtle heuristic device for interpreting social realities beyond the Hebrew Bible. This opposition first comes into focus when one notices how difficult it is to express or describe pain. Scarry examines how pain is mentioned in texts drawn from a variety of sources: medical literature, Amnesty International's reports of incidents of torture, legal briefs and transcripts from lawsuits claiming bodily damage, as well as poetry and prose. A paradox comes to light: pain is the most real and intense and undeniable experience for the person experiencing the pain, yet pain is also extremely difficult to convey to others and easy for them to deny or overlook. The presence of great pain is signaled by inchoate moans and cries, for pain has destroyed the capacity for sentences or words. The increase of pain is the disintegration of voice.

But pain is quite useful within social artifice. For example, in war the objective is to realize certain "fictions" or imaginations of power. The destruction of the bodies who resist the potential political fiction is what demonstrates the reality of its power. In torture the objective is to elicit statements from the victims that are not their own but rather fictions of the torturers. In war and torture the voices of the victims are diminished and finally annihilated by increasing the insistent reality of their bodies through inflicting pain. Because the body is vulnerable, it can be rendered voiceless. On the other hand, because the voice can deny its bodily origin in the project of becoming invulnerable, it can be disembodied. With this last observation, we come to a fact that has not been factored into Scarry's analysis. For the disembodiment of voice is *text*. Text is the way in which voice, once emerging from the fragile, historically located flesh of a human body to resonate briefly and locally, now becomes durable and escapes its historical time and place. Text is voice as artifact. While Scarry has taken most of her evidence from texts, she has not adequately taken the phenomenon of text itself into evidence.

The Body-Voice Continuum

How, then, can one relate the polarity of voice and body, which Scarry has analyzed, to textuality? If we begin with the body prior to either voice or text, then we can imagine a continuum between body and voice that runs off at right angles to the continuum between body and text. "Text" is a broadly inclusive category that includes many kinds of readable artifacts (it will be discussed more fully in the next chapter). Voice and body are opposite tendencies defining a continuum; yet, as the poles of that continuum they are still more alike (as living, realtime phenomena) than either of them is like text. Similarly, bodiliness and textuality, as we saw above, are opposite directions on a continuum of human realities that encode meaning and persist through time. Thus body and text, although poles of that continuum, are geared into each other and are more alike in their correlation as time-transcending phenomena than either of them is like voice. Body is the hinge between the two continua or dimensions. Both text and voice are in some ways alienated from the body and tend to deny their bodily origination, but in other important ways both voice and text are indissolubly tied to body.

So far, I have been fictionalizing the body by referring to it in the singular. The presumption has been that one can speak of some common underlying character of human bodily being that is always present no matter what historical-cultural context is under consideration. But that is a risky presumption. How much can we take for granted about "the" body? That all of us human bodies depend on others? That all are born and will die, and in between will often get hurt and hungry? Paradoxically, what is "the same" about bodies is that no two are "the same." To be a body, you must be different from all other bodies, both numerically and in your defining social characteristics. All bodies, of themselves, would be blank slates, yet they are never found blank.

What is meant by "body" is a socially constructed reality. It has meant different things in different eras and has been singularly receptive to redesign, as theorists have argued. For example, the redesign of the body through architectural, industrial, educational, medical, judicial, and other practices was a compelling research interest of Michel Foucault.[8] Mary Douglas also regards the body as receptive and malleable.[9] Like these and numerous other contemporary theorists, one who investigates resurrection must be interested in the body's receptivity to redesign. Yet one must discern in that receptivity a dynamic resistance, in which the body also resists and refuses certain inscriptions. Mary Douglas says that there are two bodies; "The social body constrains the way the physical body is perceived."[10] What Douglas terms the physical body, however, is, in my view, already inscribed with a version of the social body. By contrast, in order to theorize resurrection, we need to know whether we can speak of bodiliness that lies beneath all inscription and prior to it. Such a body would not be a substantially existing entity; it is more like a valence or a tropism or a tendency expressed through an actually existent (and therefore socially inscribed) body.

But the reverse also is true, for the physical body does some constraining of its own. Throughout all cultural versions, some qualities remain constant. The body is fragile, the body communicates, the body labors for its daily bread, the body is driven by emotion, the body bears other bodies, the body dies. Yet as cultural history flows along, the very interplay between body and its two alienations, voice and text, continually remakes the body. One must speak then in the plural—of fragili*ties*, communication*s*, labor*s*, hunger*s*, emotion*s*, birth*s*, death*s*—and one must speak of these as unequally distributed among bodies. A given culture at a given point in its history exhibits a distinctive configuration or footprint upon the grid of bodily realities, with its differential distribution of voice among bodies, its textual sculpting of certain bodies differently from others.

---

8. See esp. Michel Foucault, *Discipline and Punish: The Birth of the Prison,* trans. by Alan Sheridan (New York: Random House, Vintage Books, 1979).

9. See, e.g., Mary Douglas, *Natural Symbols* (New York: Random House, Vintage Books, 1973).

10. See Douglas, *Natural Symbols*, 65.

It is inherently risky to attempt to map present-day social configurations onto past eras and past relationships, even though the quest for understanding tempts us to do just that. On the other hand, if we admit plurality, if we attempt to let the distinctive body-text and body-voice configurations of other cultures stand forth while resisting the urge to assimilate them to those which are customary in our own culture, then we can gain a twofold dividend. First, the contrast between our own cultural practices and those of the other can heighten our appreciation of the special endowments of each and also suggest options for improvement. This yields a kind of dividend of discontinuity, the gain in understanding that comes from honoring differences. Second, in cases where the cultural practices under study are actually historical antecedents of our own, to pay attention to the variations is to increase understanding of how we have arrived at our own world. This yields a dividend of continuity, the gain that comes from discovering the developmental path of differentiation.

As an example, Page duBois has shown how fruitful an investigation of the body in ancient Greece can be, if only one lays aside the assumption that modern psychoanalytic theory is universally applicable. It has been customary to read pre-Socratic cultural productions through the lens of Freud's claim that male humanity is normative, while the female is defined only as lacking what the male has. But suppose, says duBois, that defining the female as the not-male is a peculiarity of recent Western culture. Suppose the earlier Greeks did not share that definition. Could one recover something of the way in which those ancient people regarded female bodies in their own right?

DuBois's research, reported in her book *Sowing the Body*, examines poetry, drama, architecture, art, pottery, and ritual from the fifth century B.C.E.[11] She identifies a cluster of metaphors that appear repeatedly in texts about women's bodies: a blooming meadow, a farmed field, a furrow, a stone, an oven, a vase, a cavern, a writing tablet. The female body is imaged as productive, protective, a workspace, a treasury.[12] This

---

11. See Page duBois, *Sowing the Body: Psychoanalysis and Ancient Representations of Women* (Chicago: University of Chicago Press, 1988).

12. DuBois's work on the seventh to the fifth century B.C.E. documents a transformation of imagery subsequent to that described by Marija Gimbutas in *The Language of the Goddess* (San Francisco: Harper & Row, 1989). Gimbutas shows that ovens, stones, and caverns figured into the imagery of the body in Old Europe from the beginnings of agriculture in the seventh millennium B.C.E. The relatively recent Greek imagery reconstructed by duBois therefore should be understood as reflecting the persistence of Old-European images after the encounter with Indo-European patriarchal cultures, into the time when the advent of literacy was occasioning another reconceptualization of the body—the one that provides the immediate background for the poietic imagination of the New Testament period.

conceptuality was the background for the transition to a literate culture, in which the productivity of the female body was transferred to the male sage, and Socrates could claim to inherit his mother's craft of mid-wifery. This remaking of body by text also presaged the political trans-formation from polis to cosmopolitan empire that subsequently threw Greek thought into ethical crisis in the Hellenistic era.[13] When we take note of these data, the dividend of discontinuity that we glean is the con-firmation that duBois was correct about the historical contingency of the contemporary psychoanalytic reading of human bodiliness. Once the male philosopher has become midwife and mother, the only distinctive-ness left to the female is to be "not male." But it was not always so.

An additional dividend of continuity comes as something of a shock for Christian theologians. The transition from autochthonous fertility to the productivity of writing is arguably the root of the Greek legacy in logic and individual personal ethics from which Christian theology has borrowed so heavily. Moreover, the metaphors of the female body re-mained contested cultural capital into the third century B.C.E., when the Hebrew Bible was being interpreted into Greek conceptual categories for the Septuagint. The literary renegotiation of those cultural markers was the rapid current through which the Bible waded as it crossed from He-brew to Greek; and when we compare the two versions today, we can see how far downstream the text traveled.

Moreover, these historically contested metaphors—sowing seed, plowing fields, pruning vines, baking bread, moving stone, entering and ex-iting holes in the earth—were still very much in play for those most influen-tial of all Septuagint readers, the authors of the Gospels. Their first-century texts represent a further stage in the resymbolization of the human body through the interplay of those metaphors. The earliest meanings of resurrec-tion, eucharist, and baptism depend upon that historically conditioned con-text. The Christian system of sacramental worship emerged as text meant to fix and sustain a new cultural configuration of bodies, a new distribution of voice.

My effort to allow for multiple versions of the human body is an ef-fort to respect perspective, not conquer it. One cannot hope to occupy some position superior to all others, from which everyone else's view can be evaluated. Our late industrial Western perspective is no more privi-leged than any other: it conceals some aspects of reality from us, while

---

13. This is to carry duBois's insight beyond where she has gone with it herself. On the philosophical crises that attended the emergence of Hellenism, see Giovanni Reale, *The Sys-tems of the Hellenistic Age*, vol. 3 of *A History of Ancient Philosophy*, trans. and ed. John R. Catan (Albany, N.Y.: State University of New York Press, 1985).

revealing others. If the concealing evokes pessimism, then let the revealing restore optimism, for there are indeed realities that stand forth very clearly to us that others have not seen. The remainder of this chapter highlights certain distinctive aspects of human bodily being that should be addressed by a theology of resurrection if it is to be both faithful to the historical data and responsive to the epistemological and metaphysical challenges of the three streams of theory mentioned above: pragmatism, materialism, and psychoanalysis. One must not elevate these aspects of human bodiliness to the status of transhistorical definition, but neither can they be dismissed as mere contingent and provisional concerns. These insights frame the possibility of understanding bodily and textual access in our world, in our day.

Materialist Approaches to Body

The materialist tradition of social analysis stems from the work of Karl Marx and follows his basic insight: that the key to understanding a society is to be sought in the distinctive practices through which it provides for the material needs of its people. The organization of labor power and material resources into systems for producing food or other commodities is called the economy. All the other human cultural activities, from art to education to religion, are interpreted as contributing toward making a favorable environment for agricultural and industrial production as well as replicating the economic system itself and the workers who make it run.

From a metaphysical point of view, materialist analysis offers scant conceptual resources for interpreting a claim about bodily resurrection. Such a claim can be read merely as part of an emotional support system that rehabilitates workers and motivates them psychologically so that they can return each day to the workplace. (More sinisterly, it could also be read as a threat invoked to extort compliant behavior and scarce resources from them.) This reading hardly seems adequate to the historical data recovered in our inductive studies, much less the data returned by history, archaeology, and anthropology. However, this reductionistic hermeneutic is not the only way for us to take the materialist critique. We can instead take it as a reminder not to neglect economic considerations and, moreover, to stay on the alert to notice the ways in which economics and epistemological factors interact.

The Marxian tradition treats knowledge as something shaped by the knowers' social position in the economic class structure of their society.

Knowledge is perspectival: what human beings can know is determined by their work.[14] What we have taken to be an objective, unbiased account of our world quite likely corresponds to the view available to those occupying places of economic privilege in our society and disseminated to everyone else through cultural indoctrination. Such a view should be challenged by the alternate views available to those who do the productive and reproductive work that keeps society going. The differential assignment of labor in a society may be made along the lines of class, but in addition it may be determined by the construction of gender and ethnicity as well. Thus materialist analysis is a doorway to understanding how knowledge is differently distributed on different sides of what I have called social frontiers.[15]

Materialist analysis can help throw light on realities that, although they have been ingeniously hidden by our customary beliefs, must be foregrounded in the claim for bodily resurrection. For example, the body is animal. It is a biological reality with physical needs and with psychological drives to fulfill those needs. We bodies stand within a food chain that links us with all life on earth. We eat. We eat other bodies, plant and animal bodies, when we can find them, catch them, coax or coerce them to abide with us, and/or raise them from the earth or from the wombs of their mothers. When we cease to eat, then other bodies will eat us in the natural process of decay within the grave, or sometimes more dramatically. Here is another dimension of the artifice of saying "the body," singular. The human body cannot exist in the singular, but only within the food chain along with the other bodies on which it feeds.

But the human niche within the food chain is differentiated. Some people produce food as well as eat it. Food producers are of two kinds: mothers nurse their infants at the breast, while farmers and herders take care of the living things that feed us after we are weaned. Mothers can also farm and herd, of course, but not all farmers and herders can nurse infants. In our complex society, the number of food producers is small in

<hr>

14. The pedagogical implications of this insight were already grasped by the community of teachers for whom the Gospel of Luke is speaking. As we saw in an earlier chapter, they invested the possibility of understanding resurrection in the possibility of working to feed the hungry.

15. For an introduction to materialist epistemological analysis, see Nancy C. M. Hartsock, "The Feminist Standpoint: Developing the Ground for a Specifically Feminist Historical Materialism," in *Discovering Reality: Feminist Perspectives on Epistemology, Metaphysics, and Philosophy of Science,* ed. Sandra Harding and Merrill B. Hintikka (Dordrecht: Reidel, 1983), 283–310. Anthropologist Karen Brodkin Sacks makes explicit the grounds for expanding class analysis into the dimensions of gender and race in her essay "Toward a Unified Theory of Class, Race, and Gender," *American Ethnologist* 16 (1989): 534–50.

comparison to the population whose place in the food chain is that of consumer only. Nevertheless society is specialized so that most people do
some productive work to provide for the nonnutritional needs of the food
producers while the latter are engaged in caring for living things. Those
other needs include shelter and clothing, health care, defense, the communications activities characteristic of a dynamic culture, and the management of the related industries of production and distribution. Thus our
economy is quite complex. The economy is the cultural counterpart of the
food chain, embracing both psychological and biological dimensions. To a
large extent, individuals base their self-concepts and sense of personal
worth on their participation in the economy through the work they do.[16]

Not every consumer does work that contributes to production. For
example, some people are too young or too old to work, or have another
disability. They are fed through the labor of others. But some able-bodied
people also decline to work. They are of two kinds: criminals and capitalists. Criminals take their sustenance without the consent of those who
produce it. Capitalists, along with financiers and managers, siphon their
sustenance out of the economic system as they manipulate the production
and distribution of goods and services. In our society, there is debate
about whether the managers' contribution toward efficiency in industry
is proportional to the rewards they reap. This debate is especially acute in
the case of managers who do not manage industry directly but rather
manage the money that finances industry.

No society comprised of human bodies can organize itself to distribute labor and food among its members in a completely egalitarian
way. Because some bodies are young while others are old, some are gestating or nursing, and many are disabled in one respect or another, human societies always are systems of inequality—which is not to say that
they are always unjust. Food and commodities are made available to

16. There are two exceptions to this rule and they constitute a social crisis in our
time: the upper class and the underclass. People of the underclass are denied access to
meaningful productive work and are offered counterfeit sources of self-valuation based on
style. People of the upper class displace personal worth into their possessions. In antiquity,
the ruling elite of the Greco-Roman cities considered leisure an essential component of humanity, and so they considered workers subhuman. From that small minority, however,
come virtually all of the literary texts that give us the familiar picture of the ancient world
as well as the ideology of the "classical" good life. By contrast, the nonliterary evidence of
carvings on tombs indicates that craftworkers and merchants took pride in their labor and
wished to be remembered for it. See, e.g., Paul Veyne's remarks on "'Work' and Leisure," pp.
117–37 of the volume he edited, *From Pagan Rome to Byzantium*, trans. Arthur Goldhammer,
vol. 1 of *A History of Private Life* (Cambridge: Harvard University Press, Belknap Press, 1987).

individuals through various practices that differ widely in efficiency, complexity, and scale. Kinship practices are among the most important of these, particularly in preindustrial societies.

Kinship is the assignment of reciprocal but nonsymmetrical social bonds between individuals. It tells you who you are. That is, the kinship system can prescribe whose labor you may utilize and who may manage your labor; whose land and livestock you will inherit and who will inherit from you; whom you may marry and who may marry you; who arranges for your social settlement through marriage and whose marriage you must provide for; who protects you when you are weak and whom you must protect. One's kin identity is correlated to one's bodily origin, needs, and destiny.

When we describe the kinship practices of an alien society, we give them an objective abstract expression that their own practitioners would not recognize. From "within" the system, it may not look like a constructed system at all. Its prescriptions may simply seem self-evident given the natural needs of human bodies. It is only from "outside" that both the conventionality and the rationality of the system may become evident. The rules of the tribe need codification only when a challenge arises—for example, when there is contact with a different set of practices or when the scale and complexity of the society grow beyond the point where kin obligations can efficiently organize to provide for the bodily needs of the increasing population. In such cases, kinship is weakened and may give way to another sort of economic system, such as feudalism or clientage.

The sheer scale of a society may overwhelm kinship structures or force their integration with other social institutions. In ancient Egypt, for example, a large population was fed through intensive agriculture and a centralized bureaucracy royally sponsored and based in the temples, for the political and religious institutions had taken over the economic managerial functions handled through kinship in simpler societies. In ancient Israel too, the centrally administered system of tithes and sacrifices functioned to provide for the needs of those without kin or land. A materialist analysis of this arrangement reminds us that, whatever else may have been involved in these cultic practices, they constituted a rational organization for distribution of scarce resources to satisfy the requirements of hungry bodies.[17]

---

17. That is not to say that the particular arrangement was the only rational one or the most rational one. Jacob Neusner finds in the Mishnah a sophisticated if unthematized appreciation of this fact. The Tannaim play off two theorizations: distributive economics, which is the more traditional system expressed in Mosaic legislation, and free-market

In our own century, several nations have experimented with alternative means of managing the production and distribution of food and other necessities. Communism and socialism are attempts to make the food chain work better by eliminating excessive rewards for managers. By the 1990s, those experiments seemed to have shown that communism did not bring efficient management. Socialist countries are tempering their economies with the cultivation of some free-market practices, just as the United States and other Western countries have tempered laissez-faire capitalism with socialistic controls. These practical experiments, and the political and philosophical debates that accompany them, take place in a world in which the population is growing faster than the capacity to produce and distribute food. While the northern hemisphere debates and experiments, the southern hemisphere multiplies and starves. The urgency of this tragic situation must not be forgotten in any consideration of human bodily being, no matter how theoretical.

Our century's economic experiments and ideological debates have largely overlooked another significant aspect of human participation in the food chain: the special place of women. Women's bodies feed the next generation by nursing, by subsistence farming, and by the seasonal tasks of food storage and the daily work of meal preparation. This real economic contribution, so apparent in ancient and traditional societies, has been curiously camouflaged in our own. The American economic system has taken the baby away from the breast. It has done so by the marketing of infant formula in the Third World, by the conscription of young mothers into the labor force in the industrialized world, and by the textual redesign of the female body as a commodity to attract the culturally engineered purchasing power of white males.

At the same time, women's labor in food preparation has been defined as non-work and therefore not significant. Obtaining food and cooking it for the family are tasks to be done *in addition to other* labor; they are invisible in the economy and can be erased from consciousness. The unrecognized, unwaged domestic labor of women is not computed in the economic equations that describe the function of individual economies, whether they are capitalist, socialist, or communist. This bodily toil of women first brings forth and then constantly habilitates the bodies of the wage earners who go forth from their homes to the workplace refreshed each morning and

economics, introduced by Hellenistic trade and urbanization. The rabbis deftly hobble the mechanism of the market in the interest of providing more equitably for the sustenance of the whole society.

return there depleted at night. The value transactions that register on economic indicators are made possible by this domestic work, yet they hide its very existence. In other words, industrial economies are organized to extract the value of the domestic labor of women without having to compensate them for it.[18]

Nutrition itself has undergone both textual redesign through advertising and chemical redesign to accommodate the needs of marketing and distribution systems. Thus eating, the activity that ought to display for us most plainly our radical connection with all living things in the food chain, actually hides and severs the links among human bodies and between people and other growing things. The dining table is one site where cultural texts remake the human body. Ancient dining practices dramatized and reinforced class distinctions in a highly visible way. In contemporary America, by contrast, the realities of farm labor and international trade are colorless, tasteless ingredients ingested with our cereal, hamburgers, and microwaved spinach.

Ethnic customs and cuisine are also under pressure from commercial advertisements representing a kind of homogenized and commodified American dining practice. The remaking of the body at meals—whether in the home dining room, in the workplace cafeteria, or at the fast-food counter—tends therefore to promote both economic and cultural oblivion as the texts of the consuming society take flesh.[19] But fortunately, flesh refuses to take completely to the texts imposed upon it. The incompleteness of their inscription underscores the fact that the body resists standardization. One might say that the body *is* refusal of sameness. No two bodies are exactly alike. We come in different sexes, colors, and abilities. Questions of gender and race arise because of this physical plurality; if there were no bodily variety among us, we would never have come up with the pseudo-analytical category of race. Yet the differences of our bodies are somehow threatening, and from this arise certain fictions—for example, that white people are not a race but just "normal," while the peoples of color belong to races; or that regular people are male, while women as a special case are a gender unto themselves; or that I speak with an accent although you do not.

The co-differentiation of human bodies continues to reassert itself in the face of concerted efforts to hide, deny, or destroy every sign of it. Mary

---

18. Sacks, *"Toward a Unified Theory of Class, Race, and Gender,"* argues for this interpretation in the case of capitalist economies.

19. This criticism of the nutritional practices of Americans who can still afford to eat overlooks, of course, the real and growing catastrophe of hunger in America.

Douglas has described three ways in which information such as this is systematically pushed out of sight, or "backgrounded." First, it may be automatically destroyed because it would otherwise contradict information commonly held to be beyond question. Second, it may be taken as completely obvious and unworthy of attention. Third, it may be assigned to the chaotic, unknowable realm of dirt, rubbish, and defilement.[20] I believe that this third variety of "backgrounding" accounts for much of the concealment of work, hunger, and other bodily realities from attention in Western humanistic bourgeois scholarship, including most theology. From this conceptual soiling arises the cultural disparagement of people of color, feminine gender, homoerotic orientation, Semitic or Slavic ethnicity, and all who sweat and struggle for their living. Yet the body resists, and asserts its distinctive interdependence against the obliteration intended by that cultural backgrounding.

Three examples can illustrate. First, the body's radical connectedness with other bodies is clearly signified on those regions of our surfaces that we normally cover. The navel marks every human body, from cradle to grave, with the sign that this human being has grown out of another and owes life to her. Breasts and genitals also mark human bodies as oriented toward connection with others. Yet we hide these bodily emblems, and we do not speak of them in polite conversation, either through reverence or because of the vulnerability that they represent.[21]

A second obliteration is attempted in relation to our hunger and our labor. These are signals of our place within the food chain, and disguising them means forgetting the human body's connection to other living bodies. But work embarrasses us, because it signals our fragility and mortality. Self-definition is pursued instead in terms of access to leisure and through non-work weekend activities. Cleanliness is an obsession, but at the same time the compulsion to make food consumption quick and tidy through plastic packaging has precipitated an environmental crisis. Our double discomfiture with labor and with waste disposal focuses on the culturally disparaged figure of the trash-collection worker, whose job is considerably complicated by pressure to come and go invisibly. No one wants to know the garbageman's name or bid him good morning.

---

20. See Mary Douglas, *Implicit Meanings: Essays in Anthropology* (London: Routledge & Kegan Paul, 1975), 3-4. This sort of backgrounding is woven into the English language itself. For example, we use the same words, "dirt" and "soil," to denote what makes surfaces unclean as well as for earth, the matrix out of which crops grow, the support of all life.

21. The camouflage of bodily differentiation and of labor is a theme ingeniously explored in Ursula K. LeGuin's novel *The Dispossessed* (New York: Harper & Row, 1974).

A third obscuring of the body comes with the "American" cultural hegemony of mass-mediated message systems. The media cloak or co-opt those distinctive ethnicities that historically have formed and are still forming the real America—to say nothing of the rest of the world. Ethnic identity is carried in the body and its practices—whether by facial features, mannerisms, customs, style, skin color, child-rearing ways, speech habits, or dress. These arise out of, and express, the particularity of the body itself. What is distinctive about one's own cultural heritage can emerge clearly only in contrast to the values of a different ethnicity, yet the very term "culture" is begrudged to any whose forebears were not European. What is taken for culture is so intolerant and insecure that it banishes alternative expressions. "White"—actually a kind of sallow peachy beige—is not content to be one color within the rainbow; it has to be the whole show, no matter how boring a show it is.

Thus the textual obliteration of the navel and of labor and of color is a hegemonic project that, curiously, never quite succeeds. The body keeps asserting itself. Blackness won't go away; that hyphen in "African-American" is permanent. The carpenters and the trash crews make noise in the morning; the cook quits; the teachers strike. And as the stockmarket trader drops his drawers to step into the hot tub, that old navel is still right there. No escape from the body this side of the grave. No escape from the bodily connection with human beings who insist on being different from oneself.

Psychoanalytic Approaches to Body

Bodily differentiation, a factor in the production of the goods needed for survival, also figures into human reproduction, that is, the raising of the coming generations and the maintenance of the social and cultural systems that will support them. Freud gave us two basic insights: that a significant portion of the mind is not available directly to consciousness and that emotional interactions during the first few years of life set the pattern for all subsequent tasks and relationships. His disciple Erik Erikson elaborated some implications of those insights for lifelong social development. Erikson's theories together with those of Jean Piaget, self-styled "genetic epistemologist," are cited in every psychology textbook, and they form the foundation of the contemporary understanding of the origin and development of human cognition.

Both Piaget and Erikson, working from different theoretical bases, explored the extent to which the mind depends on the body. Children's thinking patterns mimic their bodily behavior patterns. For Piaget, mental operations such as addition and subtraction begin as internalizations of the gestures by which the child has learned to manipulate objects in the physical world. In logic, we "do" with our minds what we have first practiced doing physically with our hands.

For Erikson, social competences also mirror physical behaviors. Erikson traced the sequential emergence of certain "sites" upon the child's body for social attention and interaction: first the mouth with the activities of sucking and biting during nursing and weaning; then the backside with the activities of "holding on" and "letting go" during toilet training; then the genitals with the activities of intruding and including as the child gains locomotor competence to stride into groups, linguistic competence to enter into conversations, and emotional competence to beguile others into mutually satisfying one-on-one relationships. As with Freud, these oral, anal, and genital stages culminate in an oedipal crisis, in which the child faces the fact of being still a child who cannot displace the parent of the opposite sex but must make an alliance with that parent in order to be apprenticed into adulthood, now deferred to the future.

Beyond the ages of orality, anality, and genitality in early childhood, and the age of latency in the grade-school years, Erikson enumerated four more ages: adolescence, young adulthood, middle adulthood, and maturity. In each of those ages the body, always embedded in social relationships, presents a new and distinctive challenge to the developing personality. When each challenge is successfully met, the person acquires a characteristic ego strength.

The psychoanalytic approach to human cognition has drawn less criticism for the overall developmental structure it projects than for certain elaborations of particular phenomena located within that structure. Working in reverse chronological order, I will redescribe significant features in the three early childhood stages: the oral, the anal, and the genital.

Freud's proposal of a genital stage remains plausible, for children do seem to want to appropriate a precocious adulthood about the age of three or four to five years. The child must settle for nonerotic love and agree to remain a child in submissive obedience to the parents after failing in the attempt to displace one of them and captivate the other. Yet there is widespread rejection of Freud's claim that little girls envy their brothers' penises and that grown women continue to define their bodily identity in terms of a genital deformity. As Page duBois's work indicates, this way of differentiating women from men is not culturally universal and may be peculiar to Freud's own social milieu. Moreover, if the women with whom Freud was acquainted did see themselves as deprived, what they envied could have been any of a variety of things other than penises. More recent work in the psychoanalytic tradition places the child's most significant personality-defining disappointment much earlier in infancy, within the oral stage, when baby must renounce certain intense desires and fantasies in regard to mother.[22]

In the same way, Erikson's description of the anal phase needs revision. Erikson noted that the ability to control one's bowels is a significant social accomplishment and leads to feelings of self-esteem.[23] Feces are the first "products" that the human being makes. It is important to praise the child for this production, while helping him or her to distinguish between the self and the work. Controlled movement of the bowels thus is the prototype of all human making, and feces are the primal product. Erikson saw that the psychic correlate of bowel control was the emotional flexibility to "hold on" to possessions, objects of affection, ideas, and projects, when appropriate; and then to "let go" of them at the proper times. The implications are not only emotional but cognitive as well. The human experience of production has a whiff of feces about it forevermore.

Erikson reports the case of a boy who had become constipated psychosomatically because he had confused the function of his bowels with what little he knew of pregnancy and the process of birth. However, Erikson did not register the obvious analogy here between the productivity of the bowels and the productivity of the womb.[24] Perhaps the self-evident importance of the penis for Erikson and Freud kept them from noticing what every mother, aunt, big sister, and baby-sitter knows about little boys. Around the age of three and one-half years, they become very curious and somewhat anxious about the apertures of women's bodies. Where does Mama do peepee? Does the baby come out from her tummy button or from where the poop comes out? These questions are posed not once but several times a day over a period of some weeks. They can be overheard in public lavatories as well as in the homes of family and friends.

22. This renunciation founds the capacity for object relations. For a psychoanalytic interpretation of Freud's own contradictory discussions of object relations, see Jane Flax, *Thinking in Fragments: Psychoanalysis, Feminism, and Postmodernism in the Contemporary West* (Berkeley and Los Angeles: University of California Press, 1990).

23. See Erik H. Erikson, *Childhood and Society,* 2d ed. (New York: W. W. Norton & Co., 1963), esp. 80–85; and idem, *Identity and the Life Cycle* (New York: W. W. Norton & Co., 1980), 67–77.

24. See Erikson, *Childhood and Society,* 53–58. Erikson helped the child by drawing a cross-section of an expectant elephant, "making it quite clear that there were two exits, one for the bowels and one for the babies" (p. 55). My observation is that different openings imply different *processes* of production and different *products* as well. Another sort of affinity between bowel and womb is expressed in the Hebrew Bible, where they are both indicators of compassion, as in Jer. 31:19 (31:20 in many English translations). The root of the verb translated "to have mercy on" is *rḥm,* which means womb when written with different vowel points. The phrase translated "my heart yearns" is literally "my bowels growl."

Little boys need to be reassured repeatedly that there is "a special hole," different from the anus, for the baby to come out. That is, they need to know that the human body is not produced in the same way that feces are produced. The child's body is not shit. It is not a product, still less an achievement. The child's body is not destined to be used like a work of human hands or like manure. What has come from "the special hole" is very special indeed, and utterly unlike an artifact.

Because the production of feces is the original physical analogue of productive labor in the cognitive and emotional life of the young child, human beings retain profound feelings of ambiguity about all the works of their hands. This is reflected in the Bible's insistence that one may not make an image of God.[25] The only permissible image of God is the unmade one, the human body itself, the product of the womb. Yet because the reproduction of babies seems to resemble the production of feces, human beings inevitably have profound doubts about the value of the body itself. The specter of disposability stalks the body wherever it turns. Human bodies are treated like consumables and disposables in the labor market, in the media, in schools, and elsewhere. The contemporary crisis of substance abuse is a symptom of a much more extensive crisis of consumption throughout Western society. The systems of production and consumption are interfering with the systems of reproduction, which include both the birthing and nurture of the rising generation and the maintenance of social systems like education and government needed by the children.

The earliest of the ego-developmental stages, the oral stage, holds a key to understanding the genesis of the global crisis of consumption. Just as the capacity for productive work has its roots in the young child's anal experiences, so physical and psychic practices of consumption are founded in the character of the child's oral experiences. Newborn infants do not distinguish themselves from their mothers, with whom they have a concrete nutritive connection through nursing. The child's ego emerges gradually but never completely from the maternal ego. Nursing is at first experienced as passive reception of satisfaction and gradually becomes more active acquisition as the baby becomes more capable of sucking, more adept at attracting attention, and more able to tolerate periods of delay. Mother and baby must negotiate these developments together. If baby were to experience no resistance or frustration in feeding, there would be no differentiation of a separate ego and no construction of objects.

The appearance of teeth is tremendously significant for the nursing pair. Heretofore suckling had been mutually rewarding. The baby now

---

25. See Exod. 20:4; 34:17; Lev. 26:1; Deut. 4:15-18; 27:15.

finds that biting feels good to one of the partners but is forbidden by the other. Teething babies learn to modulate their practices of consumption in consideration of requirements imposed by the source of their nourishment. This is how they learn that the proprietor of the breast is "someone else" whose needs also must be taken into account. Of course the child has many other opportunities to discover personal separation. Even a bottle-fed baby must adapt to the schedule of the household and to mother's periodic absence. Either way, mother becomes the first "object," that is, the first subsisting item of the world that baby constructs as a separate entity in which knowledge and love are invested. All subsequent knowing and loving will be modeled after this original relation.

In the psychoanalytic tradition, object-relations theory states that the capacity to reason emerges out of the unfolding relationship between mother and child. On its affective side, it enables the child to balance conflicts: the desire to return to a less differentiated state, against the fear of being swallowed up; the desire to use the mother ruthlessly, against an emerging rudimentary concern for her as a separate person. On its logical side, it enables the child to balance contradictions: the object is created in the mind by baby's desire but also was there previously waiting to be created; the baby in fits of rage strikes out against the object that was created, but the object survives destruction and now becomes truly useful for the first time.[26]

D. W. Winnicott has proposed that between mother and infant there is a kind of transitional space that is neither subjective nor objective. This space opens up in the process of individuation as a kind of testing ground in which the baby safely experiments with relinquishing the fantasy of omnipotent control on the part of, alternately, baby or mother. As mother more often fails to respond instantaneously to baby's every demand, the availability of so-called transitional objects (for example, a blanket or a toy) in the transitional space helps the baby to cope. The transitional space is intermediary between the illusion of omnipotence and the unyielding resistance of reality.[27] This space, like other ego phenomena of infancy, persists into adulthood. It is the breeding ground for

---

26. See Flax, *Thinking in Fragments*, 107–32. Two of the most influential interpretations of object-relations theory have been Evelyn Fox Keller, *Reflections on Gender and Science* (New Haven: Yale University Press, 1985); and Nancy Chodorow, *The Reproduction of Mothering: Psychoanalysis and the Sociology of Gender* (Berkeley and Los Angeles: University of California Press, 1978), and idem, *Feminism and Psychoanalytic Theory* (New Haven: Yale University Press, 1989).

27. Pertinent essays of D. W. Winnicott are collected in *The Maturational Processes and the Facilitating Environment: Studies in the Theory of Emotional Development* (New York: International Universities Press, 1965). See also a discussion of Winnicott in Flax, *Thinking in Fragments*.

all cultural productions, including the religious production of what Scarry termed the Prime Artifact, the deity.

The oral, anal, and genital phases are species-universal for human beings. They devolve from the normal pattern of bodily growth and the basic relations without which the baby body cannot live. Yet these stages unfold with infinite variety among peoples with different child-rearing practices. Erikson thought that distinctive weaning customs determined the typical national characteristics of peoples. To be sure, each stage is a kind of agenda, although it can be fulfilled in a variety of ways. For our analysis the agenda of the oral and anal stages frame the species-universal issues that are addressed by the first century's claim of a bodily resurrection. These issues include the status of us bodies among other items of our environment that can know and be known, eat and be eaten, make and be made.

Pragmatic Approaches to Body

A third interpretive tradition that contributes to the understanding of human bodiliness is pragmatism. If, as we have seen, a psychoanalytic approach regards the "past" experiences of childhood as present components of the body's relational repertoire, so a pragmatic approach enfolds into the body's present capacities the projected future outcomes of its ongoing practices. Pragmatism is a general orientation toward results and consequences rather than foundations and origins. The term itself comes from the same Greek root as do praxis, practice, and practical, although *pragma* throws the emphasis onto the outcome achieved by those activities. Immanuel Kant distinguished the practical from the pragmatic in his study of the human will, and this nuance was picked up and developed by the American philosophers Charles Saunders Peirce and William James at the end of the last century. John Dewey brought the pragmatic approach to the cognitive theories supporting his hugely influential philosophy of education.[28]

The basic pragmatist insight is that concepts are without meaning and truth unless one knows their concrete applications—what James termed their "cash value." The imperative of interpretation is to look for

---

28. For an overview, see John Dewey, "The Development of American Pragmatism," in his *Philosophy and Civilization* (New York: Minton, Balch & Co., 1931). For a more recent reading, see Cornel West, "The Politics of American Neo-Pragmatism," in *Post-Analytic Philosophy*, ed. John Rajchman and Cornel West (New York: Columbia University Press, 1985), 259–75. See also Richard Rorty, "Solidarity or Objectivity," in Rajchman and West, *Post-Analytic Philosophy*, 3–19.

the meaning of terms and the truth of claims in the social outcomes unfolding for those who use the terms and make the claims. John Dewey went so far as to say that what justifies a belief is its proven ability to fulfill a need.

As with materialism, considered above, we are seeking from pragmatism, not a full-blown comprehensive theory of reality, but some tools to enhance our understanding of the body. We can take from it the reminder not to neglect the consequences of the concepts and claims that we receive from our tradition. Resurrection belief is diachronic in scope, and its meaning depends on the difference it makes for the bodily realities unfolding themselves down through history. The meaning of resurrection was not complete when the Gospels were written, because all its outcomes were not yet known. Resurrection belief emerges as a response to the possibilities and threats for the body inherent in Hellenistic society, and it is still strategically proving itself in our own society.[29] To claim a resurrection for Jesus is to claim, minimally, that a certain possibility inheres within the human body itself and that Hellenistic society was one in which that possibility could be actualized. But all of the body's possible futures are precarious. They are riding upon what the body does with what is done to it as its life unfolds. We bodies wield conceptual tools whose creative effect spreads outward to color the world but also arcs back to modify us tool users ourselves. Every expressed idea is a boomerang inasmuch as it is an artifact. Every implemented metaphor comes true in its implementation.

To illustrate, let us consider again the alternate metaphors for teaching introduced above in chapter 2: planting and nursing. These describe bodies differently, and therefore they have differential effects on the bodies they describe. *Planting* is an agricultural metaphor. We speak today of the various "fields" of knowledge that comprise the modern university. Academic areas are mapped through bibliographies. The territory is defined by landmarks: the groundbreaking discoveries, the famous authors who may be said to "own the field." There are proper fences, and requirements for admission through the recognized gateways. One enters a field through an introduction, literally a leading into, in which one becomes acquainted with positions within the field.

The learners also can be regarded as a field. Teaching is the act of cultivation: plowing the field into receptive straight furrows, breaking up its resistant clods, then sowing the seed. The field needs continued

---

29. Francis Schüssler Fiorenza discusses the warranting of belief in dialogue with the pragmatic tradition. See esp. Fiorenza, *Foundational Theology* (see chap. 1, n. 4), 306–10.

cultivation while the seed matures. In due time, the crop is ready for harvest. It has become a field of knowledge again. The cycle of seasons explains why the metaphor of field can carry the two contrasting meanings: both a body of knowledge and the body of the student awaiting knowledge.

This metaphor elaborates several aspects of the teaching/learning relationship. According to the planting metaphor, the learners are relatively passive while the teacher works on them with labor that is tedious and monotonous. The objective is to increase grain: from a little seed to a plentiful harvest. The grain harvest will be owing in part to the teacher's labor but also to the timely appearance of rain and sunshine and to the application of manure. Little passion or emotion need accompany this toil. The gratification of teaching is delayed to the future of the expected harvest.

As we have seen, the sowing metaphor was a familiar theme in Hellenistic texts about teaching, and it appears in Mark 4, the parable of the Sower, with a curious twist. Under the influence of this metaphor, agricultural products tend to take on the connotation of information, learning, or knowledge. The Gospel writers play with this shade of meaning when they mention grains of wheat, bread, or wine. The Mishnah expresses Torah, or divine instruction, to a great extent as the management of cultivation, harvest, and distribution of agricultural produce.

The other pedagogical metaphor is *nursing*. Its provenance is not agriculture but animal husbandry and, in particular, herding. Today this metaphor is used less prominently for academic work than in political discourse. The herding metaphor emphasizes paths, not fences. The pedagogical term "curriculum" reflects this metaphor, for the Latin meaning of that word is "racetrack," the path along which horses run to the finish line. A movement is driven by needs and goals, not mapped bibliographically like a field. The shepherd takes the flock where it has to go to get what it needs to flourish, while avoiding or defending against dangers.

In this metaphor the learners are the animals in the flock, especially the young lambs. Teaching is leading the sheep to lush meadows and bubbling springs so that they get adequate nutrition to breed and so that the ewes can nurse their lambs. In one development of this metaphor, the teacher herself is the mother who nurses the learners until they are weaned and able to graze for themselves. This metaphor reinforces aspects of the teaching/learning relationship different from those highlighted by the metaphor of sowing. Here the learner is not passive like the earth but interactive with the teacher. The work of teaching becomes more interesting, emotionally rewarding, even passionate. The objective is not harvest but weaning: that is, the production of individuals who are strong, lusty, able to fend for themselves and eventually to reproduce and nurse others. In the herding metaphor, the teacher has greater command of the factors leading to success. Grass is in abundant supply. Water comes out of rocks in the form of a spring or a stream; no need to wait for rain. Where the field required manure to produce grass, the flock eats grass and produces manure. Thus the nursing metaphor and the sowing metaphor both situate teaching on the circle of the food chain but at opposite points.

The metaphor of birthing and nursing was also a familiar theme in classic Greek texts about teaching. In Hellenistic times, as the Septuagint translators interpreted the Hebrew Bible into Greek, this affinity between nursing and teaching put a certain spin on the concept of Israel's God. To the Hebrew imagination God was the Shepherd of Israel, its midwife, the one who knit Israel together within the womb, the one who fed Israel with nonagricultural foods: milk, honey, manna. To the Greeks, that spelled teacher. As we have seen, this was one of the factors that transformed salvation history into paideia in the Septuagint. However, in rabbinic thought, where Hellenistic influence was less pronounced, weaning signaled the time to begin a child's instruction in Torah. As we have seen, the trajectory of the nursing metaphor in some Jesus traditions effectively positions the kingdom of God prior to Torah.

As we consider these metaphors, we are doing a kind of archaeology. We are digging down through the foundations of our own understanding of teaching in order to discover what lies below. What are we recovering? We are finding *theories:* speculative expressions about the nature of teaching in the abstract. But we are also finding *practices:* certain distinctive ways of working with people and information in the teaching/learning situation. The practices and the theoretical reflections seem to be interactive. Pragmatically, we see that the practices are the embodiment of the theories.

It is well to note how the body asserts itself in both of these metaphors, which in fact are derived from the food chain of which the body is a part. Both metaphors picture teaching as a way of managing the body, a labor with the body. But both metaphors model this labor as organically productive rather than productive of an artifact. The learner was not experienced as "a work of human hands," a made thing. The learner was not raw material being "made into" something. This contrasts with contemporary Western practices, which typically design educational programs to "make citizens," or "make engineers," or "make Christians." Contemporary theorists and practitioners seem to have overlaid a manufacturing metaphor upon the earlier biological metaphors.

Thus an overdose of pragmatism seems to have engulfed and drowned pedagogical science in instrumental behavioral technology.

Secular education is awash with teaching for quantitative measurement, and the "social science" approach submerges truth in orthodoxy. What is lost here is the genuinely pragmatic insight that consequences fulfill concepts. Regardless of content, the outcome of technoscientific pedagogy is already prescribed by its controlling metaphor: manufacturing. Very different consequences unfold from the bodybuilding nutritional metaphors of farming and nursing. From a pragmatic perspective, it is irrelevant whether one of these metaphors is "correct" or "right" in some abstract sense. Of greater import is how they work, whether they work, and what kind of human life they tend to support.

In the twentieth century the human body has had a precarious career, and its survival remains in doubt. The *material* survival of the body depends upon the economic restructuring of agribusiness and the equitable worldwide distribution of food; upon the political refusal of militarism and the cooperative rebuilding of a just peace; and upon the emotional restructure of the patriarchal family so that all children can be born into safety and sustenance. But the fuller *human* survival of the body requires something more. Besides famine, war, and abuse, what threatens bodies everywhere is the contagion of texts: the risk of having oppressive meanings inscribed.

9

Scripts Written and Read

FROM THE philosophical approaches surveyed in chapter 8 we have compiled memoranda: things to bear in mind as we consider what resurrection can possibly mean for human bodies. Materialism reminded us that any knowledge is complicit with the food-distribution mechanisms of the society in which it occurs. Psychoanalysis reminded us that cognitive capacities evolve out of the nutritive and productive bodily activities that occupy the earliest years of life. Pragmatism reminded us that concepts and claims are semantically open-ended and achieve their meanings only gradually, as their consequences come into being.

These three sets of reminders derive from a consideration of what the human body is, whatever its culture or social habitat. But what is the logical status of assertions such as these? Do we have here finally a collection of culturally universal eternal verities? Are these the ashlars to lay as the foundation of a metaphysical system to end all systems? Hardly. For these memoranda concerning the body that we have collected will function merely as negative imperatives. In effect, they advise the theologian: "Don't forget that knowers eat, make things, are born, and die." They say watch out for systems constructed to hide any of those factors.

The only cultural universal here is this: what knows is always a body. The memoranda of the body, taken alone, would never enable one to compile a complete and exhaustive description of any culture. Rather, these caveats are assembled to play an auxiliary role in tempering programs of social description and analysis. They direct an investigator to inquire into the fate of the body in its various textual representations. They insist on the fragility of the body. What is most fragile about a human body is its uniqueness. Any particular body is precious because it is the only one of them there is, it can never be repeated, it is irreplaceable. Texts, as we shall see, are infinitely replicable.

What Is Text?

The contrasts drawn between body and text in chapter 8 might suggest that text could be defined now simply and tidily as non-body. But the logic of binary opposition and subordination, as we saw above, does not grasp the difference of two entities but may actually suppress it. Moreover, text is only one of several "opposites" for body, just as body is only one of several "opposites" for text. Among the other entities that have been proposed as candidates for body's opposite number are spirit, voice, and the remainder of the "nonhuman" material world. The human body could be in some sense the opposite of any of those.

As for text, once again there are multiple candidates for its "opposite." Non-text might be body, or context, or the unreadable furniture of the physical world, or what Walter Ong has termed "voicings . . . oral art forms." Ong would restrict the denotation of the term "text" to what is made with the alphabet: manuscripts and printed materials, that is, literature. According to this usage, an oral, nonliterate culture has no texts.[1] That distinction helps Ong to show how literacy appears in human history as a novel technology that transforms traditional practices of composition, memory, performance, and verification. The alphabet has speeded up the evolution of human consciousness toward the individual interiority now commonly experienced among the modern Western bourgeoisie. Yet to make his case, Ong must generalize about pure orality and pure literacy; and to construct those abstractions, he must distort the untidy middle territory in between. (Thus, for example, he insists that the Torah, which certainly looks as though it should qualify as a chirographically written text, must have "set down in writing thought forms still basically oral.") In the attempt to distinguish cleanly between a literate culture and "a primary oral culture or a culture with a heavy oral residue," Ong's analysis obscures the fact that the majority of cultures one encounters today are mixed. That "heavy oral residue" is all around us, particularly when we step outside the university and the middle class.[2]

1. See Ong, *Orality and Literacy*, 14, 33.
2. Ong, *Orality and Literacy*, 99.

This untidiness suggests that once again it may be more fruitful to explore the continuities rather than the differences. The term "text" must have a broader denotation here than with Ong. Text will include all cultural copy. In this inclusive sense, then, a recitation of an epic poem (what Ong calls an "oral art form") is *text*—text that is more or less voice-like. A book too is text: stuff-like text, text inscribed upon organic and inorganic substances as its media. A custom is text as well: body-like text, text inscribed in human behavioral practices. We never get plain old text; always it is inscribed into some medium, whether voice or paper or behavior, which accounts for its persistence in time. Neither do we get plain old bodies, but only bodies inscribed and inscribing.

The reciprocality between body and text invites a closer look. Text has its origin in a process more like the manufacture of an artifact than like the organic birthing of a human body. Text is indeed artifactual and artificial. Recalling Elaine Scarry's description of the "arcing" of creativity out toward the artifact and then back toward the maker,[3] we may note that text exhibits a similar function. Inscribed by the outward projection of human creativity, text too focuses creative energy back toward its human source, all the while concealing its own origin in human creativity. People are susceptible to texts, just as we are to other artifacts. Texts, like any other made thing, can redesign or even destroy human bodies. They can work like scalpels or weapons. Texts, then, are implements for remaking what was never literally made in the first place, the human body.

The redesign or remaking of the originally non-made body is a curious phenomenon. How is such a process even possible? It is possible because human bodies are "originally unmade" only in the abstract, while in reality every actually existent human body is always already covered with text. Human bodies live within human cultures. We are cultured, cultivated, from the hour we are born. The biology of human reproduction itself is etched with courtship customs, gender roles, the folkways of marriage and child rearing. "Prior to" these textual embellishments of the human body is only the ancestral ape. The newborn is written into the story of his or her people; their version of the world is written onto the child.

The English word "culture" recalls millennia of ruminations upon this process by means of the metaphor of farming. The practices of cultivation—plowing and planting fields to produce nourishing food—served as an analogue by which to understand how children are raised up in the nourishing traditions of their people. As we have seen, sowing became a

---

3. See chapter 8 above.

metaphor for teaching. When writing developed, it too was compared to plowing. The stylus worked in straight lines scratching through the soft wax or clay of the tablet, depositing letters, raising up a crop of meaning. These metaphors interbred, so that the fertile mind of the learner came to be regarded as resembling the receptive material of the tablet, inviting inscription by the teacher. Yet the English word "text" recalls that a contrasting metaphor must have been at work as well. Texts resemble textiles, woven from the wool of the flocks to protect and decorate the human body.

Weaving is a more complex activity than plowing and therefore may offer a more adequate metaphor with which to approach the dynamic phenomenon of textuality. In the first place, although both plow and shuttle are tools that travel back and forth, the plow works the "raw material" of earth directly, while the shuttle works across perpendicular strands that have already undergone several processes: sheering the fiber from the animal's coat, carding it, twisting it into yarn, and stringing the yarn upon the loom. (If one is weaving cotton or flax instead of wool, of course, the fiber comes from cultivation rather than the herd.) Weaving requires more patience and ingenuity; plowing requires more strength and stamina. But the complexity of weaving allows for the introduction of pattern, style, beauty, whimsy into the design of the fabric. Weaving can encode more meaning into its product than plowing can; and the cloth lasts longer than the crop. In these respects, weaving resembles writing.

But cloth most resembles text in that, once woven, it is remade several times. Perhaps the cloth is cut and stitched into a coat, a sturdy surface to protect a worker's shoulders, back, and arms. The remnants may serve as patches for a pair of jeans or as scrub rags. The coat may later be cut down for another wearer, cut off for warmer weather, then finally (but not really finally) cut up into scraps, which go into the construction of a new (but not really new) patchwork quilt under which bodies will cuddle and couple after work is done. With cultural texts too, we are continually patching new pieces onto older garments; stitching new designs out of the disintegration of previous ones; and augmenting the body's tasks of loving and working, overlaying them with intricate meanings. This phenomenon, in which cultural texts are forever recycled, is called intertextuality.

Characteristics of Text

But neither of these analogues, weaving or plowing, is entirely adequate as a model for the dynamic complexities of textual production and reproduction. The reason is that both weaving and plowing are material productions. They involve the transformation of some finite, limited quantity of matter into another form, while mass is inexorably conserved. Human creativity is expressed in both, although only weaving produces durable artifacts; yet this creativity in either case is very closely dependent on the organic fecundity of the earth.

With text, it is different. In principle a text is infinitely replicable. It copies. For all practical purposes, a copy is as good as the original. The text is mere information; although it must be carried by some material medium or other, still it makes no difference to the information whether it is written onto this piece of paper here or that one over there.

This characteristic is termed "material transcendence" by Mary Gerhart and Allan Russell, who propose it as one of four criteria that qualify an artifact to be counted as a text.[4] Thus the lines that you are reading right now can be text—because, to be the particular text that they are, they do not have to be the lines in this particular book that is in your possession but can be the lines in another copy of the book, or the electronic configuration of my word processor's memory, or the paragraph that I have scrawled in my notebook. The identity of the text is independent of the nonidentity of the various material manifestations of it. To burn a flag is not to burn *the* flag, because the flag is text and can still imprint some other piece of cloth. Thus for Gerhart and Russell, an artwork is not a text if it needs to be apprehended in its original medium—as would be the case, for example, with an oil painting.

With text, then, there is no such thing as "an original."[5] There is only copy. This raises the fascinating question of how we are to negotiate the concept of sameness. In what sense are two identical copies "the same" if in fact we can count them (one, two) and tell them apart, at least spatially? In fact, "same" turns out to be another one of those ideal predicates which never occurs in the real world. What is "same" is not material; it is pattern, algorithm, software.

Ong points out that a poet in an oral culture will claim to have recited "the same" epic in two different performances. Yet if written transcriptions of those performances are made, they can be compared to show that the two renditions were "not the same." In the meturgemanic practice of traditioning, as Bruce Chilton has shown, spoken versions of instructional materials always were adapted to the social situation of the

4. See Mary Gerhart and Allan Melvin Russell, "A Generalized Conception of Text Applied to Both Scientific and Religious Objects," *Zygon* 22 (1987): 299–317.

5. Gerhart and Russell, "Generalized Conception," 305–6. However, the metaphysical issue of "the same" lies beyond the scope of Gerhart and Russell's discussion.

recitation.[6] Moreover, even manuscript copies always differ. The ideal of textual sameness was conceived along with print technology. But as anyone who has worked on a newspaper composition floor and anyone who has transmitted an ASCII file over a modem can attest, sameness is maddeningly elusive even for the adepts of electronic literacy.

If there existed such a thing as pure text, then sameness might be within our grasp. But in fact, every text is always a little bit body. That is to say, every copy is really a version. The characteristics of the material medium upon which the text is written, and those of the writer, and those of the reader, always alter the text as they come together for its reinscription. Therefore, copy is always both production and reproduction. To copy, as we know it, is always to alter as well as to propagate. Copy, although it lies toward the text end of the continuum, falls slightly shy of perfect identity with what it copies, and it falls shy in the direction of the unique irreplicability that is characteristic of body. To put this another way: if something is original and self-identical, then it is body; for copy necessarily falls shy of sameness.

Gerhart and Russell suggest that among the advantages of copy is its ability to permit greater access than is possible with an original. The loss of the immediacy of the original is compensated by the gain in availability of understanding made possible through the copy. For example, photographic slides and videotape permit us to study great works of architecture without our traveling to distant cities. Copy facilitates access and intelligibility where the original may have been entirely opaque and beyond reach.

As a verb, "to copy" can mean to understand, to receive instructions and carry them out, or to conform oneself to another as a model. Thus human beings can copy in two ways, depending upon where the copy is written. On the one hand, I can inscribe a pattern into a medium such as paper or audiotape or the body of another. Or, on the other hand, I can receive the encoding of the pattern into my own body, gestures, and utterances. (This may happen wittingly or unwittingly.)

In the former case—let us call it hetero-inscription—one is making a text by recording an original, or replicating some preexisting text, or creating a new text according to some preexisting protocol, or doing any of these in combination. For example, one might compose a novel or transcribe the

---

6. Chilton's insights guided our investigations in previous chapters. But see esp. Chilton, *Profiles of a Rabbi*, 119–21. See also Chilton's comment in the *Bulletin of the Council for the Scientific Study of Religion* 21 (1992): 34.

periodic table of elements or tape a lecture. (The textual mediation of the Risen Lord in the Gospels involves copy of this character, as we shall see.)

In the latter case—let us call it auto-inscription—the body itself is modified to encode the pattern. That is, personal behaviors within a community are reconfigured to carry meanings. For example, marriage is a cultural text, versions of which are encoded in the daily activities of all the couples in a particular society. Other examples would be the performance of duties required in one's job, participation in a game or in a religious ritual, the application of makeup, or conformity to a style of clothing. (The bodily mediation of the Risen Lord in the liturgy involves copy of this character.) Hetero-inscription is to auto-inscription as portraiture is to mime.

Thus we see that text and body are not mutually exclusive opposites. Text comes to us embodied, while the bodies whom we meet are textured. Auto-inscription and hetero-inscription are not two distinct classes of copy. They are, rather, two tendencies or capabilities of copy, which continually affect each other. Auto-inscription, the self-sculpting through which one comes to embody cultural texts, seems to occur as a copying or revision of the hetero-inscription with which parents, teachers, and other social agents previously had designed one's behaviors and which had included the use of texts inscribed in other media as well. Human bodies, like subway walls, attract text. Bodies get marked up and overwritten continually with the distinctive texts of their cultures. At the same time, texts get copied promiscuously, without copyright, prolifically spawning unauthorized variant versions.

Production and Productivity of Copy

Yet is there not something counterintuitive about the notion that texts have in themselves a tendency to propagate? Where is the author's role? Surely the present book betrays in some way the rational intelligence of writer, editor, and agents of production and distribution at work behind the appearance of the text. The author has composed a text, although she expects that your copy of it is not identical to what she wrote (the editor will have improved the manuscript). Moreover, she knows that as you "copy" the text—take it into your mind, understand it, interpret it to yourself, digest it—you will create another book. Every reader reads his or her own book out of the text provided by the author, editor, and publisher. Like children, books take on lives of their own. They start families, breed dynasties.

Both author and readers have creative roles to play in relation to text. This brings us to the other three criteria for determining textuality, as proposed by Gerhart and Russell. Besides transcending the material in which they are inscribed, texts must be readable, retrievable, and formally produced.

Readability. To read is to decode a meaning that links into a network of meanings beyond the particular text in question. The most basic move in reading is to reconstitute statically stored potential information into a kinetic performance in which the information becomes available and interactive in realtime. To read is to access. We will return to this point below when we consider the reading of both texts and bodies.

Retrievability. This names the requirement that texts must be intersubjective; that is, it must be possible for at least two persons to consider the same object. For example, this criterion would disqualify dreams from being counted as texts, for a dream cannot be inspected by anyone other than the dreamer. While the dreamer may narrate the dream for the consideration of others, nevertheless what those others can consider is not the dream itself but the statements of the dreamer, which of course would be texts. However, that slippery word "same" has given us trouble before. Granted that in the pure realm of ideals, two pure texts could be perfectly identical, nevertheless in our own real world all the texts we get ahold of are a little bit body-like, and they fall short of that perfect "10" on the text-body continuum. No existent text is "the same" as any other. Even if I read the newspaper over my husband's shoulder, I don't read out the same stories he does. Newspaper stories are a good deal more retrievable than dreams, of course. For us, then, the Gerhart-Russell criteria yield judgments of more or less, not *sic* or *non.* Texts are characterized by being *relatively* retrievable, just as they are *relatively* transcendent from their material media.

Formality. Formality names the requirement that "in order to qualify as a text, an object must be the product of, or have been produced in accordance with, the rules and conventions of some formal system."[7] For language, that system would be grammar; for music, the scale and the rules of harmony. The formal system is a set of branching options, each carrying meaning in relation to the others. Formal systems would also include the genre of a piece of writing—for example, business letter or sonnet. Thus genre is far more than a category for sorting out the different varieties of literary works or for evaluating their excellence. Genre is the means of production of meaning for a text. The author uses genre to

7. Gerhart and Russell, "Generalized Conception," 303.

compose the text, and the readers must recognize and use the genre to get meaning from the text.

Text, then, is the site of creativity. To copy it is to receive it actively. The receptive act of reading is a distinctive uptake through genre. As Maria Harris has eloquently argued, the powers to rebel, to resist, to reform, and to love are all modes of the power to receive.[8] For Mary Gerhart, the reader is no passive consumer of meanings; rather, like an author, the reader is a laborer. The work of meaning production, carried out upon the site of the text, is *not* to make images of an original but rather to originate unique instantiations of a genre. Readers are those with genre competence, which is something more than adeptness in the technology of literacy. To read is to guess the genre of a text and then, turning the guess into a hypothesis, to grasp the pattern of the text's coincidence and deviance with respect to the conventions of its hypothetical genre. The greater one's genre competence, the more different meanings one can make of a given text, because genre promotes variant readings.[9]

Yet genre is not text. It does not manifest as any particular piece of writing that we come across. Then what is it, and where is it? Genre seems to subsist in the practices of writers and readers, as a flexible provisional consensus about expectable relationships within a work of literature. No work perfectly fulfills all the expectations; they are there to be played with and creatively stretched or broken. The actual text sometimes coincides with and fulfills the generic expectations; at other points it flouts, inverts, or disregards them. The writer presumes that the reader will "have" the genre to read this text against, with, and through. The reader presumes that the writer "had" the genre in mind as the text went down on paper. Over time, genres mutate with use, waxing and waning. Expectations change. When readers no longer "have" the genre that the writer used, the text becomes unreadable.

One could write out a list of the conventions that seem to characterize a given genre at a given point in its currency. But of course that text

---

8. See Maria Harris, *Teaching and Religious Imagination* (San Francisco: Harper & Row, 1987), 89–96.

9. Genre is a set of rules or conventions. Every actual text follows some of the rules and violates others. This variance, together with the variance inherent in the act of reading, tends to warp genres so that they change over time. See Mary Gerhart, "Genre Competence and Biblical Hermeneutics," in *Genre, Narrativity, and Theology*, ed. Mary Gerhart and James G. Williams, *Semeia* 43 (Atlanta: Scholars Press, 1988), 32–33, 38; idem, "A Proposal for Genre-Shock," *Bulletin of the Council of Societies for the Study of Religion* 17 (1988), 54; and idem, "Holocaust Writings: A Literary Genre?" in *The Holocaust as Interruption*, ed. Elisabeth Schüssler Fiorenza and David Tracy, Concilium 175 (Edinburgh: T. & T. Clark, 1984), 78.

would not be the genre itself, because the list would not generate texts. The list might help a writer or a reader to develop genric competence. But merely reading the list would not be enough; the would-be writer or reader would also have to try it out in practice.

Occasionally the excellence of a work of literature is such that it is said to represent or typify its genre, to be the last and greatest exemplification of its genre, or even to define a new genre. Such a work might be called a classic. But the idea of a classic is an unstable notion.[10] It represents an attempt to nail down in history and culture what is intrinsically variable, fertile, unpredictable. To say this in another way: a genre that produces its definitive classic, its ne plus ultra, is a genre that puts itself out of business. Other genres will move in to take over the creative edge. After the classic, any further instantiations of the genre are not fresh copy but only blatant copies, that is, they are imitations by their own admission. These sequels are unable to conceal the out-arcing projection of human creativity that made them. With their contrived character fully displayed, such artifacts become dysfunctional, unable to complete the arc and deflect creativity back upon the human reader to reinscribe him or her.

While the term "genre" is normally used in connection with literary productions, something akin to genre must be working in the production of every kind of text. The term "genre" therefore can be extended to cover all habitual practices engaged for the production of meaning within a given historical community. These genric practices are neither text nor body, but they assist in the interplay of the two. Genres are the imagination's tools: its looms for weaving the future.

Problems of Reference

Thus we see that there is a historical dimension to textuality. Texts appear in time, they have a life span during which readers have adequate

---

10. An unstable notion may often be identified by the great energy exerted in the project of stabilizing it. One thinks of David Tracy's energetic work *The Analogical Imagination: Christian Theology and the Culture of Pluralism* (New York: Crossroad, 1981). Tracy claims, "If any human being, if any religious thinker or theologian, produces some classical expression of the human spirit on a particular journey in a particular tradition, that person discloses permanent possibilities for human existence both personal and communal" (p. 14). Classics are "texts, events, images, persons, rituals and symbols which are assumed to disclose permanent possibilities of meaning and truth" (p. 68). Tracy's approach invests heavily in Heidegger's dictum that truth is the disclosure of reality, but this disclosure is construed as a public event apprehended in "the same" way by many private individuals. Thus Tracy's conception of "the classic" is vulnerable to metaphysical critiques of sameness and permanence that are quite easily made, although customarily backgrounded in polite theological company.

genre competence to read them, and then eventually the texts fade as the genres mutate and the texts themselves are overwritten by other texts.

But the temporality of textuality is much more complex than that. This complexity can be opened up by considering the straightforward and commonplace query, What is that book about? To be "about" something is (1) to refer to something, some actual or potential state of affairs; or (2) to be engaged in some work, pursuing a task, doing something. The first meaning concerns situations, conditions, that which is the case, the outcomes of what has been before now. The past is what *is*, in the sense that it is everything that cannot now be changed. A fact is a *factum*, a done thing, a *fait accompli*. Texts that are trying to be factual are referring to stabilized relationships. Even texts that refer to potential future states of affairs do so by stating what is the case in the present: that is, their possibility at present.

The second meaning of "about," according to which the text is up to something, tends to destabilize the first meaning. For the work of the text, in referring so confidently to facts seemingly independent of the text, is actually to hold those very facts in stasis and thus accomplish their factuality. To state is to stabilize, but one stabilizes what would otherwise lack stability.

This is easily illustrated in the case of history. History is not the past but rather a text about the past. The historical text purports to report events that "happened" well before a writer came along to record them. But there are no events in the past. Events are elements selected to make a narrative; other elements must have been passed over for those particular elements to be singled out.[11] The act of writing makes the events. It makes them come out (Latin *e/ex* with *venio/ventus*). If you asked me to tell you the story of my morning so far on this particular June day, I would select elements that I deemed significant to both of us. I would make these events come out: "The day dawned warm, clear, and windy. The neighbor's lawnmower awakened me. The cats asked for their breakfast, and I fed them. The newspaper held nothing of interest. I began to work on my manuscript. The mail was delivered, with one bill." (What would *not* get into my story would be the spider's completion of her web under my kitchen window, the cycling on and off of the refrigerator motor, and my daydreaming about the children, who are away visiting their grandparents. Those would have remained in the oblivion of non-events, had I not made this parenthetical insertion.)

11. This is not to deny the reality of the past but to clarify what kind of reality it is. See, e.g., the work of Hayden White, particularly "The Historical Text as Literary Artifact," in *Tropics of Discourse: Essays in Cultural Criticism* (Baltimore: Johns Hopkins University Press, 1978), 81–100; and idem, *The Content of the Form: Narrative Discourse and Historical Representation* (Baltimore: Johns Hopkins University Press, 1987).

One aspect of the creativity of writing a text is this selectivity, which literally makes events by selecting elements from the past and rendering them available in the telling. The phenomenon of reference is a creative activity. It creates the present by creating a past for it. This is not to assert that nothing exists "out there," beyond text and independent of text. It is merely to deny that such a real existence can be entirely aloof from text, *as far as human beings are concerned*. Reality is a cooperative enterprise of text and body. Body, resisting as it always does the pull toward eradication by textuality, retains a certain weight that provides ballast to keep the buoyant balloon of text from drifting off into the stratosphere. But text still takes body for a ride.

History is text, and text is artifact. That means, in Scarry's terms, that the artifact history is a fulcrum around which human creative energy swings back to reinscribe the human creators themselves. Thus what text is "about," what it is always "up to," is not only the designing of the past but the redesigning of human bodily relationships. In that sense, texts are always engaging in the construction of the future. To tell a story about what has happened is to pave the way for what can happen.

What Is Reading?

Thus the means of access to the human future are textual, but so are the means of access to the past. To access the past is to read it; to access the future is to write it. But reading and writing have more in common than one might at first suppose. To write is to copy, but to read is also to copy.

It was asserted above that reading is a creative activity, as the authoring of a new version and as the evoking of meaning from text through invoking of its genre. The reader needs a certain technological competence, which is called literacy. To perfect literacy, readers must also know how to recognize the genre of the text, to overlay the requirements of the genre upon the elements of the text, and to actualize meaning as the perceived pattern of alternating conformity and deviation between genre and actual text. (This production of meaning is not exactly the reversal of the author's act of producing the text in the first place, as we shall see.) The reader takes it upon herself to author a version of the text; thus she writes the text upon herself.

But reading is not chosen as one activity from among several options by an agent intellect. It is not "a" consciously aware activity alongside others. Reading is awareness itself; it is the way the body is with its environment. Whatever consciousness one would impute to the living human body must be framed in terms of the body's readings and writings. Reading rewrites the reader, not merely her incorporeal consciousness but her practices as well. The hetero-inscription copies as auto-inscription. Reading overwrites the body because it alters her expectations and thereby affects her future behaviors and relationships.

Thus we may regard reading as the process by which text inscribes body, the process by which bodies are textured. This is exactly the reverse of what is often naively presumed to be the case. Ordinarily one might consider it properly an author's task to put the genre to use and to produce bodily realities. We think of a fiction writer as one who makes up worlds arbitrarily and peoples them with characters of her own design. By contrast, we think of the historian as one who refrains from making up anything, although she may infer causal connections, highlight or suppress evidence, or prefer one scenario over another in the case of ambiguous evidence. Yet writing is always a reading. Both historian and novelist read the bodily realities that they find around them, and they always find those bodies already culturally inscribed. Historians, novelists, and other writers are differentiated by the different genres they use in reading those bodies. These writers copy, but they do so according to genres. As we saw, genres are customary practices, that is, working hypotheses about likely configurations of bodily relationships.

Genres tell you what to look for. The "beat" assigned to a journalist provides a good example. The newspaper editors wish to report a comprehensive account of the life of the city, nation, and world. Therefore they assign reporters to cover locations where significant events are expected to occur because such events have frequently occurred there in the past. The state legislature, the police station, and the Pentagon are typical beats. Reporters read what transpires in those contexts (through the genre of the beat) and write it up into events. It is obvious, then, that there can be nothing truly new in the news, for reporters are on the lookout only for the kind of event that has happened before or, rather, the kind of transactions that, when written up as events, have in the past been accepted by the editors as worthy of being printed. The beat, as genre, not only defines the location of what will be news but sets the agenda of who, what, how, when, and why. One must not fault the newspaper industry for what is intrinsic to the very activity of writing itself.

Of course, genres are inherently fluid, and they can be brought into play quite creatively—in an offbeat way, as it were. Yet there is a limit on the innovation that is possible through writing. Just as the printed text, or "hard copy," anchors the variation as each reader "copies," so too the writer labors with the raw material of the culturally inscribed but still quite physical human bodies that surround her. Flesh and blood can be pressed only so far before rebelling. The cultural sphere, the realm of writing and reading, is an arena of competition, negotiation, and struggle.

For example, in the days of slavery in the United States, black bodies were deeply inscribed with the practices of servitude and submission.[12] Few slaves could read printed texts. The slave system was supported in books for the white master class (including the Bible), although it was also contested in other books, those of the abolitionists. More important, the slaves themselves read out the expectations of slavery from the cultural texts that surrounded them and that inscribed the reality of slavery within their physical, behavioral acquiescence to servitude. The coercion of slavery was imposed only minimally by force of arms; it was instead quite effectively propagated genrically, through instilling within the people themselves a pernicious kind of competence for auto-inscription, a hellish cultural literacy. But at the same time something amazing was happening. In the face of the pervasive cultural text that was the slave system, sometimes a slave said no. Sometimes— often—a man or a woman of African heritage read the situation as wrong and nonnecessary; sometimes the person wrote a different meaning for himself or herself.

Now the question is, where did that come from? How are we to explain the possibility of this deliberate and profoundly creative misreading? In the case of the white abolitionist authors, we could cite a countervailing literary tradition favoring universal human rights that funded their proposal of a change in American society. This would have been a countercultural tradition, which is only to say it was still *some kind of* cultural and textual, albeit opposed to the dominant version. In the case of the slaves who authored a version of freedom for themselves, however, there was minimal access to texts that could deliver the possibility of an alternative to slavery. To be sure, Africans born free might retain their families' original gift of cultural programming for dignity and self-determination, even after the superinscription of the program of slavery. They might even transmit such a memory to generations subsequently born in bondage. But the amazing thing is that slaves without even that kind of access to a text of freedom still said no to slavery.

12. I am indebted to Professor Deborah McDowell for the startling and profound insight that slavery is a text, a sacred text, that can be read in variant ways. McDowell's lecture "African-American Women's Lives and Literature" was presented at Princeton Theological Seminary in the spring of 1988. McDowell declined to give me a copy of her text, but the audiotape is available from the seminary.

We must speak here of something unique, something utterly non-textual, asserting itself to cut through the coiling tendrils of the text of slavery. While the no-saying appears as text, a very strange and surprising text, it is the body speaking. Bereft of any text of freedom, the body yet voices resistance. The cry rises not once, but thousands of times, from thousands of isolated throats, and it echoes in millions of hearts who hearken and recognize what is being said. Lincoln's writing on a piece of paper did not free the slaves. The people did it themselves with their hands and backs and voices.

As this dramatic instance shows, body does resist text and, even in the most extreme circumstances, can eventually manage to rewrite what had seemed indelible. Or rather, "body" is what I propose to call the aspect of human being that ultimately succeeds in holding textual ambition within certain bounds.[13] As an artifact, text must conceal its bodily origin the more effectively to inscribe itself upon bodies. But the priority of the body persists, even when temporarily forgotten. Body is ultimately unlike any of the other media that are made to carry text. Although bodies always are inscribed with cultural meanings, the margins must be respected. The body has regions, as it were, that must not be inscribed. The body ultimately is not an artifact. It is receptive to cultural texts, but it is not a work of human hands. It is productive, but it is not a commodity. It is fragile, but it is not disposable. It is expressive, but it is not translatable. Text is made for the body, not the body for text.

Legitimacy

The body, then, is more than a receptive tablet awaiting the stylus, a cleared field inviting the plow. Bodies are differing, material, individual, unique, irreducible to stereotype. Bodies are also fertile, autochthonous, productive, surprising, resistant to coercion. At the same time, bodies are fragile, mortal, needful of care. They compete with one another for the scarce material resources of the earth.

But we human bodies do not compete only through the kind of straightforward physical interactions that the other animals use. We do it textually. We use textual artifacts to focus destructive power toward

---

13. This is not to say that everything worked out just fine in the case of the American slave system or in any of the other instances of extreme genocidal brutality to which human bodies have been subjected. I mean instead to highlight the resiliency of what some have called "the human spirit" and what I insist upon calling the body, the sensible partner to text.

enemies. That is to say, we designate enemies textually: we read other bodies as enemy. This is done in warfare but sometimes also in the oppositional exchanges that constitute the economy, the state, the family, the faculty, the church. Thus social relationships, whether hostile or friendly, are readings of others in which—whether consciously or not—we copy, write, author, understand them *as* our own particular self-interested versions of them.

To read other bodies, as in any other reading, one uses genre. Some of the basic genres through which we read other bodies are gender, race, and class (singular). As genres, these templates do not exist independently in the real world. They are constituted and instantiated only in the production of texts, that is, the actual genders, races, and classes (plural) that inscribe the bodies whom we encounter. For example, race is not color. Color, facial features, stature, bone structures, and hair quality all are physical properties with no intrinsic significance; however configured, these signal alike the incomparable worth of the human body itself. No two bodies are the same. But color and the other ways in which bodies vary are read into arbitrary configurations and overwritten with cultural texts. Race is the genre through which this is done. Through the genre of race are produced what one calls the races (plural).

The formal rules of this genre prescribe that some possibilities of physical difference will receive heightened attention, while others will be overlooked. All Americans have the genric competence to read race. One may not have encountered a specific racial text, however, and so might not recognize its inscription upon a given individual. Thus someone raised on the East Coast of the United States might read a new neighbor as a white woman, where the woman herself and the friends she left behind in California read brown or Chicana.

Racial texts are continually rewritten in history. To be Negro, to be black, and to be African-American are three versions, not quite the same text. In tenth-century Europe, to be Slavic and to be German were two vastly different racial scripts, although in contemporary America many people no longer can read that difference. White Americans' genric competence for reading race is no less acute than that of their medieval ancestors; but the European ethnic racial texts, while still tragically legible in Bosnia, in the United States are being rewritten into oblivion, as whiteness.

Moreover, the genre of race itself has a history. For some societies, race has been a matter of language or of tribal heritage rather than of color. One hundred and fifty years ago, the formal structures of race in America included rules for privilege and disadvantage, domination and oppression. Everyone took that for granted, even those who creatively and bravely broke the rules. More recently, we as a society have tried to disengage that hierarchical ordering from the production of racial realities and substitute for it the production of texts celebrating distinctiveness. This is much more easily said than done. The genric production of cultural disparagement can persist even after the racial texts have been nearly obliterated, as is apparent from the negative stereotyping of Slavic peoples that still pervades contemporary mass media.

Gender, too, is a genre. Gender is not sex. Sex is the reality that, prior to any cultural inscription, fits our bodies to maintain our species. Every society has the genre of gender generating male and female genders, but these are not the same genders everywhere. Manhood is inscribed differently in the United States than in China or India and differently today than during the Second World War. Gender, the genre as we have it in the United States in the 1990s, is the set of rules prescribing that some version of manhood, one of several possible gender texts, will in fact be inscribed and read out, and furthermore that some text of manhood will define relationships of labor, warfare, family, consumption, and so on. The texts of manhood and womanhood vary from culture to culture, and from time to time within cultures, even though all versions of those texts inscribed on contemporary individuals in one society will be more or less similar. But just as the gender texts change, the genre itself mutates over time. That is, the competence to read through the genre of gender "drifts": it comes to entail different practices. Thus the genric function of gender may or may not include defining who may carry out certain economic or religious or political roles.

It should be clear by now that people may be aware of different texts but unaware of the genre that produces them and renders them readable. We do not recognize the genric character of race until we notice people reading familiar racial texts very differently from the way we ourselves read them. The genric formulae of race and gender can function differently in different societies. The genric reality of class can consist in a practice of reading and inscribing *economic* relations in one society, *genealogical* relations in a second, and *cultic* relations in a third.[14] At some

---

14. Contemporary Western social science correlates class with income status, i.e., with one's degree of control over wealth and the capital and labor through which wealth is produced. Thus class for us is an economic category. In societies with different economic organization, however, especially those with little currency or with an underdeveloped market system, class may correlate more closely with kinship or religious caste, because those are the factors (and not monetary income level) that confer control over labor and other resources. Moreover, class analysis may obscure the status of someone (e.g., child or wife) who lacks economic power because of age- or gender-linked restrictions.

points in American history, in some localities, the genre of race was virtually identical with the genre of class; a racial reading served also as a class
reading. Even today those two genres, race and class, are not entirely distinct in American society.

The basic genres of race, gender, and class are the means of inscribing texts upon bodies in our society. It is vitally important to recognize
that racial, gender, and class definitions are artifacts. Although these
texts may seem to be natural, they have been put there like a tattoo on the
surface of the body. Often it is in the interest of certain bodies to suppress
the demands of certain other bodies in order the better to provide for their
own physical maintenance. Cultural texts are useful in that respect. Such
texts are recipes for the accomplishment of labor needed for survival.
They also assign different shares of the crops and the products to different categories of people, categories also defined through cultural texts.

Thus "property" is produced. Class texts are employed in the production of produce and products, but, more important, they produce the
phenomenon of property itself. We now have goods that "belong" to the
body (that is, to certain bodies), not as an arm or a leg belongs, but as separate things attached and owned through textually defined rights. Property rights are textual and therefore artifactual, artificial. They need not,
but often do, conflict with the non-textual, nonartificial right that the
body continues to assert: the body's right to food. The hungry body is
there because it was born. Its organic origin challenges the textual origin
of property, food that is "owned." We are all born hungry and naked of
property. Beyond that, it is all fiction.

The social fictions that begin at birth tend to overwrite that origin.
There are texts that inscribe some births as mistakes. Some bodies, although undeniably born, "ought not have been born," according to those
texts. These bodies are inscribed as illegitimate. In our society, the social
text of illegitimacy denies that the baby is the child of the man whose
child she is. Fatherhood, a bodily reality, is overwritten as a textual relationship. The man must feed only the children of the woman legally inscribed with his name. Only to them is he "father." Others may starve.[15]

The foregoing is a stylized, logically simplified reading of the human invention of bastardy. In American society we do provide, more or
less adequately, for the care and feeding of all bodies born among us, although we do not permit all births. The foregoing sketch illustrates the
fact that it is perfectly possible to mistake the text for the body and to read

---

15. For an enlightening survey from the perspective of comparative legal philosophy,
see Teichman, *Illegitimacy: An Examination of Bastardy* (see chap. 5, n. 18).

the text inscribed upon the body as if it were the bodily reality itself. The bastard is inscribed as "not a daughter," "not worthy of care and feeding," "not one of us"—even though she lies there screaming and kicking, just as thoroughly a baby body as anyone else in the nursery. Text thus gives identity to some bodies by denying it to others.

A price is paid for this fiction. The bastard pays by diminished access to food and other goods. But the heir pays too. The legitimate child is fed *not* simply because he is a hungry baby but because he has been inscribed as heir, as proper to his father, as property. The hunger of the heir is overwritten with economic text. Who, then, is more disadvantaged: the bastard whom somebody feeds because her cries assert her insistent bodily reality as the hungry fruit of a womb or the heir whose meals are an investment in the future prosperity of a family name? The two newborns have their identities defined in binary opposition to one another. We have bastards so that we can have heirs. But to the extent that we have bastards and heirs, we don't have babies anymore.

The inscription of the newborn as bastard or heir camouflages the body's nonartifactual status. In the same stroke, it overwrites the womb with a text that mislabels the womb's productivity. The bodily reality is that the mother's birthing of the child is radically unlike the craftworker's production of the artifact. The baby comes out of "the special hole." The body is sui generis, unique. Yet as if by obscene graffiti, the womb is renamed a factory and its fruit is designated for consumption. The consuming society needs workers and buyers receptive to inscription of cultural texts. Therefore it also needs soldiers for its wars.

Reading the Body

The differential inscription of bodies is no modern invention. The ancient world overwrote human bodies with social identities analogous to those familiar in our own experience. As might be expected, the options depended on the culture into which one was born. We can distinguish a Greek set of identities from a Semitic set, and the two sets compare in interesting ways. For both Greeks and Jews, identity was inscribed as kinship. The Greeks went on to overlay kinship with economic class, while the Jews modified kinship with cultic status. In both ethnic groups, gender texts used the vocabulary of kin-class or kin-cult identification.

The contrast between Jewish and Greek kinship assignment indicates the social, artificial character of both. For Jews, the circumstances of a baby's birth settled everything about his or her status in the people of Israel, while for Greeks, birth was merely the beginning of a process of determination. The Greek midwife presided over the birth, surrounded only by women. An important part of the midwife's role was to make the decision whether the baby was healthy enough to be allowed to live. She examined the infant before the placenta was delivered and before the umbilical cord was cut. If the infant seemed malformed or weak, the midwife would cut the cord so close to the body that the baby would bleed to death; otherwise, she cut it at a length equal to the width of four fingers.[16]

A second decision point came a few days later. If the infant lived but the father decided not to receive it into the family, then it would be exposed, that is, abandoned out of doors to die. In fact, many discarded babies did not die but were taken and raised for a life of servitude.[17] Many of the prostitutes in Athens had been abandoned infants. We know from literary references that Athenian men were haunted by fears of inadvertently having incestuous sexual relations in a brothel with an unrecognized daughter or son and so provoking divine retribution. This is a significant fear. It indicates that, in the Greek perception, kinship was fixed at birth and could not be revoked by parental abandonment; yet abandonment was possible because kin status by itself carried no claim to property or human rights. Class status, and humanity itself, were affixed to the baby only at the paternal recognition ceremony. Only leisured Greek males were read as fully human.

Why would a man decline fatherhood and decide to expose a newborn infant? By custom and law, all recognized children would inherit equally from their father.[18] The more siblings, the smaller the inheritance of each. Numerous births might mean that sons' property would fall beneath the minimum requirements for membership in the senatorial or equestrian classes, or that daughters would not find husbands of appropriate class. Among laboring people, then as now, a new baby was another mouth to feed. Food came from land, so that real estate was what counted

16. For surveys of what is known of birthing practices among the Greeks, see Valerie French, "Midwives and Maternity Care in the Greco-Roman World," *Rescuing Creusa: New Methodological Approaches to Women in Antiquity,* special issue of *Helios* 13 (1986): 69–84; Garland, *The Greek Way of Life* (see chap. 2, n. 16); and Rouselle, *Porneia* (see chap. 2, n. 16).

17. Sometimes babies were sold outright to slave traders. There is debate about the frequency of infant exposure, with some estimates ranging as high as ten percent. Girls were exposed more frequently than boys. For demographic studies, see D. Engels, "The Problem of Female Infanticide in the Greco-Roman World," *Classical Philology* 75 (1980): 112–20; idem, "The Use of Historical Demography in Ancient History," *Classical Quarterly* 34 (1984): 386–93; and Cynthia Patterson, "'Not Worth the Rearing': The Causes of Infant Exposure in Ancient Greece," *Transactions of the American Philological Society* 115 (1985): 103–23.

18. This Greek principle was known to Jews in Eretz Israel as something at odds with their own inheritance customs. See Talmud *Šabbat* 116b.

as wealth, and there was only so much land to go around. The notion that wealth also comes from trade was only beginning to take hold in the Greco-Roman period (and the notion that wealth comes from labor could not yet be thought). Thus, propertied Greeks saw no way of increasing a family's wealth other than by the opportune in-marriage of girls from other landowning families. Home-grown girls, in contrast, were vehicles for the alienation of property into other families. An infant female body was already culturally inscribed with a message for the Greek male who was deciding her fate: "Hello daughter means good-bye farm."

Among Jews in antiquity, things were different.[19] Economic transactions were subsumed into the system of religious obligations. Racial status was cultic status, and both were determined by birth. The mother's lineage was at least as important as the father's in ascertaining the baby's religious identity, and sometimes more so. In Palestinian Jewish society the assignment of kinship was organized into a hierarchy of castes: the priestly, the Levitical, the Israelite, and, at the bottom, mixed racial identities such as offspring of legally forbidden unions between Jews, of Jewish women with gentile partners, and of Samaritans. Caste status was transmitted in a family line by both parents. It could be enhanced or diminished by the choice of the spouse for one's child, or lost by marriage outside the legal requirements. Arranging proper marriages entailed inquiring into the parentage of the prospective spouses for several generations back; the requirements were most strict for the priestly caste.[20]

The Jewish caste system wrote onto bodies both rights and duties that were at once both religious and economic. The Mishnah reflects a theological theory of ownership: God owns the holy land of Israel, and people work it in partnership with God. The Temple and its scheduled castes, with their assigned rights to shares of the land's produce, represent the interest of the divine senior partner.[21] Land in Israel cannot (in theory) be permanently bought or sold but reverts back always to the lineage to whom its use was originally assigned. Harvesting customs and a system

19. Because only sons stood to inherit, Jewish daughters were no threat to property. Of course, Jews in Hellenistic cities were affected by Greek customs. Philo found it necessary to insist that Jews should not practice infant exposure.

20. At the time of the compiling of the Mishnah, in the second century C.E., there is a memory of archived legal records where people arranging marriages were required to trace families back as far as ten generations. This indicates that this way of assigning caste status was in place well before the fall of Jerusalem in 70 C.E. and the social upheaval that followed. See Miller, *Studies in the History and Traditions of Sepphoris* (see chap. 5, n. 21), esp. chap. 3, "The 'Old' 'archei." See also Neusner, *The Economics of the Mishnah* (see chap. 2, n. 20).

21. See Neusner, *The Economics of the Mishnah*, 115.

of tithing are supposed to assure that the landless poor will have a share of the crops. Regulations governing the consumption of sacrificed livestock also provide sustenance for the poor.

We do not know whether this system always, or ever, functioned satisfactorily to distribute food equitably across Eretz Israel. We do know, however, that merely being born entitled a person to food in Israel's cultural system. No matter what caste identity inscribed a baby body, it read: "I have a claim on the fruits of this holy land."

Hellenism, however, brought the possibility of other ways of reading the body. The Mishnah itself is something of an attempt to turn back the clock to a time before geopolitics and international trade introduced Israel to institutions such as absentee landlordism and imperial taxation, which extracted sustenance away from the people on the land. (It is irrelevant that there may never have been such a golden age as the Mishnah projects, an era of pure theo-economics.) The Mishnah tries to contain the influence of market forces by insisting on the observance of economic prescriptions deriving from ancient texts. It does this from the perspective of the landowning minority.[22] As we shall see, in the same situation the Jesus movements also developed counterreadings of the body, but from different social perspectives.

The Body as Reader

Our consideration of text and body now draws to a conclusion with the observation that the body, ultimate medium for the propagation of social texts, is principle of their variation as well. Receiving inscription by social meanings, the body is instantiating always a new, and more or less variant, version of those meanings. While being written upon, the body is writing (on) itself. The reciprocality at work here is already familiar to any who have labored in the teaching/learning process, which requires the active but cooperative engagement of both sides. Learners accommodate themselves to whatever the teacher is trying to impart; yet they also adapt and assimilate that so-called content to their own purposes. I have used the term "copy" to designate this reciprocality. The body copies, but its copy is necessarily "not the same" as whatever it had to read.

Both of the metaphors for the teaching/learning process current in antiquity can be applied now to copy. Nursing expresses the close cooperation between giver and receiver of information. Mother gives milk, and

---

22. This is Neusner's interpretation in *The Economics of the Mishnah*.

baby incorporates the nourishment, building up bone and muscle. The nursing interaction also gives the child the psychic raw material to develop capacities for cognition and relationship.[23] Thus the human self is grown, both physically and psychologically, out of nursing. The cultivation of crops, too, involves a kind of copy. The seed replicates, yielding a thousandfold harvest. Grain proliferates, thanks to the annihilation of the one original grain.

The term "copy," then, provides another way of expressing much of what was expressed in those two ancient metaphors—nursing and planting—but with certain differences. We lose the imagery of nutrition, but we gain the possibility of exploring the relation between artifacts and bodies, that is, between texts inscribed in nonliving media and the inscribed bodies that read them. A theory of copy can be a theory of the utility of textual artifacts for the inscription of bodies. It can be a theory of how texts are used on bodies by bodies.

This places textual artifacts in continuity with other items of material culture that anthropologists might interpret. Artifacts, as Scarry has described, function as fulcrums that deflect the out-arcing power of creativity back upon human beings to redesign or divert or enhance or diminish their bodily existence. Gospel texts and liturgical rituals alike are parts of a set of artifacts that bodies read. We bodies employ them to auto-inscribe in our flesh new versions of life's possibilities.

These artifacts themselves are versions of earlier sets of artifacts, and their meanings emerge when we place them in the cultural series in which they occur. For example, the text that links God's kingdom with breast milk,[24] once current among some sector of the Jesus movement, makes sense as a counterreading of a prevailing conceptual linkage between God's kingly governance and practices of alimentation known to us from Torah and Mishnah. The significant semantic mutation in the Jesus saying is that nursing, which fell outside the practices covered by the law, here is made the model for gaining access to the realm of God's law. If eating tithed food was the legitimate way of copying "God's kingdom" in one's bodily practices, then eating untithable food was a bootleg copy of that text, a variant version. Seaside picnics on baskets of fish were variations on the same theme.

Jewish belief in resurrection provides a second example. Burial practices in first-century Jerusalem (although, significantly, not yet in Galilee)

---

23. This is the premise of psychoanalytic object-relations theory, discussed in chap. 8 above.

24. *Gospel of Thomas* 22, discussed in chap. 2 above.

copied the Pharisaic expectation of a general resurrection of the just. Inter-ment occurred in two stages. On the day of death the shrouded body was laid out on a shelf in the family's tomb, ideally a chamber carved out of lime-stone in the side of a hill. There it decomposed for a year. The rotting away of the flesh was regarded as the cleansing of sin, that is, of all wrongness en-coded in the body. When the year had elapsed, the dry bones were collected and saved for the resurrection. They might be stacked tidily in a small stone box called an ossuary or they might be pushed off the back of the shelf to fall into a pit with the bones of previously deceased relatives.[25] In either varia-tion, the eating away of the flesh by putrefaction and by chemical interaction with the limestone was the preparation for resurrection. The bones were wiped clean and left ready to be resurfaced with flesh. Stacked upon the skeletal remains of one's kin, the bony framework or loom of the human per-sonality now awaited restringing for a divine weaving of new fabric. The bony needles were ready for God to knit new clothes of flesh. The spindles were primed to receive a freshly inscribed vellum scroll.[26]

The resurrection claimed for Jesus was again a heterodox copy of this cultural text. The Gospel write-up has two layings out of Jesus' body: at a supper table and in a tomb. The body on the table is eaten, but among friends rather than family. The body on the limestone slab is not eaten at all, for it needs no resurfacing. The texts written onto this body during its life are not to be obliterated. This flesh already is a garment fit for the kingdom. Moreover, there are no ancestral bones to keep this

25. Details as well as archaeological evidence and rabbinic texts are reported by L. Y. Rahmani in a four-part series, "Ancient Jerusalem's Funerary Customs and Tombs," *Biblical Archaeologist* 44 (1981): 171–77 and 229–35; and 45 (1981–82): 43–53 and 109–19. Further ref-erences and an insightful discussion are offered by Byron R. McCane, "'Let the Dead Bury Their Own Dead': Secondary Burial and Matt. 8:21-22," *Harvard Theological Review* 83 (1990): 31–43.

26. Stone ossuary boxes that have been found in Israel are designed to resemble a *teva* or common wooden chest in which scrolls were kept. On the oblong side of the box may be two circles, side by side, each with an inscribed rosette pattern; the circles look like the han-dles on the ends of the spindles of a rolled-up scroll laid on its side for storage. Ossuaries were made just long enough for the two thighbones to be laid in side by side, and wide enough to accommodate the skull. The rabbinic tractate *Semaḥot* 8:7 mentions that a pen and an inkwell may be placed with a burial. In a first-century tomb at Meiron an inkwell was found that had never contained ink, perhaps meant to signal that the tomb's contents lay ready for the divine writer's creative hand. The inkwell is reported by Eric M. Meyers, James F. Strange, and Carol L. Meyers, *Excavations at Ancient Meiron, Upper Galilee, Israel 1971–72, 1974–75, 1977*, 109, 118–20, but the excavators do not subscribe to the cultural anthropologi-cal interpretation that I suggest here.

body company in the tomb, and when friends arrive, they find that it has already gone. This version of resurrection is an unauthorized and deviant copy of the standard Pharisaic burial practice.

This is not to say that we have now handily recovered, in this telling, what originally happened to Jesus. The examples cited here—kosher dining versus breast-feeding, and ossuary burial versus "last supper"—merely illustrate what it means to make bodily readings and, in doing so, to introduce significant variations. It still remains to account for the genesis of such creative miscopying as well as the establishment and propagation of the new variant once it appears. That will be attempted in chapter 10.

One final detail must not escape notice here, however. When I say that the body reads or copies a text, I mean to privilege the sense of hunger and to elevate the activity of eating to full epistemological seriousness. Western philosophy in the Greek tradition has doubted the validity of what the senses tell us, although at times grudgingly accepting the evidence of the eyes or even the ears. But hunger is a sense. (I do not say taste, because taste is a luxury of the well fed.) Mother Eve hungered for knowledge of good and evil, but Philo, sated with Plato, dismissed her as a shameful glutton. Jesus hungered to eat the Passover with his friends. The text of resurrection can be read only bodily, and bodily only through the sense of hunger.

Christian Origin

Human society, now as in the past, can be viewed as an ongoing renegotiation of the demands of bodies through the mediation of texts. The constant in this picture is the body's receptivity to text, tempered by the body's reassertion of its residual bodily character in the face of textual encroachment. The fluid elements in the picture are the genres, the texts they produce, and the media that carry the texts. The latter change while the body remains the same (as only bodiliness can).

Yet bodies also are fluid. New and completely unique ones keep being born, while even the most impressively inscribed ones eventually die. The body is not a text but offers itself as a medium ready for inscription. Texts are fictions and they are temporary. For a while a text can hold or fix a stable arrangement of elements, but because genres shift and readers copy, texts deteriorate. The rate of erosion is variable. There have been periods in history of rapid renegotiation. For example, the industrial revolution and the conquest of North America entailed an energetic and extensive remapping of metaphors. Yet even the most revolutionary changes are revisions, rereadings, rewritings: copy rather than composition *de novo*.

All of this suggests a novel approach to Christian origins. Traditionally the advent of Christianity has been thought of in terms of a "Christ-event," a new beginning datable at a discrete point in time and space. The New Testament has been regarded as a collection of books referring backward to that event as if "it" were something external to the books themselves and already completed before they were begun. The books have been construed as if they were pale reflections of an original lying far off in the past, forever beyond the reader's grasp.

But it now seems more appropriate to talk of Christian origins in another way: as a rereading, a variant copying, of both scriptural and cultural texts. The "events" of Christian origin cannot be nailed down into a time line; they are, rather, many resistant, variant instances of reading common texts such as fatherhood, justice, property, maleness, femaleness, and food in an illegitimate way.[27] Christian origin is a breakthrough assertion of the claims of body. It is a cognition and a recognition of hunger. It is a rupture of the narrative closure of the story of body. It is an unauthorized reading of tomb as womb, according to which that awful hole in the earth is mapped as another "special hole" whose outcome is neither fiction nor manure.

In this approach, Christian origin is a crescendo quickening with Jesus of Nazareth in the first century. The practices attending it are recoverable through investigation of the New Testament texts. But it would also be correct to use the term "Christian origin" to designate the gathering of the young churches of the Third World in our own time. Those communities come into being through and for variant readings of the texts of their own indigenous cultures. Another instance of Christian origin would be a contemporary individual's conversion to Christianity—not at a sudden stroke but gradually through the catechumenal process leading up to baptism. The body of the new Christian undergoes reinscription as the cultural texts that have marked it are reread and overwritten.

My hypothesis is that Christian origin is not an event or a text but a generic disruption in the ongoing inscription of the human body. This disruption coincides with no actual instantiation of Christian origin but subsists rather as a protocol or set of procedures for tampering with the reproduction and the reading of embodied texts. From the canonical

27. This line of inquiry into the legitimacy of Christian origin has been cautiously opened by Jane Schaberg in *The Illegitimacy of Jesus* (see chap. 5, n. 17). Schaberg is concerned with the legal status of Mary's pregnancy. But if she is correct in her claim that the unborn body of Jesus was a textually contested site, then the stage is set for variant readings of the ecclesial body of Christ.

Gospels one can recover this protocol, this prescription of "the way things go" in Christian origin. The task here is to illuminate the phenomenon of "Christian origin" by describing the genesis of certain claims about the body of Jesus as an illegitimate variation, a misuse, a counter-competent exploitation, of the somatic genres of class, race, and gender. The task furthermore is to describe the propagation of that disruptive genric competence as the sacramental availability of the Lord to the church.

10

A Frontier Anthropology

THE CLAIM of resurrection for Jesus sprouted from the cracks in the Hellenism with which first-century Palestine was paved. Easter faith owes its genesis, stabilization, and propagation more to the fissures rending that society than to whatever structures unified it. Yet the quest to describe such unifying structures has engaged the energies of historians and cultural anthropologists alike. Their depictions of ancient societies stress general features and therefore may obscure the volatile incongruities that allowed resurrection faith to erupt. The task of this chapter is to peer through the cracks in the first-century monoliths of gender, race, and class (as conventionally described) in hopes of discovering what it meant for rock to roll in Jerusalem.

As the shoot of resurrection faith grew into a tough little ecclesial shrub, its roots pried farther into the cracks of Hellenism and coiled around great chunks of it, anchoring them for the future, giving us an impression of serene stability. That impression is textually wrought, a fiction. The Gospels reconstruct ecclesial origins as the events of founding and institution. History-producing narrative is one kind of textual productivity, but we now have to deal with another kind that compounds it: that of contemporary anthropology, with its comparative methodology.

Comparative study in the social sciences begins with two more or less arbitrary determinations: (1) of a category for comparison and (2) of a range of societies in which instantiations of that category will be sought. These two determinations effectively construct or produce the phenomena that are to be observed. For example, categories such as "honor" or "domestic space" often are invoked to describe social conventions, and it is tempting to apply these particular constructs to Jesus materials such as the saying about nursing (*Gospel of Thomas* 22) and the anointing at Bethany (Mark 14:3-9). Or again, one often reads that "the Mediterranean area" is unified by its peoples' preoccupation with the negotiation of honor and shame. Such descriptions may indeed promote understanding—if we take due care to avoid the twin traps of circular definition and ethnocentric projection of our own presuppositions onto the ancient world. But debates among anthropological theorists during the last decade or so have raised some relevant considerations that must be noted first.

Range of Comparison. When using anthropology's comparative method, one must decide how to demarcate, geographically and/or historically, some portion of humanity in order to study it. The validity of the findings will depend upon how appropriately and rigorously this is done. For example, should the land of Israel be taken as a homogeneous unit? Or should we examine Galilee apart from Jerusalem? Or would it be more appropriate to treat Palestine as a segment of some larger geographical whole? How would we define that whole? Any border is arbitrary and contrived, and exists because some group has agreed to recognize it. "The Mediterranean area," subject of much contemporary anthropology, did not exist until constructed in the 1970s through the selection of certain cultural characteristics as significant.[1]

"Mediterranean," then, is anthropologists' shorthand designation for the constellation of characteristics that certain adjacent twentieth-century societies seem to have in common (when you overlook ways in which they differ). Proximity to the sea of the same name is not enough to make a society "Mediterranean," as is evident from the exclusion of Balkan and Israeli societies from the generalizations that anthropologists propose concerning what is "Mediterranean." Among anthropological theorists, it remains an unsettled question whether so-called area studies are more likely to reinforce the ethnocentric biases of the investigators than to advance what has been recognized as the fundamental objective of comparative studies: a

1. One can observe "the Mediterranean" under construction in the literature. See Julian A. Pitt-Rivers, ed., *Mediterranean Countrymen: Essays in the Social Anthropology of the Mediterranean* (Paris: Moulton & Co., 1963); J. G. Peristiany, ed., *Honor and Shame: The Values of Mediterranean Society* (London: Weidenfeld & Nicolson, 1965); Jane Schneider, "Of Vigilance and Virgins," *Ethnology* 9 (1971): 1–24; J. Davis, *People of the Mediterranean: An Essay in Comparative Social Anthropology* (London: Routledge & Kegan Paul, 1977); David D. Gilmore, "Anthropology of the Mediterranean Area," *Annual Review of Anthropology* 11 (1982): 175–205; and idem, ed., *Honor and Shame and the Unity of the Mediterranean* (Washington, D.C.: American Anthropological Association, 1987).

correlation between characteristics of particular communities and those of humanity in general.[2]

Before placing first-century Palestine within "the Mediterranean," one first should ask whether there are grounds for presuming that its culture resembled the cultures to its west more than those to its east—with which, after all, it shared the Aramaic language in several dialects. Geography alone does not make the case. One cannot validly conclude that since Galilee and Judea lay along the coast of the Mediterranean Sea and had complex cultural and economic relations with their western neighbors, therefore their cultures *must have* exhibited the very traits that characterize twentieth-century "Mediterranean" societies. There may indeed be similarities, but let us not beg the question.

This brings up the temporal aspect of the problem of finding an appropriate scope for cultural comparison. How reliably does knowledge of the twentieth-century Mediterranean region illuminate the customs and beliefs of people who lived there some eighty generations ago? All things being equal, cultural patterns would tend to propagate themselves unchanged, owing to the inherently conservative nature of human socialization and because culture is an adaptation to the physical environment, which remains relatively unchanged over historical time. Yet all things have *not* been equal around the Mediterranean over the last two millennia. Arguably, two cultural forces—Islamic civilization and the agricultural and economic revolutions precipitated by capitalism—stand between the ancient world and the contemporary "Mediterranean area" and count against any presupposition of undisturbed cultural continuity between then and now.

Therefore, caution is appropriate when one is extracting generalizations about "the Mediterranean" from contemporary anthropological studies and applying them to first-century Palestine. The same goes for generalizations about "the Greeks" and "the Jews." In antiquity, both groups were quite diverse (and of course they overlapped). Moreover, one must weigh the relevance of the comparative data according to their temporal proximity to the first century. Even with relevant Greek,

2. Michael Herzfeld and Lila Abu-Lughod in different ways have criticized recent anthropology of "the Mediterranean," in dialogue with its proponents, especially Gilmore. See Michael Herzfeld, "Honor and Shame: Problems in the Comparative Analysis of Moral Systems," *Man* 15 (1980): 339–51; idem, "The Horns of the Mediterraneanist Dilemma," *American Ethnologist* 11 (1984): 439–54; and idem, "'As in Your Own House': Hospitality, Ethnography, and the Stereotype of Mediterranean Society," in Gilmore, *Honor and Shame and the Unity of the Mediterranean*, 75–89. See also Lila Abu-Lughod, "Zones of Theory in the Anthropology of the Arab World," *Annual Review of Anthropology* 18 (1989): 267–306.

Hebrew, and Aramaic texts available from about the seventh century
B.C.E. through the sixth C.E., there is far too little information to attempt
anything like an ethnographic description—and the literary record
likely reflects the biases and practices of the privileged, literate classes.[3]
These caveats apply even to the Gospel stories themselves.

Categories of Comparison. After one has ascertained that the Mediterranean as a cultural region and antiquity as a unified and distinct period of
human history both have been plausibly constructed, one must take care
when invoking these categories. The same goes for the interpretive pairs
"honor/shame" and "public/domestic," whose polarity displays their common theoretical parentage in structuralism and also portends their com-
plicity with theorizations of gender. The public/domestic distinction,
although commonly made in contemporary popular anthropology, recently
has been challenged on both theoretical and empirical grounds. Its basic
premise is that all human societies both understand and intend a distinction between two spheres: a public realm where important affairs are trans-
acted among members of different kin groups and a domestic realm where
inconsequential matters are taken care of, usually within a kin group. The
realms are identified with physical spaces; different rules hold in each; and
human activities neatly divide between them. Typically the public realm is
characterized as free, open, conversational, politically and economically
significant, and male. The domestic realm, then, would be unfree, hidden,
silent, politically and economically insignificant, and female.

While Aristotle distinguished *oikos* from *polis*, it is Claude Lévi-
Strauss's conceptualization of "nature versus culture" that is the modern
antecedent of the construction of public space as a universally available category. The public realm supposedly is the realm of culture and creativity,
while the domestic realm belongs to nature and necessity. Early feminist
anthropology assumed the subjection of women to be a human universal,
brought about by the confinement of women to the domestic realm because
of exegencies of reproduction. The benchmark statement of this position
was made by Michele Rosaldo.[4]

---

3. The bias inherent in the texts is a threefold problem: the ancient authors were a
cultural elite; the scribal transmitters of *these* texts (instead of others) were religiously elite;
and we who read them today do so with culturally elite interests as well.

4. See Michele Z. Rosaldo, "Woman, Culture, and Society: A Theoretical Overview,"
and Sherry B. Ortner, "Is Female to Male as Nature Is to Culture?" both in *Woman, Culture, and
Society,* ed. M. Z. Rosaldo and Louise Lamphere (Stanford, Calif.: Stanford University Press,
1974). It is tempting to map the public/domestic boundary onto the story of the anointing of
Jesus, considered above in chapter 7. The meal would be in supposedly "public" space—the
andrōn of a great house—where a woman should not go. But the *andrōn* was by no means public
in the same sense in which an *agora* was public; guests needed invitations.

Theoretical criticism of the domestic/public conceptualization follows along familiar poststructuralist lines. It is pointed out that the binary pairing creates a value and a disvalue, reductively defines the latter in terms of the former, and tends to force the data to fit the categories of explanation. Rosaldo has taken these criticisms into account in a reconsideration of her earlier statement.[5] *Empirical* criticism of the domestic/public distinction is more devastating, coming as it does from field anthropologists who find that the construct cannot be used reliably to interpret their data.[6] For example, in the archaeological record one cannot reliably identify an excavated space as "domestic" or "public" solely on the basis of topography or by the tools and furniture found within it. One must also know how an activity—spinning, calligraphy, butchering, winnowing—was understood, the scale of the activity, how it fit into marketing arrangements, and so forth. Whether the activities in question, and the spaces where they occurred, were more "public" or more "private" depended on other factors, including the gender status and the kin status of the people doing them.[7] The putative association of female gender with domestic space appears particularly tenuous; we know that in contemporary traditional societies the gender of a place can shift with the time of day and the season of the year.[8]

The question of the space in which an activity occurred or a saying was told is an extremely significant one, and it should not be foreclosed by forcing all space into the preconceived gendered interpretations of "public"

5. See Michelle Z. Rosaldo, "The Use and Abuse of Anthropology: Reflections on Feminism and Cross-Cultural Understanding," *Signs* 5 (1980): 389–417.

6. See, e.g., *Historical Archaeology* 24 (1991), a special issue edited by Donna J. Seifert entitled *Gender in Historical Archaeology*. See also Alison Wylie, "Gender Theory and the Archaeological Record: Why Is There No Archaeology of Gender?" and Ruth E. Tringham, "Households with Faces: The Challenge of Gender in Prehistoric Architectural Remains," both in *Engendering Archaeology: Women and Prehistory*, ed. Joan M. Gero and Margaret W. Conkey (Oxford: Basil Blackwell Publisher, 1991); and Louise Tilly, "The Social and the Study of Women," *Comparative Studies in Society and History* 20 (1978): 163–73.

7. On the relation between kinship and production, see Christine Ward Gailey, "Evolutionary Perspectives in Gender Hierarchy," in *Analyzing Gender: A Handbook of Social Science Research*, ed. Beth B. Hess and Myra Marx Ferrée (Beverly Hills, Calif.: Sage Publications, 1987), 32–67; Karen Brodkin Sacks, *Sisters and Wives: The Past and Future of Sexual Equality* (Westport, Conn., and London: Greenwood Press, 1979), and idem, "Toward a Unified Theory of Class, Race, and Gender," 534–50.

8. Among the Kabyle of North Africa, e.g., men are abroad in the village at different hours in different seasons. At those times, only girls and old women go to the fountain or tend the chickens. See Bourdieu, *Outline of a Theory of Practice* (see chap. 1, n. 1), 159–63, 90–91. Gender itself is not a stable category, for in some societies it varies with age and with social class. At most, one could say that masculine gender in some societies, when combined with class status, entails the ability to carry "public" space along with oneself, while female gender in some societies entails the ability to transform either "public" or "wild" space into "domestic" space.

versus "private." When ancient texts inform us that upper-class Greek homes had women's apartments where men *without* kin status did not go (the *gynaikōn*), as well as men's dining rooms where women *with* kin status did not go (the *andrōn*), it is best not to treat this as a manifestation of either a human universal or even a cultural universal. It reflects merely a kinship custom of the tiny privileged class. Jewish village homes like those excavated in Capharnaum and Meiron, in Galilee, had nothing like that.[9]

The honor/shame distinction was constructed in the 1960s as a defining cultural characteristic for the contemporary Mediterranean region. The first articulators of this construct were careful to preserve differences of nuance among cultures and among individuals within cultures. Subsequently, however, the construct has been employed in a circular argument as a criterion by which to label societies as "Mediterranean." What Western anthropologists term "honor" can differ drastically from place to place around the Mediterranean Sea, yet these different kinds of honor seem always to correlate with aspects of male gender definition shared by researchers and informants—a coincidence noted with interest by feminist readers of the ethnographic record.

More recently the constructed and tentative character of the honor/shame distinction has been altogether overlooked by some anthropologists and by several important interpreters in biblical studies.[10] This renders their work vulnerable to criticisms recently raised against the construct, criticisms that again are both theoretical and empirical. *Theoretically,* if one must select a defining characteristic for "the Mediterranean," then at least it should be some trait that is not equally or even more common in non-Mediterranean societies. Yet the honor/shame sensibility bears such a strong resemblance to Euro-American gender values that it either may be an ethnocentric projection or may simply select out values that the male researchers happened to hold in common with their informants. *Empirically,* the English terms "honor" and "shame" are but a rough approximation of the various indigenous terms that they are meant to explain, which apply in dissimilar situations. Perhaps it is only the poor translation of many different local terms into one English word that has made "honor" appear to be a Mediterranean universal. Michael Herzfeld

---

9. Compare the floor plans published by Susan Walker, "Women and Housing in Classical Greece: The Archaeological Evidence," in Cameron and Kuhrt, *Images of Women in Antiquity,* 81–91; and by Meyers, Strange, and Meyers, *Excavations at Ancient Meiron, Upper Galilee.*

10. Crossan, *The Historical Jesus,* and Jerome H. Neyrey, ed., *The Social World of Luke-Acts* (Peabody, Maine: Hendrickson Publishers, 1991), both are superb applications of social theory to the interpretation of Gospel materials, but they have too uncritically imported Mediterranean area anthropology.

proposes that "hospitality" is a better name to classify the diverse practices observed.[11] Lila Abu-Lughod finds that, while honor is exclusively linked to masculinity in the literature, with womanly shame as its mere foil, yet among Bedouin people within "the Mediterranean area" both genders participate in a discourse of vulnerability as well as a discourse of honor.[12]

In light of this critical reevaluation, the use of the honor/shame construct to interpret *contemporary* Mediterranean societies has become increasingly perilous. Moreover, this construct may obscure more than it illuminates for the *ancient* world. "Honor" often is simply a cipher for masculine gender, and so in most instances gender analysis will prove to be more productive than analysis in terms of honor and shame. Like honor, gender is not a quality or commodity that one can statically possess. It is always being wagered and waged: use it or lose it. Honor and gender are in constant negotiation. Pierre Bourdieu insightfully describes the fluid character of social exchanges and has taught social theorists to think in terms of *practices rather than qualities.* Thus, if we borrow conceptual constructs like "honor" and "domestic space" from anthropology's toolbox, we must use them carefully to ensure valid conclusions. They are not monolithic structures; they are more like games presenting numerous options, whose shifting rules we must discern.

Further, the Mediterranean of the first century was not one culture (much less "the same" culture that is there to be studied today). It was a seething society of many cultures in creative contact and conflict. For such a situation, comparative study does not mean constructing a lowest common denominator; it means tracing out those lines of contact and conflict along cultural frontiers and describing the interactions that occur across them. Where contemporary "anthropology of the Mediterranean" is questing for regional homogeneity, we should be looking instead for fractures and fault lines. That is, we should attend to the interplay of distinctive Greek and Jewish elements as well as class frictions, and at the same time we should be on the lookout for points of communication where one cultural configuration is taken up and resymbolized by another.

The overlay of Greco-Roman urbanization upon Eretz Israel was like the grinding together of tectonic plates along a geologic fault line or the

---

11. See Herzfeld, "'As in Your Own House,'" 75–89.

12. Abu-Lughod uses Appadurai's term "theoretical metonym" to criticize the way in which honor has become a gatekeeping concept that filters the discussion of Mediterranean cultures and defines the questions that can be asked of them. See Abu-Lughod, "Zones of Theory in the Anthropology of the Arab World." Other criticisms that I have summarized here are taken from Herzfeld.

convergence of weather systems into a storm front. Therefore no static description can be adequate to the realities of gender, race, or class in the society in which Jesus lived and died. To interpret the meaning of resurrection in terms of those realities, one should recognize them as heterogeneous and unstable systems in motion relative to one another—with the claim of resurrection contributing to their turmoil for several decades before coming to rest in the Gospels.

This is of course not to deny divine agency in the resurrection of Jesus. Rather, it works toward explaining why divine agency took effect precisely in the way it did, with the distinctive significance appreciated by people in that time and place. To understand what happened to Jesus, we have to understand *what the earliest witnesses can possibly have thought* had happened to Jesus. What is more, we must excavate conceptually down to a time when "*the* claim of resurrection" was not (yet) a stable monolith but only a pebble in motion across a game board. At those conceptual strata, "the kingdom of God" was a glass vial shattering; it was lava spilling from Nazareth's caldera and congealing into carvable stone; it was clay attracting potters; it was ink about to run. Fluid imagery like this must furnish and guide our own historical imaginations, displacing the solid frozen "events" and "structures" that are the legacy of naive historiography. Otherwise there is little hope of understanding the volatility of the first century or of the ecclesial life that began there.

The Means of Imaginative Production

Easter faith dawned slowly. Between Calvary and the empty tomb story, quite some time elapsed. A recent estimate that "the first Holy Saturday" lasted five or ten years seems entirely plausible.[13] During that interval between Calvary and the breach of the tomb, there emerged an intensely creative apprehension of Jesus' continuing identity and availability. That apprehension was gradual, and it was achieved through the progressive reimagination of Jesus in relation to the kingdom of God. In the preceding chapters we have excavated some components of that poiesis or imaginative makeover. These fragmentary pieces cannot by any means be strung together into a simple line of narrative development leading from before Calvary into the finished Gospel portraits. But our reconstructions have indicated decisively that the body of Jesus was a site of contention after

---

13. See Crossan, *The Historical Jesus,* 376.

Calvary. It was food for thought, meditation, rumination, prayer. The Gospel texts, meant to be that body's final inscription, are the fruit of controversy over the identity of Jesus and the means of access to him.

Today's readers of the Gospels quite likely first received those texts with social markers firmly attached: male, white, literate, bourgeois. These characteristics were typical of Western churches and their ministers in the 1940s, 1950s, and 1960s. (In those days, even the black church had not yet found the courage to accept Jesus as a man of color, nor religious women to claim the ancient teaching credential that had always been theirs.) So one can understand why we as children would start off assuming that the Jesus story was the intellectual property of white males—and that we ought to let white male authorities explain it to the rest of us. Uncritically, Sunday school pupils and Scripture scholars alike have imagined the early Jesus movement as a milieu in which men talked and wrote to men.

That fantasy has flourished in the face of the contrary assertion, in all four Gospels, that Jesus' resurrection was revealed to and through women. The men didn't get it. Or more precisely, the means to imagine what happened with Jesus were not culturally available to elite males like Mark and Paul. The capacity to conceive of the identity and accessibility of Jesus after Calvary was not evenly distributed throughout the population of first-century Palestine. Crucial components of what would become Easter faith can have crystallized only in certain social niches, and then subsequently must have been transmitted and revised in others. "Making" Jesus was a work of recognition and redesign involving the variant reading of certain cultural texts. That kind of variation is not built upon the rock; it thrives underneath and between.

As we have seen, it has been possible to recover elements of this "making" through a kind of archaeological excavation of the texts that we have received. On the one hand, perhaps this recovery ultimately will be of merely historical interest, and the "real" meaning of the resurrection will be what comes into view only at the topmost level, the surface of the scriptural texts. On the other hand, in the next chapter I will argue to the contrary that every reimagination occurring between Calvary and the last Gospel text (John's) is both theologically significant and precious to faith. The "event" of resurrection inheres in and depends on all of them, and on many others that no longer can be recovered in detail.

It matters who made Jesus, where, and how. It matters to faith no less than to history, church politics, or curiosity. The post-Calvary struggle over Jesus has left its traces throughout the Gospels, but the many dimensions of that struggle can be resolved into two for purposes of analysis here. First, there are issues of the social definition of physical space, and the spatial constraints of social exchanges. For example, womb and tomb are the bracketing physical spaces for human life, and places at table also are significant.[14] Second, there are issues of paideia, teaching. These are worked out as speech practices pursued in the various physical spaces in which the Jesus movement propagated, and finally are corralled in the canonical texts.[15]

Where Was Jesus Made?

Resurrection is a geographic phenomenon. The story of the empty tomb is sited in Jerusalem, of course, but certain key aspects of the poiesis of Jesus also correlate more finely with the topography of houses and cities. Moreover, Jesus' resurrection, in breaching a tomb, breaks through other architectural barriers (or at least it travels along the pathways of those who know how to get around such). In chapter 8 we examined the human body from several philosophical perspectives. Now we shall consider how physical space conforms to and also enforces the distinctive fragilities of the body discovered there. A bodily resurrection is one that happens in and according to the physical spaces where the body dwells.

Access to Jesus as Risen Lord is spatially generated and defined. After Calvary, Jesus does not appear everywhere, or just anywhere. He appears, for example, in the midst of people locked behind closed doors. Closure and structure in fact become conditions for the possibility of access to Jesus; even Matthew's open-air appearance, in dispatching resurrection witnesses to the ends of the earth, actually binds them tightly to teaching observance of the halakhah of Jesus. Mark's innovation, the written Gospel, is in effect a trap in which to secure the official "Jesus" by clamping down the lid on any further development of Jesus materials. The Lord escapes the tomb only to be cloistered in the texts. But the risen body does not rest easily there. The tension between text and body persists. As Risen Lord, Jesus also resists the closure imposed by the historicizing text, which would confine his identity within the events of his career before Calvary.

Every bit of information that the Gospels give us about Jesus was imaginatively refashioned by various people before being committed to

14. Kathleen Corley has developed the latter consideration in *Private Women, Public Meals.*

15. The interlacing of space with fence, body with text, where with how, achieves its ecclesial resolution in the liturgy, as we shall see in the next chapter.

the written page. Where did that imaginative re-creation take place? Scholars answer in various ways. Some think that Mark wrote out his text isolated in a kind of studio surrounded by scrolls containing earlier versions of Gospel materials.[16] Others imagine men speechifying to other men in synagogues or beneath urban colonnades, adapting stock stories to local issues. But there are indications that women transmitted Jesus materials as well. The saying recorded in the *Gospel of Thomas* 22, that nursing babies are like those entering God's kingdom, quite likely was passed along among women, perhaps from older to younger within households or on courtyards. The saying changed when it left the women's circles and was pressed into service to support pedagogical programs, as we have seen. But that this material did pass from women's space into men's space (and not the other way) is extremely significant.

The Mary story, too, must have traveled among women. If our reconstruction was correct, then the core of that story took shape when someone versed in Jewish law drew precedent for the case of Mary's son Jesus out of the case of Hannah's son Samuel. Who knew—who could possibly have imagined—that Mary would pray Hannah's Hebrew prayer? In Galilee of the mid-second century, according to the Talmud, at least one woman of rabbinic family was reputed to be a legal expert of such shrewdness and compassion that her opinions were sought by and discussed among her male relatives and the associates of the latter. On one hand, a genesis for the Mary story among women of the *Tannaim* fits the hypothesis that Jesus' mother came from a distinguished family in Sepphoris and maintained her relationship with her natal kin after she married into Joseph's family. On the other hand, certainly the transmission and the embellishment of the Mary story are owing to its retelling among women. Not only the colorful details of the *Infancy Gospel of James* version but the memory of the problem pregnancy and divine saving intervention itself would be most important to Jesus' maternal aunts, cousins, and nieces, and to young women marrying into his extended family. The legitimation of Jesus as servant and son of God is among their contributions to the embryonic Gospel tradition and to its claim of resurrection for Jesus.

Like the dominical saying about nursing, the argument in favor of Jesus' legitimacy projects spatial and class coordinates for itself. The nursing scenario suggests peasant women in the courtyard of a village *insula* or tenement, while the Hannah precedent comes from elite women in an urban mansion. Both of these are enclosed spaces that are nevertheless permeable

16. See, e.g., Mack, *Myth of Innocence.*

to certain people. The tenement courtyard welcomes people of both sexes, but the economically privileged and the religiously scrupulous would not wish to enter there. At the mansion, the *gynaikōn* or women's apartment was off-limits to men, but visiting female relatives and women workers from outside the kin group could enter. In both cases young girls, old women, and other workers had more mobility and access than privileged women of childbearing age. Thus we must postulate three kinds of important communications activities that somehow have escaped the notice of historians of Christian origins. First, women who knew Jesus talked to one another around ordinary courtyards and within the women's apartments of elite homes. Second, women circulated among others of their own class: courtyard to courtyard, mansion to mansion—and when they visited, they talked. Third, working women such as midwives, wet nurses, hairdressers, and caterers came and went in the women's apartments of the great houses. In each instance, girls and old women circulated more freely than young wives. The friendships of women provided context for the passing of Jesus traditions—quite early Jesus traditions.

What did visiting women talk about? We have more to go on for the elite class than for peasants, and more for hellenized urban families than for traditional villagers. What women did in the *gynaikōn* was weaving. Wool work was the occupation associated with the good wife among the Greeks from time immemorial. When the Greeks established their colonial city of Alexandria, they insisted on introducing sheep, despite the unsuitability of the Egyptian climate and landscape, so that women would have their accustomed weaving to keep them busy.[17] Wool work was also traditional for Jewish women, and it is one of the points of cultural compatibility that eased the adoption of Hellenism in Eretz Israel. The loom occupied a considerable portion of women's time and attention. As mentioned above, weaving is motivated by the body's need for protection, but it also trains the mind to make linear and two-dimensional connections. The weaver connects threads and composes patterns. Weaving teaches you to think in an orderly but innovative and creative way.[18]

---

17. Linen and cotton weaving were indigenous Egyptian industries. Compare the sketch of the profit-making wife in Prov. 31:13.

18. When Rabbi Eleazar ben Peraṭa was tried by the Romans on charges of teaching Torah in violation of imperial law, the prosecutor asked him why he was called master. "I am a master of weavers," was his reply. See ʿ*Abodah Zarah* 17b. In modern times, loom technology was the direct antecedent of computer software. Punched cards were invented to encode the patterns of jacquard designs in woolen mills. Charles Babbage adapted that technology for use in the "analytic engine" that he designed but could not afford to build. Women have been at the creative edge of software development since its inception. Harriet Taylor's letters to

Texts and textiles are metaphorically related realities. Walter Ong and others have shown that the advent of literacy changes how people look at the world. The habit of making texts tends to reinforce visual bias and imparts linear narrative structure to experience. What, then, may be said of the habit of making textiles? It too equips the imagination and focuses perception. Just as ancient writing was the work of covering skin (parchment) with ink, so weaving was the work of covering living surfaces with protective artificial skin. Writing selects "events" and with them fabricates a design upon the page, while weaving selects fibers and connects them into a design upon the loom. Thus the women working in a first-century *gynaikōn* in Erẹtz Israel had more than just the opportunity to talk to one another: they had the mental acuity to fabricate interesting things to say.

It is plausible that women talked with one another on a daily basis in the course of their affairs, but it is quite certain that they had contact on the occasions of major life transitions: weddings, births, illness, death. Such bodily events brought duties that, by Greek and Jewish customs, only women could fulfill. Delivering babies was the work of midwives, and they are credited as sources of the information conveyed by male medical authors. The customs of mourning and burial also involved women. Jewish women provided hospitality to mourners and washed and laid out the corpse.[19]

Women mourned for the dead—and as they mourned, they thought about what they were doing and tried to make sense of the death. Illustrations of women's poietic reflection upon death come down to us from both pagan Greek and hellenized Jewish sources. The Greeks had several traditional festivals that were observed exclusively by women. These festivals, religious in character, also were an important opportunity for women to interact with one another apart from male supervision. The Thesmophoria and the Adonia included a day of mourning followed by a celebration of new life. The theme of "mourning Adonis" inspired not only rituals but poetry as well.[20] The annual public women's observance of "mourning

---

Babbage enunciated the rudiments of programming; she was also mentor to John Stuart Mill. Admiral Grace Hopper devised the first natural-language data-processing compiler, called Flowmatic, and later developed the programming language COBOL out of it.

19. Men could also wash a male corpse but not a female one. See *Šemaḥot* 12:10.

20. Adonis was the young lover of Aphrodite, killed by a wild animal. It is thought that Adonis originally was a Babylonian deity, Tammuz. When the Greeks appropriated the story of "Lord Tammuz," they mistook the Semitic honorific term *ʾadon* for his proper name. From that same root comes the Hebrew word *Adonai*, "my Lord." The two divine names would have sounded startlingly similar to hellenized Jews.

Adonis" gave Greek women an imaginative resource through which to interpret tragedy when it entered their own private lives.

Another example of the reinterpretation of a tragic death comes down to us attached to the name of Beruriah (or Valeria), who lived in Tiberias by the Sea of Galilee in the first half of the second century C.E. Beruriah's father was Rabbi Hananiah ben Teradion, and her husband may have been Rabbi Meir. The latter was well read in Greek literature, and both were Tannaim. The teachings of all three are recorded in the Talmud. A story is told that Beruriah's two sons died suddenly on a Sabbath while their father was at the house of study. When Rabbi Meir returned home he asked to see the boys, but Beruriah put him off. Not until after he had ritually observed the conclusion of the Sabbath and had finished his supper did Beruriah approach him with a legal question.

> "Rabbi," she then said, "some time ago a deposit was left with me for safe-keeping, and now the owner has come to claim it. Must I return it?" "Can there be any question about the return of property to its owner?" said R. Meir, half astonished and half indignant that his wife should entertain a doubt. "I did not care to let it go out of my possession without your knowledge," replied Beruriah, seemingly in excuse, and, taking him by the hand, led him into the room in which the bodies of their two sons were lying on the bed. When she withdrew the cover, R. Meir broke out in tears and plaints. Gently Beruriah reminded him of his answer to her question about the return of a treasure entrusted to one for safe-keeping, adding the verse from Job (1:21): "The Lord gave, and the Lord hath taken away; blessed be the name of the Lord."[21]

Whether or not this event is historical, its presence in traditional sources demonstrates its perceived plausibility. Hellenized Jewish women could and did make imaginative use of cultural resources in order to give meaning to a tragic death. Women's interpretive practices were an accepted part of their role as mourners. Bereaved Jewish women knew why they were weeping. The decomposition of the body was thought to be painful and thereby to accomplish atonement for sin. In first-century Jerusalem, as we have seen, the process of dying was culturally completed

21. This version of the story is Henrietta Szold's. See her article on Beruriah in *The Jewish Encyclopedia* (New York: Funk & Wagnalls Co., 1906) 3:109–10. The textual sources are *Yalkut* to Proverbs 964, and the Midrash on Prov. 31:10. But compare Epictetus' *Handbook*, 11, for similar sentiments in contemporary Stoic thought. Thus, the association of this story with Beruriah may indicate that she was—or, was remembered by people who were—familiar with the secular learning of the day.

only with second burial, a year after death. The last day of grieving was the day when the bare bones were gathered and placed with those of other family members, in order to await the resurrection and the messianic age. The day *after* that one was joyful, because the body had been wiped clean of sin and was ready for God to clothe it anew with life.

Loss of the Body

In Jesus' case, that process was interrupted. The body was not given back to the family. Calvary had been a quarry in antiquity, and after executions the police dumped the bodies into any convenient hole together with some lime to cut the stench. But possibly the Sanhedrin took custody of Jesus' corpse according to the procedure recalled in Mishnah *Sanhedrin* 6:5, since the sentence of the court was not considered satisfied until the body decomposed. In the case of a criminal whose execution has been ordered by the Sanhedrin (as Jesus' was, says Mark), the body was not released to the family immediately. The court took charge of the corpse (perhaps through a delegated member like Joseph of Arimathea?), and laid it in a tomb reserved for the purpose, to undergo decomposition without the family's observing the customary mourning rituals. Only after a year would the bones be released to the family for ossilegium burial in the normal way. Thus someone facing capital punishment would expect his body to be unavailable to his family for anointing after death.[22]

In either case—limed pit or confiscation—the interruption of the dying process causes grief. Mary Magdalene, asked why she is weeping, replies: "They've taken my Master away, and I don't know where they've put him" (John 20:13).[23] This grief focuses less on the death itself, interestingly, than on the fact that, because someone prevented the body from undergoing atoning decomposition in the normal way, the family and/or disciples could not get at the bones to get them ready for resurrection and the messianic age. I suggest that such grief over loss of the body was the starting point of the reflection that culminates in a "finding" of the empty tomb and a "seeing" of Jesus as already risen from the dead.

22. On the other hand, Mishnah reflects concern over securing burial for corpses found abandoned. Burial is a timely need that can override virtually any other custom or law.

23. In John's account, Joseph of Arimathea has buried Jesus. Apparently Mary knows about that, so her three complaints about Jesus' having been "taken" and "put" somewhere all are referenced back to the emptiness of the tomb that he supposedly occupied briefly.

Grieving women's reinterpretation of Jesus' death likely lies behind Mark's story of the anointing at Bethany (Mark 14:3-9), as we saw in chapter 7. The Greek words for weeping and anointing, *myrasthai* and *myrisai,* not only sound similar but come from the same verb.[24] Luke's version of the anointing story (Luke 7:36-50) even retains mention of the tears. However, the implied setting for Mark 14:3-9 is not the *gynaikōn* at the Bethany villa but its *andrōn* or symposium room, for Jesus is said to be "reclining." Thus by the time the story becomes a written text, it has traveled significantly. This "anointing" is no longer simply the way that grieving women speak to make sense of Jesus among themselves; now it is what they have to say about Jesus to the men.

For their part, the men of a *symposion* group would be ill equipped to make the first tentative imaginative moves that started the remembered Jesus on his way to resurrection. According to Greek custom, the *symposion* was a more or less stable group of seven or eleven men who pledged loyalty to one another and met regularly for formal meals, conversation, entertainment, and drinking. These companions, or *hetairoi,* might be related by kinship, or as age mates they may have begun attending the *gymnasion* together, or both. This was an upper-class sort of association. Jesus cannot have been a regular member of such a set, in view of the indications we have of his peasant background and his dim view of Hellenistic institutions in general. Craftsmen didn't dine reclining.[25] Before Calvary, it is conceivable that Jesus could have accepted (unwittingly?) an invitation to dinner at a great house where he was meant to be part of the entertainment. That is exactly how Luke interprets the tradition of the anointing, for in his version Jesus has been snubbed as a low-class client and disappoints the host because he fails to perform as a prophet. But no way was Jesus traveling with the *symposion* set before Calvary, and no way would such men find him fit to mention at table, were he not introduced there by someone else, someone credible.

After Calvary, a tradition about Jesus "reclining" at a *symposion* must be read as an attempt to align the Risen Lord with elite institutions and practices. To recline at meals in the Greco-Roman manner, one needs a large staff and a house big enough to set apart a room for formal dining with the requisite furniture (couches and tables). Great houses had dining

24. *Myron,* "ointment," and *myrizō,* "anoint," are related to the verb *myrō,* which in the active voice means "ooze, trickle" and in the middle voice means "weep." Many of the participial forms are quite close.

25. The Mishnah mentions reclining at Passover, but that does not necessarily reflect the practice of Jesus' time and social class. Neither does the Talmud's interpretation that such reclining is required, *Pesaḥim* 108a; see also the mentions of reclining at 99b, 100a, and 101b.

rooms where men of the kin group entertained their friends along with hired women.[26] Dining was educational. It taught you who you were. In earlier times, banqueters found diversion in the antics of beggars who, in exchange for scraps, acted out the upper-class caricature of themselves.[27] In Roman times, a wealthy host would take the opportunity to humiliate the clients who, by his command, were reclining in low-prestige locations and receiving both verbal insults and poorer food.[28] Dinner could be followed by pantomime and theater; dinner itself *was* theater. The *symposion* was the means of social memory and paideia; it was the principal venue for reciting the poetry in which virtue was defined and brave deeds were immortalized in memory.[29] Peasants and slaves did not recline to eat, and it is thought that men did not recline until they entered the *ephebate*, about age eighteen.

In the Greco-Roman cities, meat came from temple sacrifices. Greek women's *domestic* cooking duties were comparatively light.[30] Slaughtering, roasting, and distribution of meat were the work of men. The term *mageiros* derives from *machaira*, "knife," and it designates the man who butchers, cooks, and carves meat.[31] *Mageiroi* hired on to work fancy banquets; we

26. In classical times, dining rooms in houses were typically square and held seven or eleven couches arranged head to toe around the walls, leaving room for a door. Entertainment would consist in discussion, recitation, and song *within* the nearly closed circle of guests. Later, the Roman *triclinium* angled the diners elbow to elbow along three sides of a square table, and the sigma-couch or *stibadium* arranged them fan-wise in a semicircle within an apse that opened out onto a large hall. Thus diners in the *triclinium* and especially the *stibadium* could be (and were) entertained by rhetors, poets, musicians, dancers, etc., who were not part of the reclining group. Some private dining halls had seven or more apses opening out onto a single large performance space. See Katherine M. D. Dunbabin, "*Triclinium* and *Stibadium*," in *Dining in a Classical Context*, ed. William J. Slater (Ann Arbor: University of Michigan Press, 1991), 121–48.

27. See Burkhard Fehr, "Entertainers at the *Symposion:* The *Akletoi* in the Archaic Period," in Murray, *Sympotica* (see chap. 7, n. 4), 185–95.

28. See John D'Arms, "The Roman *Convivium* and the Idea of Equality," in Murray, *Sympotica*, 308–20. The Lukan version of the anointing story presupposes readers' familiarity with this practice; see Luke 7:44-46. This elite men's ritual of humiliation through food and drink compares with the elite women's custom of *katachysmata*.

29. On memory as the function of the *symposion*, see Rösler, "*Mnemosyne* in the *Symposion*," in Murray, *Sympotica*, 230–37. On the *paideia* of the *symposium*, see Manuela Tecuşan, "*Logos-Sympotikos:* Patterns of the Irrational in Philosophical Drinking: Plato Outside the *Symposium*," in ibid., 238–60. On entertainment, see Christopher P. Jones, "Dinner Theater," in Slater, *Dining in a Classical Context*, 185–98.

30. See, e.g., Brian Sparkes, "The Greek Kitchen," *Journal of Hellenistic Studies* 82 (1962): 121–37 and plates IV–VII; and idem, "Not Cooking, But Baking," *Greece and Rome* 28 (1981): 172–78.

31. See Marcel Détienne and Jean-Paul Vernant, *The Cuisine of Sacrifice among the Greeks*, trans. Paula Wissing (Chicago and London: University of Chicago Press, 1986),

would call them caterers. In addition, the host had to hire women called
dēmiourgoi to prepare the sweet desserts and bake the fancy cheesecakes,
cookies, and honeyed fruit pies.[32] At a lavish banquet, apparently, guests removed their wreaths for heavy eating during the meat and poultry (or fish)
courses. Then they cleansed their hands, refreshed themselves with perfume, and rewreathed themselves. The dessert courses followed, before the
serious drinking of the *symposion* began.

We know these details from Athenaeus, who complains about variations in this "classical" order. He grumbles that at modern banquets (late
first to early second century C.E.), *mageiroi* serve you sweets when you are
ready for meat, but then after you have wreathed and perfumed yourself
again those darn women, the *dēmiourgoi,* bring on meat pies and thrushes.[33]
Male meat chefs and female pastry chefs receive equal notice. Crews of each
had to be hired to pull off a really fine banquet. They are described as
working briskly through the night to prepare the fancy foods.[34]

Much has been made in pious scholarship about the table practices of
Jesus before Calvary. Many would like to think of him as a host who

132–33. For the range of the occupation, see Guy Bertiaume, *Les rôles du mágeiros: Etude sur la
boucherie, la cuisine et le sacrifice dans la Grèce ancienne* (Leiden: E. J. Brill, 1982). Curiously, the
abridged lexicon of Liddell & Scott derives *mageiros* from *massō,* "because the baking of bread
was originally the chief business of the cook," but in light of the gender evidence the linguistic connection to *machaira* seems more likely.

32. A second-declension noun, *dēmiourgos* is feminine when preceded by the feminine
article *hē,* as here. (Compare *hē parthenos* and *hē theos.*) The term *dēmiourgos* derives from
words that mean "people's work." It applies to members of a skilled artisan class, such as
sculptors. In a culinary context it takes on the specialized meaning of "confectioner." Plato
calls rhetoric the *dēmiourgos* of belief; see *Gorgias* 453, discussed below. The exclusive masculinity of the role of the *mageiros,* the meat-carver, makes the very idea of a female butcher
grotesque and all but unthinkable in Greek. This is illustrated in two instances where a contrived feminine form of the noun appears as a special effect. The fifth-century (B.C.E.) comic
poet Pherecrates writes that a *mageiraina,* a "butcher-ine," was never yet known. The third-
century translators of the Septuagint use *mageirissas,* "butcher-esses," at 1 Sam. 8:13, where
Samuel warns the people that a king would make their daughters do such unseemly work.

33. This implies that one would expect the women chefs to be bringing in sweets to
refresh the palate after the heavier courses. See Athenaeus, *Deipnosophistae* 4.172ff., quoting
Menander's plays (4–3 century B.C.E.) as witness to earlier customs.

34. Ibid. Athenaeus tells us that in a pilgrimage center like Delos, virtually the whole
population of ordinary men and women worked in the catering trade and had names corresponding to their specialties. Collectively they were called *eleodutai,* "table dodgers," by men
of Athenaeus's class, because of the way they earned their living. Athenaeus also tells of an
old woman who worked as a food taster to protect her master from poisoning, and of a
woman supervisor of a common men's dining hall on Crete. Thus when we imagine an elegant *andrōn* banquet room in a Greco-Roman city, we must imagine women at work there—
but very few of them are *hetairai.*

welcomed everyone—rich and poor, male and female, Jew and Greek—to the table in his own home. That attractive version of Jesus originates with the elite men who knew Jesus after Calvary in their practice of a eucharist, and whose views are transmitted to us in stories with Jesus reclining at table. But it cannot be supported archaeologically or anthropologically for the period before Calvary. Village houses from the time of Jesus have been excavated in Capharnaum, in Nazareth, and elsewhere in Galilee. They are not large enough comfortably to accommodate even a card table, much less the luxurious couches needed for seven or eleven men to recline together. The Jerusalem Temple, like Greek sanctuaries and pilgrimage sites everywhere, had to provide private banqueting rooms for people to use when they went up to sacrifice. If villagers wanted to hold feasts closer to home, they would have to do it outdoors on the ground. The Gospel accounts of miraculous outdoor feedings on bread and fish reflect the meal practice of the peasant Jesus movements, as John Dominic Crossan and others have pointed out.

The availability of rentable rooms for pilgrims in and around the Temple complex in Jerusalem lends plausibility to Mark's statement that Jesus shared a formal Passover dinner there with his companions before he died. If so, it was a special occasion, and not indicative of the commensality otherwise customary among Galilean villagers. But that practice no longer is recoverable for us, especially not in the reports of how Jesus dined in Jerusalem. It is more enlightening to read those last supper narratives for what they can tell us about the people who were transmitting them after Calvary.

Death and Dining

In Mark's passion narrative the theme of death hovers over the last *two* suppers of Jesus' life. At Jerusalem, the conversation in the room upstairs introduces the notes of sacrifice and covenant to interpret the execution that would occur the next day. But at suburban Bethany, the "reclining" of Jesus already has invoked a long-standing Greek upper-class conceptual affinity between feasting and the grave. The fancy couch, or *klinē*, on which diners reclined at a *symposion* is the very same piece of furniture used to lay out a corpse. In either situation, the ornate carving and gilding of the *klinē* would show off one's wealth. Moreover, the same unguent and the same term, "anointing" (*myrisai*), are used whether the scent is for live bodies or corpses. *Myron*, even when applied for luxury, inevitably reminded Greeks of death. The playboy lifestyle, signified by wreathing and perfuming oneself, was typically contrasted with the grave that inexorably would overtake it. This association is made in several banquet epigrams that come down to us. For example:

> Let us cover our heads with wreaths and let us anoint ourselves, before others carry such to our tombs. For my part, let the bones inside me drink their fill of wine, and let dead ones soak in Deukalion's stuff (that is, water).

A similar sentiment is expressed in the following:

> If someone does not enjoy . . . wreaths and perfume, but takes a frugal supper . . . to me such a one has died, and I cautiously tiptoe past the corpse who pennypinches for the sake of the gullets of strangers.[35]

Extravagant waste was a feature of both feasts and funerals in upper-class Greco-Roman society. Moreover, the recitations and dramatic presentations staged at *symposia* were intended to reinforce the values of bravery and loyalty to one's companions, especially for times of war. The beautiful death of a hero would be an appropriate theme. This is the cultural background against which Mark's intended readers would appreciate the challenging gesture of the woman who anoints Jesus for burial and Jesus' acceptance of the challenge.

It bears noting, however, that this message—his impending death and its necessity—is delivered to Jesus and the other symposiasts from elsewhere, from outside their circle. A woman has introduced this meaning, and in doing so has suddenly focused that vague foreboding of death that would be hovering over any Hellenistic *symposion*. Her bottle of persuasive ointment (*alabastron myrou nardou pistikēs*) was concocted elsewhere and *prior to* this gathering at table. In Mark's narrative, Jesus' acceptance of this persuasive message while just outside Jerusalem prepares him for the next night's supper, his last, within the holy city. But the persuasive or belief-inducing salve itself was prepared out of sight, beforehand, among women.

We get the impression, then, that there were significant off-screen developments in the Jesus movements well in advance of the point when Jesus materials began to attain currency among reclining elite men at their *symposia*. An understanding of Jesus' identity and fate is something *brought to* the table from elsewhere by a woman—prepackaged already in

---

35. These epigrams are from an ancient collection called the *Greek Anthology,* 11:19 and 9:409.

her *alabastron*, as it were. The diners wouldn't know what "Jesus" was about without being shown this anointing for burial. They do not like it when they see it, and they accept it reluctantly if at all.

Eucharist as we know it is a formal feeding ritual. Not all segments of the early Jesus movements practiced anything like it or knew a tradition about a last supper. For example, the carriers of the sayings in the Q collection got along without any narrative depicting the supper, passion, death, and tomb. Nor did the community that produced John's Gospel hand on any eucharistic institution story. As we shall see in the next section, Mark reads Jesus' death to be a sacrificial surrendering of body and blood as pledged beforehand among *symposion* companions. This reading, valid and viable as it has turned out to be, is that of one specific elite male segment of hellenized Jewish society. Moreover, it presumes and builds upon the earlier interpretations made by others.

The table counts as one location where the figure of Jesus undergoes significant redesign in the forging of Gospel traditions. But the table is not a point of origin. There was a Jesus, and he even was risen, *before* Mark focused the events of his death with the last supper narrative.[36] Practices of sending disciples to the Lord, practices of "seeing the Lord" by keeping his teaching and even by feeding the hungry, already were in operation in several pockets of the Jesus movements. The specific claim that Jesus' tomb was found empty must be traced in terms of all those practices, and not just within the tight little three-day narrative frame that Mark has patched together. Jesus rose from the dead, although not to fulfill a bleary-eyed boast to his drinking buddies (Mark 14:23-28).

How Was Jesus Made?

You can't get from the upstairs room to the garden tomb. Nobody who eats with Jesus before Calvary is let in on the discovery of the empty tomb afterward, according to Mark's account. These were distinct traditions. I have just argued that the last supper narrative construes Jesus' death in terms of a pledge shared among *hetairoi*, or companions, at a *symposion*. Soon we shall see how a motif of sacrifice is overlaid upon that structure. But first I will contrast the Markan imagination of what happens to Jesus' body with other options that better account for the emergence of a tradition about breaking out of a tomb.

---

36. The institution narrative itself is of course pre-Markan, for it is known to Paul. Mark has adapted it from something like an early Christ cult, as Burton Mack surmises.

Bodies are receptive to textual definition, and throughout life they continue to receive social inscriptions. At the same time, the meanings ascribed to bodies always fall somewhat shy of a perfect fit. The body does the unexpected; it resists the confinements of economic class, of gender restrictions, of racial stereotypes (as we considered in chapters 8 and 9). It offers personal access and intimacy, sometimes in spite of texts that place bodies off-limits to one another. The claim of resurrection for Jesus asserts that God has overridden his death as if it were no more than a troublesome social text. God gets around death with Jesus. But stop and think. This is entirely different from the notion that Jesus bought something from God with his death. A death that is pledged to pay for a kingdom is a good thing. Perhaps such a good death needs to be memorialized in song and story, but it does not need to be gotten around or undone. However, the death that cuts off access to someone who opened up access to God is a bad thing. Means have to be found for reestablishing that interrupted access. Hence the theorizations of the availability of Jesus in hungry little ones, or in obedience to justice, or in prophetic speech—all premised upon the availability of God in Jesus.

Resurrection, in first-century Jewish religious thought, was expected as part of the new age that the messiah was going to begin. Opinions varied about the scope of this phenomenon, or whether it would happen at all. But the notion intended a mass resurrection to a restored life on earth, with graphic physical details. It did not cover the singular privilege of someone who would appear alone here and there after his own death, and then disappear altogether. Thus the culturally available imagery of "rising from the dead" was not a good fit for the case of Jesus; what was happening with him would have to be forced into that mold, with not inconsiderable warping of the mold.

What, then, was happening with the late Jesus before the women brought forth their story that he rose up and left his tomb empty?[37] He was bodily presenting himself, to the extent that people who had known him before could now recognize the sameness of Jesus in the newness of life. A bodily presentation is a fragile one, which both receives textualization and resists it. Jesus' body was being recognized in bodies of other genders, classes, and ethnicities than his own. The kingdom of God was getting around the borders and leaking through the cracks of civil, social, psychological, and physical impediments. Jesus was turning out to have been right about the permeability of society and personality for

---

37. Or if you will: What was God doing with Jesus during that time?

God. Specifically, we are told, the wonderworks of healing and exorcism continued as before Calvary. At the same time, the old camaraderie revived and the movement coalesced, broadcasting a congenial appeal that was attractive to many amid the alienating social conditions of Greco-Roman cities. News of Jesus seeped into elegant salons where the Galilean teacher himself never ventured. Things fell slowly into place as thoughtful people reviewed various scriptural precedents in the effort to comprehend the death of Jesus together with the persistence of aspects of his teaching.

Jesus didn't need an empty tomb until he became the fulfiller of prophecies thanks to the study, argumentation, and downright ingenuity of an educated few. Higher education in the Greco-Roman world meant training in rhetoric, which was the practice of persuasive speech in public affairs. Beruriah and her husband, Rabbi Meir, like numerous other Hebrew scholars, were familiar with classical texts of the Greek rhetorical tradition and with the practice of the art of persuasion. But one did not have to be a rabbi to know rhetoric; the widespread participation of Jews in the governing institutions of the hellenized cities of Palestine indicates a level of competence in argumentation, composition, and speech, on the one hand, as well as competence to hear, evaluate, and act upon public speech, on the other.[38] As we have seen, *meturgemanin* at the same time were adapting historical Hebrew texts to fit contemporary situations in their oral practice as Aramaic interpreters in the synagogues. The modern English concept of "faith" has no exact parallel in the Hebrew Bible; it derives from the New Testament's synthesis of Semitic obedience, awe, and wholehearted devotion, with Greek persuasion.[39] To believe is to allow oneself to be persuaded. *Pistis*, translated "faith," denotes both the factors that persuade and the state of having been persuaded. *Pistis* can also denote a pledge or promise to do something to

---

38. So says James Kinneavy, who also proposes that there must have been an extensive system of secondary education throughout Palestine to equip people for political participation. See James L. Kinneavy, *Greek Rhetorical Origins of Christian Faith: An Inquiry* (Oxford: Oxford University Press, 1987). The literature on Greek rhetorical influences on the rabbis is large and growing. See, e.g., Henry A. Fischel's 1966 paper "Story and History: Observations on Greco-Roman Rhetoric and Pharisaism" as well as the other early articles reprinted in *Essays in Greco-Roman and Related Talmudic Literature,* ed. Henry A. Fischel (New York: KTAV Publishing House, 1977).

39. Kinneavy would go so far as to assert that Christian faith *is* Greek persuasion. But the Greek verb *peithō,* meaning "persuade" in the active voice, also means "obey" in the middle voice, so that the derived noun *pistis,* "faith," embraces more of the Hebrew range of meaning than Kinneavy allows.

prove oneself. (In English we call that a sign of good faith; in Latin, *bona fides*.) Members of a *symposion* set looked for *pistis* from one another.

Belief was not universally esteemed by the Greeks. Plato, who deplores the rhetors, says that "rhetoric is a producer of persuasion" (*peithous dēmiourgos estin hē rhētorikē*). He distinguishes between "having learned" (*memathēkenai*) and "having been persuaded" (*pepisteukenai*) in this sense: there can be a false belief (*pistis*), but there cannot be false knowledge (*epistēmē*). Because belief and knowledge thus differ, and because both are effected by persuasion (*peithō*, as a noun), there must then be two kinds of persuasion. So Plato formulates a clarification: "Rhetoric . . . is a producer of persuasion for belief, not for instruction about right and wrong" (*hē rhētorikē . . . peithous dēmiourgos esti pisteutikēs, all' ou didaskalikēs peri to dikaion te kai adikon*). The rhetor is not *didaskalikos* but merely *pistikos*.[40]

Plato's argument was widely known and very influential in antiquity, even though it had little impact on the teaching and practice of rhetoric in the *gymnasia* and beyond. James Kinneavy, noting the involvement of Jews in the public affairs of Greco-Roman cities in Palestine, infers that rhetorical training must have been provided to equip them to participate in the polis as they did.[41] The presence of the technical vocabulary of rhetoric indicates that the Gospel texts stem from people of an elite sector of the Jesus movements who knew the lingo of the *gymnasion*. Even though women did not receive formal rhetorical instruction, they could well be characterized as *pistikai* by men who had. *Pistikēs* in Mark 14:3 and John 12:3 is the literary trace of persuasive, convincing women's speech that had the major effect of inducing the *pistis* of the christhood of Jesus. Under the influence of gender stereotyping, "persuasiveness" drifted toward "seductiveness" in subsequent retellings (Luke 7:36, 47), as the link to live verbal instruction was forgotten.[42] Traditionally in Judaism as in Greek philosophy, instruction is better than mere persuasion. Something that is *pistikos* should be treated with extreme caution. In the first century, if someone described Jesus and his group as teacher and learners

40. Plato, *Gorgias* 453a–455a. I should add that the material issue here was *marketing*: given the availability of both rhetors and philosophers in the educational marketplace, which one should you hire for your adolescent heir?

41. This training would have focused on *pistis* as both the techniques of political and legal persuasion and the conviction induced in listeners who were competent to appreciate such techniques. See Kinneavy, *Greek Rhetorical Origins*, 79–80. Kinneavy presumes too much in asserting that *gymnasia* and "synagogue schools" in the first century were as accessible as high schools are in American society. Yet he is correct in his basic thesis that *pistis* and *pisteuō* in the New Testament are borrowed from the vocabulary of Hellenistic rhetoric.

42. Compare the fate of eloquent Beruriah's legend in rabbinic tradition. The medieval commentator Rashi hands on the slander that she committed sexual improprieties with one of the students, then killed herself in remorse. See Rashi on ʿ*Abodah Zarah* 18b.

(*mathētēs*), then literate people would certainly ask what kind of teaching was going on and whether it was producing knowledge or mere belief.[43]

Who Made Jesus?

The emptied tomb is presented first as a *pistis* or means of persuasion—one that meets with less than overwhelming success. Like the *alabastron* at Bethany, the breached tomb is meant to be *pistikos* or persuasive.[44] Both tableaux concern the identification of Jesus: they figure into arguments about his status. They are means by which women undertake to convince men to accept a distinctive interpretation of the death of Jesus. The emptying of the tomb, like the emptying of the bottle, constitutes a *pistis* or deft rhetorical demonstration. It argues that Jesus' death brings God's kingdom. Or rather, the emptied tomb is a piece of someone's argument about God's inbreaking power brought near in the enduring nearness of Jesus even after Calvary.

Whose argument? Can it have been a women's argument? Yes, and it was theirs before it was anyone else's.[45] Hellenized Jewish women were quite capable of making persuasive arguments, in the technical Greek and Hebrew senses of the word. If their imaginations were stimulated by weaving, their intellects as well were trained by formal instruction in Torah and in Greek culture.

Beruriah, whose Greek name was Valeria, is one example we know. She constructed her halakhic arguments according to recognized exegetical principles. We are not told the details of the Hebrew and Greek education that she received, but much information survives about the education of upperclass girls in earlier times. Greek education made no separation of

43. This question had a formative influence on the gospel genre. Vernon Robbins shows how the Gospels portray Jesus as a teacher using the culturally available models. See Robbins, *Jesus the Teacher* (see chap. 2., n. 28).

44. *Pistikos* is a variant spelling of *peistikos*. Depending on the version you consult, you can find both spellings in Plato; e.g., at *Gorgias* 455b 4, *pistikos* in the *TLG* database, but *peistikos* in the Loeb edition. When Sextus Empiricus cites the *Gorgias* he fastidiously spells it *peistik-*; see *Adversus Mathematicos* 2:2 and 5. But Plotinus uses *pistik-*. For a contrasting argument using resurrection as a *pistis*, see Mark 12:18-27. Jesus responds by citing Torah.

45. For several decades in pre-textual Christianity, everyone knew this. However, the women's contributions toward making Jesus did not register in the subsequent texts about him. Compare the salience of Grace Hopper's creative contributions in the oral histories of computer scientists recorded in the PBS series *The Machine That Changed the World* or in the recollections offered by coworkers in obituaries shortly after her death on January 1, 1992, with her obscurity or absence from histories of programming written by people not yet born when she was laying the foundations.

the mental from the physical; both were integrated to develop the competences for one's place in society. Upper-class young men in the *gymnasion* read classical treatises for examples of how to set up cases. They fought for sport and to prepare for war. They declaimed speeches at the top of their lungs to keep themselves physically fit; it was aerobic exercise. Their sisters went to dancing school but not for ballet or ballroom dancing as we have today. Greek dance was public participation in civic religious festivals. It combined poetry, music, movement, and gesture into multimedia depictions of events significant to the community and its cultural foundations.[46]

The social function of the chorus was education as well as religious observance but not entertainment as we know it. Girls learned to speak and to move, gracefully and expressively.[47] Some would pantomime, while others recited or sang. Adolescent bodies were trained to keep one's place and to do it honor. Just as boys were ideologically oriented toward standing fast in a battle line, the ideology for girls pointed toward standing steadfastly at the loom. One's place in the pattern of society was written onto the body with this physical training, to the accompaniment of songs and recitations about the great deeds of the past. We know that Jewish men and boys participated fully in the paideia of the *gymnasia*, even in the cities of Eretz Israel itself. There is every reason to believe that Jewish girls received the parallel education that the chorus system had to offer. The design of at least one synagogue in Israel from the Greco-Roman period was fit to accommodate a chorus of chanting preteens presenting historic tableaux and circle dances before their parents and relatives. The mosaic floor excavated at Hammat Tiberias depicts YHWH/Helios amid the wheel of zodiac figures. A large circular zodiac floor from a later period has been found at Sepphoris, among other examples.

Greek girls' choruses were small, perhaps numbering seven or eleven members (interestingly, like the *symposia*). They were organized by age group and likely comprised neighbors and cousins related through their mothers. An accomplished woman taught the chorus and might even compose some of the works that it performed. The girls and their teacher loved one another. Friendships that formed when one was nine or ten years old could last a lifetime, especially if they reinforced kinship ties. The Greek custom of seclusion for upper-class women of childbearing age

---

46. These details and the details that follow are taken from Claude Calame, *Les choeurs de jeunes filles en Grèce archaïque* (Rome: Edizioni del'Ateneo & Bizzarri, 1977), vol. 1.

47. The Talmud says that when Beruriah's sister walked by, Roman aristocrats remarked, "How beautiful are the steps of this maiden." She appreciated the compliment. See *'Abodah Zarah* 18a.

did not interfere with women's friendships but encouraged them. For example, anthropologists find that in some modern-day societies that practice gender seclusion, women still meet regularly to negotiate matters of economic and cultural importance, such as the arrangement of marriages, religious observances, and the enforcement of social sanctions. Thus we can understand the schoolgirl friendships as founding networks of social influence through which elite women operated throughout their lives. The *gynaikōn*, then, was inhabited by interesting and articulate people, no matter what the men might choose to believe. Women's access to news and stimulating conversation did not depend on attending *symposia* or reclining in the *andrōn*.

There were hellenized Jewish women of the first century who had the wit and the cultural expertise to mount a creative reinterpretation of a calamitous death. But traditions about Jesus' life and teachings were transmitted as well, and gendering was a significant dimension in them. While I have just argued that elite women received paideia and participated rather fully in its benefits, nevertheless their reception was not exactly as compliant as the dominant male viewpoint would make it out to be. Women's paideia had its underside, its "muted" knowledge. This can be illustrated in the cultural construction of Greek female gender itself, and I suggest that it comes to sharp expression in certain strands of the Jesus materials.

In the predominant Greek imagination, girls were like pets. When little, they were wild creatures. They couldn't talk, and they would scamper away if a man approached. The process of educating a girl was to befriend her, calm her down, teach her to converse, and break her of her wild ways and her uncivilized spirit. That humanizing process, men thought, began with the chorus teacher but was completed by the husband. The *parthenos*, or virgin girl, in literature and art is typically imaged as wild and uncultivated. Mature women, even when domesticated, still are liable to be associated with the animality of bitch or sow. Prostitutes had pet names like Lioness or Panther, and wives were slurred as canine. Dogliness is opposed to civilization and to accepted ways of doing things (which is precisely why the philosophical critique of social conventions and pretensions was called Cynicism).

The underside or muted counterpart of such stereotyping does not come down to us explicitly in the classical tradition of elite Greek males, except for a few quotations from women's poetry. We know more about Jewish women's practices from the Talmud than we know of Greek women's practices from the entire corpus of ancient Greek literature (which is larger by several orders of magnitude), yet the reconstruction of women's Judaism is still in its early stages of discovery.[48] It is interesting that the wild and uncivilized character imputed to the Greek girl places her in conceptual proximity to workers and slaves, who were deemed subhuman all their lives. Among Jews, the law functions symbolically in a comparable way. Literate and observant men (the minority, but the source of the traditions we receive) regarded the majority as lax and little better than Gentiles. Women of observant households were, on the one hand, deemed fully Jewish, since the Jewish identity of their children depended on their own; on the other hand, they did not present tithes in fulfillment of the covenant between God and Abraham as their male relatives did, nor were they obliged to keep most of the other commandments. In that sense Jewish women, whatever their fervor and training, still were more like the ignorant unobservant peasants than like the Tannaim.

Thus the underside of Greek paideia is the wild and the inarticulate, which is symbolically identified with female gender as well as with disadvantaged social classes in general. The underside of Torah is nonobservance, including the untithability of wild foodstuffs; this too is identified with female gender and with peasants alike. To recover the muted knowledge of their societies held by the disadvantaged groups, we should look for a deviant interpretation of the underside.

We can find it in strands of the earliest Jesus traditions. The saying about nursing associates the kingdom of God with mother's milk, food that is outside the law in that it is not subject to tithe. The kingdom is entered by babies too young to have become acquainted with Torah. The fish shared in the outdoor meals of the Jesus people is wild food and so not diminished by tithe; instead, it multiplies and is a vehicle for kingdom entry. (The loaves would have been tithed twice: once as grain by the male farmer, then again as dough by the female baker—women's only tithe.) You need a teacher to enter the kingdom, but the teaching must be like sowing without cultivation. You greet the king when you greet the hungry and disabled little ones in whom he is invisible. The words you read on a page are idols; don't look, just listen for God's voice. What the lawyers reject, God can legitimate.

The overwhelming importance of food in these traditions creates enormous symbolic pressure toward a meal ritualization when the Jesus movement consolidates and institutionalizes. In hindsight we know how it

---

48. See, e.g., the contemporary anthropology of Susan S. Sered, *Women as Ritual Experts: The Religious Lives of Elderly Jewish Women in Jerusalem* (New York and Oxford: Oxford University Press, 1992).

turned out: the culturally available forms of the *symposion* and the sacrificial meal were the ones ultimately chosen, fused, and made to carry the weight of the kingdom traditions when they were reduced to written text. Much was trimmed away from the traditions in order to make them fit that hybrid ritual form, and their growing edges were cauterized. From the peasant traditions we lost those marvelously multiplying fish, not to mention the habit of taking religious authority with a grain of salt. From the women's traditions we lost the skill to weave persuasive meaning out of old texts, along with confidence that God would work changes in people through matrons.[49]

The *katachysmata* of the matrons was a discourse and a rhetorical practice before it was *myron* in the bottle at Bethany. In other words, Mark's tableau represents a memory that the christological interpretation of Jesus, which would in time become canonical, first was taught by women and took everyone else by surprise. That astonishment gradually turned into acceptance—*pistis*—through the matrons' persuasion. This persuasive feat itself was lifted up for consideration by being dramatized as an event said to have occurred one day during the career of Jesus, with the women's discourse characterized as "ointment." That packaging would come in handy for Mark, who when he wanted to make Jesus over into a self-immolating priest would need some ointment to do it. The sacrifice motif in the passion narrative may well be the legacy of an earlier Christ cult, but whatever its origin, it is the keynote in the Markan orchestration, the fuel for his soteriology. Jesus cannot have died inadvertently (like poor Adonis, gored by a pig); this christ has to sacrifice himself. He has to be a priest, so he needs a priestly anointing. Mark's Jesus is anointed like the proto-priest Aaron in (the Greek version of) Ps. 133:2: with *myron* running down over his hair and beard. Jesus is portrayed as *mageiros* as well, passing out servings of (his own) flesh at table in Mark 14:22 and receiving the victim-slayer's wreath in 15:17. These details make for the fusion of Greek and Jewish cultic traditions.

Crossan has suggested that before eucharists of bread and wine developed in Hellenistic house churches, there had been outdoor meals of bread and fish shared among peasants, going back before Calvary.[50] Fish

---

49. But the weeping and sprinkling practices of women survive as traces in the Gospel texts as well as in ritual. Baptism, the ritual for change of status, arguably owes its form in part to the woman's christening of Jesus by pouring something over his head. Foot washing in Luke and John is a modification of the woman's *katachysma*. John has Jesus mimic this gesture of foot washing in the last supper narrative, just as Mark has Jesus copy the breaking of the *alabastron* with his last breaking of bread.

50. See Crossan, *The Historical Jesus*, 367, 398–404, where earlier work by Hiers and Kennedy is cited. Crossan observes that the description of Jesus serving the fish eucharist is gendered female.

are fine for Aramaic-speaking peasants, but they cannot be used in Greek sacrifices.[51] So the ritual menu of the Christ cult is bread and wine, and now these are identified with the body and blood of the victim-sacrificer. To get the Jesus people to swallow this, Mark had to integrate it somehow with the thriving traditional practice of teaching (not priestcraft) that was known to go back to Jesus' own practice before Calvary.

That integration was engineered through the *alabastron* at Bethany. Its *myron* is *pistikon* because it is the distilled essence of a teaching program that had been burnishing the memory of Jesus with apt allusions to the Septuagint. *Pistikēs* (Mark 14:3) suggests a boldly effective rhetorical practice and repertoire that perhaps already had made their way out of the *gynaikōn*. Mark subordinates them to sacrifice, in the interest of investing Jesus' death with soteriological efficacy. The instruction (*katachysma/tôrāh*) now silently anoints the victim for his death. But bloody sacrifice is male-gendered for Greeks. When Jesus' death is turned into a sacrifice, for the first time it seems now wrong for women to have anything to do with figuring it out or grieving over his memory. Tearful matrons are banished from the banquet (although that was easier scripted than done, judging from Luke 7:38). The estrangement of women from the table is the price paid for the unification of the disparate Jesus constituencies behind the Gospel program. But ironically, it was—*and is*—the matrons' original christological speculations that make belief in the sacrifice possible. Mark says as much.

The last supper in Mark is different from other Greco-Roman sacrificial banquets in one respect: the victim whose flesh is portioned out hasn't yet been killed. Jesus takes the role of *mageiros,* serving up the body tonight and slaying it tomorrow after he has been properly wreathed for the office. At the same time, as we have seen, Mark designs this meal after the upper-class custom of the *symposion.* So Jesus, who coincidentally is victim as well as butcher, gives himself up freely to keep his *pistis* with his companions. Both *symposion* and blood sacrifice are male customs. Women do not fit culturally into either scenario. Neither does resurrection.

The resurrection has no conceptual affinity with a sacrificial reading either of Jesus' death or of the eucharistic ritual (even though a promise to rise is carelessly dropped on the way out at Mark 14:28). This imaginative

51. Because, say the Greeks, except for tuna, fish do not bleed. See Détienne and Vernant, *The Cuisine of Sacrifice among the Greeks,* 221 n. 8. Moreover, blood sacrifice was a male affair and fish reminded Greeks of female genitals. Meat eating and manhood are closely associated today among mountain villagers on Crete described by Michael Herzfeld, *The Poetics of Manhood: Contest and Identity in a Cretan Mountain Village* (Princeton: Princeton University Press, 1985).

construal of Jesus' identity and fate in terms of a sacrifice-*symposion* cannot be the root supporting the branches of resurrection faith. If you started out with this little story about a dinner for a men's club, your faith would not blossom into the empty tomb and the Risen Christ. Imagination had to run the other way. First someone had to see how Jesus was risen, then later when the men heard about it they could have their *symposion*, their blood covenant, and the rest.

Stringing the Loom

If Jesus didn't rise on the sheer brute strength of a promise to his men friends, then how? To reconstruct those first intimations that Jesus was alive after Calvary, we should recall the cultural imagery that furnished people's imaginations in first century Palestine. The Greek cultural view favored immortality of the soul, whose physical shell must perish (and fortunately so, according to the extreme Platonist opinion). For the Jews, as we saw above, the body was more important because resurrection needed bones. Ossilegium burial among Jews was intended to leave the bones ready for God to set them up again like a loom frame and weave new flesh on them in the messianic age.[52] The body in the resurrection thus would not be something completely new. Its bones would retain the individual personality, reduced to its simplest and most innocent form. Their preservation ensured continuity between the human being on this side of the grave and the new being created beyond, and also with his or her family.[53]

The bones were thought to function like the posts of a loom—or even like the spindle rollers of a Torah scroll set upright, supporting the skin (parchment) wrapped around and stretched between. Like a scroll, one's flesh carried the marks of the good deeds and sins of a lifetime. The decomposition of the flesh after death wiped out sins; the new skin that God would stretch over the bones would receive a fresh inscription.

52. This practice may have been influenced by the Greek attitude toward bones as divine property. At Greek sacrifices, the bones customarily were burned upon the altar for the deities.

53. This was the first-century belief. Later, people thought that even a small part of the skeleton would ensure identity, and eventually they understood that God did not need even that. See Rahmani, "Ancient Jerusalem's Funerary Customs and Tombs," 175. The fact that within Palestine, ossilegium burial was in the first century confined to Jerusalem (spreading into Galilee only later when refugees from the holy city fled there after its destruction) counts as evidence in favor of the thesis that the emptied tomb story developed in pre-70 C.E. Jerusalem, independently of Galilean preaching practices.

This culturally apt association between the body of a teacher and the scroll of the Torah was horribly dramatized in the martyrdom of Beruriah's father, Rabbi Hananiah ben Teradion, during the persecution of the emperor Hadrian in the early second century. Hananiah was arrested while teaching publicly from the Torah in defiance of an imperial order. The police wrapped him up in the scroll and placed him on a slow-burning pyre to die before the eyes of his students and family. When Rabbi Hananiah looked out through the smoke and saw his daughter crying, he told her not to be sorry either for himself or for the Torah and he assured her that while the parchment was disintegrating, he could see the letters of the law flying up into the air.[54]

So the story comes down to us through the generations from the people who were there. This narrative affords us a glimpse of how grieving people could imaginatively frame their groping for understanding of the fragility of the human body, the invincibility of Torah, and the faithfulness of God against the power of evil, all in a cultural context and time very close to that of the first creative reinterpretations of Jesus' death. Quite simply, Hananiah's people see that the destruction of the teacher's flesh does not extinguish his life or the instruction that was his life.

A similar interpretation would have been emotionally and imaginatively available to Jewish followers of Jesus who grieved for him after Calvary. They could comfort one another with the thought that Jesus' halakhah would survive him. We should assume that some slogan such as that fell into place immediately after Calvary, because it provides the foundation for development of claims that Jesus can be seen as Risen Lord and then eventually for claims that Jesus has experienced a personal resurrection out of his tomb.

Those developments are spurred by the peculiar conceptualization of God's kingdom among the Jesus people (which was not a factor in the comparable case of Hananiah's legend). The halakhah of Jesus projected a kind of spatial permeability. The kingdom of God was "within you," and "entering it" meant letting it enter you. The Jesus halakhah also focused a kind of time warp in which the kingdom of God was "already here." "Here," however, seemed to depend on the proximity of Jesus. So where Hananiah's students could go home and find the Torah on another scroll, and in their hearts, and in their behaviors, and in their very kitchens and pantries, Jesus' disciples couldn't do without his physical presence.

---

54. ʿ*Abodah Zarah* 17b–18a. This is one of several versions of his death.

Among the tatters of the Jesus movement left operating in Galilee after Calvary, the *discursive* practice of speaking "in Jesus' name" supported the notion that Jesus lived and worked through them despite his death. But among other Jesus constituencies, *bodily* practices now localized the perceived and perceivable presence of Jesus as living. What that post-Calvary living Jesus looked like to those groups is indicated by the catalog of disclosures in Matthew 25—feeding, clothing, healing, helping—as well as by the pounding Lukan rhythm of hunger and response. Pragmatically the content of the claim for a risen Jesus must be sought in those references. The hungry little ones, always with the church, are the reason why the resurrection of Jesus must be affirmed as bodily, absolutely, for Christian faith. There is no room for the nice wedge of metaphor to slip in between them, who are the body of the Risen Lord, and the real Jesus.

The *pistis* of the emptied tomb story is designed to protect the hungry body of the Risen Lord from the agile arguments of anyone who says the little ones aren't really Jesus. Yearning for Jesus is channeled toward the places—the bodies—where he may be found. The signpost directing inquirers is erected at the entrance to his tomb: Look elsewhere. He isn't here. For the parchment disintegrated, but the letters have flown up. The skin became transparent, but the name has copied itself all around you.

Christology,
Liturgical Theology,
and Catechetics

11

A Resurrection Theology

W RITING IN the mid-1980s, the theologian Gerald O'Collins suggested that three stances or "stations" exist from which we may approach the question of the resurrection of Jesus: the scholar's desk, where we can do critical historical study; situations of dire suffering, where we are groping for meaning and hope; and worship, where we assemble to celebrate the mysteries of our redemption. These perspectives are complementary, and none is dispensable. O'Collins writes:

> Not only historical study but also human hope and Christian worship open up ways for considering Jesus' resurrection. . . . Those who attempt a purely academic approach and refuse to remember prayer and suffering are sure to go wrong. Their intellectual efforts to grasp resurrection can stand in the way of the resurrection working in them and on them.[1]

An adequate theology of resurrection uses all three sources: historical narrations, the claims of wounded and needy people, and claims made in the liturgical assembly. This rule holds true for twentieth-century resurrection theology, because it was *already* operative in the first century. The Gospels themselves are theologies of the resurrection that adopt the same three stances—historical reinterpretation, care for the body's needs, and worship—as they weave together the same three kinds of sources that we still look to today: stories already in circulation about events of Jesus'

---

1. See Gerald O'Collins, *Jesus Risen: An Historical, Fundamental and Systematic Examination of Christ's Resurrection* (New York: Paulist Press, 1987), 2–3.

life and death, claims arising from the sufferings of members of the early communities, and claims made in their various worshiping assemblies.

All three kinds of input were living and volatile at the time of the Gospels' writing. But as the ink dried, the texts congealed into material that could be pondered in a scholar's study while the life of hope and prayer went on someplace else. This happens. It was already prone to happen in the first century. We who like to read also like to believe that we have the whole story under control when we finish a book. The Gospels therefore are ingeniously designed to deflate the reader's arrogance. They refuse to deliver their referent, the Risen Lord. They tease, but they ultimately redirect the reader's attention away from the desk and out toward the table.

"The table" is my shorthand for what O'Collins calls "stations," especially the second and third kinds—that is, all the places where human hungers are recognized and agonized over and all the places where Christians negotiate the sacramental liturgy. But "the" table is an insidiously simplified term. In chapter 10, I argued that the elite men's custom of the *symposion*, once fused with the male-gendered practice of blood sacrifice and flesh eating, provided the culturally viable core around which Mark organized other independent aspects of the Jesus kingdom traditions, including many that had to do with peasants' and women's feeding practices. This fusion, dramatized as the last supper, constitutes the foundation narrative for eucharistic liturgical practice. It identifies Jesus as self-immolating priest, the victim whose death keeps faith with man and God while buying peace between them.

The grandeur of this interpretation would completely crowd out some other, older but humbler tables, had Mark's text ended where it should have, with the burial of the hero. But no. Guess what. Jesus doesn't stay dead; so much for the blood covenant. In 16:1-7, Mark admits he knows about this fatal flaw in the sacrifice scheme, the report of a resurrection. Yet he *shouldn't* know about it at all if he were telling the truth in v. 8, where he alleges that the women who found out about the emptied tomb *were too scared to tell anybody.* But this is not a fib. It is the writer's skillful signal that this text is a constructed thing, one that calls for readers with comparable wit and daring. Mark takes a hatchet to the fiction of the sacrifice-*symposion* that he has just rendered; then he turns around and breaks his hatchet, in full view of the reader.[2]

---

2. In an earlier chapter, we saw something comparable in Luke's Easter narrative, which is a story about how a story cannot convince people about the resurrection of Jesus.

What to Disbelieve

In light of this double deconstruction, where does Mark "really" want us readers to stand in relation to the death and resurrection of Jesus? What are we supposed to *dis*believe? Should we disbelieve the *symposion*-sacrifice interpretation presented in the last supper and the passion narrative, on account of the report that the appeasing death so soon came undone? Or should we disbelieve the part about the tomb, because Mark had no way of knowing about it if all the details he reports are indeed accurate? Or should we disbelieve that the story ends where Mark ends it and, in view of his earlier intimations of a resurrection, go ahead and make up a more satisfying ending?[3]

Take your choice. I chose to disbelieve that these narrative jolts are accidents. At the very least, Mark is declining to favor decisively either the last supper cultic tradition or the emptied tomb tradition. In forging an alliance of traditions, he is preserving their variance and not entirely submerging one beneath the other—even when that means loss of narrative coherence. We (like Matthew and Luke) have run through the Markan rendition so many times that the speed bump between passion and emptied tomb is worn quite smooth. Their incongruity is lost in familiarity and can be recovered now only with difficulty, through analysis and cultural reconstruction.

But I think that something more can be inferred here. At the stratum of Christian history when Mark wrote, the resurrection of Jesus was plurally understood but not unanimously accepted. Not everyone who invoked the name of Jesus, for whatever reason, thought of him as Risen Lord, and not everyone who thought of Jesus as Risen Lord subscribed to an event of tomb emptying. If distinctive feeding practices were attached to the name of Jesus, still there was great variety among them, and they had not yet been amalgamated into a bread-and-wine eucharist for men.

On the one hand, these findings are moot. The ecclesial connection that we have today with those people and their practices is carried entirely through the textual compromise first engineered by Mark and by the liturgical and charitable practices that his text supported and disciplined. It is pointless to second-guess the choices that were made by the founding generations. We know the Lord only through them; it is their version of the

---

3. Rewriting was the response of several ancient readers of this frustrating text. Alternate endings have been appended in the canonical version of Mark, while Luke and Matthew also added appearance stories to their Markan source.

Lord whom we recognize among us today. On the other hand, why not take and cherish *all* of the information that the texts have to give us? If Mark's Gospel manifestly confounds every attempt to read it as a straightforward journalistic report, why keep trying? If what's "on the desk" tells us to look at what's "at the table" when we want to see Jesus, then what transpires at the table becomes a component of the reality of the resurrection, *as meant by the text.* There is a paradoxical identification of Jesus with hungry little ones and with bread to feed them. This is more than a textual identification or labeling; nevertheless the texts that want to be "about" it can be so only by paradoxical and oblique textual strategies.

Therefore what Gospels do is build up portraits of Jesus with one hand and strike through them with the other. In the portraiture they carefully compose the anecdotes and the teachings to yield a definitive outline of Jesus. Then in a brilliant transgression of that identification, they color outside the lines, as it were: they break their own closures by having Jesus identify with what he is not. Access to "Jesus" requires rupture of the final closure that comes to any human life, the seal on the tomb.

Access to Jesus after Calvary was not at first the product of Gospel texts; it preceded them by many years. Yet the texts are components in the intergenerational transmission system that stabilizes the possibility of access to Jesus ever after. These are curious stabilizers. What they stabilize is instability: the impossibility of text to fence the space of risen life, even while life is impossible without the fence. Thus the intellectual practices of reading and writing theology text must open out onto compassionate practices of caring for suffering human beings and also onto aesthetic practices of liturgical celebration that propagate the presence of the Lord to the church. The interfacing of these three sorts of practices constitutes the church's knowledge of Jesus as Risen Lord.

The Risen Lord manifests in time and space, according to the Gospels. The kingdom of God has anthropological coordinates. In chapter 10 we visited some of the real-life first-century stations of suffering and hope where Jesus was made, such as the *gynaikōn* and the tenement courtyard. In that inquiry, were we prying where we were not meant to go? Did we trespass beyond gates that the Gospel texts meant to stay forever safely shut, and did we see things that our ancestors wanted to hide from us? In other words, does our discovery of the madeness of Jesus defeat the Gospels' historicizing project—or fulfill their design? Can the first-century churches have intended to show us how to make Jesus? Yes, exactly. It is the recipe of the kingdom of God.

We were indeed meant to have the information that is available through anthropological and literary analysis of the Gospel narratives.

The textual studies presented in the preceding chapters have all been "archaeological" in their attempt to excavate historical strata beneath the surface contours of ancient Gospel texts. We have discovered certain distinctive poietic practices contributing to the portraiture of Jesus, along with certain distinctive initiatory practices for leading people toward the Jesus so portrayed. The texts are fictions. They are built to fix or stabilize the outcome of those practices. They frame the portraits and the approaches. Their narrative enframing must be understood for what it is. It is not a videotape. It is not a fossil. It is not a lie. Instead, it is more like a vehicle, a portal, or software. In more traditional terminology, it is a path. As the Johannine Jesus says, "I am the way."

That aphorism must not be heard nostalgically. It should not be read as an engraved invitation for a sweet trip down memory lane, where everything will be comfortingly familiar. There is scant comfort in the Gospel. There is massive disruption. What is fixed and held in uneasy equilibrium within the Gospel portraits of Jesus is the potential to overwrite the programs that produce human identities day by day in society. Those programs are the programs of race, class, and gender. In an earlier chapter, I argued that those realities normally function as genres for the social inscription of human bodies. They are tremendously powerful. They prescribe who lives, who dies, who rules, who serves, who eats, who starves. Any given society is characterized by a specific configuration of racial, economic, and reproductive practices. These compose a kind of text, that is, a dynamic message system encoded upon all the bodies within that society. In contrast, the Gospels do not simply project some alternative configuration or text. Rather, they tamper with the genric encoding mechanism itself. They are not a replacement program but a virus in the programming.

What is narratively enframed in the Gospels' Jesus stories is a "Jesus" who reaches out beyond the frame. These frames are permeable. They are dimensional, so that processes occurring "beneath" the framing, in their past, can break through the surface of the framed tableaux and erupt into ongoing human history. You lay your eyes upon the page to read the Gospel text, and next thing you know it's clutching you by the throat. You peer into what you took to be a window upon peaceful bygone days whence came the rules for life, but what you see is your own reflection scowling back out at you, and over its shoulder a mob of unruly strangers who mean to march you into a future that is not what you had planned at all. It's not a pretty picture for you. Who are all those people? Who let them into the Jesus story? Where are they going with him? Where are they taking *you?* A cloud of witnesses got ahold of Jesus. He in the lap of mammy church, and she don't look like no lady Michelangelo carve.

Now, as in the first century, the body of Jesus lies in hands other than those that wield the pen. His identity depends as much on what they make of him as on what we writers make of him. The Gospel portraits of Jesus do their enframing not only as a kind of biographical profiling of a historical figure but also as a fixing of certain communicative processes as they were historically engaged for the compilation of that portrait. The portraits thus include practices of caring for the hungry and practices of teaching that point to community activities of caregiving and cultic celebration. They include as well the practices of referring back to classical Scripture and classical figures like Samuel, Moses, and Isaiah and conscripting them to serve the community's interests. Third, they include practices that I have been calling poietic: production through imaginative variance. The identity of "Jesus" is riding upon all these practices of identification. His body, his very real and personal being, is given over into their hands for inscription. His body could not be transhistorically available to us were it not given over, entrusted to strangers, and radically set at risk in this textually precarious way.

Who Jesus is can be contagious only in this way. He becomes copy so that he can copy. He depends upon being read. His availability depends upon a distinctive kind of literacy or competence with texts. I have used the term "hetero-inscription" to describe the creation of a version, that is, the rewriting of a text from one medium to another. "Auto-inscription" is the writing of a text upon oneself. The poietic production of the Gospel texts, then, was a hetero-inscription of Jesus: into ink and papyrus, out of flesh and blood—but not out of materially "the same" flesh and blood of the man living before Calvary. That was long gone. The Jesus finally inscribed with Markan ink already had been inscribed into the bodies, words, and practices of very many people. He already was carried and gestated in them for several decades. He was in their midst bodily before he was enframed on parchment. They auto-inscribed him. Moreover, they hetero-inscribed him *for the purpose of* propagating the possibility of auto-inscription, that is, remaining able to rewrite him into many more hearts and hands and voices.

Why use the term "inscribe" rather than "remember"? Because it allows us the metaphysical leeway to work differently with the verb "to be." A memory of a person is not equivalent to the person. A memory is a mere image or reflection, so the person and the memory are not "the same." In contrast, a text has a capacity that Mary Gerhart and Alan Russell have called "material transcendence." Two versions of a text, although necessarily written into different media, nevertheless can be the same. We can recognize the sameness between the two materially separate versions.

The meanings are available to anyone who has the literacy, the competence, to read them. As long as the literacy or competence is maintained among the reading community, the text can be replicated and made ever more widely available. Yet no two versions are ever *materially* the same; the medium introduces variations, while the reader recognizes the identity of versions through the variation of media.

Can a person be a text? The author of the prologue to John's Gospel thought so. In an earlier chapter, I argued that bodies always are being socially inscribed, while at the same time bodies always are resisting inscription. Every human person's body, then, as it goes through life, bears text uniquely produced by the interaction of socially mandated hetero-inscription, modulated by selective auto-inscription. We write the texts we receive onto ourselves, but we write them as our own distinctive personal variations.

Can Jesus be a text? The authors of the Synoptic and Pauline last supper narratives thought so. In their stories, Jesus writes himself onto the common nutritive media of bread and wine. He inscribes what he is— "body, blood, soul, and divinity," as the catechism put it—upon a medium that had been like his body only remotely and metaphorically. With the eucharist, "Jesus" textually enters the food chain; and he enters it at woman's place, as a body that nourishes. The Jesus of bread and wine is the same as the Jesus of flesh and blood, but now there is more of him to go around. Jesus is recognizable in the breaking of the bread, if one has the basic eucharistic textual competence to read him there. The church has the task of delivering him in bread and wine but also of training people in "eucharistic literacy," as it were, so that they will know whom they are getting.

The textual literacy that enables people to read Jesus, to recognize the sameness, is what is meant by resurrection faith. It is the ability to "see the Lord." As literacy, this competence presupposes material variation: "sameness" perceived in, and precisely because of, difference. The body of Jesus today has to be materially different if he is to be textually the same. Our ancestors in faith chose the technology of text as the delivery system for the body of Jesus. It was not the only option they had to choose from. People in the ancient world knew very well how to preserve bodies in their material sameness. There are scores of mummified corpses still with us from Egypt, and most of them are far older than Jesus. Indeed, there are Christian relics moldering all over Europe. But the body of Jesus is not with us like some crumbling souvenir, like a faded flower pressed nostalgically between the pages of a venerable old book. He is as alive as the screaming foundling in the AIDS ward. He is as fresh as challah on Friday night.

Genric Disruptions of Race and Class

The availability of Jesus to the church after Calvary is bodily, but it is bodily *because* it is textual. The bodily availability of the Risen Lord depends on a distinctive kind of literacy, or ability to read. Moreover, this has been so in the church since long before Mark wrote anything down in ink. We know that the literacy of resurrection faith predates the canonical Gospels, because we find stories in Mark's Gospel in which demonstrations of that literacy already are caught within the pre-textual frame that enframes "Jesus." This special literacy consists in an ability to read bodily texts against the grain of the genres of race, class, and gender that, day in and day out, are operative in the inscription of bodies within society. This is a counter-generic literacy. It is the ability to read resistively, in a mode that disrupts the reproduction of society's scripts. We don't get any Jesus "before" such a reading praxis has swung into action; it is already fully operative at the earliest recoverable levels of the texts.

Texts, as we saw in an earlier chapter, can be generally described with four criteria suggested by Gerhart and Russell. They are (1) "formally produced," which means that a template or pattern (such as a genre) has been invoked in the making of the text. Every actual text both coincides with and deviates from the genre that it instantiates, and this variance accounts for the gradual evolution of the genre itself. In the case of human bodies, I argued that race, class, and gender are important genres invoked in the writing of individual and group identities and that as genres those realities tend to mutate slowly as time passes.

Because a reader must, to some extent at least, share competence to work with the formal structure according to which text was produced, another criterion appears: (2) "readability." The text remains alive as long as people have the competence to decode it and link it into a network of corroborating meanings within their society. Readability leads into writability, for text entails the possibility of copy. To copy is to understand, to uptake and auto-inscribe what the text says into oneself. Text has a proclivity to copy itself, to get itself copied. Although it is pattern, it must also be physically available in some way for the reading. This leads to another criterion: (3) "retrievability." By this the text is publicly offered and objectively available to whoever has the requisite competence to read it. Yet text cannot be dependent upon its material medium. If the information would be lost or mutated beyond recognition by translation into another medium, then it is not a text in Gerhart and Russell's reckoning. Thus the final criterion is (4) "material transcendence," whereby in principle the text can be infinitely replicable. Many versions can be produced, entailing much variance, yet retaining the identity of the information.

The "Jesus" enframed within the Gospel stories that we have examined fulfills all of these criteria. The writing, reading, rewriting, and rereading of this Jesus was a long-term project of the infracanonical church. The Gospel texts freeze and enframe slices of the process in action at various points in its evolution. Excavating these surfaces, we have seen how the social genres of race, class, and gender have been productively, poietically invoked to produce them. But the writing of "Jesus" according to those genres has also radically mutated the genres themselves. The mutations have been massive but not unopposed. The struggle over "Jesus" that is still so evident in the Gospel texts is largely a struggle to overhaul the semantic machinery of his production. While some Jesus people were smashing racial oppression, others were trying to patch it together again. While some were tampering with the class system, others were trying to restore privilege. While some were overturning gender relations, others were hushing the women who had begun to speak. These were not three separate arenas of struggle; they were all components of the tug-of-war over the body of Jesus. This curious genric phenomenon has emerged in our textual archaeology.

It seems a safe generalization to say that all societies use the genre of race for the differential inscription of the bodies of their members, even though societies produce widely differing racial texts. Jewish identity, for example, is inscribed through the bodily genre of race. We have seen that three major versions of Jewish racial identity were written in the three overlapping language communities of first-century Palestine: the scholarly and liturgical Hebrew, the everyday village Aramaic, and the cosmopolitan business-oriented Greek.

The society into which the Jesus movements erupted already was quite racially mixed. Many Jews carefully guarded their distance from Gentiles, but many others wanted to become as Greek as possible. A plastic surgeon could make a living at reversing circumcisions. It may have been a valid boast, at some point in the early history of the churches, that *"in Christ* there is neither Jew nor Greek"; nevertheless the same thing was certainly true in a number of other locations as well. Moreover, by the time of Constantine, in Christ there was no Jew *at all*. Semitic versions of ecclesial life were systematically suppressed in the empire, leaving only the European.

Greek Christianity was well on its way to subduing other ethnic versions by the end of the first century. The New Testament is Greek literature. We have no Hebrew or Aramaic or Coptic or Latin testament (translations of Greek originals aside). It is all the more striking, then, that this Greek literature conveys a rejection of paideia as the model for introducing people into the Christian life. Catechesis was designed to be a curious hybrid kind of teaching: a noncultivation in which the seed of the word was planted to grow without human assistance, contrary to the Greek pedagogical practice. And contrary to Jewish practice, catechesis would also be a nursing: a collaboration with nature, transpiring in a state of preliteracy, before the learner was able to bite into textual food like the Torah. The eucharist ingeniously combines these inversions of the two teaching metaphors: cultivation and nursing.

Racial identity in the United States is associated with skin color. Color was less important in the ancient world than for us, but it may have been a factor in the early Christian overwriting of racial texts. The story of the anointing at Bethany, in which "Jesus" receives his messianic identity, is situated in the house of someone whose skin is the wrong color: white. In Hebrew legal texts, skin that takes on the color of snow or of dead bones is considered a disgrace and warrants isolating someone outside the people of Israel. Miriam was punished for criticizing her brother Moses by having her face turned white (Num. 12:10; see also Exod. 4:6). Therefore, to place Jesus narratively in the house of Simon "the leper" is not to have him philanthropically visiting the sick. The term that white people have translated as "leper" really indicates anyone with pathologically pale skin, which in the ancient Near East was considered rather repulsive. This detail of the story, then, defies the conventions of racial disadvantage.

Racial purity was an important issue in the litigation of the legitimacy of Jesus. Although we do not know the exact customs in force in Galilee in the early part of the first century, rabbinic law determines the racial status of a child by rules very different from those governing inheritance and legitimacy in modern Western societies. For the rabbis, being born to an unwed mother does not in itself make a child a bastard. Such a child's status depends instead on whether its mother is a Jew, whether she identifies the father, and whether a marriage between them would have been legal. If the father is marriageable, then *no matter whether he is a Gentile or a Jew,* the baby is still a Jew as long as it is born to a Jewish mother. The baby would be a *mamzer* only in a situation in which laws against adultery or incest would have prevented the marriage of its parents. If the mother cannot or will not tell who the father is, then the child is called a *shetuki,* "undisclosed," and circumstantial evidence must be sought.[4]

Because Jewish racial identity was constructed differently from that of modern gentile societies, Jesus would have been *no less a Jew* had Mary or her family declared that his conception resulted from rape by a

4. See Teichman, *Illegitimacy,* 138–40.

goy legionnaire. This casts an extremely interesting light on their refusal to declare a human father, whether the gentile rapist or Joseph. It was a refusal to certify racial purity in *either* of the two legal ways that lay open in the case. This refusal thus counts as a costly, and therefore important, challenge to the genre of race. "The power of the Most High" casts its shadow against the reproduction of racial identity and in favor of miscegenation. Divine fatherhood for Jesus is thinkable, in Jesus' society, *only* as an interruption of the genric propagation of racial identity.

As anthropologists often observe, kinship can be culturally construed as being carried in fluids. For example, we may think of siblings as related "by blood" or of paternity as conveyed through semen. This is an ethnocentricity of ours and is not taken for fact in every culture. However, it so happens that blood and semen were indeed considered kinship-identifying fluids in both Jewish and Greek cultures. These fluids were implicated in the construction of kinship and ethnicity, but coincidentally they were components of male gendering as well. Female-gendered fluids, such as mother's milk and tears, were thought inconsequential for kinship. (Having a wet nurse who was a slave and/or a foreigner, for example, was considered not to affect an heir's racial or kin status.) Thus there is both racial and gender significance in the fact that some Jesus traditions associate fluids such as milk, tears, perfume oil, or baptismal birth waters with kingdom entry and the corresponding change in someone's personal status. This employment of fluids of the "wrong" gender not only overrides preexisting kinship but does so with female-identified fluids, making the latter more efficacious than blood or semen for the kingdom of God. This has the double effect of subverting both ethnicity and the gender system.[5]

We have seen how the notion of the kingdom of God was highlighted in Aramaic popular piety. Among the Jesus movements, the figure of "Jesus" was gradually overwritten upon "the kingdom" and soon completely displaced it. As the stories were told, "approaching Jesus" came to mean the same thing as "entering the kingdom of God." Already in the Scripture of Isaiah and in the practices of the Diaspora synagogues, Gentiles had been welcomed into God's covenant. Now, in the telling of the Jesus stories, we see some interesting conflicts about exactly who can be allowed to get near to "Jesus." An issue was made out of various categories of people: street children, people with disabling conditions,

---

5. In the final synthesis of the last supper narrative, a compromise fluid—wine—takes the place of both mother's milk and the male-gendered blood of sacrifice from the antecedent Jesus traditions. At Jesus' death, what flows forth from his breast is the combination of blood and water.

eunuchs, tax collectors (especially if they were physically diminutive Grecophones like Zacchaeus), prostitutes, menstruating women, people with
Greek names—and our friends the Bitch-Cynics, who were a triple threat
as heterodox Gentiles lacking the good manners to disappear during menstruation. Insofar as there were racial, eugenic, and nationalistic overtones to the controversies about these groups, their appearance in
narrative association with Jesus also resists the cultural "business as
usual" of the propagation of racial texts.

The language differences in first-century Palestine were, to a considerable extent, correlated with differences in social and economic class and
in political sympathies. To converse and write in Hebrew required leisure
time for study as well as a means of livelihood that did not take up too
much of one's attention. Although they were a cultural elite, the sages
were not necessarily well-to-do. In Sepphoris, the rabbis worked at manual crafts to keep their minds free and independent. Hebrew wisdom
never disparaged labor the way the Greeks did.[6]

Greek was the language of the cities and of traders. Everyone in
Galilee knew a little, to deal with salesmen and magistrats when necessary. Aside from its commercial uses, Greek was cultivated by a smaller
cadre of Hellenists who wanted a window on the outside world to the
west. The aristocratic class, with international connections in the western
Diaspora, had Greek as a mother tongue. Aramaic was the language of the
villages, but then some villages were larger than the Hellenistic cities and
some villagers were quite prosperous. Moreover, Aramaic was the language of international scholarship and trade used in the eastern Diaspora.
Toward the middle of the first century, then, as the Jesus movements
branched out beyond Palestine, the two international languages in which
Jesus material spread were *koinē* Greek and dialects of Aramaic.

Labor was a different reality in Greek than in the Semitic languages.
The Greek laborer was not fully human; and as a general rule Greek gods
did not work. In contrast, we have seen how a Hebrew legal case sought to
identify Jesus as the slave son of the Lord, with solid Scriptural precedent.
But when this identification, first written by means of the Hebrew genre
of class, was variantly read out through the Greek genre of class, new
meaning was generated. A notion that had not been a particularly novel
idea became in translation an overnight sensation. The difference in ontological status inscribed in Greek between human *despotēs* and subhuman
doulos now was overlaid upon the difference in ontological status ascribed

---

6. But see the evaluation of occupations in the book of Sirach.

to divinity versus humanity. Jesus was theorized now by Greeks, using their bodily template of class, as a divine son who had humiliated himself and "come down," taken on an inferior status, and "lifted up" humanity to a new plane of being. By becoming a slave, the son had set us miserable slaves free—at least figuratively, and at least in a text produced and read out through the Greek genre of class. If all were set free, then "In Christ there is no slave or free" came as the conclusion to the syllogism. In practice, of course, that proved to be a bit too revolutionary, so Paul and other leading theorists were quite willing to retract it.

Hunger, too, is a phenomenon inscribed upon human bodies through the genre of social class. People negotiate and struggle to get themselves different places of access to the economic food chain. But the halakhah of Jesus inverts the chain. Hunger is now designated as the baseline competence for hearing God's word and for access to the Risen Lord. You could "see him" only by coming into contact with hunger: by being hungry and by feeding the hungry. You could "enter the kingdom" only if you rooted and snuffled around for it like a hungry infant wanting to nurse. God's kingdom was imaged as the table where there are places for everyone, and everyone has the place of honor, and everyone gets enough. The only table like that is the breast, the table where someone smiles and says, Eat my body, and where the little child has the place of honor forever. There is to be no weaning from that table, no turn away from easy nourishment toward difficult jawboning over the Torah. Hunger is the new literacy of the kingdom, the competence imparted by the Teacher. All you'll ever need to know, you can guzzle right here. God has leaking teats.

Thus hunger is proof of election and readiness for God; it is not the mark of divine censure. This inversion of the meaning of hunger is massively destabilizing not only to the religious-knowledge industry but to industry in general. It horrifies the urban aristocracy with good reason. Besides retheorizing the meaning of their privilege in rather uncomplimentary terms, it takes Deuteronomy seriously enough to threaten the economic base of international trade. God said don't work for anybody but God (Deut. 5:9); therefore the text "messianic" cannot be written onto any collaborationist political program. "Jesus" belongs to the hungry. Even in prison, you can ask questions that will let you find him. Even in the dark, with this neo-Deuteronomic program you can still hear God.

The economic and cultural indicators of divine favor now all are reversed. The bodies of workers can no longer be read as economic resources, raw material. The human body ceases to be a geopolitical commodity. Deuteronomic resistance to unlimited labor now focuses into a different sort of worship. God sends bread, once again. The body is nourished for permanence. Its ultimate meaning is not to return to the soil and rot. The body is not a farm to cultivate, and it is not manure. The commodification of human labor is reversed, because the grave is only temporary. There is to be a new sabbath, an eighth day, for celebrating the fruition of labor. Women's labor at childbirth, as well as the labor of all workers, is rewritten as a struggle already won, a permanent achievement. Jesus, having risen, is the firstborn of many.

Genric Disruption of Gender

When we try to track back through the stages of the poietic identification of Jesus, we find women's imaginations at every step of the way. "Jesus" is conceived, explained, challenged, anointed, mourned, and recognized as risen by women. Each of these poietic modifications happens to "Jesus," but *not to him alone,* for each revision is also a revision of womanhood itself as a gender text. In poietically producing and reproducing "Jesus," women alter the genre of gender by which they themselves are socially produced as women. "Jesus" is their bootstrap to salvation.

Whatever happened between Mary and God, that is where we have to go to find any sort of beginning to the quickening of the Christ-event. In the canonical annunciation tale as well as in the extracanonical one, Mary is already bucking genric pressure when she calls herself the Lord's slave. Only Hannah had done that before. All of the *ᶜebedîm yhwḥ* in Scripture were men. If Mary answered God in Hebrew, perhaps she dared pronounce not one forbidden word but two: the divine name and the feminine form of *ᶜebed.*

This event of poietic meaning-making really happened whether its agent was the historical Mary or whether we can know only that the literary-historical character "Mary" emerged as its artifact. *Someone* counter-genrically imagined the possibility of a female *ᶜebed yhwh,* and that imagination coincided with the conception of "Jesus." The sexual availability of the mammy, the *ʾāmāh,* was rewritten as the possibility of mothering another Samuel. The anointing of the messiah began that way. Or so says the canon. God did not touch humanity where the touch was not wanted. God was invited in. This conception was in no way facilitated by the text of feminine gender current in Mary's world, which gave rapists access to virgins. It had to happen against the grain of that text. It was a counter-poiesis, that is, a resistance made by one female body against the cultural tide inscribing the common text of womanhood.

When the historical Jesus talked about the kingdom of God, he may or may not have said that people entering it were like babies nursing. What is historically certain is that *somebody* was telling the story of Jesus using that line. Somebody at some relatively early point in some Jesus group was imagining God's kingdom with that metaphor. That poietic production was a rewriting of the text "kingdom of God." Equally significantly, it was at the same time a rewriting of what it meant to be a breasted body and to suckle. This too was a rewriting against the grain of the genric prescriptions for how woman's body could be inscribed in that society.

Perhaps this warp of gender was introduced by the historical Jesus; or perhaps we can say with certitude only that this gender revision was part of the poietic production of the literary figure "Jesus"—and even at that, a stage of his production that did not even make it into the frame of the canon. Yet my study of this metaphor indicated that the canonical tradition could not have produced the "Jesus" who welcomes little children, or the "Jesus" who admonishes Nicodemus to get born again, unless somebody first rewrote the meaning of the gestating, lactating body. The poietic specification of access to Jesus happened together with a massive revision of the text of Jewish womanhood. Before that poietic event, Jewish breasts had to be left behind when the study of Torah commenced, at the age of weaning; and bodies with breasts were not to study Torah at all. Now, the availability of Jesus is depicted by imagining a table like the maternal breast, where all are welcome and where his body is the food. Access to God's kingdom is imagined as nursing. Such things simply cannot be asserted rationally without a wholesale revision of the gender text of woman's body.

The stroke that connects messianic destiny with death, while affixing both to Jesus, also is attributed to a woman. The Markan tableau can hardly be a historically reliable record, showing us an event that happened one day when a woman named Jesus "Christ" by breaking a vial of ointment over his head. The symbolism of the pantomime is too perfectly contrived not to have been staged, dramatically or narratively, after the fact. What, then, was "the fact"? My hypothesis has been that the anointing of Jesus first was a catechesis among women. After Calvary, they read his body as a broken jar. They thus identified his body with their bodies, his fate with their own fates.

How was this catechetically done? What was the catechesis like? In economic terms, like an extravagant wasting of expensive ointment it would have had a negative impact upon a woman's future security. The *breaking* of the vial indicated a point of no return. In symbolic terms, however, much more was at stake. A jar was a symbol of the female body for the ancient Greek imagination.[7] It could contain the means to sustain life, in the form of grain or other foodstuff. Ancient European cultures had also buried bodies in huge ceramic vases, folded in fetal position. It is thought that the first writing was iconic marking on the outside of a jar to indicate the contents. All of these meanings are pulled together in the alabaster flask smashed at Bethany. The pantomime reprises the elements of the catechesis it is designed to represent. That catechesis can be reconstructed as having stated that four things are irrevocably broken in the identity and death of Jesus: containment by writing, the shell of the tomb, woman's body as commodity packaging, and the economic order. This fourfold breaking is made equivalent to what christhood means for Jesus. That is why his death is inevitable. He is to die in childbirth. From the breaking open of his body is to come forth new life: his own new life and that of the disciples whom he bears in resurrection.

Or rather, from the perspective of the women catechists working after Calvary, Jesus *already has* died in childbirth. His death has birthed new bodies, but he has also lived on to nurse them. The anointing at Bethany is sited at a table, because the table is where this messianic identification of Jesus had to be negotiated and judged. The catechesis is controversial. It is a women's thing; who can trust it? Any of the four breakings, taken alone, is a hard enough saying in itself. (1) The economic implications of christhood for Jesus were explored above, in terms of the counterinscription of class. (2) Women's refusal of commodity status for their bodies would obliterate the gender texts constructing personal and family identities across the society. Jesus has overwritten his own body with a woman's text by offering it as nourishment; may women also then identify themselves with the risen body of the Lord? Must they too have places at the Lord's table? (3) How dare anyone conceptually disturb the sacredness of the tomb? How can it be said that someone has broken out of his grave? May women overwrite the reality of the tomb and designate it a womb? May mother earth, long subdued by patriarchal myth, now safely be allowed this new fecundity? What can be made of women's testimony that a grave has brought forth the Risen Lord? (4) The breaking of the written word is the most unsettling of all. Race, class, and gender have been sacred texts. They have been the laws supporting social reality. What strange wisdom insists now upon smashing those venerable stones? Moreover, the most important stone among evangelists has been the engraving of "Jesus" into stories of events that happened in the past. That

7. See duBois, *Sowing the Body* (see chap. 8, n. 11), esp. 46–49 and 130–66.

sculpting has held "Jesus" still for study, kept him stable as a base for social construction. That stone, too, must be smashed. The women catechists
bust Jesus out of any carved structures—*pesĕlîm*—designed to hold him.

Individually, these are awesome breakings. Taken together, the
Markan narrative makes them coincide with recognition of the messianic
identity of Jesus and orients the whole complex toward its mirror image,
the eucharistic institution within the last supper narrative. Mark places
no women at that messianic banquet (and neither does any other New Testament author). No women are there to see Jesus identify himself with
food and give himself away. In my opinion, this reflects a reliable historical memory. Women did not recline to eat with Jesus before Calvary (nor
did anyone else). There may have been a custom of commensality among
Jesus' friends, but women were not welcome to partake in it.

This presents us with a nice historical puzzle. At some point, the
original exclusionary practice was changed and women got to eat the
crumbs that fell from the table. We must ask: when, and by whose authority? Who broke into the circle and convinced the guys that "in Christ
there is neither male nor female"? In fact, the guys never have been completely convinced. Yet undeniably, the crumbs were made available. The
eucharist overwrote the gender definition of the female body at least to
the extent that women's hunger came to be recognized.

The gospel tradition is ambivalent about whether the eucharist is the
definitive poietic identification of Jesus' body. This ambivalence is evident in the omission of a eucharistic institution narrative from the Johannine account of the last supper. In John's story, the identity chosen by
Jesus is symbolized instead through the foot-washing ceremony. Earlier,
John (like Luke) has retold the messianic anointing of Jesus as a foot washing too. The "example" that Jesus gives in John 13:15 was first given to
him in John 12:3 by a woman (just as the dominical bread breaking of
Mark 14:22 mimics the woman's jar breaking of Mark 14:3). Washing feet
was work for a womanslave or a wife, so once again the genre of gender is
violated in order to express the bodily identity and availability of the
Lord. As at the Synoptic last supper, where Jesus is more the *dēmiourgos* or
caterer than the symposiast, here in this Johannine last supper he is both
symposiast and *ʾāmāh*.

Recognizing Jesus after Calvary

The Gospel narratives draw solid outlines around the figure of "Jesus."
They state who he was. They specify him. They give his vital statistics,

like an identification card. The Gospels are the standard mug shots, the "wanted" posters hanging on the wall of the church. When someone comes along now claiming contact with the Risen Lord, the Gospels are the baseline against which to evaluate the claim. They are designed not simply for remembering Jesus but for recognizing him and catching him. Thus Jesus is "made" through the Gospels: identified but also multiplied.

Besides being ID cards, these texts are recipe cards. Besides descriptions of Jesus, they supply information about the ecclesial practices to be followed in approaching Jesus. As I have argued throughout the preceding chapters, the Gospel narratives give directions for traveling to where Jesus may be seen as well as criteria for certifying whether the one who comes into view there is the real Jesus. Moreover, they are adamant in their assertion that the Gospel text itself does not deliver Jesus. "He is not here." The mug shot is not the face. Look for the face among faces, and the living one in the midst of life.

Very often in the Gospel narratives, life is sited at a table. The table of the Jesus communities was not a peaceful place. Table imagery seems to stand for all the contested territories, especially that of the Lord's body itself. What, then, is the "table" of the early Christian communities? It is at least three things. First, the Christian table is a table of new laws, a new Torah. It is the halakhah of teachers like Matthew, who, while professing to have preserved each tiniest stroke of a letter, extensively renovated the cornerstone text "kingdom of God." It is the impulse to codify Jesus, not just in fluid gossipy haggadah but in solid stony graven text. It is the slab supporting Jesus when his career has been completed, his last word uttered, his mouth closed. It is perfectly horizontal. (This flat table is O'Collins's first station, the academic study.)

Second, the Christian table is a cultic center where thanksgiving or eucharist is made. It is the site of recognition of the Lord "in the breaking of bread." It is where people gather in fear and hope, where the Risen Lord suddenly materializes even if doors are shut tight. It is the breast of God, where each littlest child rests in the place of honor forever. It is the feet of Jesus, where instruction flows sweet as kisses and clean as tears. This table is also at once a grapevine, and a cup, and a jar, and a well of living water, and an altar. So it is a slippery slope. (This inclined table is O'Collins's station of prayer.)

Third, the Christian table is what people have in common who think they have nothing in common. It is the leveling of all flesh by the body's innate fragility and the ravages of time. It is a tabulation of race, class, and gender that reduces privilege to nought. It is the lowest common human denominator—hunger, disability, need—depicted in a riveting tableau of the universal deathbound human condition. The Christian table is the home of the homeless, the larder of the poor. And theirs only. It is a convergence and a thrust. It is both a funnel and a wedge. (This tornado-spun table is O'Collins's station of hope.)

I find it curious how easily one's attention can focus within a narrow band of these meanings, while blotting out the rest of the spectrum. When the Gospel narratives mention a table, the typical reader's reflex is to imagine a nice dinner party with oneself lounging alongside Jesus. Yet Jesus was betrayed by someone in exactly that position.[8] For Jesus, the table was a risky place. He gave himself away at table—all "three" of them. Table transactions signal the start of the diffusion of Jesus' body: in word and narrative, in cult and sacrament, and in social inversion.

To understand that Jesus is copy who copies, one must first comprehend the layered meanings of "the Christian table." What hinders our comprehension is our preoccupation with commodities. This is a cultural disability that the modern Western reader invariably brings to the Gospel texts. We tend to translate whenever possible into terms of consumption, containment, procurement, and marketable goods. This bias dominates our perception of Jesus.

With this bias, we miss entirely the *table* in the "first" table or new law by assuming that the textual delivery system that packages "Jesus" is Jesus himself. Like a toddler with a birthday present, or a preschooler in the cereal aisle, we confuse the box with the substance. Approaching the "second" or eucharistic table, our commodifying bias reduces Jesus to a bonbon, a goodie that I can get for myself. At the "third" table, we regard the poor as problems to which some surplus commodities should be applied as remedy, to clear them up. We do not see how they are flesh of our flesh, transubstantiated now into the body of Christ, indispensable to the possibility of our ever looking Jesus in the face.

The Western theological enterprise has proceeded along lines warped by this commodifying bias. At the scriptural table, the interest of doctrinal theology has been to define and to broker canonical texts. At the eucharistic table, the interest of sacramental theology has been to ensure valid delivery systems for grace. At the charitable table, the interest of social ethics has been to manage the poor, with a view to "developing" them and making them "like us." All of these interests are exploitative. Exploitation is not evil. It is just embarrassing, because it is a project whose success is always its failure. The bread crumb messiah is

---

8. Or by two such, if one counts cowardly Peter along with Judas.

a permanent temptation for the church, but he is just another idol unless the vial breaks.

To meet the Lord "at table," you have to know how to behave. The church knows how. In chapter 4, I suggested that the church addresses words of guidance and encouragement to all who are seeking Jesus. What the church says to Jesus seekers is exactly what Matthew's Easter angel says to the women: "Do not be afraid. Approaching this slab, this tomb, this narrative is already the first step, even though you must discover that Jesus is not contained therein." Seeing the Lord is a special composite competence, a distinctive literacy. It cannot be infused, revealed, or downloaded; it must be demonstrated, built up, and practiced.

We have, then, three tables, as it were, at which to acquire this competence, and we must become adept at all three. The table of the *Gospel narratives* teaches us to retain and process "factual" information about who Jesus was. That skill is essential for recognizing him. But if we learn no other skill, then we imagine Jesus as someone from the past, dead and gone now although nostalgically remembered. We will miss seeing Jesus in the present because we will think of him as only a historical figure. The table of *worship* equips us to taste the volatility of the power of the spirit flowing through a community at prayer. That skill too is essential for recognizing Jesus, but it is not sufficient in itself. If all we can do is pray, we will start seeing "Jesus" everywhere, and we will hear him saying whatever we like. The table of *solidarity with the poor* trains us in the literacy of hunger. When that competence is added to charismatic sensitivity and factual recall, then we begin to approximate a receptivity to what the gospel traditions intend by the phrase "seeing Jesus."

It should be clear that I am not talking about some achievement that is guaranteed to follow upon the completion of a checklist of prerequisites. I am talking about the church's ancient longing for the Lord. Ecclesial access and Christic identity are defined together; each is wagered upon the other. But the longing for the Lord is also a refusal to settle for anyone else.

The poignant intensity of this longing is evident in many of the Gospel Stories, especially those whose central theme is "seeing Jesus." The church whose wisdom is embodied in those stories is our own church: it is standing here on the same side of Calvary where we are standing. This church grieves for what was taken at Calvary and longs to see the Lord again. This church remembers Jesus through tears; it lets its catechesis flow while weeping. The Gospel stories may be projected back to the other side of Calvary, into the time when Jesus spoke directly with his friends before he died. But those stories are fictions, whose intention is to dramatize how people get to see Jesus *now*, after Calvary.

We have already made a careful examination of several of these vignettes. Some have had to do with making a physical approach toward the Lord—as when little children clamber into the lap of the Teacher, or John the Baptist sends people to Jesus in various ways, or women looking for the body of Jesus receive curious instructions at his empty tomb. Another set of stories concerned the specification of the identity of Jesus—as when the Mary story explores what it means to be the new Samuel and God's slave son, or the story of the desert trial pits two traditions of divine commissioning against each other. Both identity and access were at issue in the stories of the anointing at Bethany, in which a woman enters an *andrōn* to get near Jesus so that she can rewrite his identity entirely.

But numerous other stories pursue the same themes and can be mentioned briefly here to corroborate the findings of our earlier studies: Bartimaeus, Mark 11:46-52; Zacchaeus, Luke 19:1-10; some Greeks who want to meet Jesus, John 12:20-22; as well as the Easter appearances in Matt. 28:1-10, 16-20, and in Luke 24:13-53, considered earlier. In all of these, the first step is *to want to see who Jesus is,* and it typically is taken in the midst of a misapprehension. John's Gospel has twin recognition stories with women seeking something from holes in the earth, John 4:5-42 and 20:11-18; both women are disappointed and frustrated before being recognized by Jesus and then recognizing him. Mark's Gospel also has three appearance stories appended, Mark 16:9-18; but these no longer are *recognition* stories. Paul too comes up with an appearance story for himself, because it is so important for teachers to have seen Jesus. We have several versions of Paul's vision, which differs from the Gospel accounts of seeing Jesus in some important respects. Paul's vision was not preceded by instruction or by any sympathetic information about Jesus. Paul did not particularly want to see Jesus. Paul did not recognize the Lord and had to ask Jesus who he was in the midst of the "vision." Whether Paul ever developed the competence "to see the Lord" remained a matter of contention in the Jesus movements for quite some time.

Who Will Roll Away the Stone?

The nature of the material we have been examining is such that, on the one hand, its meaning cannot be pinned down with precision or mapped neatly as having originated within a particular historical situation; while, on the other hand, its very design provokes one to indulge in a kind of imaginative free association to pursue wisps of connotation and allusion. It could hardly be otherwise in an analysis of the poietic productivity of the human imagination. When the dust clears, nevertheless, some facts remain. It is beyond doubt that the recognition of a messianic identity for the crucified Jesus occurred along with a massive, and untidy, unraveling of the social genres of race, class, and gender. This recognition happened after Calvary, and with the significant involvement of women and workers. It was a bodily renegotiation, a struggle over the human body. The battle was staged in proximity to a "table," access to which was contested.

I have employed the metaphor of the "tug-of-war" to describe this struggle. Surely it is an oversimplification to reduce the "sides" to two and the "struggle" to a single dimension. Yet I believe that it is valid to identify two major contrasting tendencies in the early, infracanonical negotiation of the identity of Jesus and the means of access to him. One tendency worked toward stabilizing "Jesus," giving him a definite profile, certifying the facts about him. This tendency preserved a solid identity for him and located it firmly in the past. The other tendency worked to break Jesus out of the past so as to experience his powerful presence as close, confrontational, volatile, and personal.

These tendencies are held in unstable tension, and neither succeeds without the other. The text of Scripture is woven of these perpendicular threads. We would not get "Jesus" were he not wrapped in the delivery blanket of this scriptural fabric. Yet his shroud is made of the very same material. The place to look for the Risen Lord is not in the past, not in the text. The rending of the textual veil must be accomplished, countertextually, if Jesus is to rise.

12

Copy Who Copies

CHRISTIAN ORIGIN happens continually, and always with the contrapuntal structure of enframing and frame breaking. The dawning of Easter faith in the life of a catechumen or a community today resembles what happened soon after Calvary. Jesus, remembered in definite outline from the past, is recognized amid ongoing life in terms of that memory. The project of certifying identity works at cross-purposes to the project of opening access; a social genre is called into play, only to be transgressed. The canonical recognition stories insist that the Risen Lord could be made out because he was the "same" Jesus intimately known to his disciples before Calvary, while also insisting that his life and powers after Calvary were radically new. The Gospels impose definition upon the character of Jesus and closure upon his career, but, as I have argued, those narratives have seams designed to split.

Origins for Easter faith today, in individual lives as well as in young churches, display this characteristic tension between the frame-up and the escape of Jesus as Risen Lord. We tell the catechumens our old stories about who Jesus was, but not so authoritatively that the hearers must discredit any words or deeds or needs of the Lord occurring tomorrow. We train their bodies in the traditional disciplines of worship and good works, but must expect their auto-inscriptions to vary from our models. The propagation of access to the Risen Lord, down through the generations and out across the nations, depends on remembering Jesus as maker and made of the kingdom of God. The purpose of our remembering is to realize that his making also continues. God's is a kingdom of variations.

A great deal is at stake in the question of access to Jesus. Quite early in the history of the church, and well before the Gospels were written down, Jesus was aligned with God in the Christian imagination and system of belief. That is, Jesus was regarded as one who had—and could share—access to God. In Jesus, God meant to draw near to human beings. Jesus' proclamation of God's kingdom was a claim that God was "near" or "here" or "within." Jesus was known to be, in some way, the vehicle or gateway that made this claim real.

But Jesus died. Death is the end of access. The dead are available to us only in very restricted ways. We, the living, remember what they said and did; but dead people do not say or do anything further. Death closes life, and with it, one's availability for relationship. Jesus really did die. The Marys and others saw him die, and they watched his tomb long enough to make certain that he was truly dead and gone. The women watched until it was time for the limestone slab and walls to do their work: *sarka phagein,* eat the flesh (from which comes the word "sarcophagus"). Yet in a bold reversal, proto-Christian communities connected eating Jesus' flesh with life, not decay. For them, the body was back; and its mouth was working, because they were hearing new words of Jesus from the Christian prophets.

Calvary was a breach in the availability of God through Jesus, and it is essential to realize that the early churches stood on the same side of that breach as we do today. After Calvary, Jesus was no more reachable for them than he is for us. The Gospels are "about" access to one who died. The genric intent of Gospels is to communicate the means of approaching someone dead, someone for whom the normal interpersonal means of contact no longer operate. The object or term of that access is someone risen, someone who keeps on talking and touching after death—not in spite of *sarka phagein* but because of it.

Since the first century, the church has known and employed certain strategies for opening the possibility of recognizing Jesus as Risen Lord. There are both bodily and textual strategies. The bodily strategies are embedded in the sacramental rituals celebrated by the worshiping assembly, while the textual strategies motivate the catechetical teaching and learning of the Scriptures. As always, body and text form two poles of one continuum: ritual and story belong to two complementary and nonexclusive sets of practices.

But they are not "original" in the sense that they would preexist the reflective effort to understand and evaluate them that we today call "theology." From the first moments when they appear on the screen of Christian memory, the eucharistic ritual as well as the narratives of Jesus' career already are interlaced with theological interpretation, as we have seen. With the New Testament the trajectory of theological development already is well along on its course, as a historical mediation to us of the possibility of seeing Jesus as Risen Lord. But that theological-textual mediation is not a self-sufficient delivery system, for there are two other trajectories, both bodily, in operation as well. The *liturgical* tradition reflectively embroiders and interprets the availability of Jesus after Calvary and hands it down to us as a bodily competence. And the disciplines of *care*—elaborated in works of charity, mercy, almsgiving, solidarity—likewise develop their own trajectory that passes on to us the practices disclosing the Lord's presence in the resistance of children, women, and men against their sufferings.

Theology, liturgy, and solidarity—each of these is a strand in the cable that links us back to the first people who saw Jesus risen and transmits their competence down to us. Yet each strand itself is braided with elements of the other two. Thus Gospels, as reflective texts, refer to early feeding rituals and to practices of healing, even as they compose their "facts" about the career of Jesus. Theology in its historical development continues to do the same kind of braiding. While reflecting upon the Gospel texts, it pulls in strands of contemporary liturgical and charitable practices, for those also are sources of valid information about what God did and continues to do in Jesus.

Because this is a book (not a mass or a hospice), I am naturally concentrating on *the textual interpretation of* both textual and bodily practices of identifying and accessing Jesus as Risen Lord. I trust the reader to understand that no book could deliver complete information; those who want to see the Lord must devote themselves to the liturgy and the poor (better yet, the liturgy *with* the poor) as well as to printed texts. Here I will do what a writer can, which is to consider the part that theology has played, and should play, in propagating the availability of the Lord to the church.

The Theology of Charity

One startling discovery comes clear at the outset. In the history of Christian theology, which has flowed largely from the pens of well-fed people, there is no theological tradition reflecting on the practices of care for the poor. Saints who sought the Risen Lord in the hungry little ones did not theorize about it. Theorists did not write about it. Biographies of monarchs and missionaries may mention that they fed the poor or nursed the sick. While such behaviors are praised as (eccentric but) virtuous, they have never been brought into mainstream Christology's discussions of the identity and availability of the Lord. Even when someone insisted that she or he had *seen* Jesus as a beggar, the report was consigned to the marginalized discourse of "spirituality," mystical theology, fancy, or fable. It did not count. That is, while the competence to see the Lord in the hungry little ones continues unabated in the living church, one never would know it from reading historical or contemporary mainstream Christology.[1]

Sacramental Theology

Within the first century of the church's existence, sacramental access to Jesus underwent institutionalization, becoming cultic ritual observance, the liturgy. It is somewhat anachronistic to use the term "sacrament" at all for experiences that occurred earlier than the third century, when the Latin author Tertullian borrowed the terminology of military induction to discuss Christian practices connected with baptism. The earlier Greek term was *mysterion*, which expresses an affinity with other cultic experiences familiar in the ancient world. Yet even that term does not reach back to the earliest layers of Christian history and experience. Moreover, even the term "theology" itself is anachronistic if applied to early Christianity's reflective practice, since that term took on a meaning resembling its modern usage only about the twelfth century. While proto-Christians claimed to experience in their baptisms and eucharists a bodily availability of the Risen Lord, and while they also thought and taught about those experiences, "sacramental theology" is our term, not theirs.

So it is only through a wholesale telescoping of twenty centuries of richly varied experience that any general statements at all can be made. Yet given this caution, one observes that the classical questions in sacramental theology ultimately have boiled down to "how," the question of the mode of possibility. (This also was Mary's question in Luke 1:34: *pōs*, that is, how? How can Jesus come here and be in me and grow in me? In Luke's text the mother voices the archetypical question about the origin of Jesus' life.)

One can distinguish three nested clusters of possibility questions in the ongoing discourse of sacramental theology.[2] First, there are core questions of

---

1. This is a harsh overgeneralization, but I let it stand in order to call attention to the anomaly that it underlines. Some theologians have argued that both the marginalized texts of "Christian spirituality" and its practices should be brought into the mainstream of the academic theological tradition. Twentieth-century theologies of liberation also intend to make both the practice and the theorization of solidarity the focal point of their work. Nevertheless, both mystical and liberation theologies still are treated as afterthoughts to systematic theology. Or when one is tentatively admitted, the other is shut out.

2. Karl Rahner itemizes the traditional concerns of sacramental theology as follows: (*a*) the foundation of the sacraments by Christ; (*b*) the common nature and the differences between

power and causality. Whose action is the sacramental ritual? What is the relation between divine and human activity? What is the character of the eucharistic "real presence"? How does Jesus "get into" the bread and wine; and how do we know? What does the water do in baptism? How can water accomplish such a thing? How do the sacraments affect us?

Branching out from these causality questions are the questions of institution and authorization. Sometimes these are invoked arbitrarily to short-circuit the investigation of the first cluster of questions—for instance, with the claim that Jesus is "in" the bread *simply because he said that he would be* or that the water works because Jesus said that it would. Or less simplistically, one traces the possibility of historical and ecclesiological connection between Jesus of Nazareth and the sacramental rituals practiced by a particular congregation today. One asks who can validly and licitly administer sacraments, and who can give or withhold such certification.

At the margins of significance are found the third classic cluster of questions, those having to do with ritual details concerning the composition of the elements employed, the rubrics and texts of the rites themselves. Here arise issues of the proper matter and form. One asks what is absolutely necessary in order to enact the sacrament, and what aspects of the ritual are merely expressive or decorative but not constitutive. How is this bread, wine, water, washing or eating different from the usual kind? How are they the same? How does this symbolic communication differ from secular instances of symbolic communication? And must it?

In this tangle of questions, certain presuppositions define the field of the discourse. The most striking feature emerging here is that we are dealing with questions of the possibility of something already taken for a reality. Like Mary in Luke's annunciation story, the church is asking "how can it be" that Jesus is bodily present, not "whether it can be." This is a questioning in faith, not of faith. Certitude about access to Jesus is the context but not the object of inquiry. *That* Jesus is present, active, and available within liturgical celebrations is beyond question for the church. However, such ecclesial certainty does not put the issue of Jesus' presence

---

the sacraments; (*c*) the relationship among the seven sacraments; (*d*) efficacy; (*e*) administration; (*f*) sacramental expression of the church as the presence of grace; and (*g*) eschatology. See the conclusion of his article on "Sacraments" in *Encyclopedia of Theology: The Concise Sacramentum Mundi*, ed. by Karl Rahner (New York: Seabury Press, Crossroad Books, 1975). Alexandre Ganoczy suggests that the fundamental questions in sacramental theology since the Council of Trent have had to do with efficacy, institution, number, necessity, administration, and reception. See Alexandre Ganoczy, *An Introduction to Catholic Sacramental Theology*, trans. by William Thomas and Anthony Sherman (New York: Paulist Press, 1984).

beyond question for the scholarly investigator, who is intrigued to note the foundational status of the perceived reality of Jesus' presence within ecclesial discourse about its possibility.

Yet at points in the historical unfolding of the discussion, the weight of the *that* often has distorted the investigation of the *how*. These points remain sensitive, sore points in sacramental theology today. The church is touchy about them; they are avoided, or shielded from too-rigorous investigation. Not surprisingly, some of these areas coincide with the deepest wounds of the Reformations, which both sutured and fractured the body of Christ. Yet wounds do not heal without attention, light, air, and care. It is high time to attend to several key issues whose investigation has been foreclosed or distorted in medieval and modern sacramental theology.

One of these issues comes into focus in the scholastic formula *significando causant*, "they cause through signifying." This formula means to link two assertions: that the sacraments are signs of realities beyond themselves and that the sacraments are *causally involved* in putting Christians in touch with those same gracious realities. Moreover, the formula implies that the latter depends on the former; that grace comes to people in the sacraments precisely because they are signs. The signing or symbolizing of the reality is simultaneously the causing of the sharing of the reality with the person for whom the signing is done.

So far, so good. The "reality" at play here is God's gracious opening of access to God through Jesus. God has "caused" this once and for all; the signifying ritual does not have to cause it again but only occasions the availability of Jesus within a particular situation after Calvary. The sign realizes the reality. But this notion raises fears that *significando causant* is no different from magic or wishful thinking, where saying so makes it so. Pursuing the possibility question in this way seems to jeopardize the reality, the certitude of Jesus' availability.

Therefore scholastic and modern theologians have recoiled from the implications of symbolic causality and have retreated in two directions.[3] Tracking these retreats discloses two additional issues that have undergone distortion. One retreat has been toward psychology. It has seemed safe to construe symbolic signification as a psychological phenomenon,

---

3. In the generations since the Second Vatican Council, rigorous metaphysical inquiry into the issue of sacramental symbolic efficacy was postponed as the church struggled with the pastoral assimilation of liturgical and catechetical reforms and with the ecumenical détente escalated by the council. Two recent studies reopen the serious investigation of this issue: L.-M. Chauvet, *Symbol et sacrement: Une relecture sacramentelle de l'existence chrétienne* (Paris: Editions du Cerf, 1987); and Bernard J. Cooke, *The Distancing of God: The Ambiguity of Symbol in History and Theology* (Minneapolis: Fortress Augsburg, 1990).

with the ritual construed as an interpersonal encounter between Jesus and the believer. Yet it only "feels like" an interpersonal encounter; what it really "is" still has to be described in metaphysical language, since one fears that intrasubjective or psychological realities may be less sturdy than philosophical ones. Thus sacramental theology must bifurcate into a "soft" pastoral discussion of the individual's private, subjective, devotional appropriation of liturgical experience and a "hard" ecclesiological discussion of the church's public, objective, self-realizing provision of liturgical experience. The latter is privileged over the former as more important and more reliable; yet both are truncations of the phenomenon of symbolic communication.[4]

The other retreat from the investigation of symbolic causality flees in the direction of stabilizing the symbol by forcibly translating it into words that supposedly are equivalent in meaning.[5] This option as it were downshifts ritual on the scale between body and text, displacing it toward word or text and reducing its bodily sacramentality. Thus one asserts that word and sacrament are really the same thing, or that ritual is merely a different kind of word. This is a bid to clean up the messy unwieldiness of physical symbols, by containing their meaning within words that can be more easily handled, manipulated, controlled, and understood. If the legitimate meanings of the symbol can be certified, then illegitimate meanings are easily identified and excluded. But this forced translation of physical symbols into words leaves behind a residue of nostalgia for the beauty and poetry of the simple rustic symbols. Nostalgia for symbols can be safely indulged once the symbols themselves have been declawed, housebroken, and secured on the leash of words. Yet the ambition for verbal control of symbol severely truncates sacramental communication.[6]

So far, three significant distortions in the discourse of sacrament have been unfolded: a recoil from the connection between signifying and causing, leading on the one hand into the bifurcation of liturgy into the opposing dimensions of the psychological versus the real and on the other hand into the quest for verbal control of symbol.

A fourth wrinkle in the discourse of sacramental theology has to do with time, but it too stems from a desire to shore up the reality of God's

4. This option in sacramental theology is exemplified in the work of Edward Schillebeeckx, more about which below.

5. An especially astute example of this is Margaret Mary Kelleher's impressive proposal of "horizon analysis" as a method for studying liturgical phenomena. See Margaret Mary Kelleher, "Liturgical Theology: A Task and a Method," *Worship* 62 (1988): 2–25; and idem, "Liturgy: An Ecclesial Act of Meaning," *Worship* 59 (1985): 482–97.

6. This option in sacramental theology is exemplified in the work of Karl Rahner, discussed further below.

availability in Jesus. This distortion settles for a naive and premodern view of the temporal dimension of human experience. As a general premise, this option in sacramental theology construes God's availability as an act or event, which has a definable beginning and end and which is placed into the human past. "It" "happened" "then." This premise means to establish a temporal location for the reality of God's gracious availability and to establish that location at a temporal distance from ourselves. (As we shall see presently, doctrinal theology has made a similar move.)

The conceptual gain from this move is a heightening of the facticity and definiteness of the reality. But it also entails considerable loss, for the periodization of God's availability is accomplished by tearing the fabric of human space and time. First, one must imagine God suspending physical laws to intervene in human reality from outside it. One must further imagine that God did this in a finite and countable number of instances during the two millennia B.C.E. and then again definitively during the first century C.E. One must imagine these interventions as starting and stopping. Thus one conceptualizes certain original divine violations of human temporality. The sacramental theology that paints such a picture of history is not content then to allow the ripples of these supernatural break-ins to propagate naturally down through history into our present day. Natural historical mediation will not do for such supernatural intrusions. Therefore the liturgy cannot be an ordinary recalling of great events. Instead, each sacramental celebration must be *another* special intervention by God into human time and space. Having located God's act "then," we must rip our own "now" out of the fabric of human reality and patch it onto "then." The liturgy not only celebrates the past but revisits it as well. There is no room, conceptually, to celebrate the present in its own right. One loses track of the value of human history, and one loses the possibility of meaningful engagement with it.

Finally, the contemporary discourse of sacramental theology is hung up on the issue of action. There is concern to assert that the human beings who celebrate the sacraments do not personally cause the realities that they celebrate. But if the liturgy is an action, who is the doer of the action? It cannot be a private action by the individuals involved. To avoid making that claim, it is asserted instead that the one who acts is Jesus Christ. From this follows the assertion that it is the body of Christ, or the church, which acts on his behalf. The church becomes the subject of the sacramental ritual.[7] Yet the church cannot be a subject; it is not a big self who

7. Kelleher, e.g., writes, "An assembly engaged in the performance of liturgy acts as a collective subject" ("Liturgical Theology," 7).

thinks, feels, perceives, decides. To make the church a subject trivializes the subjectivity and freedom of the believers themselves and diminishes the political significance of their collectivity and solidarity.[8]

Each of these five incongruities in the discourse of sacramental theology reflects a fear, a failure of nerve. (1) The alienation of the *significando* from the *causant* is owing to fear of manipulation, of falling for a lie. (2) The exclusion of psychological, subjective matters from the realm of what can be counted as objectively real is a symptom of the fear of emotions, feelings, and their power to sway judgment. (3) The digitalizing of symbols into verbal approximations betrays a fear of loss of identity and control. (4) The override of the structures of human historical mediation evidences a fear that time is not permeable to God's influence, as other creatures are. (5) The hypostatization of the church into an agent of sacramental celebration manifests fear of the creative political potential of the human subject.

These five flights are understandable but not necessary for protecting faith, because Matthew's Easter angel has said, "Don't be afraid." Human gullibility, human fragility, the fertility of human imaginations, human temporality, and human freedom—these are frightening, but the church is told to take courage. Sacramental theology can work through these aspects of human bodily being; it does not have to detour around them.

Doctrinal Theology

The church's experience with the word as a means of reaching Jesus is, to say the least, well documented. The Gospels tell Jesus' story; they "give" Jesus to the reader in story form. More subtly, these texts are also about how one gives others access to Jesus in story form. The scriptural texts reflect the church's experience of telling the Jesus story for at least forty years without texts. As we have seen, they divulge reflective information about how words have functioned, post-Calvary, to occasion the recognition of Jesus as Risen Lord.

Matthew, Mark, Luke, and John did not call it theology when they provided such information. Nevertheless their work belongs within the history of doctrinal theology, although not at its very beginning. Ahead of them stand the generations of Christian prophets and teachers who

8. The human being as free, productive, politically creative "subject" has been a central teaching of the philosopher pope, John Paul II, especially in *Laborem exorcens* and *Sollicitudo rei socialis*. See the comments of Gregory Baum, "The Church against Itself," in *World Catechism or Inculturation*, ed. by Johann-Baptist Metz and Edward Schillebeeckx, Concilium 204 (Edinburgh: T. & T. Clark, 1989), xiii–xv.

received Jesus' own teaching and elaborated and systematized it so they could introduce newcomers into this body of wisdom. The creative contributions of those pre-textual Christian teachers were massively formative of the Christian tradition.

Thus the story of the Christian story begins well before the writing down of the Gospels, and it continues after their completion, throughout history until the present time. The story always has been "about Jesus" *and* "about how one comes to know Jesus." The impulse toward narrative and text seems to be a distinctive feature of the Christian tradition. That is, the making, reading, and remaking of text is a constitutive structure of the availability of Jesus as Risen Lord. This impulse has given the church a variety of genres: the collection of aphorisms, the gospel, the creed, the treatise, the dogmatic definition, the summa, the anathema, the catechism, the hymn, the sermon, the prayerbook, the audiotaped or video talk, the encyclical, the theology textbook. Each of these genres has emerged historically and delivers its message by playing its own distinctive kind of language game, demanding its own distinctive kind of competence. Amid these we can discern that which generated these genres: the drive to narratize and to textualize, as a component of the continuing availability of Jesus to the church.

Historically, each generation's discourse about the story of Jesus has become part of that story itself for ensuing generations. As was the case with sacramental theology, here again within doctrinal theology one can discover certain biases or distortions of discourse. These are connected with the forgetting of the ways in which the Christian story was put together and still continues to be put together. Earlier I suggested that sacramental theology's distortions stem from and disclose an ecclesial interest: the desire to stabilize the factual, trustable, real availability of Jesus within the sacraments, in the face of certain threatening dimensions emerging in the pursuit of questions about symbolic causality. Here within the discourse of doctrinal theology something similar is at work.

By doctrinal theology is meant a set of activities as well as their outcomes: the selection and abstraction of certain elements from Christian Scripture, the refinement of those elements by philosophical means into declarative statements, and the arrangement of those statements into a systematic presentation that is asserted to be true in itself and also representative of its scriptural source. Doctrinal theology is both the process and its product. Its prototype is the baptismal creed, which is a handy narrative summary of the events and assertions of the Christian Bible. The exegesis of Scripture usually has been a component of this discourse as well. Doctrinal theology is never finished; later formulations draw upon earlier ones as well as upon the Scripture. This discourse is like a stream gushing down through Christian history. The new Christian is baptized in this stream of doctrine as well as in the waters of sacramental initiation.

If the recurrent question within sacramental discourse was the *how* of the possibility of symbolic causality, then within doctrinal discourse the classic question is *location,* both spatial and temporal. Where and when has God acted to reconcile human beings?

As before, one discerns three nested bundles of "where" and "when" questions. At the core are those which prompt the Christian revision of salvation history. How does the Hebrew Scripture get to be an "old" testament for some people? What grounds are there to refocus the Law, the Prophets, and the Writings upon Jesus of Nazareth and the church? What elements of the life and death of Jesus can be identified with God's intention to save human beings? What is revelation; how did it "close"; how did it even "open"? What does it mean to locate God in the man Jesus of Nazareth?[9] Surrounding these originary locatings in time and space another set of doctrinal questions clusters. These have to do with the meaning of those times and places which happen *not* to be the special locations of the originary revelation. What applications are possible "here and now" of what happened in that special privileged "there and then"? Can Scripture become the word of God for people today? What does Jesus have to do with us? (Sacramental theology itself often is brought into this cluster of doctrinal questions.) At the margins of doctrinal theology are practical and eschatological questions. What is God going to do with today's people, and when is God going to do it? What is the relation between human political creativity and the divine creativity?

Once again, we are interested more in the general shape of the discourse than in the particular questions. Doctrinal theology is defined and circumscribed by what is *never* questioned within it: Jesus' status as the definitive localization of God's activity.[10] The identification of Jesus

9. The logical difficulties that attend the project of locating, or relocating, God's activity in time and place are considered by Farley, *Ecclesial Reflection* (see chap. 2, n. 1), esp. chaps. 3 and 4. That discussion is condensed in "Scripture and Tradition," by Edward Farley and Peter C. Hodgson, in *Christian Theology: An Introduction to Its Traditions and Tasks,* ed. Peter C. Hodgson and Robert H. King (Philadelphia: Fortress Press, 1982).

10. The definitiveness of Jesus is indeed questioned today in the context of Christianity's dialogues with other world religions and ideological systems. However, I would not place this questioning within doctrinal theology. By the same token, to say that the "that" of Jesus' availability in sacrament remains unquestioned within sacramental theology is merely to assert that such a question occurs only in discourse that is no longer sacramental theology but another discourse.

founds the spatially and temporally determined access questions (just as reality founded possibility in sacramental theology). Yet again there are sensitive points at which the free pursuit of "where" and "when" questions in relation to God's grace has threatened to destabilize ecclesial certitude about Jesus' Christic identification. As doctrinal theology avoids such points, distortions are introduced into the fabric of the discourse. This has been true historically and is becoming more acutely apparent in our own time.

These distortions are not benignly academic. The genocidal atrocities of the twentieth century were made thinkable and possible through tactics of discourse not unlike those with which doctrinal theology detours around the confrontation between the distinctiveness claimed for Jesus and the plurality of conflicting claims in a multicultural world. The Holocaust itself was initiated in Christian discourse. That is to say, communities that identified with Jesus, from those of Matthew and John through those in modern Europe, have oppressed Jews and others defined as outsiders, justifying their oppression by reference to the Christian story. To object that anti-Semitism and genocide are "not Christian" is to beg the question.

Therefore the need is especially urgent to bring to light several issues in doctrinal theology that have been foreclosed in the attempt to protect the uniqueness of Jesus—a well-meaning attempt that is both shortsighted and unnecessary. The first issue that calls for attention is the problematic character of salvation history itself. To select certain contours of the past and identify them as "events" in which "God acted" is a move fraught with all kinds of metaphysical difficulties, not the least of which is the use of the past tense itself in connection with the deity. Yet doctrinal theology has staked its viability on the assumption that there were certain events of Christian origin, locatable as discrete points upon a historical time line. Those events are understood to have happened, in the sense of being completed, before an account of them was written down. The Gospel texts, then, are construed in doctrinal theology as referring to events that are extratextual, that is, outside the Gospel text, prior to it, and independent of it.

When, as often happens, the texts present variant versions of an alleged event, the resources of biblical scholarship are called out and historical-critical methods are invoked to try to identify the "original" or earliest fragment of the tradition. Yet many contemporary biblical scholars resist being drafted into the service of such a project, for consensus is growing that an original version cannot be found. On the other hand, the quest for historical-Jesus material has brought vastly improved understanding of the historical strata of social formations and practices in the primitive Christian communities. But those data have yet to be assimilated by theology, which persists in its futile quest to capture historical events through whatever textual versions of them can be placed closest in time to their supposed occurrence. The reality of Jesus, who is the location of God's saving availability, is constructed as something prior to all of the textual versions. He is thought of as standing in their past, that is, elsewhere and unreachable *except as the referent of texts.*

A second issue emerges from this one. If the events of Christian origin were over even before the Gospels were written, then certainly they are long gone by now. Revelation is closed, and into its place has stepped authority. If the resurrection is an event that happened a long time ago, then one's access to the Risen Lord must be through a third-person account of resurrection from an authorized witness. Thus authority and authoritative transmission become tremendously important, inasmuch as they are the vehicle for access to resurrection for those of us born since the year 30 C.E. God's saving action in Jesus is translated into information, packaged in doctrine, and wrapped in an apostolic mandate. The contents of this package are imagined to be perfectly preserved in stasis, unaffected by the transmission process that delivers them across the centuries and the oceans. This arrangement maximizes control and ease of handling and minimizes the possibility of surprise when the package is opened. Christian life is conceived in terms of verbal message and verbal response.

From the insistence that God's act lies in the past and has been completed, a third issue arises: the discontinuity of the structures of human history. "Now" has to be radically different from "then," that special time when Jesus was alive and God was with humanity. Theologians since Matthew, Luke, and John have been trying to smooth out this wrinkle in logic by devising some theory about how Jesus or his Spirit could remain with the church but in some manner subordinate to the privileged era of Jesus' lifetime. If some such derivative presence of God is maintained, or if (as in the sacramental version of this issue, introduced above) a patch of the twentieth century is ripped out and stitched onto the first century, one might still have a plausible way for God to be active in our time. Nevertheless God would not be doing anything new, unique, or important. God's really important acts would remain the church's past.

The last two issues needing attention here are more textual than temporal. The Gospel texts are narratives. Narratives focus attention beyond themselves toward a story line purportedly in their past. In doing this, narratives deflect attention away from themselves; they do not want the reader to notice that they are artifacts, fictions, creations. To be sure, a fiction is not a deception, and this redirection of attention is simply a characteristic of narrative. Doctrinal theology colludes with this narrative intent of the Gospels. It overlooks their textuality in favor of the events they describe but is polite enough not to notice how those very descriptions all the while are constituting the events by telling them.

Thus the "content" of the Gospels that typically receives attention in theology comes exclusively from their story lines, their surface features. This content is not always received uncritically by theology, for elements of the Gospel narratives are compared with information gleaned from secular historical sources. Yet the doctrinal theologian avoids reading the narrative content against the textuality of the Gospels themselves, that is, reading the Gospels in the context of their composition, their social situation, and function. Thus doctrinal theology focuses on Jesus in the background and loses sight of the prophets, teachers, and other proto-church figures surrounding him. The role of teachers and teaching in the mediation of the presence of Jesus thus has remained invisible to doctrinal theology. But the recovery of the Christian teaching practices from the Gospel traditions must occasion a major refocus of the doctrinal enterprise.

One more issue connected with the theological denial of the textuality of the Gospel texts needs mentioning here. Doctrinal theology demands that the Gospels do more than text can do: deliver facts. The one fact that the texts actually could deliver is the one that theology overlooks: the bare fact of their textuality itself. The Gospels as we receive them are four portraits, four versions, of Jesus. They agree on relatively few factual details. This is abundantly obvious in a comparison of the divergent accounts of even such a significant "event" as the finding of the emptied tomb. But the supposed "factual disagreement" embarrasses theology. Immense effort is expended in a quest to reconcile the stories, to have not four versions but one superversion to override the others. This move is countercanonical, to say the least. It expresses a naively simple view of truth as correspondence between declarative statements and past states of affairs—as if such a thing were possible. It demands a strictly literal reading of the Gospel texts, in which they are made to parody themselves. It robs the Gospels of nearly every scrap of artistry and guile, and thus it disables them.

Each of these five distortions in the discourse of doctrinal theology reflects a fear, a turning back from the challenge of revelation, a withdrawal from reality. (1) The stabilization of Christian origins into definable events of the past betrays a fear of the volatility of the human future, the becoming of the present. (2) The freeze-drying of the "contents" of these "events" into immutable doctrinal statements shows a fear that their nourishing potential might otherwise spoil. (3) The estrangement between "now" and "then" shows how much we fear the living God (Mark

12:27), or, rather, it shows our fear that a living God is not a God we can live with. (4) The erasure of the artifactual character of the canonical texts is evidence of fear of the living God's finest creation: the living human creator. (5) The suppression of variation among canonical and postcanonical versions of Christianity manifests a fear of the otherness of the bodily or culturally other—a fear that reads variation as deviation.

But Matthew's angel (who, after all, is giving voice to the knowledge of how to find the Risen Lord) says, "Don't be afraid." Our open-endedness, our hunger for substance, our espousal to a dangerously living God, our textual creativity, and our variance—these terrifying characteristics of the humanity that we have received are the signposts toward the humanity that God means to give us in the life to come and that God already has given to Jesus as risen Lord. Doctrinal theology must not avert its gaze from these aspects. The way to understanding lies through them, not around them.

Rethinking Foundations

The almost instinctive flight of both the doctrinal and the sacramental theological enterprises from the destabilization of Easter cannot be eliminated, but it can be diagnosed and treated. Resurrection phobia develops from too much work on texts and not enough play with the kingdom's little ones at the eucharistic banquet. I have two recommendations. First, those who would write faithfully about the resurrection of Jesus should circulate among Gerald O'Collins's "three stations," spending as much time at the tables of hope and prayer as they spend at their desks. (That's all I can say about that from here at *my* desk.) Second, at our desk work we should employ tools of analysis appropriate to the phenomena that we are trying to understand. If the Gospels and the sacraments are works of art, then we need to be listening to contemporary aesthetic theorists. If they invoke human systems of meaning, then we need the help of anthropologists. If they figure into the institutional reproduction of the church as well as the propagation of practices of gender, race, and class, then the full range of contemporary social interpretive theory should be brought to bear. It won't hurt faith. To do any less through fear is to doubt the reality of Jesus as Risen Lord.

A brave resolve to face historical facts is characteristic of some of the best recent work in foundational theology—which is ironically "foundational" chiefly in calling the possibility of ecclesial and epistemological foundations into serious question. Francis Schüssler Fiorenza catalogs and critically assesses the ways in which the resurrection appearances narrated in the Gospels have been cited by theologians during the last two centuries. He finds that some writers have treated the appearances as objects of faith alongside numerous items prescribed for belief. For others, the appearance narratives have had the special role of grounding faith itself; in this sense they are cited foundationally. In regard to *appearance narratives,* Fiorenza shows, foundations heretofore have been built upon the *appearances,* construed as historical events that in some sense make a beginning for Easter faith. Fiorenza would build instead upon the *narratives* insofar as they may be taken as reports of credible witnesses who should be trusted.[11] Pheme Perkins too surveys the theological uses that have been made of the resurrection. But first through careful analysis of the New Testament texts she identifies several earlier kinds of affirmation about a risen Jesus that predate the empty tomb narratives. She thus in effect disables their fictive project of stabilizing that version of what happened to Jesus.[12] Gerald O'Collins makes the provocative proposal that resurrection be interpreted as disclosive of the power of divine love.[13]

These tentative moves away from reliance on resurrection as *foundation* for ecclesial structures, practices, and beliefs are all well and good. But they are not yet close to what is needed: an account of resurrection as that which also *disrupts* structures, practices, and beliefs. As we have seen, the possibility of recognizing the Risen Lord always propagates as the interplay between a framing and a violation of the frame. Access to Jesus after Calvary depends on his paradoxical identification with the community and with its suffering but hoping least members. And that happens in the liturgy. Thus foundational theology, as it has been called, has to redesign itself by becoming a liturgical theology as well.

The breaking of the tomb of text is accomplished day by day in the Christian liturgy. The Gospels as Scripture are only one component of what is required in order for the church to have access to Jesus as Risen Lord and for the Lord to have access to us in the church. The Gospels themselves admit as much, especially when they are recounting how

11. See Fiorenza, *Foundational Theology* (see chap. 1, n. 4), 5–55. But the direction of Fiorenza's work is away from foundation building altogether and toward the theological securing of faith through three mutually reflecting activities: historical reconstruction, examination of retroductive warrants, and epistemological evaluation in terms of relevant background theories.
12. See Perkins, *Resurrection* (see chap. 1, n. 4), 391–420.
13. See O'Collins, *Jesus Risen.* O'Collins's survey of ancient, medieval, and recent theologies of resurrection is less critical than Fiorenza's and Perkins's, but his constructive work moves furthest beyond the project of foundation building.

people get to meet Jesus. As we have seen, recognition narratives emerge as dramatizations designed for demonstrating a competence, a practice. They show how people do this thing called seeing the Lord. As little dramas, they are meant to be watched by those of us who stand at a distance. We are the spectators. We get from the tableaux the kind of knowledge that spectators get, and that in Greek is called *theōria*: theoretical knowledge. *Watching Mary* see the Lord is not the same as seeing the Lord, but it does impart the theory or objective knowledge of what seeing the Lord would have to be like. The theory gleaned from the canonical narratives states this: that seeing the Lord is a praxis and that the body of the Risen Lord whom one sees is identified with the body of Jesus the crucified through a poiesis.

In the same way, the narratives about the sayings and doings of Jesus before Calvary are dramatizations designed for use in certifying whether the one seen after Calvary as Risen Lord is really Jesus of Nazareth, the crucified. They are meant to convey theoretical, historical knowledge. Reading the stories, one cannot tell how many other minds that knowledge passed through, how many people already used it to "make" the Risen Lord, before it got written up into the Gospel texts. It is "previously owned" theory. Because it has been used, the church knows it works. The Jesus stories are already poietic receptions of who he was, and they overlay their historical information with the traces of several generations of practical accessing of it.

Scholarly inquiry whose goal is to strip off the patina of ecclesial poiesis and praxis in order to lay bare the original surface of "the historical Jesus" may be extremely fine and valuable. But there is something precious to be recovered as well from the originary poiesis and praxis that peel away. They are not corrosion of the surface or static on the line; they are the line itself. Without them, there is no access to the Risen Lord for us. The theological recovery of the competence to "see the Lord" has to be a reconstruction of the poietic practices of the early, infracanonical ecclesial communities.

Thus the narratizing of "Jesus" is not a distortion; rather, it is a structural component of his availability as Risen Lord to the churches. However, it is not the *only* component. The narrative construction has to be broken up again by the same sort of processes, the same poietic ecclesial practices, that produced the narratives in the first place. This construction deconstructs itself. This enframing of "Jesus" circumscribes a surface *so that* the one thus bounded can violate the boundary. The inscription of the body of "Jesus" has to happen but only so that the body can break out of the tomb of text.

The Gospels set things in order, but in a disruptive way. Jesus is copied not in order to close the book on him but so that he can overwrite an ever-expanding community of human bodies. To imagine this, one has to keep in mind the superimposition of the "three" Christian tables. Book is bread is the needy little ones. Each one keeps the others from closing in upon itself. Because of the book, we know that the bread is more than bread. Because of the bread, we know that the book is not about the past. Because of the needy little ones, we know what to do with the book and the bread.

The availability of Jesus as Risen Lord has to be understood as a relation of these three. The efficacy that binds them to him should be understood as an intertextuality, a copying of Jesus. He is the copier and he is what is copied. Consideration of this aesthetic causality should be brought into the mainstream of the theological discussion that guides the life of the contemporary church.

Constructive proposals already have been made in sacramental theology and in secular aesthetic theory. Three approaches to the theorization of aesthetic efficacy can be considered here: aesthetic efficacy as reference, as symbolization, and as intertextuality. Traditional theories, in the pondering of the connection between communication and effect, have built on the assumption that the relation between word and reality may adequately be understood as one of *reference*. When one thing "refers to" another, the two are ontologically separate, and one determines or causes the other. These referential theories typically assume that God and people are separate realities, external to each other at the level of their very being. More recent theories of *symbolic causality* have sought to understand how sign and reality, although distinct, can also in some way be internal to one another. They have conceptually positioned the divine and the human in closer association. Most recently, the contemporary discussion of *intertextuality* has foregrounded some novel ways of conceiving an efficacy of identification between texts and bodies. The motif of "overwriting" that I have played with throughout this book is taken from that discussion. The theological appropriation of these textual theories is only just beginning. It conceptualizes divine agency as a phenomenon of productive meaning.

Efficacy as Reference

The basic premise of reference theories is that the meaning of sacramental ritual has been translated or lifted out of something else in a kind of point-for-point correspondence. The ritual that one performs today is regarded as an "ordinance" that the Lord once commanded. His command is understood to point forward in time to one's action today, while this action today refers back in time to that earlier command. The ritual is efficacious—it "works"—by virtue of the obedience motivating its accomplishment and the promise of the Lord. But the efficacy itself is understood to operate outside normal human spatiotemporal reality.

In the Western church Peter Lombard, a twelfth-century scholastic, was the first to explain sacramental action in terms of cause. Thomas Aquinas described the working of sacraments by juxtaposing the notions of cause and sign, without accounting for the dynamic connection of cause and sign. Sacramental efficacy was simply attributed to the mysterious power of Christ without further question. Theologians following Aquinas continued to investigate the sacraments' being as signs independently of their being as causes. Various accounts of sacramental efficacy are reviewed and cataloged by Bernard Leeming in his 1956 textbook. The viable theories inevitably attribute the power behind the working of the sacraments to some mysterious and divine causality inhering in the will of Jesus Christ. Leeming rejected "perfective" theories of sacramental causality, which hold that the sacramental ritual directly causes the grace of the sacrament. He favored "dispositive" theory, according to which the ritual first produces a symbolic reality (the *res et sacramentum*) through which grace is then bestowed. By contrast, Leeming criticized "physical" and "intentional" theories on grounds that they reduce the efficacy of sacramental symbolism to a mere imparting of knowledge, and he attributed the production of grace to either the efficacy of the physical elements themselves or the efficacy of God's intention working independently of the symbols.[14]

An able spokesman for the tradition of efficacy through reference, Leeming found an impenetrable mystery in the transformative power of the sacramental word. He could only liken this efficacy to that of God's utterance in creation and to the miracles of Jesus. He pointed to a mysterious divine power, presumably projected from beyond the human time-space continuum, as the source of sacramental efficacy. For example:

> Christ's words are effective because they are his; and sacraments are effective because they are Christ's words, and form a unity of power with him. . . . Christ's word in sacraments is effective because of what is expressed, because he expresses it. . . . All this . . . may

14. See Bernard Leeming, *Principles of Sacramental Theology* (Westminster, Md.: Newman Press, 1965), 283–345.

seem to leave unsolved the original question: How can a sign produce an effect other than knowledge? The answer must be that there is here a mystery.[15]

In light of the development of textual studies since Leeming wrote, I am inclined to locate that mystery within the why of God's decision to communicate life to human beings; the how today seems rather more intelligible.

A contemporary example of a reference theory of efficacy is the "horizon analysis" proposed by Margaret Mary Kelleher. With a philosophical basis in Bernard Lonergan's generalized empirical method, liturgical horizon analysis employs a series of questions that thoroughly describe a ritual in its relation to the community celebrating. The "basic units" to be interpreted are "ritual symbols: objects, actions, relationships, words, gestures, and arrangements of space."[16] The referring that is at work here is pointing from these items outward across space to elements of the community's life, and not so much backward in time to events of the first century, as with older reference theories.

Efficacy as Symbolization

Reference and symbolization are contrasting ways of accounting for the metaphysical status of an artifact or a ritual action. In cases of *reference,* the ritual transpiring here before us derives its meaning from some referent or agent that is imagined as distant in space or time, not present at all. The bridging of the spatial or temporal distance happens only in intention; text and referent are kept ontologically separate, and there is no doubt which is which. In cases of *symbolism,* however, what transpires here

15. See Leeming, *Principles,* 353–54. See also the postconciliar work of Raymond Vaillancourt, *Toward a Renewal of Sacramental Theology,* trans. Matthew J. O'Connell (Collegeville, Minn.: Liturgical Press, 1979). Vaillancourt identifies three functions of the sacrament: "Proclamation or revelation, realization or actualization, and finally celebration" (p. 91). He says that it is difficult to relate those three functions and especially "to elucidate this connection between efficacy and signification" (p. 100).

16. In encoding observations as data, the analysis digitalizes these basic units. In my opinion, this must result in a truncating distortion of the phenomena. Moreover, the metaphor of "horizon" betrays the visional orientation of this approach, an orientation that entails distance between observer and observed, and a flattening of the phenomena onto the two-dimensional surface of the retina. Walter Ong and others have contrasted the visional approach with the three-dimensional aural-oral approach. When hearing is chosen as the primary epistemological metaphor, the knower is understood to be immersed in and surrounded by the phenomena. For Kelleher's introduction to her approach, see "Liturgical Theology: A Task and a Method," 2–25, and "Liturgy: An Ecclesial Act of Meaning," 482–97.

before us is construed as some sort of shadow or hypostasis that shares in the being and agency of the absent thing that it represents. Efficacy by symbol differs from efficacy by reference in that the symbol is construed as a vehicle of real presence. Some of the most creative and pastorally fruitful work in twentieth-century theology has employed the theory of symbolic efficacy.

The German theologian Karl Rahner developed an influential theology of symbol by wedding the German Idealist philosophical tradition with neo-Thomism. His work in ecclesiology, Christology, and trinitarian theology helped to prepare the ground for the Second Vatican Council and to facilitate its reforms afterward. In several of the areas of his interest, Rahner made use of a peculiar category of being that he called the *Realsymbol*. Rahner conceived of this as the self-expression of an entity into a medium that is other than itself. The entity must so express itself in order to be itself. This expression, or *Realsymbol,* is not something separate and independent from the entity symbolized. The two do not exist apart; they are not even numerically "two," so it never becomes necessary to demonstrate how there could be an efficient material causality connecting them. Because the *Realsymbol* and its originating entity share being, the causality linking them can be described as formal, performative, and intrinsic.[17]

Rahner employed his invention the *Realsymbol* in positing an analogy of relationship. When he said that there is a "realsymbolic" relation between God's transcendental self-gift, on the one hand, and its categorial actualization in a sacrament, on the other, he meant that that relation resembles the causal relation between a whole human person and that person's body—a relation that he regarded as intrinsically, formally, and performatively causal. The human body is the *Realsymbol* of the whole human being because it is the particularizing expression of that person, encountered in a definite time and place.

On that analogy, Rahner said that God's self-gift comes to humankind through a chain of realsymbols: the humanity of Jesus Christ, the church, the sacraments, and particular experiences of sacramental liturgical celebrations. In his later writings, Rahner depicted the sacramental realsymbol

---

17. Rahner sketches his theory of the *Realsymbol* inconclusively in "Zur Theologie des Symbols," *Schriften zur Theologie,* vol. 4 (Einsiedeln: Benziger, 1960), 275–311. There is an English translation in *Theological Investigations,* vol. 4 (Baltimore: Helicon Press, 1966), 221–52, but it obscures the distinctions among important technical terms. Developments in Rahner's theory of *Symbolsursachlichkeit* can be traced in several other essays published in vols. 3, 4, 8, 10, and 14 of *Theological Investigations;* and in *Kirche und Sakramente* (Freiburg: Herder, 1960), trans. by W. J. O'Hara as *The Church and the Sacraments* (London: Burnes & Oates, 1963).

as a time- and place-specific utterance and hearing of God's word, in liturgy, which expresses grace that, while it was always there before, paradoxically is still the happening of "more" grace. Thus the sacrament, like the church itself, is an embodiment of God's outreaching uplifting grace.

Where Rahner used the church as analogue and model of the symbolic presencing of God in sacrament, Edward Schillebeeckx used Jesus himself but imagined in a transhistorical way. Schillebeeckx also developed an important approach to systematic theology based on symbolic efficacy, in which Christ is "the sacrament of the encounter with God" (as the title of an early work has it). Unlike Rahner, however, Schillebeeckx attempted to integrate his theoretical work with contemporary historical-Jesus research. In part owing to Schillebeeckx's engagement with scholarship in other fields, there seem to be two distinct and independent theories of sacramental symbolic efficacy operating in his work. One of them elaborates experiences of divine creation and the other interprets experiences of human creativity.[18]

In his earlier work, Schillebeeckx treated symbol as a link between heaven and earth. Symbol functioned incarnationally, as it were, and was imagined as a point where God's presence pierces the material world so that God may become active and available in the human present. To recognize such points—persons, things, events—for what they are is to have a creaturely experience, that is, an experience of one's own or another's being as being from God.

Although conducive to profound mystical insight, this early conception of symbol proved inadequate to certain challenges of modern political theory. It could describe the identity of activity between a long-ago, faraway Jesus and the here-and-now actions of Christians only by positing some divine prerogative whereby space and time were overcome. The divine will operated outside the structures of human historical being, to endow Jesus' acts with a special transhistorical boost that could reinsert itself in any subsequent time or place as the sacramental church. The early

---

18. Edward Schillebeeckx' 1952 masterwork *De Sacramentele heilseconomie* was condensed, updated, and republished in Dutch in 1959, and then in English as *Christ the Sacrament of the Encounter with God* (Kansas City, Mo.: Sheed Andrews and McMeel, 1963); this is the most representative example of his early approach to symbolic efficacy. Another influential volume, translated as *The Eucharist* (New York: Sheed & Ward, 1968), also belongs to that period. A new direction can be detected in *God the Future of Man* (New York: Sheed & Ward, 1968) and *The Understanding of Faith* (New York: Seabury Press, 1974). Schillebeeckx's mature work, informed by contemporary historical-Jesus research, is found in *Jesus: An Experiment in Christology* (New York: Seabury Press, 1979) and *Christ: The Experience of Jesus as Lord* (New York: Seabury Press, 1980).

Schillebeeckx did not yet theorize the church as a mediating factor working within the normal processes of human history. Instead, the church was reified as an institution and conceived as a kind of legal proxy for the absent physical body of Jesus. The sacraments, as institutional functions, took the place of Jesus' bodily gestures.

Metaphysically naive as these theories of Rahner and the younger Schillebeeckx may sound today, they were important conceptual steps beyond the referential theories that had been in place since the twelfth century. Schillebeeckx's own understanding of symbolic function continued to expand as he investigated and pondered the historical mechanisms by which the human future is made. As he observed the natural everyday efficacy of the political enactment of meaning, which substantially modified both the social and the material world, he began to describe a second or political dimension of sacramental symbolic function, in which the symbol works to link the present and the future. Symbol then became for him an ideal conception of the future, projecting itself upon the present reality, generating a "contrast experience," and moving human beings to action. When that ideal vision derives from a remembrance of Jesus or proclamation of God's kingdom, then the creative praxis incited can be experienced as an instance of human creativity empowered by God. Thus God's action works inside the normal human (psychological and political) mechanisms of building the future symbolically.

Yet the two understandings of symbolic function persist in uneasy tension in Schillebeeckx's mature work. Neither fully resolves the problem of finding and describing the sacramental principle of identity between what Jesus did and what Christians do. The problem of stating a coherent theory of sacramental symbolic efficacy hinges directly on the problem of conceiving divine agency and the metaphysical status of the deity. On the one hand, Schillebeeckx continued to regard the whole created world as a medium of communication from God, a medium in which God is immediately present. God permeates all creatures without displacing them; therefore, all creatures symbolize God. Most especially, wrote Schillebeeckx, God permeates the humanity of Jesus, so that God is most intensely present and active in Jesus. Similarly, the sacramental liturgy of the church is also a special intensification of God's ubiquitous presence. The experience of grace grows out of the fundamental experience of one's own createdness and of the creaturely status of all that is. The nonnecessary gratuity of existence, its giftedness, is the matrix for the special, liturgical experience of grace in the sacraments and also for the unfathomable "Abba experience" that Jesus enjoys with God. The liturgy heightens the symbolic value of selected created things and selected actions of creatures. Thus their natural ability to symbolize or present God is greatly amplified. I would call this theory "incarnational," because it seems to make an analogy between sacramental symbolic efficacy and the efficacy through which God is supposed to be personally present, active, and available in Jesus.

On the other hand, Schillebeeckx alternately conceptualized God in the human future, guaranteeing the success of the political processes through which human beings progressively perfect society and promising that reconciliation and justice will be achieved. In this view, the political upbuilding of the human world is fueled by what Schillebeeckx termed contrast experiences, that arise in critical negativity when a symbolic vision is projected upon present circumstances. The vision reflects both the future and the present, and so it anticipates and mediates reconciled meaning into current reality. The experience of grace, according to this theory, grows out of the foundational experience of one's own creativity, one's innate ability to refashion the world into something better, thanks to the insight and the impulse that the contrast experience affords.

In Schillebeeckx's mature work, then, the remembrance of Jesus' life and death, and of God's victory in him, supplies the symbolic utopian vision in light of which Christian emancipatory action can be taken. The sacramental liturgy *applies* that vision to present human suffering, thus unmasking it as nonnecessary and setting liberation in motion. At the same time, the liturgy is a continual reminder that human beings can never claim to have arrived at the last word, the final liberation. The last word is an eschatological word, and as such it belongs to God. Thus sacraments are symbols that bring the human future to presence. They link the theory of the Christian creed to the praxis of building a just society. I would call this second of Schillebeeckx's two theories the "political" one, because the analogue in secular experience on which it relies is the efficacy of the utopian vision in generating social change.[19]

Bernard Cooke has recently published a sweeping study of symbolic efficacy, which traces the propagation of divine presence throughout the history of the church. For Cooke, presence is a personal reality, and the presence of God to humanity can be conceptualized in three ways: in terms of periodic divine interventions in human affairs, as ongoing participation in life and activity, or as a dwelling in which God visits people and makes friends. The basic unifying symbol of Christian experience, for

---

19. These theories of symbolic efficacy are analyzed in excruciating detail in my 1983 doctoral dissertation, *Aesthetic Catechetics: An Approach via the Effective Symbol as Described by Schillebeeckx, Rahner, and Heidegger* (Ann Arbor, Mich.: University Microfilms International, 1984).

Cooke, is the mosaic of human history itself.[20] Rather than craft and defend a single metaphysics, as did Rahner, or a bifurcated metaphysics, as did Schillebeeckx, Cooke complements his treatment of the historical career of Christian symbolic efficacy with a survey of contemporary developments in cognate fields that must shape future theological efforts: anthropology, psychology, and linguistics and literary criticism.

Although theories of symbolic efficacy are designed to soft-pedal the distinction between symbol and symbolized, or effect and cause, nevertheless they depend on the doubtful premise that the thing presented, here and now, really exists, independently, *somewhere else.* This methodological blind spot advertises itself throughout the work of the theorists of symbolic efficacy. A handy, if perhaps unfair, illustration can be taken from the opening of Cooke's *Distancing of God.* Chapter 1 begins: "The first generation of Christianity was one marked by the immediacy of the Easter experience." *Easter?* Say what? "Easter" is the question, not an answer. But any approach by way of symbol must take it for granted that there *was* an Easter experience, which was and remains a stable enough quantity to merit its definite article, "the." The theorist of symbol sees no need to investigate what "Easter" was; nor has he left himself any conceptual maneuvering room in which to launch such an investigation if he wanted to.[21] Terms such as "God" and "grace" and "Christ" tend to function in Rahner's and Schillebeeckx's work as "Easter" functions for Cooke: as convenient points of departure, uncriticized foundations. Both reference theories and symbol theories of sacramental efficacy, then, conceive of the divine contact with the human as an incursion from without. Schillebeeckx's later theorization attempted to situate God within the structures of human political efficacy by means of the "contrast experience." Nevertheless Schillebeeckx insisted that God waits for humanity out there ahead of all time, at the eschaton.

To enable itself to talk about the efficacy of worship at all, then, theology has traditionally construed sacrament as an act of a God who was

---

20. See Cooke, *The Distancing of God.* Like Schillebeeckx, Cooke has been a major benefactor to twentieth-century theology and has remained in productive dialogue with developments in related scholarly fields. See, e.g., Bernard J. Cooke, *Ministry to Word and Sacraments: History and Theology* (Philadelphia: Fortress Press, 1977); and idem, *Sacraments and Sacramentality* (Mystic, Conn.: Twenty-Third Publications, 1983).

21. If not altogether unfair, it is surely unwise of me to single out for criticism Cooke's opening premise of an "Easter experience"—when my own point of departure in this book was the comparable premise that early Christians had practices of "seeing the Lord." The difference in our approaches, however, is that I have presented a detailed historical examination of what it must have meant for the earliest Christian generations to "make" Jesus or "see the Lord."

positioned outside creation and who reached into our reality to do something to us. Edward Farley calls this "the monarchical metaphor" of God's relation to the world.[22] Traditional theories of sacramental efficacy that invoke this metaphor, whether explicitly or tacitly, may be termed "incursive" theories, because they have posited a divine intrusion or incursion—an ultimately mythical conception. The "grace" that is the "effect" of worship must then be conceived as owing to Jesus' arbitrary volitional identification of himself with impersonal elements, and through them with the persons participating in the rite who desire that identification.

Efficacy as Intertextuality

It seems preferable, on both metaphysical and scriptural grounds, to theorize efficacy in a nonincursive way. Metaphysically, the referential and symbolic-presence approaches require a special realm for God beyond the universe and special exemptions from universal laws for divine agency. Furthermore, the possibility of interface between that other reality and this one where we live is difficult to account for. Even in this our own familiar world, the notions of "presence" and "reference" have begun to crumble. Moreover, a nonincursive theory would accord with the depiction of the origin of Jesus offered in the Gospel stories. Luke knows of no divine invasion at the conception of Jesus. Whatever violence might have transpired, God's act of begetting Jesus was written up as gentle, cooperative, and, as we have seen throughout this book, eminently textual. The word that became flesh was *yes,* and Mary said it.

In contrast to the incursive, monarchical conception of God's act through symbol, there are resources for theorizing a nonincursive, intertextual approach to sacramental efficacy in the contemporary scholarship of literary theory, phenomenology, and communications. Elaine Scarry, in work already introduced in chapter 9, has analyzed the function of artifacts as they impart meaning to human bodies. The artifact is first made by an outflow of human creativity from the body into elements of its material world. Sited, focused, and deflected back by means of the artifact once made, that creativity re-creates the human body itself. The artifact is a machine for overwriting the body. Scarry borrows extensively from Heidegger's work on technology and art in articulating her theory, but she refines and develops his insights profoundly. In her view,

---

22. See Farley, *Ecclesial Reflection,* 29–30.

the artifact stabilizes the meaning act that produced it, magnifies its effect, and replicates it continually.

Texts are artifacts, as I have argued throughout this book. They are produced poietically, and they then function to revise and overwrite the bodily reality of those who read them. Written texts are in continual exchange with bodily texts. Sacraments too are artifacts. Both the ritual liturgical actions and the material elements handled within those rituals appear as versions or readings of that which is also inscribed in scriptural texts, the bodily accessibility of Jesus. The assembly of worshiping Christians itself is also a kind of text: the triply genre-violating text that states that this body of Christ is neither slave nor leisured, Jew nor Greek, female nor male.

What is more, as artifacts these texts inscribe meaning onto the bodies of those who make themselves available for this transformation. The connection holding among the Jesus who died on Calvary, the "Jesus" produced in the Gospels, the church, the eucharist, and the poor, is one of rereading and rewriting, auto-inscription and hetero-inscription. That is, it is intertextual. There is no substantial "X" that can be isolated as a disembodied untexted meaning and held up for inspection as "the" essence of Christic reality. There is no transcendental referent of the Gospel or the liturgy. We get only these versions. Whatever the Christ is, it is highly contagious, but it doesn't survive outside texted bodies.[23]

Yet one's attachment to the "reference" theory of narrative dies hard. We need help in conceiving the truth and reliability of narrative and liturgy otherwise than as a pointing to something else out there distinct in space and time. The phenomenologist David Carr suggests that the truth of story consists in its ability to come true. Carr regards story as radically practical. The function of narrative is to facilitate action. To do anything at all, one must plan the act by adopting a future-retrospective viewpoint, that is, by grasping it within a story. The story works to bring into reality that which is planned.[24] Carr writes:

23. In the words of Herbert Schneidau, the transcendental signified may be described as "an absolute that means something all by itself beyond the play of differential systems." See Herbert N. Schneidau, "The Word against the Word: Derrida on Textuality," in *Derrida and Biblical Studies,* ed. Robert Detweiler, *Semeia* 23 (Chico, Calif.: Scholars Press, 1982), 5–28, esp. 11.

24. See David Carr, *Time, Narrative, and History* (Bloomington, Ind.: Indiana University Press, 1986). See especially the discussion on pp. 18–44. For a brief presentation of these insights, see David Carr, "Narrative and the Real World: An Argument for Continuity," *History and Theory* 25 (1986): 117–31. See also Stephen Crites's earlier essay "The Narrative Quality of Experience," *Journal of the American Academy of Religion* 39 (1971): 291–311.

To perform or carry out an action is to achieve its end. The achievement is the *resolution* of a certain suspense engendered by the contingency of the action. The notion of suspension and resolution, of
course, is often associated with music and reminds us of our example
of the melody. Action begins with a divergence between what is the
case and what is to be done, a divergence that has to be overcome and
which, but for my action, would remain. . . . Completion of the act is
thus not only a *temporal* closure, which brings a certain sequence (of
movements, for example) to a close, but the *practical* closure of a gap
between envisaged or protended result and reality.[25]

This is in some ways reminiscent of Schillebeeckx's view of a divine vision projected upon human reality, producing the "contrast experience."

Carr says that both the actions we undertake and the experiences we
undergo already are shaped like stories before we reflect upon them. Following Husserl, he argues that to hear a melody, one always retains the
notes immediately past while anticipating the ones to come. Likewise in a
tennis serve, one's involvement has this "melodic character" of grasping
the middle of one's gesture along with what has already been done and
what is about to be done. Carr places action at the genesis of story. Human
beings can act only by adopting a future-retrospective stance in regard to
the action, so as to see where we are going with it. We must grasp the act
as fitting into some story in order to be able to carry it out. This is the case
even for actions of greater duration than a tennis serve and also for collective actions of a social group as well as for individual actions. Narrative is
a strategy for controlling and making sense of reality, because narratives
arise from the need to act, to conduct human affairs. What is being said
here is more than the assertion that a myth of origins gives a people identity and direction. Rather, the spontaneous generation of stories is intri-
cately involved in the micromanagement of life. Stories arise from actions
to make further actions possible.

This insight of Carr's suggests a solution to the dilemma posed by
"reference"—a concept not only metaphysically suspect but utterly inadequate for theorizing sacramental access to Jesus. If text is story, and story is
action-oriented, then there seems to be a way to get from text to reality,
albeit not to the reality of *the past*, that is, of that which irrevocably *is*. Although any extratextual referent within the what-has-been remains irrevocably unreachable, the opposite is the case for *what is not-yet*. While no
transcendental signified as such exists for the text, the text itself exists for

25. Carr, *Time, Narrative,* 49.

the sake of the production and reproduction of extratextual reality: practices, social structures, human character, and so forth. The text exists as an implement for overwriting bodies. The function of texts has to do with the human future, not the human past. To write and read is to bring into reality.

Carr goes on to describe how story functions in the constitution of the self. The individual achieves identity through unifying the three viewpoints of his or her "life story": narrator, audience, and protagonist.[26] Far from being an extratextual reality referred to by the story or standing behind it, the self is as it were a byproduct of the story, arising as the whole intended when the three viewpoints are grasped in their unity. This is not to say that the self is an artifact; rather, artifacts such as stories are intrinsic to the coming-into-being of the human being as self.

In fact, Carr has reinforced this point in his choice of the two examples that illustrate the narrative structure of experience and action. For a melody is not just any chance raw experience, and a tennis serve is not a completely independent action.[27] The melody, and the game of tennis itself, already are textual artifacts. They are *copies*—dramatized versions— of experience and action, respectively. They disclose to us, *artificially*, what experience and action are. They also disclose, thanks to Carr's able reading, what the self is: precisely someone who plays with narrative and whom narrative sets into play.[28]

The efficacy of narrative artifacts, which Carr describes on an interpersonal scale, can be shown to operate amid large populations as well, through mass media. George Gerbner's studies of televised drama show that so-called entertainment has a decided influence on the expectations and decisions of viewers. Gerbner emigrated to the United States from his native Hungary during the Second World War and received his training in communications science in this country. His empirical work has been as

26. Carr, *Time, Narrative*, 58, 73.

27. That is to say, Carr could have chosen (but did not) as his illustration of experience a *non*-artificial experience such as listening to running water, or a *non*-artificial action such as wandering through a forest. In contrast, the artifacts of a melody and tennis already have been designed with the beginning-middle-end structure deliberately built into them.

28. Carr suggests that communities also attain their unity, identity, and endurance in much the same way individuals do: they are constituted narratively. He goes so far as to say that the group itself becomes a subject. See Carr, *Time, Narrative*, 122. This seems an insupportable analogy, for a community like the church does not unify itself by unifying the three narrative viewpoints at all. The church is not a subject-actor but rather a way of being that is *en*acted when the ecclesial activities of proclamation, celebration, and care are undertaken. Sacramental celebration is one sort of activity that brings about the church. This I take to be the gist of the "portraiture" of ecclesiality presented by Farley in *Ecclesial Reflection*.

controversial as it is fascinating, but what is of particular interest here is the theoretical explanation that he offers in order to interpret his data.[29]

For Gerbner, the study of communications can be organized into three enterprises. (1) *Institutional process analysis* focuses on the political and economic relationships among groups like sponsors, labor unions, and media managers who collaborate in the creation of programming. (2) *Message system analysis* focuses on the components of the programming itself, particularly the kinds of characters represented and the typical fates they meet in the programming. (3) *Cultivation analysis* focuses on the correlation between the features of the fictional world in the programming that one absorbs and the expectations one subsequently entertains concerning the "real world." So through message system analysis, Gerbner has shown that the world of television drama deviates in specific ways from the real world as described in U.S. census data or crime statistics. For example, on television the percentage of the population over age sixty is much smaller than in the U.S. census, while older people are much more likely to be sick, crazy, or victims of violence than in real life. Then, through cultivation analysis, Gerbner has shown that when the beliefs and choices of people who watch a great deal of televised drama are compared with those who watch little, the expectations and behaviors of the high viewers resemble the television world, while low viewers form expectations more in keeping with reality. As Gerbner says, the mass-mediated messages have "cultivated" beliefs and attitudes, and these lead to decisions about the conduct of personal and political life. The sign brings about what it signifies. To pursue the example given, high television viewers show relatively low regard for the elderly in responses to interviews.

This phenomenon of "cultivation" at work through the mass media is a kind of aesthetic efficacy, although as a scientist Gerbner stops short of asserting what he cannot actually observe: a *causing* of behavior by communication. In cultivation, Gerbner sees the world revealed as what it is *not*, through a kind of self-fulfilling prophecy in which future behaviors are conformed to the distorted images in televised stories (as people's

29. Gerbner signaled the beginning of his impressive researches in "Toward 'Cultural Indicators': The Analysis of Mass Mediated Message Systems," in *The Analysis of Communication Content*, ed. George Gerbner et al. (New York: John Wiley & Sons, 1969), 123–32. The research is longitudinal, with periodic technical reports available from the Annenberg School of Communications at the University of Pennsylvania and summaries published occasionally in the *Journal of Communication*. See, e.g., George Gerbner et al., "The 'Mainstreaming'" of America: Violence Profile No. 11," *Journal of Communication* 30 (1980): 10–29. Gerbner's work has been substantiated in other parts of the world; see G. Melischek et al., *Cultural Indicators: An International Symposium* (Vienna: Akademie der Wissenschaften, 1983).

"buying power" is put at the disposal of the sponsors). In Carr's view of narrativity, on the other hand, equally artificial stories constitute the self as they make action possible. In both cases, any "reference" to what is (that is, to "the past") is insignificant compared to the bringing into being of new realities, new identities and identifications. The enframing of "the past" functions to produce a future.

But I have argued that the enframing at work in Christian narratives and sacraments is unstable and bound to split open. It is dehiscent. Its provisional stabilization sets up a picture of the past only to shatter the pastness of what is pictured. The metaphor of dehiscence recalls how pods split open at their seams and spray seeds into the autumn wind.[30] The dehiscence or seam splitting of the Gospels is a tendency they have in common with certain contemporary aesthetic products, and one that has not gone unnoticed by literary critics. The self-mocking, self-exploding potential of artworks has been examined by the historian and philosopher Alan Megill. Megill's thesis is this: "Works of art in the postmodern mode demonstrate an ontological concern, continually asking what it is to be a sculpture, a play, a novel, a painting."[31]

This suggests an innovative hermeneutic approach to reading ecclesial artworks such as the Gospels and the sacraments. Arguably, Matthew's Gospel takes for its principal theme the question, *What is it to be a Gospel?* The Matthean text persists in asking, What does it mean to be a narrative that both identifies Jesus as Lord and also provides a means of access to this recognition and to him? Matthew's Gospel is an edition or copy of Mark that introduces not only many sayings of Jesus unknown to Mark but also an explicit concern about the function of authoritative teaching. The teacher, or scribe trained in the reign of God, brings forth things old and new from the storehouse (Matt. 13:52). There is what Jacques Derrida calls *différance* in such teaching.[32] It is not burdened with slavish duplication. Yet not one iota, not one dot of previous text can pass

---

30. See Taylor, *Erring: A Deconstructive A/Theology* (see chap. 3, n. 14), 6, 92.

31. Alan Megill, *Prophets of Extremity* (Berkeley and Los Angeles: University of California Press, 1985), 263.

32. Jacques Derrida has authored an essay entitled "Différance," but it is no introduction to this slippery concept. See Jacques Derrida, *Margins of Philosophy,* trans. Alan Bass (Chicago: University of Chicago Press, 1982), 3–27. Différance is the ability or latitude for two texts to be versions of one another without being "the same," and without having one be the original and the other be the copy. We tend to talk and write as if the relations of identity and difference were absolutes and were mutually exclusive; however, this is a convention. Relationships are much more subtle than that. Meaning subsists in the différance, or variance of terms from one another.

away (Matt. 5:18). The teacher is to have no authority, not even the title of master (Matt. 23:8). Yet this teacher's text presumes to impose closure upon the words of Jesus so that no new ones can be added—added by the charismatic prophets who were, in Matthew's time, still able to evoke the real-time presence of the Risen Lord by wonder-working, eucharistizing, and speech "in Jesus' name." Matthew's Jesus is not really still "present," despite the closing promise of the Gospel. The text asserts that authority resides in the words of Jesus, but at the same time this teaching text retains authority over those very words and adjusts them to fit purposes of its own.

In the same vein, we can read Christian worship as text that continually asks, *What is it to be worship?* —that is, to be an inscribing of bodies that purports to unite people and God. Liturgy always plays with questions: Who are we? What are we doing? Where is God? Worship is by no means the mere spontaneous outer expression of some inward preexisting extraliturgical relationship. Rather, the relationship itself is at issue, at wager, at risk in the celebration. The Eucharist celebrates not so much the actuality of past events—life, death, resurrection—as the possibility of resurrection experience ("seeing the Lord") within its own text. During and through sacramental worship, resurrection itself ceases to be some sublime transcendental signified that happened "back then" and now is a datum, a *fait accompli.* But what, then, does resurrection become? We must ask about the validity of the liturgy, not in terms of its alleged correspondence to alleged events of the past that now are closed off and external to it and ourselves, but rather in terms of its creative potential to copy onto our bodies and into their practices the patterns that are textually mediated in the Gospels.

God's Action

The theology that can make sense in the postmodern situation will not be one that insists on a God beyond text or on causality from beyond the textual world. Sacramental efficacy, like all of "God's acts," must be reconceived as an intertextuality, that is, a revising of texts in light of other texts, an issuing of more texts, more significations. Derrida and others criticize "logocentric thought" that clings to the myth that there is a plan somewhere faraway against which we are to judge our own reality.[33] They

---

33. See Taylor, *Erring,* esp. 58–59; see also Jacques Derrida, *Of Grammatology,* trans. G. C. Spivak (Baltimore: Johns Hopkins University Press, 1974), esp. chap. 1.

discredit the idea of a preexistent Logos, one who is "the original" to whom earthly patterns conform—for there are no originals, only copies. In the postmodern age, it is futile for theology to insist on such a Logos; just as it was futile for theology in the modern age to insist on a God who intervened from beyond to cause empirical effects in the physical world. As modern theology worked out a "place" for God in the "depth dimension," postmodern theology must work out a place for God in/as some dimension of textuality.

The Jesus of the Synoptic Gospels has declined to be the transcendental signified, the original, against whom the little ones, as copies, might be compared in order to discover that they are not he. Rather, the earliest versions of Jesus that we can find already are identified with the little ones. Yet this is not to say that they are "the same" as he.[34] Rather, he is available in them and can be found and recognized in them.

What, then, makes recognition possible? In human experience, recognition is the insight that identifies someone here present but unknown with someone known previously but thought now to be absent. You need both elements—the past known and the present unknown—so that the present can become known as being another version of the past known. Therefore you do need some definite information about the past. In Jesus' case, you need to know details of his life, message, and work; this is what the Gospel narratives purport to give. That is why they seal the record of Jesus in an attempt to preclude the possibility of infinite variations in the things he might say. But these definitive portrayals are given for the sake of present recognition, so that someone or something presently encountered can be identified with the real Jesus.

The enframing of Jesus did not conclude with the Gospels. It continued as the impulse toward formulation of creeds, toward dogmatic definition, toward systematic theology, and toward critical analysis of Scripture and dogma. Each successive wave of discursive enframing put greater distance between the real Jesus and the present. But running counter to the enframing impulse in every age of the church has been the impulse toward

---

34. It is curious that the term "the same" can never be used in an absolutely proper sense. Two things cannot really be the same, or they would not be two things. On the other hand, to say "it is not the same" is to say "it is not it." Both sameness and lack of sameness seem to be impossible predicates. Related to this puzzle is Mark C. Taylor's critique of such a thing as a book in chap. 4 of *Erring*. He says that a book tries to mime the world; yet: "Perfect mimesis is no longer mimesis. If imitation were to realize itself completely, it would negate itself by actually becoming the thing imitated. Mimesis, therefore, necessarily bears witness to its own failure" (see p. 82).

liturgical celebration of Jesus' immediacy—a celebration that overcomes the distancing of the narrative campaign and sets Jesus loose in the present. The imaging of resurrection in worship puts the lie to the proclamation that Jesus got up and went a long time ago. It means to restore his rising in realtime.

In the trinitarian theology elaborated over many centuries out of the Gospels, the one whom John called Logos is also a version of God—that is, God's copy. The Logos as God's copy is a reimagination of how God companions humanity in a nonincursive way, that is, not as a being would impact another, separate being. We say in effect that *God copies* when, affirming the doctrine of the incarnation, we say that God is available in Jesus, and when, affirming the doctrine of the resurrection, we say that the real Jesus is available to us despite the narrative removal in time and place that is necessary to preserve his identity.

Jesus is copy who copies. The Gospels identify Jesus with needy little ones. To see or recognize the Risen Lord is to see him in them. To reach them is to reach him. But the Gospels also inquire into the dynamics of recognizing Jesus mystically, spiritually present during worship. These two possible modes of Jesus' availability, through care and through cult, mutually support each other and are secured in each other. The Gospel texts do indeed point "beyond" themselves, toward a Risen Lord who is extratextual in certain specific ways. But they qualify those ways quite carefully. It is not that the Risen Lord is the "transcendental signified" for the texts, in the sense of standing independently in the past where they can "refer to" him. *He cannot be both past and risen,* for to be past means not to be active and available now. The canonical texts decline to identify the Risen Lord as one who is available through stories as what is past. Rather, he is on the loose beyond the canonical texts. The name of Jesus, a text, attaches itself to persons and to experiences of empowerment that turn up day by day in the infinitely varying career of the church. The referent of the Gospel texts, so to speak, is toward versions of themselves being continually inscribed into human activities: that is, toward ongoing discoveries of the Risen Lord that they make possible.

We can theorize sacramental worship as the deconstruction of resurrection. That "of," indicating that "resurrection" is in the genitive case, can have two senses: an objective and a subjective. In the *objective* sense, resurrection as the tale of a vacated tomb gets deconstructed. The story of an event confined within the past, as Easter morning, falls apart. When resurrection is made the object of a deconstructive reading, one is brought to the realization that resurrection cannot have been an event in the past. One is tempted to conclude that resurrection therefore has no reality at all. But in the *subjective* sense of the genitive, when the tale itself is exercising deconstructive force, what falls apart are the structures bounding human availability. The liturgy is the means of crossing the eschatological frontier. It overcomes the opposition between what is "Jesus" and what is not. Sacramental liturgy is the means of assimilating to Jesus many persons, communities, and even material elements that, according to our accustomed narrative time line, could not possibly have supported any such connection.

Resurrection, then, is "about" the availability of Jesus as Risen Lord in the activities of caring for the poor and celebrating the liturgy. It is "about" renovating the body-inscribing genres of race, class, and gender. In view of the practical intentionality of any narrative, one might assert that the appearance narratives were designed to support historical first-century activities of care and cult and do not report whatever transpired two mornings after Jesus died. Yet such an assertion would itself founder on its own attempt to constitute the "event" of such a designing! Better, then, to say that relationships of coequal, symbiotic intertextuality obtain among these texts: the emptied tomb itself, the canonical Gospels, the activities of caring for needy little ones, and the ritual celebration of the sacramental liturgy. These are versions of the same reality: four renditions of a Christic pattern. The sacramental cult is text rendering other texts.

We may theorize resurrection, then, as the rupture of human temporal existence, from the inside out. Ordinarily death itself does not destroy human being; rather, death organizes it. Human being is unique, as Heidegger saw, in that it is a "being toward death."[35] Belief in resurrection is a belief about time, that is, about the structures of human availability as they are conditioned by our experience of time. Death has meant becoming part of the past, and access to the past cannot be had on the same terms as access to the present. Beyond violating the laws of biology, therefore, resurrection violates the laws of phenomenology. It disobeys the laws of access to the past, that is, to what is. This disobedience is not merely epistemological or psychological, but metaphysical, given that the being of people is really transformed by the way their bodies are written. Resurrection deconstructs the narrative structure by which we grasp the past. Ironically, the resurrection of Jesus also was relegated to the past very early in the history of the Christian community, which turned resurrection into a story about events that had happened to other people.

---

35. The clarification of human time consciousness was a major contribution of Heidegger's phenomenology; see Martin Heidegger, *Being and Time*, trans. John Macquarrie and Edward Robinson (New York: Harper & Row, 1962).

We may theorize worship as replications of the pattern of Jesus' relationship with God in multiple media. In sacramental communication, God's offer of reconciliation and its human acceptance in Jesus Christ become available through effective interpretation in the media of song, gesture, speech, textiles, sculpture, architecture, water, bread, fire, incense, oil, salt, and wine. Worship is scripted and inscribing artifact. If *only* story were working in worship, worship could not give access to Jesus: Jesus would be locked into the past just as securely as any other "transcendental signified," and story wouldn't reach him. What's happening in worship is more subtle and profound: an identification of the Jesus of the past with someone unrecognized in the midst of the church. The possibility of access to this "one who stands among you whom you do not know" (John 1:26) depends on resurrection's rupture of temporality.

A Personal Future

In examining the possibility of recognizing Jesus as Risen Lord, this discussion has left untouched the issue of most acute concern as each of us faces the certitude of our own death. What will happen *to me?* Traditional belief in the resurrection of Jesus has envisioned him as surviving Calvary to be reunited with his Father in the love of the Spirit. We who are looking for the Risen Lord have been hoping that death would be the gateway to a new home and to renewal of loving relationships with those who have gone through the gate before us: with Jesus, sure, but also with parents and companions and others whom we loved in life. What happens to that hope, now in the midst of all this fancy aesthetic efficacy, inscription of bodies, and rupturing of foundations? It is all very nice that Jesus could be recognized by his bereaved disciples after Calvary—but could he recognize himself? Did his personal awareness continue; was *he himself* still around to enjoy whatever happened after Calvary? Did he come out of the tomb laughing? *Will I?*

These questions are profoundly important. But they may be pursued only on the basis of a faithful reconsideration of the ecclesial traditions (such as I have tried to offer in this volume); they cannot be allowed to preempt it. For now, I will defer these questions in the same way Jesus did. On the issue of personal resurrection, the Synoptic Jesus shrugs off speculation and refers inquirers to Moses. The Torah declares the permanance of each human body with the ancient affirmation that we are created in God's image. God is the God of the living: Abraham, Isaac, Jacob, and your parents and mine. Resurrection is the aesthetic consequence of our divinely designed, *bodily* imaging of God.

Bibliography

Abu-Lughod, Lila. *Veiled Sentiments: Honor and Poetry in a Bedouin Society.* Berkeley and Los Angeles: University of California Press, 1986.

———. "Zones of Theory in the Anthropology of the Arab World." *Annual Review of Anthropology* 18 (1989): 267–306.

Achtemeier, Paul J. *Mark.* Philadelphia: Fortress Press, 1975.

Adan-Bayewitz, David. "Kefar Ḥananya, 1986." *Israel Exploration Journal* 37 (987): 178–79.

———. "Kefar Ḥananya, 1987." *Israel Exploration Journal* 39 (1989): 98–99.

———. "Kefar Ḥananya, 1989." *Israel Exploration Journal* 41 1991): 186–88.

———. *Common Pottery in Roman Galilee: A Study of Local Trade.* Bar-Ilan Studies in Near Eastern Languages and Culture. Ramat-Gan: Bar-Ilan University Press, 1993.

Adan-Bayewitz, David, and Isadore Perlman. "The Local Trade of Sepphoris in the Roman Period." *Israel Exploration Journal* 40 (1990): 153–72.

Afshar, Haleh, ed. *Women, State, and Ideology: Studies from Africa and Asia.* New York: Macmillan, 1987.

Archer, Léonie J. "The Role of Jewish Women in the Religion, Ritual and Cult of Graeco-Roman Palestine." In *Images of Women in Antiquity,* edited by Averil Cameron and Amélie Kuhrt, 273–87. Detroit: Wayne State University Press, 1983.

———. *Her Price Is Beyond Rubies: The Jewish Woman in Graeco-Roman Palestine.* Journal for the Study of the Old Testament Supplement Series, no. 60. Sheffield: JSOT Press, 1990.

Ardener, Shirley, ed. *Perceiving Women.* New York: John Wiley and Sons, 1975.

Arthus, Marilyn. "Women in the Ancient World." In *Conceptual Frameworks for Studying Women's History: Four Papers,* by Marilyn Arthus, Joan Kelly-Gadol, Renate Bridenthal, and Gerda Lerner, 1–15. Bronxville, N.Y.: Sarah Lawrence College Women's Studies Publications, 1976.

Aune, David E. *Prophecy in Early Christianity and the Ancient Mediterranean World.* Grand Rapids: William B. Eerdmans, 1983.

———. *The New Testament in Its Literary Environment.* Philadelphia: Westminster, 1987.

Avi-Yonah, Michael. *Hellenism and the East: Contacts and Interrelations from Alexander to the Roman Conquest.* Jerusalem: Hebrew University, 1978.

Bagatti, Bellarmino. *The Church From the Circumcision: History and Archaeology of the Judaeo-Christians.* Publications of the Studium Biblicum Franciscanum, smaller series, no. 2. Translated by Eugene Hoade. Jerusalem: Franciscan Printing Press, 1971.

———. *The Church From the Gentiles: History and Archaeology.* Publications of the Studium Biblicum Franciscanum, smaller series, no. 4. Translated by Eugene Hoade. Jerusalem: Franciscan Printing Press, 1971.

Balme, Maurice, and Gilbert Lawall. *Athenaze: An Introduction to Ancient Greek.* New York and Oxford: Oxford University Press, 1990.

Barth, Fredrik, editor. *Ethnic Groups and Boundaries: The Social Organization of Culture Difference.* Boston: Little, Brown and Company, 1969.

Batey, Richard A. "Jesus and the Theater." *New Testament Studies* 30 (1984): 563–74.

———. *Jesus and the Forgotten City: New Light on the Urban World of Jesus.* Grand Rapids: Baker Book House, 1991.

Bauer, Walter, comp. *A Greek-English Lexicon of the New Testament and Other Early Christian Literature.* Translated and adapted by William F. Arndt and F. Wilbur Gingrich. 2d ed. Chicago: University of Chicago Press, 1979.

Baum, Gregory. "The Church Against Itself." In *World Catechism or Inculturation,* Concilium no. 204, edited by Johann-Baptist Metz and Edward Schillebeeckx, xiii–xv. Edinburgh: T & T Clark, 1989.

Bell, Catherine. *Ritual Theory, Ritual Practice.* New York: Oxford University Press, 1992.

Berchman, Robert M. *From Philo to Origen: Middle Platonism in Transition.* Chico, Calif.: Scholars Press, 1984.

Bergen, Ann. "Language and the Female in Early Greek Thought." *Arethusa* 16 (1983): 69–95.

Bertiaume, Guy. *Les rôles du mágeiros: Étude sur la boucherie, la cuisine et le sacrifice dans la Grèce ancienne.* Leiden: E.J. Brill, 1982.

Bertram, Georg. "*paideuō, paideia . . .*" *Theological Dictionary of the New Testament* 5: 596–625. Compiled by Gerhard Kittel, edited by Gerhard Friedrich, and translated and edited by Geoffrey W. Bromiley. Grand Rapids: Eerdmans, 1964–74.

Blackman, Philip. *Mishnayoth*. 6 vols. London: Mishnah Press (L. M. Schoenfeld), 1955.

Blair, J. "Private Parts in Public Spaces: The Case of Actresses." In *Women and Space: Ground Rules and Social Maps*, edited by Shirley Ardener, 205–28. London and New York: St. Martin's Press, 1981.

Bourdieu, Pierre. *Outline of a Theory of Practice*. Translated by Richard Nice. Cambridge: Cambridge University Press, 1977.

Boring, M. Eugene. "How May We Identify Oracles of Christian Prophets in the Synoptic Tradition? Mark 3:28-29 as a Test Case." *Journal of Biblical Literature* 91 (1972): 501–21.

Brown, Cheryl Anne. *No Longer Be Silent: First Century Jewish Portraits of Biblical Women*. Gender and the Biblical Tradition, Louisville: Westminster/John Knox, 1992.

Brown, Peter. *The Body and Society: Men, Women, and Sexual Renunciation in Early Christianity*. New York: Columbia University Press, 1988.

Bultmann, Rudolf. "New Testament and Theology." In *Kerygma and Myth: A Theological Debate*, by Rudolf Bultmann, Ernst Lohmeyer, Julius Schniewind, Helmut Thielicke, and Austin Farrar, edited by Hans Werner Bartsch, translated by Reginald H. Fuller, rev. ed. New York: Harper & Row, Harper Torchbooks, 1961.

———. *History of the Synoptic Tradition*. Rev. ed. Translated by John Marsh. New York: Harper & Row, 1963.

———. *"peithō . . ." Theological Dictionary of the New Testament* 6: 1–11. Compiled by Gerhard Kittel, edited by Gerhard Friedrich, and translated and edited by Geoffrey W. Bromiley. Grand Rapids: Eerdmans, 1964–74.

———. *"pisteuō . . ." Theological Dictionary of the New Testament* 6: 174–228. Compiled by Gerhard Kittel, edited by Gerhard Friedrich, and translated and edited by Geoffrey W. Bromiley. Grand Rapids: Eerdmans, 1964–74.

Calame, Claude. *Les choeurs de jeunes filles en Grèce archaïque*. 2 vols. Rome: Edizioni del'Ateneo & Bizzarri, 1977.

Cameron, Averil, and Amélie Kuhrt, eds. *Images of Women in Antiquity*. Detroit: Wayne State University Press, 1983.

Cameron, Ronald D., ed. *The Other Gospels: Non-Canonical Gospel Texts*. Philadelphia: Westminster, 1982.

Carnley, Peter. *The Structure of Resurrection Belief*. Oxford: Clarendon, 1987.

Carr, David. *Time, Narrative, and History*. Bloomington: Indiana University Press, 1986.

———. "Narrative and the Real World: An Argument for Continuity." *History and Theory* 25 (1986): 117–31.

Castelli, Elizabeth A. *Imitating Paul: A Discourse of Power*. Louisville: Westminster/John Knox, 1991.

Charlesworth, James H. _Jesus Within Judaism: New Light from Exciting Archaeological Discoveries._ New York: Doubleday, 1988.

———, ed. _The Old Testament Pseudepigrapha._ Garden City, N.Y.: Doubleday, 1985.

Chauvet, Louis-Marie. _Symbol et sacrement. Une relecture sacramentelle de l'existence chrétienne._ Paris: Éditions du Cerf, 1987.

Chilton, Bruce D. "The Transfiguration: Dominical Assurance and Apostolic Vision." _New Testament Studies_ 27 (1980): 115–24.

———. _A Galilean Rabbi and his Bible: Jesus' Use of the Interpreted Scripture of His Time._ Wilmington: Michael Glazier, 1984.

———. _God in Strength: Jesus' Announcement of the Kingdom._ Sheffield: JSOT Press, 1987.

———. _Profiles of a Rabbi: Synoptic Opportunities in Reading About Jesus._ Brown Judaic Studies, no. 117. Atlanta: Scholars Press, 1989.

———. "Recent and Prospective Discussion of Memra." In _From Ancient Israel to Modern Judaism: Intellect in Quest of Understanding,_ vol. 2, edited by Jacob Neusner, Ernest S. Frerichs, and Nahum M. Sarna, 119–37. Brown Judaic Studies, no. 173. Atlanta: Scholars Press, 1989.

———. _The Temple of Jesus: His Sacrificial Program Within a Cultural History of Sacrifice._ University Park: Pennsylvania State University Press, 1992.

———, trans. _The Isaiah Targum._ Wilmington: Michael Glazier, 1987.

Chodorow, Nancy. _The Reproduction of Mothering: Psychoanalysis and the Sociology of Gender._ Berkeley: University of California Press, 1978.

———. _Feminism and Psychoanalytic Theory._ New Haven: Yale University Press, 1989.

Claassen, Cheryl, editor. _Exploring Gender Through Archaeology: Selected Papers From the 1991 Boone Conference._ Monographs in World Archaeology 11. Madison, Wis.: Prehistory Press, 1992.

Clark, Gillian. _Women in the Ancient World._ New Surveys in the Classics, no. 21. Oxford: Oxford University Press, 1989.

Cohen, Shaye J. D. _From the Maccabees to the Mishnah._ Philadelphia: Westminster, 1987.

Cole, Susan G. "Could Greek Women Read and Write?" In _Reflections of Women in Antiquity,_ edited by Helene P. Foley, 219–45. New York: Gordon and Breach Science Publishers, 1981.

Conkey, Margaret W. and Janet D. Spector. "Archaeology and the Study of Gender." _Advances in Archaeological Method and Theory_ 7 (1984): 1–38.

Connerton, Paul. _How Societies Remember. Themes in the Social Sciences._ New York: Cambridge University Press, 1989.

Cooke, Bernard J. _Ministry to Word and Sacraments: History and Theology._ Philadelphia: Fortress Press, 1977.

———. _Sacraments and Sacramentality._ Mystic, Conn.: Twenty-Third Publications, 1983.

————. *The Distancing of God: The Ambiguity of Symbol in History and Theology.* Minneapolis: Fortress Press, 1990.

Corley, Kathleen. *Private Women, Public Meals: Social Conflict and Women in the Synoptic Gospels.* Peabody, Mass.: Hendrickson Publishers, 1993.

Craig, William Lane. *Assessing the New Testament Evidence for the Historicity of the Resurrection of Jesus.* Vol. 16 of *Studies in the Bible and Early Christianity.* Lewiston: Edwin Mellon Press, 1989.

Crites, Stephen. "The Narrative Quality of Experience." *Journal of the American Academy of Religion* 39 (1971): 291–311.

Crossan, John Dominic. "Kingdom and Children: A Study in the Aphoristic Tradition." In *Semeia* 29, edited by Daniel Patte, 75–95. Chico, Calif.: Scholars Press, 1983.

————. *Sayings Parallels: A Workbook for the Jesus Tradition.* Philadelphia: Fortress Press, 1986.

————. *The Cross That Spoke: The Origins of the Passion Narrative.* San Francisco: Harper & Row, 1988.

————. *The Historical Jesus: The Life of a Mediterranean Jewish Peasant.* San Francisco: HarperSanFrancisco, 1991.

Daremberg, Charles, and Edmund Saglio. *Dictionnaire des antiquités grèques et romains.* Paris: Hachette, 1877–1919.

Davidson, Benjamin D. *The Analytical Hebrew and Chaldee Lexicon: Consisting of an Alphabetical Arrangement . . . with Grammatical Remarks and Explanations.* London: Bagster and Sons, n.d.

Davis, John H. R. *People of the Mediterranean: An Essay in Comparative Social Anthropology.* London: Routledge & Kegan Paul, 1977.

D'Arms, John. "The Roman *Convivium* and the Idea of Equality." In *Sympotica: A Symposium on the* Symposion, edited by Oswyn Murray, 308–20. Oxford: Clarendon, 1990.

Dean-Jones, Leslie. "Menstrual Bleeding According to the Hippocratics and Aristotle." *Transactions of the American Philological Association* 119 (1989): 177–92.

Derrida, Jacques. *Of Grammatology.* Translated by G. C. Spivak. Baltimore: Johns Hopkins University Press, 1974.

————. "Différance." In *Margins of Philosophy,* translated by Alan Bass, 3–27. Chicago: University of Chicago Press, 1982.

Des Bouvrie, Synnøve. *Women in Greek Tragedy: An Anthropological Approach.* Oslo: Norwegian University Press, 1990.

de Ste. Croix, G. E. M. *The Class Struggle in the Ancient Greek World From the Archaic Age to the Arab Conquests.* Ithaca: Cornell University Press, 1981.

de Strycker, Emile. *La form la plus ancienne de Protévangile de Jacques: Recherches sur le Papyrus Bodmer 5 avec une édition critique du texte grec et une traduction annotée.* Brussels: Société des Bollandistes, 1961.

Detienne, Marcel, and Jean-Paul Vernant. *Cunning Intelligence in Greek Culture and Society.* Translated by Janet Lloyd. Atlantic Highlands, N.J.: Humanities Press, 1978.

―――. *The Cuisine of Sacrifice Among the Greeks.* Translated by Paula Wissing. Chicago: University of Chicago Press, 1989.

Dewey, John. *Philosophy and Civilization.* New York: Minton, Balch & Co., 1931.

Donaldson, Terence L. *Jesus on the Mountain: A Study in Matthean Theology.* Journal for the Study of the New Testament Supplement Series, no. 8. Sheffield: JSOT Press, 1985.

Douglas, Mary. *Natural Symbols: Explorations in Cosmology.* New York: Random House, Pantheon Books, 1970.

―――. *Implicit Meanings: Essays in Anthropology.* London: Routledge & Kegan Paul, 1975.

duBois, Page. *Sowing the Body: Psychoanalysis and Ancient Representations of Women.* Chicago: University of Chicago Press, 1988.

―――. *Torture and Truth.* New York and London: Routledge, 1991.

Dunbabin, Katherine. "*Triclinium* and *Stibadium.*" In *Dining in a Classical Context,* edited by William J. Slater, 121–48. Ann Arbor: University of Michigan Press, 1991.

Ebner, Eliezer. *Elementary Education in Ancient Israel During the Tannaitic Period (10–220 C.E.).* New York: Bloch Publishing Company, 5716/1956.

Engels, D. "The Problem of Female Infanticide in the Greco-Roman World." *Classical Philology* 75 (1980): 112–20.

―――. "The Use of Historical Demography in Ancient History." *Classical Quarterly* 34 (1984): 386–93.

Erikson, Erik H. *Childhood and Society.* 2d ed. New York: W. W. Norton & Company, 1963.

―――. *Identity and the Life Cycle.* New York: W. W. Norton & Company, 1980.

Farley, Edward. *Ecclesial Reflection: An Anatomy of Theological Method.* Philadelphia: Fortress Press, 1982.

Fehr, Burkhard. "Entertainers at the *Symposion*: The *Akletoi* in the Archaic Period." In *Sympotica: A Symposium on the* Symposion, edited by Oswyn Murray, 185–95. Oxford: Clarendon, 1990.

Fiorenza, Francis Schüssler. *Foundatonal Theology: Jesus and the Church.* New York: Crossroad, 1984.

Fischel, Henry A., ed. *Essays in Greco-Roman and Related Talmudic Literature.* New York: KTAV Publishing House, 1977.

Fitzmeyer, Joseph A. *The Gospel According to Luke (I–IX): Introduction, Translation, and Notes.* The Anchor Bible. Garden City, N.Y.: Doubleday, 1981.

Flax, Jane. *Thinking in Fragments: Psychoanalysis, Feminism, and Postmodernism in the Contemporary West.* Berkeley: University of California Press, 1990.

Forbes, R. J. *Studies in Ancient Technology.* Vols. 3 and 4. Leiden: Brill, 1955 and 1956.

Foucault, Michel. *Discipline and Punish: The Birth of the Prison.* Translated by Alan Sheridan. New York: Random House, Vintage Books, 1979.

Freire, Paulo, and Donaldo Macedo. *Literacy: Reading the Word & the World.* Critical Studies in Education Series. South Hadley, Mass.: Bergin & Garvey, 1987.

French, Valerie. "Midwives and Maternity Care in the Greco-Roman World." In *Rescuing Creusa: New Methodological Approaches to Women in Antiquity,* special issue of *Helios* 13 (1986): 69–84.

Freyne, Sean. *Galilee from Alexander the Great to Hadrian, 323 B.C.E. to 135 C.E.: A Study of Second Temple Judaism.* University of Notre Dame Center for the Study of Judaism and Christianity in Antiquity, no. 5. Wilmington: Michael Glazier, 1980.

———. *Galilee, Jesus, and the Gospels: Literary Approaches and Historical Investigations.* Philadelphia: Fortress Press, 1988.

Gailey, Christine Ward. "Evolutionary Perspectives in Gender Hierarchy." In *Analyzing Gender: A Handbook of Social Science Research,* edited by Beth B. Hess and Myra Marx Ferrée, 32–67. Beverly Hills: Sage Publications, 1987.

Ganoczy, Alexandre. *An Introduction to Catholic Sacramental Theology.* Translated by William Thomas and Anthony Sherman. New York: Paulist Press, 1984.

Garland, Robert. *The Greek Way of Life: From Conception to Old Age.* Ithaca: Cornell University Press, 1990.

Gesenius, William. *A Hebrew and English Lexicon of the Old Testament.* Translated by Edward Robinson, edited by Francis Brown, S. R. Driver, and Charles A. Briggs. Oxford: Clarendon, 1955.

Gerbner, George. "Toward 'Cultural Indicators': The Analysis of Mass Mediated Public Message Systems." In *The Analysis of Communication Content: Developments in Scientific Theories and Computer Techniques,* edited by George Gerbner, Ole R. Holsti, Klaus Krippendorff, William J. Paisley, and Philip J. Stone, 123–32. New York: John Wiley & Sons, 1969.

Gerbner, George, Larry Gross, Michael Morgan, and Nancy Signorielli. "The 'Mainstreaming' of America: Violence Profile No. 11." *Journal of Communication* 30 (1980): 10–29.

Gerhart, Mary. "Genric Studies: Their Renewed Importance in Religious and Literary Interpretation." *Journal of the American Academy of Religion* 45 (1977): 309–25.

———. "Genre as Praxis: An Inquiry." *PreText* 4 (1983) 273–94.

———. "Holocaust Writings: A Literary Genre?" In *The Holocaust as Interruption,* Concilium, no. 175, edited by Elisabeth Schüssler Fiorenza and David Tracy, 75–79. Edinburgh: T & T Clark, 1984.

———. "Genric Competence and Biblical Hermeneutics." In *Semeia* 43, edited by Mary Gerhart and James G. Williams, 29–44. Atlanta: Scholars Press, 1988.

————. *Genre Choices, Gender Questions.* Oklahoma Project for Discourse and Theory Series, no. 9. Norman: University of Oklahoma Press, 1992.

Gerhart, Mary, and Allan Melvin Russell. *Metaphoric Process: The Creation of Scientific and Religious Understanding.* Fort Worth: Texas Christian University Press, 1984.

————. "A Generalized Conception of Text Applied to Both Scientific and Religious Objects." *Zygon* 22 (1987): 299–317.

Giddens, Anthony. *Central Problems in Social Theory: Action, Structure and Contradiction in Social Analysis.* Berkeley and Los Angeles: University of California Press, 1979.

Gilmore, David D. "Anthropology of the Mediterranean Area." *Annual Review of Anthropology* 11 (1982): 175–205.

————, ed. *Honor and Shame and the Unity of the Mediterranean.* Washington: American Anthropological Association, 1987.

Gimbutas, Marija. *The Langauge of the Goddess.* San Francisco: Harper & Row, 1989.

Gow, A. S. F., trans. *The Greek Bucolic Poets.* Cambridge: Cambridge University Press, 1953.

Grant, Jacqueline. *White Women's Christ and Black Women's Jesus: Feminist Christology and Womanist Response.* Atlanta: Scholars Press, 1989.

Gray, John. "The Massoretic Text of the Book of Job, the Targum and the Septuagint Version in Light of the Qumran Targum (IIQtargJob)." *Zeitschrift für die Alttestamentliche Wissenschaft* 86 (1974): 331–50.

Green, Peter. *Classical Bearings: Interpreting Ancient History and Culture.* London: Thames and Hudson, 1989.

Green, Stanton W., and Stephen M. Perlman, editors. *The Archaeology of Frontiers and Boundaries.* New York: Academic Press, 1985.

Grossberg, Lawrence. "Cultural Studies Revisited and Revised." In *Communications in Transition: Issues and Debates in Current Research,* edited by Mary S. Mander. New York: Praeger, 1983.

Grossfeld, Bernard, trans. *The Targum Onqelos to Deuteronomy.* Wilmington: Michael Glazier, 1988.

Habermas, Gary R., and Antony G. N. Flew. *Did Jesus Rise From the Dead? The Resurrection Debate.* Edited by Terry L. Miethe. San Francisco: Harper & Row, 1987.

Halton, Thomas Patrick. "Paideia, Christian." *New Catholic Encyclopedia* 10: 862–64. New York: McGraw-Hill, 1967.

Harrington, Daniel J., and Anthony J. Saldarini, trans. *Targum Jonathan of the Former Prophets.* Wilmington: Michael Glazier, 1987.

Harris, Maria. *Teaching and Religious Imagination.* San Francisco: Harper & Row, 1987.

————. *Fashion Me a People: Curriculum and the Church.* Philadelphia: Westminster, 1989.

Hartsock, Nancy. "The Feminist Standpoint: Developing the Ground for a Specifically Feminist Historical Materialism." In *Discovering Reality: Feminist Perspectives on Epistemology, Metaphysics, and Philosophy of Science,* edited by Sandra Harding and Merrill B. Hintikka, 283–310. Dordrecht: Reidel, 1983.

Harvey, David. *The Condition of Postmodernity: An Enquiry into the Origins of Cultural Change.* Cambridge, Mass.: Basil Blackwell, 1980.

Heidegger, Martin. *Being and Time.* Translated by John Macquarrie and Edward Robinson. New York: Harper & Row, 1962.

Hengel, Martin. *Judaism and Hellenism: Studies in Their Encounter in Palestine During the Early Hellenistic Period.* Two volumes. Translated by John Bowden. Philadelphia: Fortress Press, 1974.

Herzfeld, Michael. "Honor and Shame: Problems in the Comparative Analysis of Moral Systems." *Man* 15 (1980): 339–51.

———. "The Horns of the Mediterraneanist Dilemma" *American Ethnologist* 11 (1984): 439–54.

———. *The Poetics of Manhood: Contest and Identity in a Cretan Mountain Village.* Princeton: Princeton University Press, 1985.

———. "'As in Your Own House': Hospitality, Ethnography, and the Stereotype of Mediterranean Society." In *Honor and Shame and the Unity of the Mediterranean,* edited by David Gilmore, 75–89. Washington: American Anthropological Association, 1987.

Hess, Beth B., and Myra Marx Ferrée, eds. *Analyzing Gender: A Handbook of Social Science Research.* Beverly Hills: Sage Publications, 1987.

Hobson, Deborah. "Women as Property Owners in Roman Egypt." *Transactions of the American Philological Association* 113 (1983): 311–21.

———. "The Role of Women in the Economic Life of Roman Egypt: A Case Study from First-Century Tebtunis." *Classical Views* 28 (1984): 373–90.

Hodgson, Peter C., and Robert H. King, eds. *Christian Theology: An Introduction to Its Traditions and Tasks.* Philadelphia: Fortress Press, 1982; newly updated edition, 1994.

Jaeger, Werner. *Paideia: The Ideals of Greek Culture.* Three volumes. Translated by Gilbert Highet. New York: Oxford University Press, 1943–45.

———. *Early Christianity and Greek Paideia.* (Cambridge: Belknap Press of Harvard University Press, 1961.

Jameson, Frederic. *The Political Unconscious: Narrative as a Socially Symbolic Act.* Ithaca: Cornell University Press, 1981.

Johnson, Susanne. "Education in the Image of God." In *Theological Approaches to Christian Education,* edited by Jack L. Seymour and Donald E. Miller, 124–45 and 276–77. Nashville: Abingdon, 1990.

Jones, Christopher P. "Dinner Theater." In *Dining in a Classical Context,* edited by William J. Slater, 185–98. Ann Arbor: University of Michigan Press, 1991.

Joshel, Sandra. "Nurturing the Master's Child: Slavery and the Roman Child Nurse." *Signs* 12 (1986): 3–22.

Kasher, Aryeh. *Jews and Hellenistic Cities in Eretz Israel: Relations of the Jews in Eretz Israel with the Hellenistic Cities During the Second Temple Period (332 B.C.E.–70 C.E.).* Tübingen: J. C. B. Mohr, Paul Siebeck, 1990.

Kelber, Werner. *Mark's Story of Jesus.* Philadelphia: Fortress Press, 1979.

———. *The Oral and the Written Gospel: The Hermeneutics of Speaking and Writing in the Synoptic Tradition, Mark, Paul, and Q.* Philadelphia: Fortress Press, 1983.

Kelleher, Margaret Mary. "Liturgy: An Ecclesial Act of Meaning." *Worship* 59 (1985): 482–97.

———. "Liturgical Theology: A Task and a Method." *Worship* 62 (1988): 2–25.

Keller, Evelyn Fox. *Reflections on Gender and Science.* New Haven: Yale University Press, 1985.

Keuls, Eva. *The Reign of the Phallus: Sexual Politics in Ancient Athens.* New York: Harper & Row, 1985.

Kingsbury, Jack Dean. *The Christology of Mark's Gospel.* Philadelphia: Fortress Press, 1983.

Kinneavy, James L. *Greek Rhetorical Origins of Christian Faith: An Inquiry.* Oxford: Oxford University Press, 1987.

Kloppenborg, John S. *The Formation of Q: Trajectories in Ancient Wisdom Collections.* Philadelphia: Fortress Press, 1987.

Kloppenborg, John S., Marvin W. Meyer, Stephen J. Patterson, and Michael G. Steinhauser. *Q Thomas Reader.* Sonoma, Calif: Polebridge, 1990.

Koester, Helmut. "*physis* . . ." *Theological Dictionary of the New Testament* 9: 251–77. Compiled by Gerhard Kittel, edited by Gerhard Friedrich, and translated and edited by Geoffrey W. Bromiley. Grand Rapids: Eerdmans, 1964–74.

———. *History, Culture, and Religion of the Hellenistic Age.* Vol. 1 of *Introduction to the New Testament.* Hermeneia: Foundations and Facets. Philadelphia: Fortress Press, 1982.

———. *History and Literature of Early Christianity.* Vol. 2 of *Introduction to the New Testament.* Hermeneia: Foundations and Facets. Philadelphia: Fortress Press, 1982.

Kraemer, Ross Shepard. "The Conversion of Women to Ascetic Forms of Christianity." *Signs* 6 (1980): 298–307.

———. "Non-Literary Evidence for Jewish Women in Rome and Egypt." In *Rescuing Creusa: New Methodological Approaches to Women in Antiquity.* Special issue of *Helios* 13 (1986): 85–102.

———. *Her Share of the Blessings: Women's Religions Among Pagans, Jews, and Christians in the Greco-Roman World.* New York: Oxford University Press, 1992.

———, ed. *Maenads, Martyrs, Matrons, Monastics: A Sourcebook on Women's Religions in the Greco-Roman World.* Philadelphia: Fortress Press, 1988.

Kuhrt, Amélie, and Susan Sherwin-White, eds. *Hellenism in the East: The Interaction of Greek and Non-Greek Civilizations from Syria to Central Asia After Alexander.* Berkeley: University of California Press, 1987.

Langer, Susanne K. *Philosophy in a New Key.* Cambridge: Harvard University Press, 1942.

Lapide, Pinchas. *The Resurrection of Jesus: A Jewish Perspective.* Minneapolis: Augsburg, 1983.

Lawler, Michael G. *Symbol and Sacrament: A Contemporary Sacramental Theology.* New York: Paulist, 1987.

Leeming, Bernard. *Principles of Sacramental Theology.* Westminster, Md.: Newman, 1965.

Lefkowitz, Mary. "Influential Women." In *Images of Women in Antiquity,* edited by Averil Cameron and Amélie Kuhrt, 49–64. Detroit: Wayne State University Press, 1983.

LeGuin, Ursula K. *The Dispossessed.* New York: Harper & Row, 1974.

Lenski, Gerhard E. *Power and Privilege: A Theory of Social Stratification.* New York: McGraw Hill, 1966.

Lesko, Barbara S., ed. *Women's Earliest Records From Ancient Egypt and Western Asia.* Proceedings of the Conference on Women in the Ancient Near East, Brown University, 1987. Atlanta: Scholars Press, 1989.

Levey, Samson H., trans. *The Targum of Ezekiel.* Wilmington: Michael Glazier, 1987.

Levine, Amy-Jill, editor. *"Women Like This": New Perspectives on Jewish Women in the Greco-Roman World.* Atlanta: Scholars Press, 1991.

Lloyd-Jones, Hugh, trans. *Females of the Species: Semonides on Women.* Parkridge, N.J.: Noyes Press, 1975.

Loffreda, Stanislao. *Recovering Capharnaum.* Jerusalem: Edizioni Custodia Terra Sancta, 1985.

Longstaff, Thomas R. W. "Nazareth and Sepphoris: Insights into Christian Origins." In *Christ and His Communities: Essays in Honor of Reginald H. Fuller,* edited by Arland J. Hultgren and Barbara Hall, 8–15. Anglical Theological Review Supplementary Series, no. 11. Evanston: Anglican Theological Review, 1990.

Mack, Burton L. "The Kingdom Sayings in Mark." *Foundations and Facets Forum* 3 (1987): 3–47.

———. *A Myth of Innocence: Mark and Christian Origins.* Philadelphia: Fortress Press, 1988.

———. "The Anointing of Jesus: Elaboration Within a Chreia." In *Patterns of Persuasion in the Gospels,* 85–106. Sonoma, Calif.: Polebridge, 1989.

Mack, Burton L., and Vernon K. Robbins. *Patterns of Persuasion in the Gospels.* Sonoma, Calif.: Polebridge, 1989.

Malina, Bruce J. *The New Testament World: Insights from Cultural Anthropology.* Atlanta: John Knox, 1981.

————. *Christian Origins and Cultural Anthropology: Practical Models for Biblical Interpretation.* Atlanta: John Knox, 1986.

Malina, Bruce J., and Jerome H. Neyrey. "Honor and Shame in Luke Acts: Pivotal Values of the Mediterranean World." In *The Social World of Luke-Acts,* edited by Jerome H. Neyrey, 25–65. Peabody, Mass.: Hendrickson Publishers, 1991.

Manns, Frederic. "An Important Jewish-Christian Center: Sepphoris." Translated by James F. Strange and circulated privately for the University of South Florida Excavations at Sepphoris. In *Essais sur le Judeo-Christianisme,* Studium Biblicum Franciscanum, Analecta no. 12, 165–90. Jerusalem: Franciscan Printing Press, 1977.

Martin, Clarice J. "Womanist Interpretation of the New Testament: The Quest for Holistic and Inclusive Translation and Interpretation." *Journal of Feminist Studies in Religion* 6 (1990): 41–61.

Martos, Joseph. *The Catholic Sacraments.* Message of the Sacraments, no. 1. Wilmington: Michael Glazier, 1983.

Martyn, J. Louis. "The Covenants of Sarah and Hagar." In *Faith and History: Essays in Honor of Paul W. Meyer,* edited by John T. Carroll, Charles H. Cosgrove, and E. Elizabeth Johnson, 160–92. Atlanta: Scholars Press, 1990.

McCane, Byron R. "'Let the Dead Bury Their Own Dead': Secondary Burial and Matt 8:21-22." *Harvard Theological Review* 83 (1990): 31–43.

————. "Bones of Contention? Ossuaries and Reliquaries in Early Judaism and Christianity." *The Second Century* 8 (1991): 235–46.

McCane, Byron R. *Jews, Christians, and Burial in Roman Palestine.* Ann Arbor, Mich.: University Microfilms International, 1992.

Megill, Alan. *Prophets of Extremity: Nietzsche, Heidegger, Foucault, Derrida.* Berkeley: University of California Press, 1985.

Meier, John P. *A Marginal Jew: Rethinking the Historical Jesus.* Vol. 1, *The Roots of the Problem and the Person.* New York: Doubleday, 1991.

Melischek, Gabriele, Karl Erik Rosengren, and James Stappers, eds. *Cultural Indicators: An International Symposium.* Vienna: Verlag der Osterreichischen Akademie der Wissenschaften, 1984.

Meyers, Carol L. *Discovering Eve: Ancient Israelite Women in Context.* New York: Oxford University Press, 1988.

Meyers, Eric M. "The Challenge of Hellenism for Early Judaism and Christianity." *Biblical Archaeologist* 55/2 (1992) 84–91.

Meyers, Eric M., Carol L. Meyers, and Ehud Netzer. "Sepphoris (Ṣippori), 1985 (I)," *Israel Exploration Journal* 35 (1985): 295–97.

Meyers, Eric M., Ehud Netzer, and Carol L. Meyers. "Sepphoris, 'Ornament of All Galilee'." *Biblical Archaeologist* 49 (1986): 4–19.

————. "Sepphoris (Ṣippori), 1986 (I)," *Israel Exploration Journal* 37 (1987): 275–78.

————. "Sepphoris (Ṣippori), 1987 and 1988," *Israel Exploration Journal* 40 (1990): 219–22.

———. *Sepphoris.* Winona Lake, Ind.: Eisenbrauns, 1992.

Meyers, Eric M., and James F. Strange. *Archaeology, the Rabbis, and Early Christianity: The Social and Historical Setting of Palestinian Judaism and Christianity.* Nashville: Abingdon, 1981.

Meyers, Eric M., James F. Strange, and Carol L. Meyers. *Excavations at Ancient Meiron, Upper Galilee, Israel 1971–72, 1974–75, 1977.* Cambridge: The American Schools of Oriental Research, 1981.

Michaelis, Wilhelm. *"horaō . . ." Theological Dictionary of the New Testament* 5: 315–82. Compiled by Gerhard Kittel, edited by Gerhard Friedrich, and translated and edited by Geoffrey W. Bromiley. Grand Rapids: Eerdmans, 1964–74.

Micks, Marianne H. *The Joy of Worship.* Philadelphia: Westminster, 1982.

Miller, Robert J. "The Inside Is (Not) the Outside: Q 11:39-41 and Thomas 89." *Foundations and Facets Forum* 5 (1989): 92–105.

———, ed. *The Complete Gospels.* Sonoma, Calif.: Polebridge, 1992.

Miller, Stuart S. *Studies in the History and Traditions of Sepphoris.* Leiden: Brill, 1984.

———. "Sepphoris, the Well Remembered City." *Biblical Archaeologist* 55/2 (1992) 74–83.

Murray, Oswyn, ed. *Sympotica: A Symposium on the* Symposion. Oxford: Clarendon, 1990.

Neusner, Jacob. *The Economics of the Mishnah.* Chicago: University of Chicago Press, 1990.

Neyrey, Jerome H., ed. *The Social World of Luke-Acts.* Peabody, Mass.: Hendrickson Publishers, 1991.

Nickelsburg, George W. E., Jr. *Resurrection, Immortality, and Eternal Life in Intertestamental Judaism.* Harvard Theological Studies, no. 26. Cambridge: Harvard University Press, 1972.

O'Collins, Gerald. *Jesus Risen: An Historical, Fundamental and Systematic Examination of Christ's Resurrection.* New York: Paulist, 1987.

———. *Interpreting the Resurrection: Examining the Major Problems in the Stories of Jesus' Resurrection.* New York: Paulist Press, 1988.

Ong, Walter J. *Orality and Literacy: The Technologizing of the Word.* London: Methuen, 1982.

Ortner, Sherry B. "Is Female to Male as Nature Is to Culture?" In *Woman, Culture, and Society,* edited by M. Z. Rosaldo and Louise Lamphere, 67–87. Stanford: Stanford University Press, 1974.

Overman, J. Andrew. *Matthew's Gospel and Formative Judaism: The Social World of the Matthean Community.* Minneapolis: Fortress Press, 1990.

Padel, Ruth. "Women: Model for Possession by Greek Daemons." In *Images of Women in Antiquity,* edited by Averil Cameron and Amélie Kuhrt, 3–19. Detroit: Wayne State University Press, 1983.

Page, D. L., ed. *Further Greek Epigrams: Epigrams Before A.D. 50 From the Greek Anthology and Other Sources.* Cambridge: Cambridge University Press, 1981.

Parpart, Jane L., and Kathleen A. Staudt, eds. *Women and the State in Africa.* Stanford: Stanford University Press, 1989.

Patterson, Cynthia. "'Not Worth the Rearing': The Causes of Infant Exposure in Ancient Greece." *Transactions of the American Philological Society* 115 (1985): 103–23.

Peristiany, John G., ed. *Honor and Shame: The Values of Mediterranean Society.* London: Weidenfeld and Nicolson, 1965.

Perkins, Pheme. *Resurrection: New Testament Witness and Contemporary Reflection.* Garden City, N.Y.: Doubleday, 1984.

Pitt-Rivers, Julian A., ed. *Mediterranean Countrymen: Essays in the Social Anthropology of the Mediterranean.* Paris: Moulton & Co., 1963.

Pomeroy, Sarah B. *Women in Hellenistic Egypt from Alexander to Cleopatra.* New York: Schocken Books, 1984.

Rahmani, L. Y. "Ancient Jerusalem's Funerary Customs and Tombs." Four parts. *Biblical Archaeologist* 44 (1981): 171–77 and 229–35; and 45 (1981–82): 43–53 and 109–19.

Rahner, Karl. "Zur Theologie des Symbols." In *Schriften zur Theologie,* vol. 4, 275–311. Einsiedeln: Benziger, 1960.

———. *Kirche und Sakramente.* Freiburg: Herder, 1960. Translated by W. J. O'Hara, as *The Church and the Sacraments.* London: Burnes & Oates, 1963.

———, ed. *Encyclopedia of Theology: The Concise* Sacramentum Mundi. With portions translated by John Griffiths, Francis McDonagh, and David Smith. New York: Seabury, Crossroad, 1975.

Rajchman, John, and Cornel West. *Post-Analytic Philosophy.* New York: Columbia University Press, 1985.

Reale, Giovanni. *The Systems of the Hellenistic Age.* Vol. 3 of *A History of Ancient Philosophy.* Translated and edited by John R. Catan. Albany: State University of New York Press, 1985.

Renfrew, Colin. *Approaches to Social Archaeology.* Cambridge: Harvard University Press, 1984.

Richter, Gisela, and Marjorie J. Milne. *Shapes and Names of Athenian Vases.* New York: Metropolitan Museum of Art, 1935.

Robbins, Vernon K. "Pronouncement Stories and Jesus' Blessing of the Children: A Rhetorical Approach." In *Semeia* 29, edited by Daniel Patte, 43–74. Chico, Calif.: Scholars Press, 1983.

———. *Jesus the Teacher: A Socio-rhetorical Interpretation of Mark.* Philadelphia: Fortress Press, 1984; Minneapolis, 1992.

———. "The Reversed Contextualization of Psalm 22 in the Markan Crucifixion: A Socio-Rhetorical Analysis." In *The Four Gospels: Festschrift Frans Neirynck,* edited by Frans van Segbroeck *et al.*, 3 vols. Bibliotheca Ephemeridium Theologicarum Loveniensium, no. 100. Louvain: University Press, Uitgeverij Peeters, 1992.

Robinson, James M. *"Logoi Sophōn*: On the Gattung of Q." In *Trajectories Through Early Christianity*, edited by James M. Robinson and Helmut Koester, 71–113. Philadelphia: Fortress Press, 1971.

Rosaldo, Michele Z. "Woman, Culture, and Society: A Theoretical Overview." In *Woman, Culture, and Society*, edited by M. Z. Rosaldo and Louise Lamphere, 17–42. Stanford: Stanford University Press, 1974.

———. "The Use and Abuse of Anthropology: Reflections on Feminism and Cross-Cultural Understanding." *Signs* 5 (1980): 389–417.

Rösler, Wolfgang. *"Mnēmosynē* in the *Symposion."* In *Sympotica: A Symposium on the Symposion*, edited by Oswyn Murray, 230–37. Oxford: Clarendon, 1990.

Ross, Susan A. "The Aesthetic and the Sacramental." *Worship* 59 (1985) 2–17.

———. "Church and Sacraments." In *The Praxis of Christian Experience: An Introduction to the Thought of Edward Schillebeeckx*. Edited by Robert Schreiter and Catherine Hilkert. San Francisco: Harper & Row, 1988.

———. "'Then Honor God in Your Body' (1 Cor 6:20): Feminist and Sacramental Theology on the Body." *Horizons* 16 (1989) 7–27.

Rouselle, Aline. *Porneia: On Desire and the Body in Antiquity.* Translated by Felicia Pheasant. Oxford and New York: Basil Blackwell, 1988.

Runciman, W. G. *A Treatise on Social Theory.* Vol. 1, *The Methodology of Social Theory.* Cambridge: Cambridge University Press, 1983.

Runia, David T. *Philo of Alexandria and the* Timaeus *of Plato.* Leiden: Brill, 1986.

Sacks, Karen. *Sisters and Wives: The Past and Future of Sexual Equality.* Westport Conn.: Greenwood Press, 1979.

Sacks, Karen Brodkin. "Toward a Unified Theory of Class, Race, and Gender." *American Ethnologist* 16 (1989): 534–50.

Safrai, Shmuel, and M. Stern, editors. *The Jewish People in the First Century: Historical Geography, Political History, Social, Cultural and Religious Life and Institutions.* Volume 2. Compendia Rerum Iudaicarum ad Novum Testamentum. Philadelphia: Fortress Press, 1976.

Sawicki, Marianne. "How to Teach Christ's Disciples: Jn 1:19-37 and Mt 11:2-15." *Lexington Theological Quarterly* 21 (1986): 14–26.

———. "Recognizing the Risen Lord." *Theology Today* 44 (1988): 441–49.

———. *The Gospel in History: Portrait of a Teaching Church.* Mahwah, N.J.: Paulist, 1988.

———. "Educational Policy and Christian Origins." *Religious Education* 85 (1990): 455–77.

———. "Tradition and Sacramental Education." In *Theological Approaches to Christian Education*, edited by Jack L. Seymour and Donald E. Miller, 43–62, 265–70. Nashville: Abingdon, 1990.

Scarry, Elaine. *The Body in Pain: The Making and Unmaking of the World.* New York: Oxford University Press, 1985.

Schaberg, Jane. *The Illegitimacy of Jesus: A Feminist Theological Interpretation of the Infancy Narratives.* San Francisco: Harper & Row, 1987.

———. Response to Clarice J. Martin's "Womanist Interpretation of the New Testament: The Quest for Holistic and Inclusive Translation and Interpretation." *Journal of Feminist Studies in Religion* 6 (1990): 74–85.

Schaps, David M. "The Woman Least Mentioned: Etiquette and Women's Names." *Classical Quarterly* 27 (1977): 323–30.

———. *Economic Rights of Women in Ancient Greece.* Edinburgh: Edinburgh University Press, 1979

Schillebeeckx, Edward. *Christ the Sacrament of the Encounter With God.* Translated by Paul Barrett, revised by Mark Schoof and Laurence Bright. Kansas City: Sheed Andrews and McMeel, 1963.

———. *The Eucharist.* Translated by N. D. Smith. New York: Sheed and Ward, 1968.

———. *God the Future of Man.* Translated by N. D. Smith. New York: Sheed and Ward, 1968.

———. *The Understanding of Faith.* Translated by N. D. Smith. New York: Seabury, 1974.

———. *Jesus: An Experiment in Christology.* Translated by Hubert Hoskins. New York: Seabury, 1979.

———. *Christ: The Experience of Jesus as Lord.* Translated by John Bowden. New York: Seabury, 1980.

Schneidau, Herbert N. "The Word Against the Word: Derrida on Textuality." In *Semeia* 23, edited by Robert Detweiler, 5–28. Chico, Calif.: Scholars Press, 1982.

Schneider, Jane. "Of Vigilance and Virgins: Honor, Shame, and Access to Resources in Mediterranean Societies," *Ethnology* 9 (1971): 1–24.

Scholes, Robert. "Toward a Curriculum in Textual Studies." In *Reorientations: Critical Theories and Pedagogies,* edited by Bruce Henricksen and Thaïs E. Morgan. Urbana: University of Illinois Press, 1990.

Schreiter, Robert J. *Constructing Local Theologies.* Maryknoll, N.Y.: Orbis, 1985.

Schüssler Fiorenza, Elisabeth. *In Memory of Her: A Feminist Theological Reconstruction of Christian Origins.* New York: Crossroad, 1984.

Schweickart, Patrocinio P. "Reading, Teaching, and the Ethic of Care." In *Gender in the Classroom: Power and Pedagogy,* edited by Susan L. Gabriel and Isaiah Smithson, 78–95. Urbana: University of Illinois Press, 1990.

Scott, Joan W. "Gender: A Useful Category of Historical Analysis," *American Historical Review* 91 (1986): 1053–73.

Seeley, David. *The Noble Death: Graeco-Roman Martyrology and Paul's Concept of Salvation.* Journal for the Study of the New Testament Supplement Series, no. 28. Sheffield: JSOT Press, 1990.

———. *Deconstructing the New Testament.* Leiden: Brill, 1994.

Seow, Choon Leong. *A Grammar for Biblical Hebrew.* Nashville: Abingdon, 1987.

Sered, Susan Starr. *Women as Ritual Experts: The Religious Lives of Elderly Jewish Women in Jerusalem.* New York: Oxford University Press, 1992.

Seymour, Jack L., and Donald E. Miller, eds. *Theological Approaches to Christian Education.* Nashville: Abingdon, 1990.

Seifert, Donna J., ed. *Gender in Historical Archaeology.* Special issue of *Historical Archaeology* 24 (1991).

Simon, Erika. *Festivals of Attica: An Archaeological Survey.* Madison: University of Wisconsin Press, 1983.

Skinner, Marilyn, ed. *Rescuing Creusa: New Methodological Approaches to Women in Antiquity.* Special issue of *Helios* 13 (1986).

Slater, William J., ed. *Dining in a Classical Context.* Ann Arbor: University of Michigan Press, 1991.

Smallwood, E. Mary. "The Jews in Egypt and Cyrenaica During the Ptolemaic and Roman Periods." In *Africa and Classical Antiquity,* edited by L. A. Thompson and J. Ferguson, 110–31. Ibadan, Nigeria: Ibadan University Press, 1969.

Sourvinou-Inwood, Christiane. *"Reading" Greek Culture: Texts and Images, Rituals and Myths.* Oxford: Clarendon, 1991.

Sparkes, Brian. "The Greek Kitchen." *Journal of Hellenistic Studies* 82 (1962): 121–37 and plates 4–7.

———. "Not Cooking, But Baking." *Greece and Rome* 28 (1981): 172–78.

Sperber, Daniel. *Roman Palestine 200–400: Money and Prices.* Ramat-Gan: Bar-Ilan University, 1974.

———. *Roman Palestine 200–400: The Land.* Ramat-Gan: Bar-Ilan University, 1978.

Strange, James F. "Two Aspects of the Development of Universalism in Early Christianity: The First to the Fourth Centuries." In *Religion and Global Order,* edited by Roland Robertson and William R. Garrett, 35–46. New York: Paragon House, 1991.

———. "Six Campaigns at Sepphoris: The University of South Florida Excavations 1983–1989." In *The Galilee in Late Antiquity,* edited by Lee I. Levine, 339–55. New York: The Jewish Theological Seminary of America, 1992.

Strange, James F., and Thomas R. W. Longstaff. "Sepphoris (Ṣippori), 1983." *Israel Exploration Journal* 34 (1984): 51–52.

———. "Sepphoris (Ṣippori)—Survey, 1984." *Israel Exploration Journal* 34 (1984): 269–70.

———. "Sepphoris (Ṣippori), 1985 (II)." *Israel Exploration Journal* 35 (1985): 297–99.

———. "Sepphoris (Ṣippori), 1986 (II)." *Israel Exploration Journal* 37 (1987): 278–80.

Strange, James F., Dennis E. Groh, and Thomas R. W. Longstaff. "Sepphoris (Ṣippori), 1987 (II). *Israel Exploration Journal* 38 (1988): 188–90.

———. "Sepphoris (Ṣippori), 1988," *Israel Exploration Journal* 39 (1989): 104–6.

————. "University of South Florida Excavations at Sepphoris: The Location and Identification of Shikhin." Part 1. *Israel Exploration Journal* 43. Part 2, with a contribution by David Adan-Bayewitz. *Israel Exploration Journal*, 1994.

Szold, Henrietta. "Beruriah." *The Jewish Encyclopedia* 3:109–10. New York: Funk & Waggnalls, 1906.

Taylor, Mark C. *Erring: A Postmodern A/theology*. Chicago: University of Chicago Press, 1984.

Tecuşan, Manuela. "*Logos-Sympotikos*: Patterns of the Irrational in Philosophical Drinking: Plato Outside the *Symposium*." In *Sympotica: A Symposium on the Symposion*, edited by Oswyn Murray, 238–60. Oxford: Clarendon, 1990.

Teichman, Jenny. *Illegitimacy: An Examination of Bastardy*. Ithaca: Cornell University Press, 1982.

Theissen, Gerd. *Sociology of Early Palestinian Christianity*. Translated by John Bowden. Philadelphia: Fortress Press, 1978.

Tilly, Louise. "The Social and the Study of Women." *Comparative Studies in Society and History* 20 (1978): 163–73.

Tracy, David. *The Analogical Imagination: Christian Theology and the Culture of Pluralism*. New York: Crossroad, 1981.

Tringham, Ruth E. "Households with Faces: The Challenge of Gender in Prehistoric Architectural Remains." In *Engendering Archaeology: Women and Prehistory*, edited by Joan M. Gero and Margaret W. Conkey, 93–131. Oxford: Basil Blackwell, 1991.

Vaillancourt, Raymond. *Toward a Renewal of Sacramental Theology*. Translated by Matthew J. O'Connell. Collegeville: The Liturgical Press, 1979.

Van Bremen, Riet. "Women and Wealth." In *Images of Women in Antiquity*, edited by Averil Cameron and Amélie Kuhrt, 223–82. Detroit: Wayne State University Press, 1983.

Walde, D., and N. Willows, editors. *The Archaeology of Gender*. Proceedings of the 22d Annual Chacmool Conference. Calgary: The Archaeological Association of the University of Calgary, 1991.

Vardiman, E. E. *Die Frau in der Antike: Sittengeschichte der Frau im Altertum*. Vienna: Econ Verlag, 1982.

Vernant, Jean-Pierre. "At Man's Table: Hesiod's Foundation Myth of Sacrifice." In *The Cuisine of Sacrifice Among the Greeks*, by Marcel Detienne and Jean-Paul Vernant, translated by Paula Wissing, 21–86. Chicago: University of Chicago Press, 1989.

Veyne, Paul, ed. *From Pagan Rome to Byzantium*. Translated by Arthur Goldhammer. Vol. 1 of *A History of Private Life*. Cambridge: Belknap Press of Harvard University Press, 1987.

Walker, Susan. "Women and Housing in Classical Greece: The Archaeological Evidence." In *Images of Women in Antiquity*, edited by Averil Cameron and Amélie Kuhrt, 81–91. Detroit: Wayne State University Press, 1983.

Warren, Michael. *Faith, Culture, and the Worshiping Community.* Mahwah, N.J.: Paulist, 1989.

———. *Communications and Cultural Analysis: A Religious View.* Westport, Conn.: Bergin & Garvey, 1992.

Wegner, Judith Romney. *Chattel or Person? The Status of Women in the Mishnah.* New York and Oxford: Oxford University Press, 1988.

Weiss, Johannes. *Die Predigt Jesu vom Reiche Gottes.* 3d ed. Edited by Ferdinand Hahn. Göttingen: Vandenhoeck & Ruprecht, 1964. First edition, 1892, translated and edited by Richard Hyde Hiers and David Larrimore Holland as *Jesus' Proclamation of the Kingdom of God.* Philadelphia: Fortress Press, 1971.

West, Cornel. "The Politics of American Neo-Pragmatism." In *Post-Analytic Philosophy,* edited by John Rajchman and Cornel West. New York: Columbia University Press, 1985.

White, Hayden. "The Historical Text as Literary Artifact." In *Tropics of Discourse: Essays in Cultural Criticism,* 81–100. Batimore: Johns Hopkins University Press, 1978.

———. *The Content of the Form: Narrative Discourse and Historical Representation.* Baltimore: Johns Hopkins University Press, 1987.

Williams, Dyfri. "Women on Athenian Vases: Problems of Interpretation." In *Images of Women in Antiquity,* edited by Averil Cameron and Amélie Kuhrt, 92–106. Detroit: Wayne State University Press, 1983.

Williams, Sam K. *Jesus' Death as Saving Event: The Background and Origin of a Concept.* Harvard Dissertations in Religion, no. 2. Missoula, Mont.: Scholars Press, 1975.

Winkler, John J. *The Constraints of Desire: An Anthropology of Sex and Gender in Ancient Greece.* New York and London: Routledge, 1990.

Winnicott, D. W. *The Maturational Processes and the Facilitating Environment: Studies in the Theory of Emotional Development.* New York: International Universities Press, 1965.

Wrede, William. *Das Messiasgeheimnis in den Evangelien: Zugleich ein Beitrag zum Verständnis des Markusevangeliums.* 3d ed. Göttingen: Vandenhoeck & Ruprecht, 1963. First edition, 1901, translated by J. C. G. Greig as *The Messianic Secret.* Cambridge: Clarke, 1971.

Wylie, Alison. "Gender Theory and the Archaeological Record: Why Is There No Archaeology of Gender?" In *Engendering Archaeology: Women and Prehistory,* edited by Joan M. Gero and Margaret W. Conkey, 31–54. Oxford: Basil Blackwell, 1991.

Zlotnik, Dov, trans. *The Tractate "Mourning"* (Śemaḥot). New Haven: Yale University Press, 1966.

Index of Ancient Texts

OLD TESTAMENT

Genesis
3 81

Exodus
4:6 288
20:4 208
21:10 101, 105, 112, 115, 116
31:14 35
33–34 123
34:17 208

Leviticus
26:1 208

Numbers
6 117
12:6-8 123
12:10 288

Deuteronomy
4:15-18 208
5 133, 141, 142, 143
5–8 132, 136
5:9 291
6 133, 134, 140–41, 142
6:4 131
6:7 131
6:9 148
8 133, 134, 135
8:19 138, 141, 142, 143
22:23-27 114
27:15 208

1 Samuel
1–2 101, 108
1:11 107, 112, 116
1:16 117
2:1-10 107
3:10 117
8:13 260

Job
1:6 134
1:21 256

Psalms
11:7 123
17:15 123
48 132, 138
50 132, 133, 134, 135
50:12 136
72 133, 142–43, 144
86 116
86:16 101
91 132, 133, 134, 135, 138, 141
91:11-12 140
91:14 130
91:14-15 101, 113, 140
116 116
116:16 101
123:2 101
132 133, 135
133:2 271

Proverbs
20:13 158
31:13 254

Isaiah
6:1-10   123
40   70
40:3   70
40:6   70
42–55   116
56:3-7   104

Jeremiah
31:19, 20   207

Ezekiel
13:9   64

Joel   101, 104

Amos
9:1   123

Zechariah
12:10   93

NEW TESTAMENT

Matthew
1:21   111
3:3   70
3:14   68
3:16   68
3:16-17   68
4:1-11   131
4:9   143
4:23—6:29   88
5–7   88
5:17-19   86
5:18   332
5:19   64
7:15-20   62
7:21-23   63, 86
9:34   151
9:35   64
9:35-38   85
10:1-14   85
10:1-15   64
10:40-42   86
11:2-15   68
11:3   69
11:4   69
11:5   74
11:9, 14   69
11:10   69
12:33-37   86

13:18-23   86
13:24-30   64
13:24-30, 36-43   86
13:52   56, 64, 85, 331
14:12   68
15:21-28   155, 156
15:29-39   88
17:1-9   88
18:3   45, 47
18:5   86
19:14a   45
19:14b   45
23   85
23:1-28   64
23:8   332
23:34-35   63
24:3—25:46   88
25   275
25:31-46   63, 87
26:6-13   154, 156
26:7   163
26:9   161
28:1-10, 16-20   87, 299
28:5   78–79
28:8-10   88
28:17-18   88
28:18-20   64, 88

Mark
1:1   168
1:1—3:6   59
1:10   171
1:10-11   68
1:14-15   168
1:24   170
1:24-25   174
2:21   171
2:22   170, 171
2:27   34, 35
3:6   170, 175
3:7—12:44   60
3:11-12   174
3:19   174
4   58–59, 62, 212
4:2b-9   57
4:8-10   57
4:11   57
4:13   57
4:14   57
4:26-29   57
5:4   170

5:7   170, 174
5:25-34   171
5:34   172
6:3   31
6:20   169
6:29   68
6:41   171
6:45—8:26   156
7:24-30   155, 156
7:25-30   171
7:29   172
8:19   171
8:29   170
8:30   170
8:31   175
8:31-35   170
8:35   168, 170
9:31   175
10:13, 16   47
10:14   46
10:14a   45
10:14b   45
10:14-15   49
10:14-16   55
10:15   45, 47
10:21   169, 172
10:29   168
10:33   175
10:45   61, 175
11–16   177
11:18   170
11:46-52   299
12:9   170
12:18-27   267
12:26-27   36
12:27   314–15
12:37   169
12:41-44   172
13:1—16:8   60
13:5-37   168
13:10   168
14   172
14:1-2   174
14:3   150, 163, 168, 170, 266, 272, 295
14:3-9   152, 154, 156, 172, 244, 258
14:4   170
14:4-5   169
14:5, 7   161
14:6   150
14:7   169
14:8   150, 161, 169

14:9   150, 151, 168, 169, 176, 178
14:10   176
14:10-11   174
14:11   169, 176, 178
14:12   177
14:16   169
14:17   178
14:21   176
14:22   150, 171, 271, 295
14:22-24   177
14:23-28   263
14:25   177, 178
14:28   272
14:30   179
14:41   178
14:44   178
14:44-45   176, 177
14:45-46   178
14:53, 64   172
14:61-62   170
14:61-64   174
14:63   171
14:65   173
14:66-72   179
15:1   177
15:13-14   169
15:15   174
15:15-25   150
15:17   271
15:17-19   173
15:26   50
15:32   174
15:38   171
15:39   174
15:40   171
15:41   171
15:43-46   172
16:1-8   171, 280
16:4   150
16:9-18   299
22:3-6   174
24:14-16   174

Luke
1:26-38   106
1:34   304
1:46-55   106
3:10-14   68
4:1-13   131
7   163
7:36, 47   266

7:36-50   154, 156, 258
7:38   177, 272
7:44-46   259
8:1-3   156
8:49-56   90
10:38-42   155, 156
11:1   67
11:27   42
14:1-14   90
15:11-32   90
15:20   177
16:19-31   90, 155, 156
18:16   45
18:17   45, 47
22:15-18   90
22:47-48   177
23:49   159
24:1-11   84
24:5   84
24:10-11   84
24:11   160
24:13-53   299
24:22-24   84
24:30-31   89
24:35   89
24:36   89–90
24:41-43   90
24:45   90
24:51   10

John
1:15   69
1:19-37   68
1:21   69
1:23   70
1:26   336
3   48
3:3, 5   45
3:4   45, 48
3:29   67
4:5-42   299
11   90
11:1-44   155
11:1-45   156
11:35   92
12   163
12:1-8   154, 156
12:3   266, 295
12:20-22   299
13:3-17   160

13:15   295
13:34-35   160
14:27   160
20:11-18   299
20:13   10, 257

Acts
1:9   10
2:14   156
6:1-5   90
6:2   91
7:55-56   90
7:56   10
9:3-6   10
9:3-9   91
9:18-19   91
10:40-41   89
20:37   177

1 Corinthians
11   91
11:4-16   161

Galatians
4   55

Hebrews
12:5-11   55

Apocrypha and Pseudepigrapha

Judith
11:5   100
12:12   105

Sirach
9:1-9   158
25:15-17   158
42:9-10   112
42:13   190

2 Maccabees
7:27   42

Philo

Philo, *De specialis legibus*
2.60-70   34
2.71-111   34

Philo, *On the Account of the World's Creation Given by Moses*
46–59   81

RABBINIC LITERATURE

'Abodah Zarah
17b   254
17b–18a   274
18a   268
18b   266

Kallah 51a   113

Kelim 30:4   166

Ketubot 6:4   166

M. Ketubot
5:5   39
60a   42

Pesaḥim
99b   258
100a   258
101b   258
108a   258

M. Qiddušin 1:1   41

Šabbat
6:3   166
62a-b   166
116a   118
116b   234

Sanhedrin
6:5   172, 257
19b   49

Šemaḥot 12:10   255

TARGUMIC MATERIAL

Targum Onqelos
Deut. 6:9   148

EARLY CHRISTIAN WRITINGS

Protevangelium of James
(Infancy Gospel of James)   80, 110, 118,
                               119, 120, 253

6:13   110
11:1-3   106–7, 109, 111

Gospel of Thomas
22   43, 237, 244, 253
22:1-2   37, 48
22:2   44, 45
22:3   45, 47
22:4   45, 48

Q   118
4   128, 134
4:1-13   131, 132, 143, 147
4:3, 9   142
4:4   134, 135–37
4:5-7   141–45
4:8   145–46
4:9-11   138–39
4:10-11   143
4:12   139–41
12:13   128

Secret Gospel of Mark   154

GREEK LITERATURE

Aristophanes, *Plutus* 764–801   162

Athenaeus, *Deipnosophistae*
2.76.15   162
4.172ff.   260
9.61.10   162

Epictetus, *Handbook,* 11   256

Greek Anthology
9:409   262
11:19   262

Plato, *Gorgias*
453   260
453a–455a   266
455b 4   267

Plato, *Theaetetus*   49

Index of Subjects and Names

'Ābad. *See* Slavery; Work
Abigail, 100
Abu-Lughod, L., 245, 249
Access
  as possibility for bodily encounter, 6, 7
  conditions for, 7
  to God, 28, 306, 307–8
  to Jesus, 6, 7, 252, 282, 301, 316
Achtemeier, P. J., 177
Adan-Bayewitz, D., 14
Andonia, 255–56
Adonis, 255–56
Africa
  contact with Eretz Israel, 19
  contributions to Hellenistic culture, 14
  European exploitation of, 13
  first-century Palestine compared with, 13
African studies, 12, 13
Afshar, H., 12
Alabastra (perfume bottles), 165–66, 262, 263, 267, 293–94
  See also Stones
Alexander the Great, 18
Alexandria, 14, 19, 97–98, 102
'Āmāh. *See* Slavewomen
'Ānah. *See* Bowing; Sexual abuse
Andrōn (men's hall). *See* Meals
Angelic dialogue
  Jesus', 124–46
  Job's, 134–35
  Mary's, 106, 109–13

Anointing, 261
  Jesus', 150–57, 160–67, 170–74, 178, 244, 246, 258, 262, 263, 293, 294, 299
  qualifications for, 130
Anne, Saint, 110
Anthropology
  of Mediterranean society, 244–46, 248, 249
  method of, 3, 244–46
Aphrodite, 255
Apollonius of Tyana, 67
Aquinas, Thomas, 319
Aramaic. *See* Languages
Ardener, E., 21
Ardener, S., 21
Aristophanes, 162
Aristotle, 243, 246
Artifact
  feces as first, 207–8
  functioning of textual, 237
  God as, 193, 210
  history as, 226
  metaphor of, 188–90
  phenomenology of, 191–93
  sacraments as, 327
  text as, 217, 327, 329
  See also Poiesis
Arts, in Greek culture, 268
Asclepios, 67
Athenaeus, 162, 260
Aune, D. E., 18, 53, 54, 67, 85

Authority
  conflicts of, 140
  Jerusalem's, 117
  Jesus', 87–88
  messianic, 130
  of church leaders, 10
  teachers', 87
  textual, 137
  Torah's, 130

Babbage, C., 254
Baking
  tithing dough before, 41
  See also Tithing
Balme, M., 15
Banquets. *See* Meals
Baptism, 304, 310–11
Batey, R. A., 32, 127
Bat qôl (echo voice)
  and angels, 111–12
  and kingdom, 70
  and prophecy, 110–11
  definition of, 69
  information delivered by, 80
Bauer, W., 48
Baum, G., 309
Bertiaume, G., 260
Bertram, G., 33, 55
Beruriah, 256, 265, 266, 267, 268, 274
Bible
  versification of, 136
Biblical studies, method of, 4
Blood, 153
  See also Fluids
Body
  and food chain, 199
  and text, 191–94, 229
  as reader, 226–27
  divine image in, 208
  ethnicity of, 205
  fate of Jesus', 180–81, 250–51, 284
  genres of, 232
  inscription of, 180, 217–18, 220–21,
    227–33, 239, 286
  irreplaceability of, 190, 208, 215–16
  irreplicability of, 220
  Jesus' resurrection, 264–65
  loss of Jesus', 175, 257–61
  manyness of, 194–95, 199
  metaphors of, 196–97

  nonartificial character of, 192–93, 208,
    229
  nonself-sufficiency of, 204
  openings of, 207–8
  person symbolized as, 189–90
  problem of defining, 187–90
  resistance of, 195, 203–4, 213–14, 227–29,
    236, 239
  resurrection claims refer to, 186
  social design of, 195
  soul versus, 187–88
  transmitter of practices, 10
  uniqueness of, 194–95
  voice versus, 194
  worshiping assembly as, 9
Boring, M. E., 85
Bourdieu, P., 3, 247, 249
Bowing
  bodily, 146
  cultic, 99, 124, 143, 161
  metaphorical, 149
  pedagogical, 144
  psychological, 104–5, 107–8, 112, 172
  physical, 112, 121–22, 124, 137, 141, 142,
    143, 160, 163
  sexual, 115
Bread
  breaking, 170–71
  insufficiency of, 136
  Jesus as, 285
  See also Food
Brown, P., 103, 110, 161
Bultmann, R., 52, 125
Burial
  customs, 255, 256–57, 273
  See also Ossuary burial; Resurrection

Calame, C., 268
Calvary
  access to Jesus changed by, 8, 9, 10, 28,
    29
  access to Jesus foreclosed by, 56
  access to Jesus limited by, 79, 82
  theology of, 114
Cameron, A., 248
Cameron, R. D., 110
Canon, biblical, 2
Carr, D., 327, 328, 329, 331
Caste. *See* Class
Castelli, E. A., 61, 166

Catechesis, 287–88
  definition of, 52, 163
  inductive, 74–75
  kerygma versus, 52
  liturgical, 71–75
  women's, 163
  See also Fluids; Teaching
Catechetics, 6
Chauvet, L.-M., 306
Childbirth. *See* Bowing, physical
Chilton, B. D., 18, 28, 30, 44, 52, 54, 69, 70, 88, 97, 105, 127, 219, 220
Chodorow, N., 209
Chreiai (soundbites), 34, 67, 128–29
Christian origins, 5, 240–41
Church, 298
  as mother, 5, 8, 9, 10
  as subject of sacramental ritual, 308–9, 322–23
  definition of, 1, 2, 5
Cities, 13, 31
Classes
  and work, 12
  economic, 12, 146
  frontier crossing among, 22
  genre of, 230, 231, 241
  genric disruptions of, 286–92
  social practices of, 9, 151–52
Companions, mealtime, 152, 171
Conkey, M. W., 247
Cooke, B. J., 306, 324, 325
Copy
  definition of, 220, 286
  Jesus as, 97, 284, 318, 334
  metaphysics of, 219–21, 222, 226
  production of, 221
  teaching as, 236–37
  See also Text
Corley, K., 171, 252
Crites, S., 327
Crossan, J. D., 12, 37, 81, 92–93, 151, 248, 250, 261
Crucifixion
  as scandal, 7
  poiesis of, 180
  political use of, 180
  See also Calvary; Jesus of Nazareth, death of
Cultivation, 330–31
  See also Farming; Sowing

Curriculum, canonical designs for, 71–74
Cynics
  Christian, 158–59
  Christian prophets as, 53
  description of, 158–59
  Jesus liked by, 159
  Jesus sounds like, 113
  paideia opposed by, 62
  women, 158–59

D'Arms, J., 259
David, 100
Davis, J. H. R., 244
Death, 335
  and anointing, 171
  necessity of Jesus', 152
  noble, 61, 166
  poiesis of Jesus', 169
Demiourgoi, 260
  Jesus as, 295
Derrida, J., 331, 332
Detienne, M., 259, 272
Dewey, J., 210, 211
Dining. *See* Meals
Dirt, 204
  See also Knowledge, concealment of
Disciples of Jesus
  as sources of information, 7
  kingdom hindered by, 47
  languages of, 15
  women as, 22
Donaldson, T. L., 88
Dogs, 157, 158
  girls like, 269–70
Douglas, M., 195, 206, 294
Drama
  and oral expansion, 129
  liturgical, 109, 110, 119–20, 147
  Markan poiesis as, 179
  pantomime, 152, 155, 157, 163–64, 165–66, 167, 168, 170, 171, 172–73, 179
  See also Theater
Dramatization. *See* Oral performance
duBois, P., 196, 206, 294
Dunbabin, K. M. D., 259

Easter
  See Jesus of Nazareth, post-Calvary availability of; Resurrection
Eating. *See* Food; Hunger

'*Ebed. See* Slaves
Ebner, E., 42
Education
    children's, 32
    cultural influences on, 65
    gymnasion as institution of, 32, 268
    of Jewish girls, 268–69
    Mark's, 55–56
    slavery for, 103
    See also Halakhah; Paideia; Torah
Efficacy
    as intertextuality, 326–32
    as reference, 318–20
    as symbolization 320–26
    sacramental, 332–33
Eliezer, Rabbi, 42
Engels, D., 234
Eretz Israel
    contact with Africa, 19
    Greco-Roman urbanization of,
        249–50
Erikson, E. H., 205, 206, 207
Ethnicity, bodily expression of, 205
Eucharist, 8, 9, 263, 280, 296, 302,
    304–5
    See also Bread, Fluids, Meals

Faith. *See* Pledge
Fall, Alexandrian invention of, 81
Farley, E., 27, 58, 311, 326, 329
Farming, 13, 62
    See also Sowing
Feet. *See* Fluids, bathing
Fehr, B., 259
Fiorenza, F. S., 315, 316
Fischel, H. A., 265
Fish. *See* Food, wild
Fitzmeyer, J. A., 111, 125
Flax, J., 207, 209
Fluids
    and civil power, 162
    bathing, 153
    blood, 153, 280, 289
    eucharistic, 177
    instructional, 161
    kinship carried in, 289
    matron's shower, 161–62
    menses, 172
    mother's milk, 289
    oil, 162, 164
    persuasive, 152, 165, 177

saliva, 157
tears, 154, 157, 289
washing, 160
    See also Wet nursing
Food
    and Mishnah, 201
    at banquets, 260
    body as, 199
    crumbs of, 157, 159, 295
    distribution of, 201–2
    in rituals, 270–71
    insufficiency of, 135. *See also* Bread
    knowledge dependent on, 81
    knowledge through, 89–90
    producers of, 199–200
    promise of, 135
    redesign of, 203
    wild, 57–58, 81, 151, 237, 270
    See also Meals
Forgiveness, 153, 157, 160
Frontiers
    crossing of social, 22, 171
    linguistic, 20, 80–81
    Lukan, 159
    modeling society through, 20
    sayings that cross, 29
Foucault, M., 195
French, V., 234
Freud, S., 196, 205, 206, 207
Freyne, S., 14, 135

Gailey, C. W., 247
Galilee, 13, 31
Ganoczy, A., 305
Garland, R., 38, 39, 234
Gaze
    as abusive, 9
    theory as, 11
Genders
    definition of, 231
    frontier crossing among, 22
    genre of, 230–31, 241
    genric disruption of, 292–95
    social practices of, 9
Genres
    bodily, 230, 232, 286
    church, 310
    definition of, 222
    productivity of, 222–24, 227
    social, 224
Gerbner, G. 329, 330

Gerhart, M., 188, 219, 220, 222, 223, 284, 286
Gilmore, D. D., 244, 245
Girls, like pets, 269–70
  See also Parthenos
Gimbutas, M., 196
Gospel
  definition of, 7
  Markan definition of, 168–69, 179
Gospels
  and portraits of Jesus, 282–84
  and rabbis, 118
  as artifacts, 8
  as artwork, 331
  as innovation, 29
  as narratives, 313–14
  as resurrection theologies, 279–85, 309
  committed to writing, 8
  composition of, 8, 29–30, 54, 73, 119–21, 124–26, 153, 166–67
  history of, 82, 83
  kinds of, 7
  textuality of, 5, 6, 7
Grant, J., 100
Gray, J., 18, 19
Greek. *See* Languages, traits of various
Grief. *See* Mourning
Grossfeld, B., 148
Gynaikōn (women's quarters)
  activities in, 39, 153, 164, 254, 255
  city as, 171. *See also* Women, seclusion
    of wealthy

Ḥaburah (fellowship). *See* Meals
Hadrian, 274
Haggadah
  definition of, 34
Halakhah
  definition of, 34
  food distribution by, 40
  of Jesus, 274
Halton, T. P., 32
Hannah, 100, 104, 108, 109, 112, 115, 253, 292
Harrington, D. J., 105, 106, 109
Harris, M., 223
Hartsock, N. C. M., 199
Hearing
  divine sonship as, 131
  failure of, 137

God requires, 134
  information delivered by, 80–81
  insufficiency of, 93
  knowing God by, 140
  knowledge through, 122–23, 136–37, 145, 147
  resurrection certified by, 92
  revelation through, 131
Hebrew. *See* Languages, traits of various
Heidegger, M., 224, 326, 335
Herod Antipas, 32, 114
Herzfeld, M., 244, 248, 249, 272
Hetairoi, 258
History
  as theory, 11
  definition of, 225
Hobson, D., 38
Hodgson, P. C., 311
Holocaust, 312
Holofernes, 105
Honor/shame, as interpretive pairs, 246, 248–50
Hopper, G., 255, 267
Housing. *See Insula*
Humility. *See* Bowing, psychological
Hunger
  and class, 291
  and covenant, 135
  and hearing, 136
  and resurrection, 90–91, 199
  and teaching, 62–63
  and women, 90–91, 295
  as competence, 83
  credentialing through, 134
  epistemology of, 134
  information delivered through, 81
  kingdom entered through, 63
  knowledge through, 90, 92, 131, 239
  legitimation of, 232–33
  revelation through, 136

Identity, as historical determination, 6
Idols. *See* Vision
Illegitimacy, 232
Imagination. *See* Poiesis
Imperialism, 12, 13, 14
Industrialization, effect on kinship, 13
Insula (tenement), 40, 253–54
Intertextuality, 218, 318, 326–32
  See also Textuality

Jaeger, W., 32
James, W., 210
Jamnia, 130
Jesus of Nazareth
    abuse of, 9, 175, 180
    and Nicodemus, 48
    anointing of, 150–57, 160–67, 170–74,
        178. *See also* Anointing, Jesus'
    as bread, 285
    ascension of, 10
    as instructor, 139
    as Risen Lord, 281, 282
    as sacrifice, 271
    as teacher, 59–66, 266
    burial of, 10
    death of, 5, 7, 60–61, 263, 264, 267, 294
    divine sonship of, 116, 135, 138, 139
    historical knowledge of, 2, 6, 7, 10, 75, 82,
        97, 114
    identification of, 5, 29–30, 250, 284,
        311–12
    inscription of, 284, 285
    kindness to, 172, 178
    kingdom displaced by, 47, 60, 66
    kingdom monopolized by, 49–50
    kinship issues concerning, 113
    legitimacy of, 113–17, 115–18, 253
    makeover of, 8
    packaging of, 149–50
    parentage of, 96, 98, 113, 129
    post-Calvary availability of, 78–79, 250,
        252, 264, 274–75, 282, 286, 306, 310, 317,
        318
    recognition of, 72, 83–84, 295–99, 302,
        309
    reconstructions of, 7
    reimagination of, 250, 251
    remembering of, 9
    risen body required for, 76
    Spirit of, 85
    table practices of, 260–61
    temporal limitations of, 10
    traditions passed by women, 253–57
    writing of, 287
    See also Resurrection
Johanon, Rabbi, 118
John Paul II, 309
John the Baptist, teaching modeled by,
    66–76, 299
Jones, C. P., 259
Joseph of Arimathea, 257
Joshel, S., 38

Joshua, Rabbi, 42
Judith, 100, 105

Kabyle, 247
Kant, I., 210
Katachusmata (matron's shower). *See* Fluids
Kelber, W., 52, 53, 85, 128
Kelleher, M. M., 307, 308, 320
Keller, E. F., 209
Kerygma, 51–52
Keuls, E., 162, 166
Kingdom of God
    access to blocked, 47
    and food, 237
    and paideia, 56–57
    as metaphor, 28
    as periphrasis, 28
    children comprise, 4–7
    conceptualization of, 27
    cynic perspective on, 43
    displaced by Jesus, 30, 47, 55, 75–76
    entry into, 37, 43, 46, 253, 270, 291, 293
    hindrances to, 48
    Jesus monopolizes, 49–50
    Jesus seeks, 44
    Markan definition of, 168, 176, 179
    pregnancy as model of, 48
    security versus, 171
    Tannaim recognize, 66
    Torah secondary to, 42
    voice announcing, 70–71
King, R. H., 311
Kingsbury, J. D., 168
Kinneavy, J. L., 265, 266
Kinship
    and class, 231
    and inheritance, 41, 50, 234
    and law, 145
    and legitimate birth, 113, 115
    and slavery, 103, 116
    and villages, 13, 40
    and wet nursing, 39, 40
    and work, 201
    as economic system, 13
    inscription of, 233–36
    Jesus', 129
    Mary's, 115
    patrilinear, 99
Kloppenborg, J. S., 53, 125, 126, 135
Knowing
    and work, 198
    bodily templates for, 205–10

developmental stages of, 206–10
economical factors in, 198–99
hearing as, 122–23, 129
organs of, 122–23
seeing as, 129
Knowledge
concealment of, 204–5
social conditions of, 185–86
unconscious, 205
Koinē (common Greek). *See* Languages,
traits of various
Koester, H., 35, 127
Kuhrt, A., 248

Labor, 13, 99
See also Work
Land
and poverty, 135
divine gift of, 136, 142
divine ownership of, 235–36
inheritance of, 41
male ownership of, 42
Mishnaic theory of, 41
Langer, S. K., 167
Languages
as indexes of ethnicity, 15, 20
comparative practices of, 127–29
of first-century Palestine, 15, 290
traits of various, 16–18, 31, 80–81, 98–99,
101–6, 121, 137, 140, 158, 204
translation difficulties, 20, 129
uses of various, 20, 21
Last Supper, 261, 272, 280, 281, 295
Lawall, G., 15
Lazarus, 92, 157, 159
Leeming, B., 319, 320
Lefkowitz, M., 162
LeGuin, U. K., 204
Leitourgia (public sevice), women's, 162
Lenski, G. E., 12
Levey, S. H., 54
Lévi-Strauss, C., 246
Literacy
genric, 223–24, 286
technology of, 216. *See also* Text
See also Vision, knowledge through
Liturgical studies, 6
Liturgy, 72–73, 304, 308, 316, 323, 327, 332,
335
Logos, 333, 334
Lombard, Peter, 319
Lonergan, Bernard, 320

Mack, B. L., 54, 57, 58, 61, 118, 128, 152, 166,
167, 253, 263
Mageiros, 159–60
Jesus portrayed as, 271
Making, modalities of, 8
See also Poiesis
Mammy. *See* Slavewomen; Wet nursing
Manns, F., 118
Martha, 157, 159
Martin, C. J., 100
Martyn, J. L., 49
Marxism. *See* Materialism
Marx, K., 198
Mary
language of, 106
parentage of, 115
story of, 98, 106–13, 253
Mary Magdalene, 257
Materialism, 198, 215
McCane, B. R., 238
McDowell, D., 228
Meals
and culture, 203
banquet customs, 259–60
children's, 157
entertainment at, 152, 153, 158, 259
eucharistic, 151, 167
haburot, 152–53
kinswomen excluded from formal, 171
men's, 171, 258
reclining at, 258–59, 261, 262, 295
ritual, 166
sacrificial, 270–72
symposia, 151–52, 153
valedictory, 177–78
See also Last Supper
Meat
Jesus as, 9
liturgical use of, 73
See also Sacrifice
Megill, A., 331
Meier, J. P., 4, 111, 114
Meir, Rabbi, 256, 265
Memoranda, philosophical. *See*
Materialism; Pragmatism; Psychoanalytic
theory
Memra (divine word), definition of, 105–6
Menander, 260
Menasiah, Simeon b., 35
Mendora, 162
Menstruation, 290
sabbatical dimensions of, 36

Messiah. *See* Anointing
Metaphor
    definition of, 188
    machine as, 189
    manufacturing as, 214
    sowing as, 211–14
    tool as, 189
    vehicle as, 189
    wet nursing as, 211–14
Meturgeman (interpreter)
    John the Baptist as, 71
    practices of, 53, 106, 111–12, 219,
        265
    role in synagogue worship, 17
Metz, J.-B., 309
Meyers, C. L., 40, 99, 238, 248
Meyers, E. M., 32, 40, 238, 248
Michaelis, W., 123
Midwifery, 234, 255. *See also* Pregnancy
Miller, R. J., xiii, 58, 109, 126, 168
Miller, S. S., 115, 235
Minim (heretics), 118, 145
Mishnah
    as reflecting Hebrew scholarship, 16
    definition of, 65–66
    ethnographic information in, 40
    land in, 41
Modeling. *See* Social relations, conceptual
        models
Mourning
    women's, 78, 92–93, 152, 164–65, 255–58,
        272, 274
    See also Fluids, tears
Murray, O., 152, 259
Mystagogy. *See* Catechesis, liturgical

Name
    divine, 111, 123, 130–32, 135, 138, 140,
        143, 145, 146–48
    forgotten, 151, 159
    Markan use of, 176
    power of Jesus', 56, 63, 75, 85–86, 87
    unmentionable, 160
    See also Periphrasis
Nature, 34–36
    versus culture, 246
Nazareth, relation of Sepphoris to, 31
Neusner, J., 40, 201, 235, 236
Neyrey, J. H., 248
Nicodemus, 48, 293
Nursing. *See* Wet nursing

Obedience
    covenant and, 134
    life through, 141
    mountains signifying, 87–88
    of Jesus, 152
    rewards for, 89
    resurrection certified through, 87–88,
        91
    vision as, 123
    women's, 88
O'Collins, G., 279, 296, 297, 315, 316
Oil. *See* Fluids
'Ónah (overlay). *See* Slavewomen, rights of
Ong, W. J., 137, 216, 219, 255, 320
Orality. *See* Voice
Oral performance
    dogs', 155, 156–57
    drama as, 147
    eucharistic, 165–66
    expansion as, 129–132
    lyric, 152
    of Targums, 17
    pantomime versus, 173–74
    practices of, 146
    reading as, 222
    repertoire for, 155–57
    rhetorical practices in, 127–29, 158
    sayings source in, 126–27, 166
    sites for, 128
    temptation as, 124
    women's, 165
Ortner, S. B., 246
Ossuary burial, 238, 273

Paideia
    as punishment, 33, 46–47
    catechesis and, 44–45, 52, 62
    class indicated by term, 34, 35
    definition of, 32
    in *symposion*, 259
    opposition to, 33
    rejection of, 55
    sowing as, 65
Pain, 193–94
Palestine
    first-century culture of, 243–45
    languages of, 15
    races in first century, 14
Pantomime. *See* Drama
Parpart, J. L., 12
Parthenos (virgin girl), 260

Passover dinner. *See* Last Supper
Patér kai poiétés (father and maker),
    God as, 9
Patriarchy. *See* Kinship, patrilinear
Patterson, C., 234
Paul (Saul), 91
Peirce, C. S., 210
Perata, Eleazar ben, Rabbi, 254
Periphrasis
    divine name and, 28, 105–6, 111
    sexuality and, 104–5
Peristiany, J. G., 244
Perkins, P., 5, 52, 316
Person
    ambiguity of term, 187
    body as symbol of, 190
Pharisees, 64–65, 85, 130
Philo, 34, 55, 81, 97, 235, 239
Physis. *See* Nature
Piaget, J., 205
Pietà. *See* Church, as mother
Pistikes, 266, 272
Pistis (means of persuasion), 265–66, 267,
    271
    of emptied tomb story, 275
Pitt-Rivers, J. A., 244
Plato, 260, 266
Platonism
    and Bible, 19, 33, 81
    Philo's, 239
Pledge
    anointing as, 164
    dramatized, 157
    Eucharist as, 164
    Jesus makes, 153, 170, 178
    matron's shower as, 161–62
    symposiasts', 152
Plotinus, 267
Poiēsis (making)
    bodily, 190
    church's, 97
    definition of, 11
    dramatic, 132
    God's, 97
    growing versus, 188–89
    Mark's, 164, 167, 174–79
    portraiture as, 6, 250
    satiric, 126, 128
    spirit and, 121
    transforming social practices, 5
    women's, 163

Poor
    availability of, 178
    care of, 303, 335
    Jesus versus, 169
    rights of, 101, 141
    salvation for, 144
Practices, inscription of, 217
    See also Anthropology, method of
Pragmatism, memoranda of, 210–14, 215
Praxis, definition of, 11
Prayer
    Greek, 107
    Hebrew, 27–28, 101–2, 107, 115
    Mary's, 116
    poiesis during, 119
Pregnancy
    disparagement of, 158
    kingdom compared to, 48–49
    metaphoric use of, 197
    poiesis of, 207–8
    problem, 113–15
    rights to, 101, 105, 107
Property, origin of, 232
Prophecy, 53
Prophets, 85–86, 127
Proskyneō. *See* Bowing
Prostitutes. *See* Companions
Psychoanalytic theory
    hermeneutic use of, 196
    memoranda of, 205–10, 215
    object relations in, 209–10, 237
Public/domestic, as interpretive pairs,
    246–48
Punishment. *See* Paideia

Q. *See* Sayings source
Questions, teaching through, 74

Rabbis, authority of, 17
Races
    conflict among, 14
    destination of, 230
    frontier crossing among, 22
    genre of, 241
    genric disruptions of, 286–92
    in Roman Empire, 14
    social practices of, 9
    See also Ethnic diversity
Rahmani, L. Y., 238, 273
Rahner, K., 189, 304, 305, 307, 321, 322, 323,
    325

Rape, as usucaption, 41
  See also Sexual abuse
Rashi, 266
Reading, 221–22, 223, 226–27
  See also Vision, knowledge through
Reale, G., 197
Realsymbol, 321–22
Rengstorf, K. H., 128
Resistance
  bodily, 35
  reading as, 223
Resurrection
  and burial practices, 237–38, 273
  as competence, 5, 6
  as geographic phenomenon, 252
  as quilting, 96
  copy and, 221
  definition of, 1, 4, 5, 6, 79, 83, 85, 335
  incompleteness of, 211
  metaphors of, 238
  modes of teaching, 53
  nonsense of, 160
  revealed to women, 251
  theology of, 120, 279–300
Resurrection faith, 301
  Hellenistic roots, 243–50
Rhetoric, 85, 265–66
  See also Oral performance
Robbins, V. K., 49, 54, 59, 60, 61, 128, 267
Robinson, J. M., 127
Rorty, R., 210
Rosaldo, M. Z., 246–47
Rösler, W., 152
Rouselle, A., 38, 234
Russell, A. M., 188, 219, 220, 222, 284, 286

Sabbath, 35–36
Sacks, K. B., 199, 203, 247
Sacraments. *See* Theology, sacramental
Sacrifice
  animals for, 73, 134
  Jesus' death as, 154, 263, 270–72
  See also Fluids, blood; Meat
Sadducees, 36, 130
Šāḥah. *See* Bowing; Prayer
Saldarini, A. J., 105, 106
Salvation
  definition of, 141
  life as, 136
  promise of, 135
  time of, 129

visibility of, 137, 138, 147
witnessing, 134
Sameness. *See* Copy
Samuel, 110, 253, 260, 284, 292, 299
Šārēt (cultic service). *See* Bowing, cultic
Sayings Source (Q)
  composition of, 53, 127–48
  hypothesis of, 37
  politics of, 141
  prophets and, 53
  puzzles concerning, 125
  textual status of, 131
  uses of, 126
Scarry, E., 191, 192, 193, 194, 217, 237, 326
Schaberg, J., 100, 113, 114, 240
Schaps, D. M., 160
Schillebeeckx, E., 307, 309, 322, 323, 324, 325, 328
Schneidau, H. N., 327
Schneider, J., 244
Scott, B. B., x
Seeing. *See* Vision
Seeley, D., xiii, 61
Seifert, D. J., 247
Šēm. *See* Name, divine
Šᵉmaʿ. *See* Hearing
Seow, C. L., 15
Sepphoris, 19, 31, 33, 113, 114–15, 130, 268
Septuagint
  God as teacher in, 62
  Lukan use of, 107–12
  peculiarities of, 19
  philosophical tenor of, 33
  polemic use of, 129–46
  slavery in, 102
  Targums compared to, 19
  translation of, 19, 197
Sered, S. S., 270
Service. *See* Slavery; Work
Sewing, sowing and, 218
  See also Weaving; Work
Sexual abuse
  ambiguities of, 101–2
  and Mary, 113–15
Shekhinah (divine dwelling), definition of, 105–6
Simonides, 158
Šiphah. *See* Slavewomen
Slater, W. J., 259
Slavery
  foundlings raised for, 38
  freedom from, 140

Greek, 102–3
household, 103
Israelite, 99–100
textuality of, 228–29
to God, 111
See also Work
Slaves
as brides, 161
humanity denied for, 103
rights of, 100, 112
sexual abuse of, 104
sexual availability of, 103
sources of, 234
Slavewomen
God's, 100–101, 104, 112, 116
halakhah concerning, 39
prayer of, 107
rights of, 100–104, 116
sexual availability of, 10
terms for, 100
Smallwood, E. M., 14
Social relations
conceptual models of, 20, 21
minorities and, 21, 22
Social science, 3
comparative study in, 243–50
Social theory, 4
Son of God. *See* Jesus of Nazareth,
parentage of
Sonship
devil's divine, 134–35, 142
hearing and, 136
instruction and, 141
Jesus', 138
life and, 143
messianic, 142
Soul, 187
See also Body
Sowing
metaphor of, 217–18
sewing and, 218
subversive, 86
teaching as, 57–59, 65, 197, 211–14,
217–18, 237
See also Farming
Sparkes, B., 259
Spirit
God's, 117
impediments to, 160
gynaikōn permeable for, 164
of Jesus as agency, 5
text and, 216

Staudt, K. A., 12
Stephen, 90
Stones
broken, 150, 157
false gods as, 145
information in, 149
law written on, 135
Strange, J. F., xii, 32, 40, 118, 238, 248
Study. *See* Learning
Suckling. *See* Wet nursing
Symbol
as link between heaven and earth, 322
body as, 189–90
presentational, 167–68, 172–73
Symbolic causality, 318
Symposion (drinking party), 258, 259, 261,
262, 263
See also Meals
Synagogues, worship practices in, 17
Szold, H., 256

Table
and sacramental liturgy, 280
Christian, 296–98, 318
cynics lay siege to, 159
dining, 155, 157, 164
Jesus at, 263
Jesus copied at, 238
politics of, 160
reclining at, 258–59
Talmuds, 16
Tammuz, 255
Tannaim (sages), 16, 253
Targums (translations)
committed to writing, 17
English versions of, 17
familiar to early Christians, 18
liturgical use of, 53–54, 106
Septuagint compared to, 19
use in biblical exegesis, 18
use in synagogue worship, 17
Taylor, H., 254
Taylor, M. C., 58, 331, 332, 333
Teachers
authority of, 87
criticism of, 134
hindrances by, 67
profile of, 59–61
prophets versus, 63–64
Teaching
abuses in, 85
and drama, 128, 157

Teaching *(Continued)*
    copying as, 236–37
    criteria for success of, 72
    divine, 136
    failure of, 56–58, 62, 64
    locations for, 131
    media of, 147
    women's, 152, 163
Tears, 92–93
    See also Fluids
Tecusan, M., 259
Teichman, J., 113, 232
Temple, 130, 138–39, 172
Temptation
    as mezuzah, 148
    Jesus', 124–26
    reconstrucory script of, 132, 133,
        134–35, 141–43
Teradion, Hananiah ben, Rabbi, 256, 274
Tertullian, 161, 304
Text
    and body, 191–94, 229
    and spirit, 216
    and textiles, 255
    and voice, 216–17, 194
    and world, 216
    artifactual character of, 217, 237, 327
    classic, 224
    defining, 216–18
    Jesus as, 284–85
    production of, 218–19, 221
    readability of, 286
    reference by, 225
    replicability of, 219
    selectivity of, 225–26
    temporality of, 224–25
Textuality
    and temporal access, 226
    criteria of, 220–22
    weaving as, 218
Theater
    at dinner, 259
    design of, 126
    in Sepphoris, 31–32
    programs presented in, 127–28
Theology
    doctrinal, 309–15
    liturgical, 135–36, 138, 143, 144,
        146–47
    method of, 4
    of charity, 303–4

resurrection 279–300
    sacramental, 304–9, 311, 318, 319, 320–23
Thēoria. *See* Theory
Theory, definition of, 11–12, 317, 318
Thesmophoria, 255
Thirst, 123–24
Tithing, 41, 42, 81, 235–36, 270
Torah (instruction), 33
    connotations of term, 139
    definition of, 123
    fluidity of, 163
    Jesus as, 149
    textuality of, 216
Torture
    inscription and, 180
    of Jesus, 9, 173–74
    weapons for, 193
    See also Gaze; Paideia, Pain; Sexual abuse
Tracy, D., 224
Trade, 12, 13
Tringham, R. E., 247

Usucaption, 41, 47

Vaillancourt, R., 320
Valeria. *See* Beruriah.
Van Bremen, R., 162, 171
Varus, 114
Vernant, J. P., 259, 272
Veyne, P., 200
Village
    contacts with cities, 13, 14, 31
    homes, 248
    kinship in, 13, 40
Violence, 158, 229–30
    See also Sexual abuse; Torture
Vision
    and false gods, 122, 124, 145
    and God's name, 123
    criterion of, 140
    divine name as, 131
    information delivered by, 80
    knowing as, 122
    knowledge through, 89–90, 91–92, 136–37
    learning through, 147
    obedience as, 123
    prophets and, 123
    tears and, 164–65
Voice
    and text, 194, 216–17, 270
    body versus, 193–94

devil's, 174
efficacy of, 180
God's, 137, 145, 270
life signified by, 148
redistribution of, 197
resistive, 229
See also Hearing

Walker, S., 39, 248
Weaning, 42
Weaving, 218, 224, 238, 254
Wegner, J. R., 39, 41
Weiss, J., 28
West, C., 210
Wet nursing
    and ego development, 208–9
    and food chain, 199–200
    and kinship, 39, 40
    and usucaption, 42
    customs of, 38
    cynic perspective on, 43
    embarrassment by, 42
    free-lance occupation of, 38–39, 40
    grammatical instability of, 43
    metaphoric use of, 37, 253
    mishnaic law concerning, 39
    saying about, 244, 270
    slavewomen's, 39, 100, 289
    teaching as, 65, 211–14, 236–37
    weaning from, 208–9
    See also Fluids; Food, wild
White, H., 225
Winnicott, D. W., 209
Women
    and food, 199–200
    and food chain, 202
    and hunger, 90–91
    arguments of, 101, 102, 116–17, 157
    as disciples, 22
    authority of, 161–62
    communication activities of, 253–56
    dangerous, 190
    disparagement of, 157–58
    doglike, 156–60

food produced by, 42
foreign, 156–57
friendship among, 22
halakhah concerning, 41
Lukan policy for, 156–60
management of markets by, 13
obedient, 88
poiesis of, 150–54
portraiture of, 158
seclusion of elite, 162–63, 171, 253–54
theology of, 114
traditions of, 114
work of, 202–3
See also Mourning, women's
Word, insufficiency of, 120
Words
    efficacy of, 86
    futility of, 169
    incomprehensibility of, 159–60
    insufficiency of, 83–84, 89, 91
    pantomime versus, 171
    power of, 93
Work
    and kinship, 161, 201
    and knowledge, 121–24, 198
    compulsory, 142, 146
    distribution of, 200
    for God, 121, 124
    freedom from, 140–41
    laws concerning, 99
    limits to, 145
    mandatory, 143
    paid, 143
    sewing, 192
    slave's, 100, 143
    varieties of, 121
Worship, 336
    See also Liturgy
Wrede, W., 168
Writing
    and weaving compared, 255
    sowing as, 218
    See also Text
Wylie, A., 247